'For those of us who missed the Sixties, Virginia Nicholson catapults this era to roaring, authentic life. Rich with intimate voices and a keen-edged analysis of the public perceptions at work, this book brilliantly evokes the struggle between the urgent change and the heavily freighted forces of tradition that defined this singularly compelling decade. Read it. It is unputdownable' Priya Parmar

'A hugely ambitious, kaleidoscope of a book, written in a sympathetic but also hard-headed tone that captures squalor and tragedy as well as glamour' Richard Vinen

'Sparklingly readable . . . Having read Nicholson's magisterial and sensuous overview of the decade, I feel I'm floating above the Sixties (a bit like Lucy in the Sky) and looking down on them with a new understanding' Ysenda Maxtone Graham, *The Times*

'The stories are terrific' Rosie Boycott, *Financial Times*

'Sparkling . . . there is a wonderfully diverse range of voices . . . we have a long way to go, but reading this book made me grateful for how far we have come' Daisy Goodwin, *Sunday Times*

'Clever . . . absorbing' Bel Mooney, *Daily Mail*

'Beautifully narrated' Sara Maitland, *Guardian*

'Nicholson is good at reminding us that it wasn't such fun in the sticks' Lynn Barber, *Daily Telegraph*

'It is her enthusiasm as much as her scholarship that makes this such a beguiling read' Joan Bakewell, *Spectator*

'Absorbing and moving' *Country Life*

ABOUT THE AUTHOR

Virginia Nicholson was born in Newcastle-upon-Tyne, grew up in Yorkshire and Sussex, and studied at Cambridge University. She lived abroad in France and Italy, then worked as a documentary researcher for the BBC. A Fellow of the Royal Society of Literature, her books include the acclaimed social histories *Among the Bohemians*, *Singled Out*, *Millions Like Us*, and *Perfect Wives in Ideal Homes*. She is married with three grown-up children and lives in Sussex.

How Was It For You?

Women, Sex, Love and Power in the 1960s

VIRGINIA NICHOLSON

PENGUIN BOOKS

PENGUIN BOOKS

UK | USA | Canada | Ireland | Australia
India | New Zealand | South Africa

Penguin Books is part of the Penguin Random House group of companies
whose addresses can be found at global.penguinrandomhouse.com.

First published by Viking 2019
Published in Penguin Books 2020
001

Typeset by Jouve (UK), Milton Keynes
Printed and bound in Great Britain by Clays Ltd, Elcograf S.p.A.

A CIP catalogue record for this book is available from the British Library

ISBN: 978–0–241–97518–3

www.greenpenguin.co.uk

To my daughters

Contents

List of Illustrations

Integrated illustrations

Inset illustrations

Prelude

Look around. And imagine. Imagine the old as they once were, fifty years ago, in the 1960s.

Was the pensioner in the supermarket queue a Mod back then, posturing on the pillion of a Lambretta? Was the lady serving her at the checkout her sworn adversary, a Rocker, hanging out in black at the Ace Café? Did the elderly woman walking her little dog in the park once stride with a banner, yelling slogans till she was hoarse, at the front of an anti-war demonstration? Does the tired-looking grandmother on the bus still treasure her collection of Biba frocks in smudgy plums and earth colours – though the label never made anything above a size 10? What about the stout assistant working in the charity shop – might she once have seen a flying saucer, back when she was a skinny chick in batik, spaced out on marijuana? And is that matronly figure dozing opposite you on the train dreaming of her long-gone student days, being seduced over late-night Nescafé to the sound of Jethro Tull?

Secrets, intimacies, insights, disillusionments, memories. For our mothers, our grandmothers, for ourselves – and for countless women born after the end of the Second World War – the intoxicating colours, potent soundtracks, intense ideals, extreme clothes and unfamiliar freedoms of the 1960s contributed to the moulding of their early lives. This book tells their story.

Of course, by no means all the young women of this generation were radicals, fashion leaders or utopians. Some took their own stand in rejecting the permissive consensus. Others had personal struggles to contend with, deeply held beliefs that were at odds with the prevailing current, or were leading lives remote from the public collisions between young and old, hip and square, fringe and Establishment that we have come to associate with the 1960s. Yet for all of this generation, the simple fact of having been young in that decade has given their lives a different dimension from those the sixties left behind, or those who, like me, were a bit too young to keep up.

This book is in part a personal one. I was born in 1955. As I enter my seventh decade, the need to make sense of a time that I both lived through and was barred from has prompted me to find out more about the women whose experience might have been my own – if I'd been ten years older, and a bit braver. Have I missed out, have I been their beneficiary, or have I in truth had a narrow escape?

But I also intend it as a homage to those women, giving them voice, value and visibility, and celebrating them, while the memories are still alive.

★

Many important books have been written about the 1960s. They are mostly by men. They range from Bernard Levin's lofty overview *The Pendulum Years* through Arthur Marwick's magisterial *The Sixties* to Dominic Sandbrook's *White Heat*, while the great historian David Kynaston has left his many fans in 1962, still waiting for him to complete his encyclopaedic account of post-war Britain. To all of these and more I owe a debt, but this history – like others I have written – stands apart from theirs because it is about women, and is narrated from a woman's perspective.

One might imagine that stepping across the threshold from the monochrome fifties to the psychedelic sixties would be to enter a new, egalitarian era. But for the young women growing up in it, the post-war world promised much while delivering little. Sex was taboo outside marriage. Unwed mothers were shunned, contraception was reserved for wives and pre-marital intercourse was only for sluts. The younger generation were hungry for sexual freedom, but for women that freedom would come with a price tag. Mid-decade, we start to recognise the tentative beginnings of the Women's Liberation movement.

Any history must have dates, data and documents as its foundation – but how best to breathe life into that impersonal repository of facts? Here, as always, I turn to memory, and the human voice.

Memory is subjective, and I have not attempted to be definitive. My aim has been to uncover how it actually felt to be a young woman at that time. I also take the view that the apparently trivial can often tell us more about the past than great men and their milestones. My own 1960s time capsule would contain nylon macs, false eyelashes, menthol cigarettes, Babycham, tubular frame furniture, transistor radios, innovations like tights and avocado pears, patchouli oil – and *Top of the Pops*. For me, they reveal the texture of everyday life in a way nothing else can.

How did I select my interviewees, and what is my version of events? The cliché of the 1960s is that it was a decade whose radiant light show sprinkled everything it touched with stardust: a time of space travel and utopian dreams, but above all of sexual abandonment. That story needed to be told, but it is far from the whole story. Early in the research period for this book I realised that not everyone felt the prevailing culture of permissiveness was for them. Their voices had to be heard too, otherwise my account of the 1960s would be warped and one-sided. A student who attended Hull University in 1967 remembered: 'It was incredibly dull. Everything reached Hull about five years after it reached everywhere else . . . girls were wearing miniskirts, but in Hull I'm sure they'd never heard of them.' Clothes will play a conspicuous part in this book. For many women – and men too – in the 1960s, clothes defined who you were, and who you weren't, just as shops, pop songs, magazines and films held up a mirror to a newly prosperous society. But this was also a time when capitalism was having image problems; many were questioning its macho associations with war, hate and greed, and asking: could we not replace centuries of male domination with the gentler, more 'womanly' virtues of anti-materialism, peace, love and spirituality? I wanted, too, to unpick some myths, so I talked to women who didn't fit our received idea of the savvy, liberated Mary Quant-wearing 'chick': like a nanny, a journalist, a Girl Guide leader, a council worker, a rural housewife and a bunny girl. Nearly forty women invited me into their homes, responded to letters and phone calls, trusted me and talked to me about their lives during that decade (some of them have asked for their identities to be disguised).

The conversations I had were many and various. I travelled to Liverpool, to the flatlands of north Lincolnshire, to a Yorkshire suburb, to a sleepy Wiltshire market town and the deep valleys of the West Country. I found some contributors not far from my front door;

others in city flats or sheltered accommodation. Their answers to my questions were surprising, funny and in many cases intensely moving. Often in those conversations there were moments when I knew I was sharing a memory of extraordinary significance to my interviewee, as barriers were lowered and the years seemed to melt away. These were experiences that, for some, had barely been mentioned for the greater part of their adulthood. Others, through the prism of their private lives, shed light on historical landmarks such as the thalidomide scandal, the Cuban missile crisis or the LSE riots. I encountered regional accents, privilege, glamour and disadvantage, side by side with comedy, honesty and tears. In these pages we will follow such women's stories. Here are just a few of them as they are today.

*

'I'm a sixties woman – for the rest of my life,' says Kimberley, who was born in 1951. 'There's not many sixty-five-year-olds like me. I go to see reggae bands, rock bands – all sorts. I don't really fit in with my age group!

'I'm a party animal. And I'm still partying on.'

Kimberley speaks with the vestiges of a suburban London accent. She now lives in a flat in Hastings, from the windows of which you can catch a glimpse of the chalk cliffs that rise above the town. Her surroundings and appearance leave you in no doubt about her claim. She's dressed in a floor-length red and orange caftan printed with pineapples. An ethnic pendant dangles from a leather thong around her neck. But her broad, lined, unmade-up features speak of struggle, survival, experience and character.

'Well, I have had a really interesting life. I've certainly got a book in me!' she says cheerfully. The flat's interior – like her colourfully eccentric clothes – hints at a complex story. African figurines jostle for space in the alcoves with books: Clare Ungerson's *Women and Social Policy*, suffragette Hannah Mitchell's autobiography *The Hard Way Up* and *Women against Violence against Women*, by Dusty Rhodes and Sandra McNeill. Red fairy-lights festoon the mirror, and geometric fabrics alleviate the surfaces. Kimberley opens the window so that she can smoke and talk without disturbing her sleeping guest in the next room, a homeless Jamaican lesbian whom she's invited to stay temporarily until she can find a place.

Then the story begins: 'I was a wild child . . .'

★

Theresa: you only have to enter her room to pick up on her sense of style. The walls are white, but pattern is everywhere: framed, semi-abstract prints, ethnic wool-embroidered cushions. Above all, the planes of her own dynamically colourful ceramics burst forth with moulded birds, palm fronds, fish and fruit. These jugs and platters seem – like their creator, who dazzles in scarlet tights, pink lipstick and a multi-coloured bandeau – to originate in a sunnier climate than that of north London.

In 2016 Theresa was seventy. All her life she's been balancing two inheritances, bequeathed by her Jamaican father and her Scottish mother. In the 1950s, growing up as the only little brown girl in Cornwall for miles wasn't always easy. From the earliest age she's been coping both with the contempt levelled at the 'half-caste', and irrepressibly curly hair. Like ambient music, her racial origins are hard to ignore, an insistent refrain underlying her loves, her career, her talent. But the teenage Theresa around 1960 sang to another key. 'Oh my God, yes, the music was important to me! The rock'n'roll thing was beginning. My friend Jean and I were mad about Cliff Richard, Marty Wilde and Elvis Presley. I even went to see Cliff Richard – he was my idol. And I screamed till my nose bled. I saw the Everly Brothers too. I adored them, absolutely adored them. Jean and I learnt to sing "Dream", in harmony. We used to sing it on the school bus, over and over and over and over, absolutely pitch perfect . . .' Melodious, hypnotic, repetitive: the swoony lyrics bound Theresa, and countless teenagers across the country, in a rhapsodic spell of wishful thinking.

★

Mary is nearly eighty. Once, her looks used to be compared to those of the top tabloid honeypot of her day, Christine Keeler. In 1968, when she was thirty, the *Hull Daily Mail* pictured Mary, not in a sexually provocative pose, but vehement, arresting – in mid-sentence, arm outstretched to make her point, wearing a boxy leather jacket and rock'n'roll eyeliner.

Today, the feline eyes and striking bone structure remain, but Mary is lame, and the glossy backcombed hairdo has lost its bounce. She struggles with mobility, and needs a Zimmer frame to potter from kitchen to sitting room. In old age, after a spell away from her north-eastern roots, she has returned to the flat watery Humber estuary, with its great windswept skies that carry a briny tang of the North Sea. Mary's life is basic now. The terrace cottage she lives in is appointed for one occupant, with a huge comfortable armchair, TV and coffee table, but little else. The kitchen betrays a lack of concern with formal meals. Mary sometimes forgets the things she needs.

But she hasn't forgotten her youth; and her spirit, her outspokenness and her dirty laugh transport one from the slightly underventilated sitting room to a more blustery and tempestuous time. When it comes to remembering the past, she's sharp as a pin. In 2017 her home town, Hull, was European City of Culture; in the sixties it was a backwater, a world away from the neon-lit and pleasure-seeking capital. In Hessle Road, heart of Hull's fishing community, the smell of salt, tar and herrings was perpetually in Mary's nostrils. She grew up in abject poverty, daughter of a fisherman, the only girl in a family of eight brothers.

Girls were seen as insignificant. Mother always favoured the boys. The men had to be served first. They had a naturally bigger appetite, so they were given more. I was left waiting.

And the way my mother spoke to me . . . If we had an argument, she would say – pointing her finger – 'You ought to remember where you're from, who you are, and *don't* expect too much of life, 'cos you *won't get it*!' She was terrified of my father. He was a drunkard, a cruel drunkard. He'd beat her black and blue – and in front of us children too. We'd cower under the furniture when he'd be kicking her.

You would think with all that I would grow up to be the most downtrodden, insignificant female. But I think it put iron in my soul. And maybe that's why I turned out the way I did . . .

★

Margaret is a reluctant rebel. If it hadn't been forced on her by circumstances, she and her husband Billy would most likely have led unexceptional lives, wary of authority, adrift in the world of their social 'betters'. Margaret never knew her father. He was killed in the war when she was a baby. Her mother remarried. Exactly eight years later her 'second dad' was killed in a work accident. The eldest of three, she learnt about maternal responsibility when their mother was forced to take factory and auxiliary nursing jobs to support her daughters. Margaret, at the age of ten, became aware that they were no longer 'a whole family'. With her mum absent at work, she now had to learn to take on a mother's role, weighing up the household budget against the family's needs, making decisions. It was a lesson that would prove invaluable.

Today, Margaret, Billy and their grown-up son David live in an impeccable bungalow on a hill overlooking the South Yorkshire town of Barnsley. Framed family photographs scatter the shelf tops; visible reading matter is mostly escapist thrillers. Where the walls aren't textured with Artex they are papered with a simple, sinuous design of modern red flowers to complement its counterpart in the seat cushions. Dressed in trousers and a stripy top, Margaret is bustling, upright and beady-eyed. When two men arrive to mend the washing machine, she deals with them briskly. She is matter-of-fact, no-nonsense, practical, with a firm grip on the set of values she inherited from her mother: self-respect, sobriety, respectability and respect for your elders. Margaret talks in her cadenced Scots about how she met Billy Hogg at the age of just fifteen. They went to the pictures together and got married two years later, in July 1959. By January 1960 she was happily, and healthily, pregnant. That was the year everything changed.

*

Anthea took the trouble to come and meet me at the station. But as we hadn't met before she had sent me a brief description of herself: 'I'm medium tall, slim, fair haired, seventy-one and hair "up"!' Even if she hadn't, I would have had no difficulty recognising her from the correspondence we had had. Standing on the platform was a slight, beautiful, unmade-up woman wearing neutral clothes and a boldly arty necklace. She exuded energy and sincerity, and welcomed me with a melodious, educated voice.

I had been seeking somebody who felt they were in opposition to the mainstream. Anthea told me by email that she had been an active clergy wife, and that as an English Literature student at Reading University in the 1960s she had met Mary Whitehouse, founder of the Clean-Up TV Campaign. 'I do seem to fit your brief pretty exactly,' she wrote. 'You will probably cause me to recall matters that I haven't considered for a long time . . .'

Anthea drove briskly out of the city and in twenty minutes its suburbs gave way to deep lanes spilling over with summer foliage. Soon we were seated with coffee in her light-filled conservatory. Anthea pulled out historic press cuttings from her student days, when she had written articles challenging the 'anything goes' permissiveness of the era. 'Now, I don't know where you want to begin . . .' she said.

*

Beryl's speaking voice is a gentle, but distinctively nasal Scouse, with a tuneful lilt to it. At nearly seventy, singing is still her reason for getting up each morning. She has no plans to give up and, for those who remember her glory days in the sixties, she's still out there, giving them a piece of the action.

All her life, Beryl has depended less on glamour and glitz than on talent and personality – a choice whose wisdom is proved as the girlish freshness of her early years has given way to a rounded, friendly attractiveness. Beryl's neutral sitting room, in a north London flat, demonstrates how little appearances matter to her. The only nod to décor is a modest arrangement that one might describe as a shrine, set against one wall, with flowers and a tea-light, the intimation of some profound inner life. Her lack of make-up and her tomboyish clothes – ripped skinny jeans, trainers and a grey marl hoodie – tell the same unpretentious story, though a curly top-knot, unleashing dark auburn tresses which bounce around her face, gives a hint of frivolity. Yet Beryl, barely over five feet tall, has a contained energy. She might jump up at any minute and start bopping.

Beryl lived her early years in Liverpool to the sound of popular song. Her first memory is hearing American female vocalist Jo Stafford on the radio, singing the souped-up hit folk song 'Shrimp Boats'. Home back then was an urban slum in a run-down Georgian terrace. Her mother had a total of ten children, by (she thinks) four different men. Even when they moved to a bigger house, the kids were three to a bed. 'So radio was, well, my sort of escapey bit from those tough surroundings . . . The thing is, I think that probably from the age of nine or ten, I went, "I'm going to sing." And I had this thing inside of me, no matter what. And me mum thought I was mad. She'd say, "What are you talking about? Sing? It's impossible . . ." And they only had boy bands then. So she'd say, "It's not a proper job! You're a girl, for a start . . ."'

★

June 1963: Caroline, aged thirteen, had managed to get tickets to see the Beatles, at their one and only live appearance at the old Odeon cinema in Guildford. Some say that 'Beatlemania' began that night. Alongside her, over fifteen hundred excited teenagers crammed the auditorium. Till then, audiences had generally listened respectfully to the performers. It was not the done thing to interrupt. The Guildford audience broke the rules. 'The screaming was so loud, you really couldn't hear them. Not a word. They sang "Love, love me do". I can remember the excitement – and feeling frustrated too, because I wanted to hear them – and I was sitting quite far back. And no, *I* didn't scream. I was far too well brought-up to do that! At that point I was still very much my father's daughter . . .'

In those early days of the sixties, as a shy and inhibited teenager, Caroline didn't question her privileged background. She has travelled a long road since then. Today she's preparing a healthy salad in her prettily rustic kitchen and, though she professes to loathe it, one could equally well imagine her, with her fabulous looks and easy manner, slotting comfortably into the dinner-party scene in West Sussex. The fact is that the outer appearance of this animated, stylish and assured woman betrays little of the inner forces that drive her.

But towards the end of the sixties, something happened. And that thing derailed her known world. 'It's led me down paths I never would have gone on otherwise. I've spent a lifetime trying to make sense of everything I experienced then, and following a totally different direction than had been planned for me. So, I've been integrating that experience ever since, all my life.'

★

These seven women are now rising seventy, or older. The lives of many more will figure in this book. They may be our grandmothers, or our mothers. They may be us. Their formative years intersected one of the most intense decades ever: the 1960s.

During it, these women measured their identity against such defining moments as the *Lady Chatterley* case, the Profumo Affair, the introduction of the birth-control pill (if you were married, that is) and the miniskirt, the Moors murders and the Abortion Act. At its end, in February 1970, five hundred women arrived in Oxford to attend the first ever National Women's Liberation Conference, held at Ruskin College, and later that year Germaine Greer's landmark book *The Female Eunuch* was published. At that time, Britain was still years away from having its first woman prime minister, working women were earning an average 25 per cent less than men and marriage had never been more popular.

If, as women, we want to understand our world today, we should surely lift the cloak of invisibility from the shoulders of the women who shaped it.

1960

Brides

The 1960s got off to a glorious start, with a great big traditional wedding.

Crowds of half a million converged on central London. A Pathé News film crew captured the neon lights of Piccadilly Circus, the illuminated clock face of Big Ben, cheery Cockneys celebrating by eating jellied eels and having a knees-up in Lambeth, heraldic décor, double-decker buses and flag-waving children. 'Here is London in her pride . . .' pronounced the reverent commentator in plummy tones. The ancien régime and its subjects were *en fête*.

On a sunny morning in May 1960, the cameras preserved for posterity the moment when the Queen's sister, Princess Margaret, alighted from the Glass Coach outside Westminster Abbey, radiant in the beauty of her floating tulle veil and white silk wedding dress. A fanfare of trumpets sounded as she approached the altar to join her handsome groom, Antony Armstrong-Jones. The service was conducted in front of two thousand guests by the Archbishop of Canterbury, following the wording from the Book of Common Prayer:

> Margaret Rose, wilt thou have this man to thy wedded husband . . .?
> Wilt thou obey him and serve him, love, honour and keep him, in sickness and in health; and, forsaking all other, keep thee only unto him, so long as ye both shall live?

and she replied:

> I will.

For the first time in four centuries of British history a king's daughter was marrying a commoner.

It was also the first time a royal wedding had been broadcast on television, and twenty million viewers tuned in that day to watch the occasion. I was one of them, though I was only four. However, we were not among the 79 per cent of households who, in 1960, owned a TV set. Instead, my mother picked me up early from my nursery school, and took me with her to watch it on a boxy wooden set at the home of some fortunate friends who did. In crackly black and white, the occasion nonetheless had a fairy-tale splendour.

But in May 1960 some people close to the newlyweds could already foresee the way it would go, and on that day of blue skies were predicting storms ahead. Though their temperaments were both mercurial, he was too bohemian and she was too traditional. He would not love, and she would not obey. The accident of birth played a part too; a number of foreign royals closed ranks and declined the invitation to attend the princess's wedding to a jumped-up photographer.

Just five years earlier, the combined male élite of Church, state and press had demanded that the beleaguered princess renounce her love for the divorced Group Captain Peter Townsend. By 1960, even as she plighted her troth to Armstrong-Jones, the tables were beginning to turn, with the Establishment itself under attack. A new and unimaginable world was beginning to take shape under its censorious gaze.

Fear accompanied the clashing of values and the questioning of roles. Male citadels began to put up defences, build stronger walls.

In the sixties, a power struggle started which still hasn't been won.

*

Just a month after the princess's wedding, another Margaret – Margaret Forster – finished her last exam at Oxford and, leaving her legs bare, put on a simple white cotton dress. Deliberately opting out of the whole church-and-flowers-and-trumpets charade that had been paraded before the nation in Westminster Abbey, she and her boyfriend underwent a simple ceremony in an Oxford register office. Afterwards, the newlyweds had lunch in a pub in Woodstock.

It had been three years since this Margaret's escape from her narrow-minded background in a proletarian neighbourhood of Carlisle. Since then she had acquired much useful knowledge about barrier forms of contraception from her fellow students at Somerville

College, meaning that she could – unlike previous generations of women in her family – have all the fun of sex without having to face the 'often fearful consequences'. But in the late 1950s, sparing her strait-laced parents the reality of her sex life committed Margaret to a series of elaborate lies involving much research, collusion and post-dated picture postcards. These somehow convinced her mother that she was *not* actually spending the holidays with her boyfriend the journalist Hunter Davies in Manchester, but was innocently travelling around Germany and Italy with a posse of girlfriends. However, finding a place where she and Hunter could cohabit after she had graduated proved much harder. Initially, they saw no reason to fudge their relationship, but were turned away by potential landlords from flat after flat. 'In the end it had to be on with the Woolworths ring and the pretence that I was Mrs Davies, which I detested.' The lying finally got too complicated.

> If marriage was nothing to us but everything to our mothers, why not just get married?

And so they did.

Later that summer, Margaret's mother, Lilian, came down from Carlisle to visit the happy couple in north London. But when she stepped into their new home, it seemed to her that her familiar universe had been turned topsy-turvy.

Lilian Forster's life in Carlisle had always consisted of drudgery. She had married, brought up her family, cooked, shopped and cleaned her house with little money and almost no labour-saving appliances. Her own home had no washing machine, and smoky open fires. Without a car, shopping in town involved large wicker baskets and a bus ride. But in the early sixties the younger generation was embracing the rapid progress of domestic technology with joyful enthusiasm while, between them, Hunter and Margaret had negotiated a very modern domestic deal.

Shortly after their marriage, the couple took delivery of a shiny Electrolux refrigerator. Its significance as a household revolution had to be spelled out to Lilian. It would mean not having to shop for fresh food more than once a week – '. . . the darling fridge would keep everything fresh'. This explanation was met by Lilian with baffled silence. After much thought, she questioned how anybody could carry home a week's worth of heavy shopping. Simple, replied her daughter. Hunter would be supplied *with a list*, and get everything *in the car* – at the same time as dropping the washing off *at the launderette*.

> There was an even longer silence . . . then she exploded, said it wasn't *right*, a man shouldn't be shopping and going to launderettes, what-ever they were.

What was it that so perturbed Lilian? Not just the new appliances and the car, the fitted carpet and the shiny steel sink, thought her daughter. It was 'the equality of our marriage' that jangled and jarred with her understanding of the traditional sex divide. Lilian resisted, but she could sense that the certainties of her life were starting to crumble. Her fortress and power base, the home, and the relation-ships that underpinned it, were becoming unrecognisable. She and her generation had lived through the Second World War; they had fought, endured and won. But passive, and passé, they were now the baffled onlookers.

*

Margaret Forster was just twenty-two years old when she got mar-ried. Princess Margaret was less typical of her generation, in marrying at a relatively late age: she was twenty-nine.

Over the last half-century, the age of brides has risen steadily. Today, a substantial majority of women who marry do so at the age of thirty-plus. Sixty years ago, the reverse was the case, with numbers of very young marriages at an all-time high. The authors of the government's Crowther Report (1959) pinpointed 'the fact that, for an increasing number of girls, marriage now follows hard on, or even precedes, the end of education'. In 1959 and 1960, half the women in the country were married before they were twenty-five, over 26 per cent of them were under twenty and, overwhelmingly, they mar-ried men from their own socio-economic band.

True, the dash to the altar at this time paralleled another less hur-ried dash, into higher education. New universities were opening their doors, and women felt welcomed by them. But for many a teenager the lure of marriage was intense, and provoked much opining and soul-searching by the commentariat as they watched large numbers of young women pulled between a domestic destiny and wider horizons.

The herd mentality of the young brides was underscored in a survey, published in 1962, which quoted a teenager saying that 'what she wanted to *have* was a wedding ring, what she wanted to *do* was to get married, what she wanted to *be* was a wife and mother'.* 'There is little doubt,' wrote the survey's author, 'that marriage and maternity is the central objective of the "average" girl and that all other ambitions are ordered round this objective in an entirely rational way.' That claim was confirmed by a later survey, which showed that aspirant husband-catchers aged between fifteen and twenty-four spent more on cosmetics – and bras – than all other age groups put together.†

Far from seeking to upturn the pre-war marital status quo, the post-war generation of women took it for granted that romantic love had only one natural outcome.

> I can't even remember the specific decision to get married. It just seemed a progression . . . [In the sixties] it was just accepted that if you went out with someone for a long time and you got on, then you'd get married . . .

recalled one woman. And another:

> I got married in 1959, straight out of college . . . I was just twenty-one. I was terribly in love with my husband, so I thought I ought to marry him.

---

* Thelma Veness, *School Leavers: Their Aspirations and Expectations* (1962). Veness's sample of 107 girls was asked, 'At what age do you expect to get married?' At the secondary modern school seventy-three out of eighty-two (89 per cent) girls saw themselves getting married between the ages of twenty and twenty-five. That proportion was a little lower among more educated girls at the technical or grammar school, where nineteen out of twenty-five (76 per cent) expected to be married in their early twenties.

† Peter Laurie, author of *The Teenage Revolution* (1965), explains, 'The connection with husbands, potential and actual, was clear.' Only 16 per cent of married women used mascara, against 44 per cent of unmarried.

The mass culture of the day, particularly pop music, fed the notion that romantic love led speedily and inevitably to matrimony. The symbol of commitment, the wedding ring, has a special place in early 1960s pop lyrics, positioning it firmly in the teen mindset of the time, as in Martha and the Vandellas' 'Third Finger Left Hand'. And echoes of *Romeo and Juliet* float from the plaintive notes of Welsh pop vocalist Ricky Valance's 1960 number 1 so-called 'death disc', 'Tell Laura I Love Her', in which the promise of a wedding ring ends in tragedy.*

More often, a happier future lies in wait. The Everly Brothers, in their jaunty and hugely successful rock number 'Claudette', get great mileage from rhyming her name with 'pretty little *pet*', and 'the best loving that I'll ever *get*'. But by verse three we've reached 'I'm gonna ask my baby if she'll marry me . . .', and the final couplet is an affirmative '. . . rest of my life / . . . brand new wife'. Lyrics expressing eternal commitment could ensure number 1 hits, with even diehard rock'n'rollers like Elvis Presley distilling lifelong devotion into a law of nature ('Like a river flows – surely to the sea / Darling so it goes / Some things are meant to be'). The Ronettes, however, with 'I'm So Young' ('They say our love is / Just a teenage affection / But no one knows / Our hearts' direction . . .'), and Bob B. Soxx and the Blue Jeans, with 'Not Too Young to Get Married', had their fingers even more on the pulse.

The topic dominated women's magazines. An academic study analysing the subject matter of bestselling weekly titles like *Woman* and *Woman's Own* allotted percentages to the themes of their feature coverage. In the early 1960s 'Getting and keeping your man' was the magazine theme that consistently made double figures, while a breakdown of role characteristics showed up 'Wife', 'Mother' and 'Marriage Fixated' as the highest scorers. The researcher then dissected and scored the magazines' content for values and goals. Here, 'Romantic love', 'Male finding/keeping' and 'Happy marriage/family' all came top.

The right hand of convention and the left hand of culture squeezed

---

* This was a cover version of Ray Peterson's original. The BBC considered teenage tragedy songs tasteless, and refused to play them, but Radio Luxembourg was less squeamish. Many other American songs of this ilk were never released in the UK.

many a couple like Margaret and Hunter into marriage. But the pattern was starting to change.

Hearth and Home

The Britain of 1960 was a nation in transition. To appreciate the strange plant now germinating, we have to do a little digging into the past.

Many women like Margaret Forster who reached adulthood in the 1960s were born during the war or during the period of austerity that followed it. So childhood memories of the time tend to start with post-war rationing and the piecemeal reappearance of pleasures like fruit and sweets. Early recollections also often include the ubiquitous visible reminders of the conflict. Cities presented a dreary, unpainted face to the visitor – cracking façades and bomb sites – while the countryside bore witness with concrete defences, prefabs and disused army camps. Men born before 1939 – elder brothers or boyfriends – continued routinely to be called up to serve two years' National Service.* The recent war's mythologies lived on in Britain's collective memory. Many a housewife still recalled the depressing round of misery-inducing substitutions with which meals were achieved: root vegetables, whale, dried egg. Khaki battledress, hair above the collar and Utility fashions remained too close for comfort. War meant blackout curtains, queues and gloom. It also meant listening to your father or uncle's war reminiscences, absorbing the vocabulary of the regiment, with its discipline and esprit de corps, its hierarchies, its unquestioning obedience, its moral certainty.

The war had also given birth to the Welfare State. Sir William Beveridge, its founding father, was a progressive. Nevertheless, he had been born in 1879, and he spoke for a generation of men whose views on women had been formed in the nineteenth century. Beveridge's reforming initiative enshrined in law an essentially discriminatory

---

* National Service was phased out from 1957. The last call-ups were issued in December 1960, and the last National Servicemen left the Armed Forces in May 1963.

vision for women. He and many like him saw housewives as the pillars supporting the British way of life. They were indispensable – but unpaid. Spelling out this orthodoxy, he wrote: 'Housewives as Mothers have vital work to do in ensuring the adequate continuance of the British Race and of British ideals in the world.' And despite increasing numbers heading for the workplace, it was still considered normal to hold the view that women who did so were wrong and misguided. One noble lord told Parliament, 'If I had my way I would introduce a law forbidding young mothers with children to leave them all day and go out to work.'

This deeply rooted Establishment vision could not be eradicated overnight. On so many fronts, our society conspired to keep women caged and indoors.*

One of these was the perennially popular *Daily Mail* Ideal Home Exhibition, which in the post-war period was one of the most loved yearly events of the calendar, feeding the public appetite for dream houses. The mid-1950s building boom made picture windows, fitted kitchens, central heating and perfect plumbing a reality for families in new towns like Stevenage, Basildon, Harlow and Hatfield; and more of their ilk were on the way.

However, Ideal Home modernity was set against a backdrop of stagnation. And while the space-age, labour-saving dream might come true for some, for far more, drudgery was their lot. Even in 1960, in isolated and forgotten pockets of the country, women were living lives that were more medieval than mid-twentieth-century. In his book *Britain in the Sixties: The Other England* (1964) the journalist Geoffrey Moorhouse uncovered a way of life not usually associated with affluent modern Britain. He told of remote East Anglian communities where sewerage or mains drainage would not be provided until 1968 at the earliest. When the housewife wanted to empty the sink in her cottage she would have to put a bucket under the plughole to catch the waste water, then carry it out and empty it in the garden. Lavatories came in the form of heavily disinfected tin containers, often housed in small cubicles in the kitchen, whose contents were

* My earlier book, *Perfect Wives in Ideal Homes: The Story of Women in the 1950s* (2015), explores and describes this post-war world.

collected weekly by 'the bumble cart'. For many urban dwellers too, conditions were primitive. Moorhouse visited the Manchester suburb of Openshaw, where it was estimated that for 20 per cent of families living in rented accommodation, the only way to take a bath was to visit the in-laws – once a week. In this down-at-heel neighbourhood, the sound of women's clogs was still heard on the cobbles. The louring factory walls blocked light from the windows, and it wasn't worth bothering to hang your laundry out to dry, or leaving your baby to sleep in a pram in the backyard, as emissions from the chimneys would cover them both in smuts.

A diehard form of domesticity, inherited from the days of Mrs Beeton, was deeply ingrained in many communities. The 1960 *Guide to Housework* (published by the Institute of Houseworkers) laid down a list of 'every day' jobs to be carried out in the well-regulated home, including brushing the stairs, polishing brass door furniture and dusting banisters daily. On top of that, there were the weekly tasks, with the cleaning of sitting room, kitchen and bedroom determined with clockwork regularity. For many a housewife, washday had to be Monday, with all the week lying ahead for the subsidiary tasks of drying and ironing. Other days were allocated specifically to tasks like 'Market' and 'Doing your front'. This last, particularly in the north of England, often involved the curious ritual of 'donkey-stoning': using a tablet to treat and whiten the stone doorstep onto the street. It was hard work, done on hands and knees, but well into the 1960s was a matter of great pride to those who undertook it. For many mothers, preparing 'real wholesome food' for their families was also non-negotiable. 'You didn't think twice about cooking a meal. You did proper dinners and proper puddings. Pastry was made from scratch, and vegetables came with earth and slugs on them, possibly from one's own garden.'

As a new decade dawned, the centrality of home showed few signs of diminishing.

> When the evening fire glows, when the house becomes a home, then it seems to me that this is perhaps the path to true happiness . . .

rhapsodised one happy housewife, while recognising that her comfortable hearth was the result of long and tedious efforts.

In 1960 the demarcations between home and the world of work still lay on either side of the conventional gender divide, and many women saw this as the way God intended. But subjection was breeding rebellion. For the writer Fay Weldon, home in the early sixties was a place of demons. Fay married Ron Weldon, a much older man, who took it for granted that, since men who did housework were to be despised, his wife would be the homemaker – never mind that she also had a job. But the obnoxious Ron refused to let Fay have a washing machine, because they were noisy. Instead, twice-weekly, she had to make time after work to haul her bags of socks and shirts to the Coin-Op launderette. Ron described his ideal woman as 'barefoot, pregnant, and up to her elbows in soapy water'. Soon after, Fay wrote a surreal play – 'a historical document of a time now gone' – in which the heroine is lying on her deathbed, surrounded by visitors who are personifications of her daily life: Shopping, Washing, Cleaning, Dusting and Cooking. These odious guests bicker, carp, berate her and accuse her of preferring one over the other. The last visitor, Socks, turns up late '– bitter, faded and twisted, to deal the final death-blow. Between them, they finish her off.'

*

Alongside the Ideal Home, the England of my childhood idolised the Ideal Mother. As fundamentals go, motherhood could hardly be more central to post-war women's self-image.

This ideal mother was beatified in children's books, advertisements, popular media and literature. I was schooled with the help of Ladybird's much-loved 'Learning to Read' series, in which Mother takes Peter and Jane shopping, and Father is the breadwinner. A doll or a cooking set was on every girl's Christmas wish-list, while the homely television soap opera *Coronation Street*, which began in 1960, peopled by working-class matriarchs, gossips and community rocks, was quickly clasped to the national bosom.

Illegitimacy rates were rising steadily at this time. Moral panic around teenage and working mothers betrayed the anxiety felt about erosions to 'normal' family life, and women themselves bought into the heavy pressure to be stay-at-home mums. In 1959, barely 20 per cent of women with children aged between five and ten were working

Jane gets a doll, and Peter gets a car. In 1960, that was the way God intended.

full-time, while those doing part-time jobs numbered less than a quarter of this sample. In the complete absence of state nursery provision for pre-schoolers,* the remainder consigned a high proportion of their waking hours to the tasks associated with childcare: food preparation, toileting, endless laundry and play; they were aided in this by the dedicated producers at the BBC, who from the 1950s gave Britain's children the gently reassuring strands *Watch with Mother* on television, and *Listen with Mother* on radio ('Are you sitting comfortably? Then I'll begin . . .'). They were also encouraged in their efforts by one of the most successful books of all time, Dr Benjamin Spock's *Baby and Child Care* (first published in 1946), whose sales were at a zenith in the sixties. Departing from the clock-watching and punishment recommended by previous childcare gurus, Spock emphasised the rewards of child-centred intimacy, instinct and leniency. 'It is when a mother trusts her judgement that she is at her best,' he said.†

* The Pre-School Playgroups Association was started as a grassroots voluntary organisation by a young mother, Belle Tutaev, in 1961.
† Spock's preference for giving love and affection over regimentation would later damage his reputation, leading to questionable accusations that he had corrupted a generation and led them down the path to permissiveness.

A generation of girls was now growing up with little to challenge the status quo. 'It never struck me,' remembered one middle-class woman, who turned thirteen at the beginning of the 1960s, 'that my mother could do anything but look after the house, cook, write shopping lists (*1lb toms, a nice lettuce, 1 t-roll*) and thumb lick through pattern books at the drapers.'

*

This thirteen-year-old remembering her mother was named Mary Ingham. Mary, who grew up in the Midlands, also recalls the huge gulf of understanding about sex:

> Our mothers had mostly married in white, with clear consciences, in their twenties . . .

she explains. But they never discussed any sexual practicalities with their daughters. At school Mary and her friends were taught some biological basics, but nothing that was exactly 'user-friendly'. Garbled versions did the rounds. For example, when she and her fellow pupils were called for their medical, it was rumoured that the doctor could tell if you were a virgin by looking at your nipples.

Nearly *every* woman I interviewed for this book volunteered the fact that they had been given zero information about sex; though, it must be admitted, one Lancashire schoolgirl found out about childbirth in the most practical way imaginable:

> Miss Green, who taught us Domestic Science, had clearly been assigned to tell the girls what was what, while the boys did woodwork. And in Miss Green's class we had to knit a uterus. I've still got the pattern for it! It was a four-needle exercise, with scraps of wool in different colours. And if you knew how to cast on you were supposed to put a nice ribbed bit at the bottom for the cervix. But even then, some of us didn't know how to cast off, so it got longer and longer, with endless dropped stitches.
>
> And then we had to get a tennis ball and push it through this uterus. And then Miss Green said, 'Well, now you know how a baby is born.'

And that was all very well, but of course what we wanted to know was, well, how does it get there in the first place?

These voices are more typical:

– My periods started at home and I thought I was dying! I told my mother. She just gave me a sanitary towel and didn't say anything.

– I thought I came out of a tulip . . .

– My mother just tutted a lot. She couldn't bring herself to talk about anything like that. They never did, in those days.

But in the late autumn of 1960, Mary and her generation were about to be hit by a revelation.

Lady C

Just like her contemporaries quoted above, eighteen-year-old Clare Lane was given 'no information about sex at all' by her parents. It didn't stop her getting informed herself, by going to bed with her boyfriend. In any case, her conscience was untroubled, since she had grown up in a family who leant towards tolerance. And in October 1960 her father, Sir Allen Lane, founder and chairman of Penguin Books, publicly declared those liberal values and risked prosecution, by standing in court as a representative defendant in the legal cause célèbre of the year, the trial of D. H. Lawrence's erotic novel *Lady Chatterley's Lover*. Clare sat in the Old Bailey to watch her father take the stand.

The story is now well known, of how the unexpurgated edition had been published by Penguin that summer, only to be prosecuted, in a test of the new Obscene Publications Act 1959. And one of Mervyn Griffith-Jones's opening remarks for the prosecution was to earn him immortality – of a sort:

Would you approve of your young sons, young daughters – because girls can read as well as boys – reading this book? Is it a book that you would have lying around in your own house? Is it a book that you would even wish your wife or your servants to read?

For Clare Lane the gravity of her father's situation barely registered. 'It all felt very grey. The penny didn't drop really that he could have gone to prison. I think I was living in a kind of bubble. I was doing a typing course in Kensington at the time, and living in Holland Park. They were the boundaries of my world.'

But also watching from the gallery of the Old Bailey was another woman – not so young as Clare Lane – for whom the trial was of compulsive interest. Sybille Bedford sat with her press colleagues, 'shaking with anguish and fury . . . I felt so desperately strongly about it – it was like being in the war'. Bedford already had a reputation as a novelist. But the law was an early love, and as a child she had harboured a secret ambition to be a barrister. This was not to be, since the profession discriminated against women. In 1960 fewer than one hundred women practised at the Self-employed Bar – '[We] were considered to have the wrong voice for it.' For her, the *Lady Chatterley* trial, with all its flaws and hyperbole, was an education in her chosen career as a writer of fiction. But perhaps, though she didn't refer to this, another factor in the trial that she must have found compelling was its challenge to conventional, prudish morality. Sybille Bedford had had a short-lived marriage, but was primarily lesbian. In her time, and in her world, the norm was still vanilla heterosexuality. *Lady Chatterley's Lover* – with its depictions of transgressive sex – threw down a gauntlet to the sexual conventions of the post-war world. An acquittal must have had personal relevance to a woman whose loves were still shrouded in privacy and shame.

From her vantage point, Sybille scrutinised the jury, projecting hope onto their anonymous faces:

> The twelfth acting juror in this trial was a most educated-looking woman, with an alive and responsive face, and she may well have been the kingpin in the decision of that jury. Of course we shall never know . . .
>
> Most of them looked like pleasant people. The women seemed at their ease. There were two of them besides the twelfth juror; one very pretty young woman with a gentle face – ought one to pin hopes on her? – and one middle-aged, more of the housewife type. The second day she had appeared without a hat. A favourable sign?

To her joy, the defence mobilised an impressive line-up of witnesses, including Clare's father and a roll-call of the great and the good from the worlds of literature, religion and the arts. Their conviction and eloquence were decisive:

> For us, who waited on that day [wrote Sybille] it was a long three hours before we heard – still incredulous in relief – those words: Not Guilty. A ripple of applause broke out . . .

It was 2 November 1960. On that day a pupil in Mary Ingham's class scrawled 'Congratulations, Lady C' across the blackboard. The young English mistress took it in her stride, but the elderly puritanical spinster who taught them scripture took one look and had it promptly wiped off with a duster.

But she couldn't stem the tide. Bookshops across the country reported queues outside at opening time, and quickly sold out of copies. The controversy – and sales – were stoked when an elderly lady missionary, watched by a posse of photographers, publicly burned a copy of the book outside an Edinburgh bookshop. Clare Lane's father became suddenly and hugely wealthy. Clare, with her sophisticated background, was slightly bemused by the fuss. 'Mellors and Lady Chatterley didn't provide me with any information I didn't already have. Actually, Henry Miller's books, which I'd also read, are a lot more explicit! As far as I was concerned, Lawrence's novel just felt like an imaginative way of describing something I knew about already.' For her and her family, the trial and its impact were neutralised by unshockability and self-mockery. Having successfully floated Penguin, Sir Allen happily paid for Clare to have a generous twenty-first birthday party, at which the guests were entertained by the iconoclastic songwriter Sydney Carter:

> *When I was on the jury once*
> *I had to read a book,*
> *And when I came out of the court*
> *I wore a wicked look.*
> *'Oooh, tell us all about it Syd,'*
> *The barmaid said to me –*
> *'What did the gamekeeper do today*
> *To wicked Lady C?'*

From November 1960, Lady Chatterley's physical gratifications – 'complete and unexpurgated' – were legally available between soft covers for just 3s 6d.

Meanwhile, consumed with curiosity, Mary Ingham walked straight into the newsagent's shop on her way home from school and ordered a copy for 3s 6d. After it arrived she covered the novel's notoriously recognisable cover with brown paper, concealed it at the back of a pile of text books – 'I couldn't risk taking it home . . .' – and secretly read the naughty bits:

> Then as he began to move, in the sudden helpless orgasm, there awoke in her new strange trills rippling inside her. Rippling, rippling, rippling, like a flapping overlapping of soft flames, soft as feathers, running to points of brilliance, exquisite, exquisite and melting her all molten inside. It was like bells rippling up and up towards culmination. She lay unconscious of the wild little cries she uttered at the last.

Mary was now fourteen. For her, the mystery that Lawrence's novel unveiled was that 'Lady C' was not lying back, thinking of England, she was having 'an incredible physical experience'. Here was a free, disinhibited woman who loved to be aroused, loved to give pleasure, loved to succumb to it, loved the feelings it gave her. And this was new. For Mary, sex was still to come. But she and many like her made up their minds then and there that, when it did, it was going to be fun.

New Arrivals

In early November 1960, while the nation's liberal-minded reading public were celebrating the Penguin victory, a young woman in a working-class neighbourhood in Edinburgh was facing the knowledge that nothing life could throw at her would ever be tougher than her present challenge.

We earlier caught a glimpse of Margaret Hogg as she is today in a Barnsley bungalow, fifty-four years after her eldest son David was born in a hospital at Leith near Edinburgh in October 1960. Margaret and Billy Hogg had married in July 1959, when she was just seventeen. The couple lived with her mother, in Burdiehouse, to the south-east of Edinburgh. Within weeks of the wedding Billy, who was in the RAF, was posted to Germany. In January, after his leave, Margaret missed her period, and started to feel sick. Then a bronchial infection set in. After missing a second period, Margaret braved the icy weather and took herself off to the doctor's.

> I had a right cough. And he says to me, 'Is there any chance that you could be pregnant?' And I says, 'Well, yes, I've missed two.' And he says, 'The reason I ask is, I need to give you something for this cough. And I need to put a sedative in it, because if you go on coughing like that, you could miscarry.'

Miscarrying was not a risk Margaret was prepared to run with this, her first and entirely wanted baby.

> I took the medicine, and the cough went away. And for the rest of my pregnancy my mother said she'd never seen me look as well in my life. I was blooming, and I never had any more sickness. And all that was going through my mind at that time was, it doesn't matter what baby you have, so long as it's hale and hearty.

All appeared well. Soon after the four-month mark the baby started to stir in her womb. Margaret acquired a cot and a set of terry nappies, and started knitting.

On Monday 24 October Margaret woke in the morning with a sore back. 'I got up to go to the toilet and I thought, I don't feel right, and the next thing I vomited.' By midday she was on her way to the hospital in an ambulance. There, the procedures were straightforward. First she was examined, then shaved, then she was given an enema and a bath, before being parked in a ward. Nothing much happened. She slept. Towards evening the pains increased and she got a strong urge to push. At ten minutes past eleven that night, Margaret Hogg's baby was delivered by a midwife.

> And there was a doctor there as well. And then all I heard was, '*Ohh!*'
>
> And I said, 'What's wrong?'
>
> 'Oh,' she says, 'nothing dear, nothing for you to worry about,' she says, 'Baby's just a little bit blue . . . So we're going to take him away to give him a bit of oxygen and sort him out.'
>
> So I thought, 'Fine.' And I says, 'What have I got?'
>
> And she says, 'A little boy . . .'

The baby was whisked away. Margaret was dopey with gas and air, the only pain relief she had had. Though dimly aware that she hadn't heard her infant cry, she tried to put worries from her mind. The medical authorities had told her nothing was the matter, and who was she, a relatively uneducated eighteen-year-old, who had merely worked in a shoe shop till she got married, to question them? After a cup of tea she was put to bed. Exhausted after her labour, she mustered the energy to ask the nurse attending her, 'When can I see my baby?' The reply was reassuring. He was quite pink now and breathing fine, and she would see him next day.

But in the morning the medical staff began to produce excuses. First it was, 'When you've had your breakfast.' The tea trolley came and went. Margaret washed. At ten o'clock the doctors appeared on their ward round. Respect was owed to these authoritative beings, but by now Margaret was becoming increasingly impatient. 'I still haven't seen my baby yet!' she pleaded. And the doctor said, 'Haven't you, Mrs Hogg?' A discussion ensued, couched in incomprehensible medical terms. It was all above her head. Please, she begged, when would she see him? 'Shortly . . .' came the answer. And the morning wore on. More than twelve hours after she had given birth, her mother and mother-in-law appeared bearing magazines. It was outside visiting hours. Why now? They had been summoned by a phone call, they explained. 'And I says, "Well I haven't seen Baby yet, and I'm getting annoyed. I don't even know how heavy he is!"' Looks were exchanged. There was something unspoken in their discomfort. They left, promising to return.

More hours passed, and a nurse arrived with her lunch. 'By now I was beginning to lose it . . .' Desperation gave her appeals renewed urgency. Margaret was beginning to learn that, to get what you wanted, you had to make yourself heard:

'Look,' I says, 'I'm beginning to get annoyed now,' I says. 'I havnae seen my baby yet,' I says, 'He's fourteen hours old,' I says. 'What's going on?'

'Oh,' she says, 'The doctor is coming round after you've had a nap,' she says. 'Doctor'll talk to you about Baby then.' And I says, 'NO, Doctor'll NOT come after I've had a nap,' I says. 'Doctor'll come NOW.'

'Oh,' she says, 'Doctor is busy . . .' I says, 'I don't care how busy Doctor is.' I says, 'If Doctor doesnae come to me,' I says, 'I'll go to him.'

Her threat had its effect. In due course the nurse reappeared to collect the lunch tray, with a doctor in tow. 'I believe you want to see me, love?' This time Margaret was determined to get a straight answer out of him. She wanted to see her baby, she explained, and she wanted to see him <u>now</u>. She wanted to know what, if anything, was wrong with him, why he had not been brought to her, and whether he was dead. 'Oh, NO *NO no no no* . . .' was the emphatic answer.

And I says, 'Well, bring him!'

The doctor sat on the bed. He said he thought they needed to have a little talk. Then he proceeded to tell Margaret that unfortunately her baby hadn't developed properly. The baby, it seemed, had phocomelia. The word meant nothing to her. She asked him to tell her in English. Two things were the matter, he explained. Her baby had been born with a club foot. Also, he had only one eye. The other one hadn't developed. That was all. And then he told her that she was to have her nap, and afterwards, the nurse would bring her baby to her.

So I must admit, that was the one time, the one and only time, that I cried myself to sleep.

And when I woke up my blood pressure and my temperature were up, and the staff nurse came and said, 'You need something to calm yourself down with, Mrs Hogg.' And I says, 'No,' I says, '<u>I just need to see my baby</u>.'

So I think I must have waited ten minutes . . . and they came back and walked into the room with this little wrapped-up bundle. And they put him on the bed, and then they walked out.

So I picked him up – and I had a good look at him, and I says, 'Well,' I says, 'you've been a long time coming to see me.' So I says, 'Are you going to say hello to your mummy?'

Margaret was holding her child in her arms; and he was waking up. It was the moment she had been waiting for. His one eye opened. But no, this wasn't how it should be. The eye was asymmetrical, its oval distorted at one end into a curious pear-shape, with the iris at the bottom. And now she saw that his feet, too, were indeed maimed. One of the tiny extremities protruding from the bundle showed signs of the pronounced inward curvature that comes with a club foot, the toe strangely bent back. And yet, after her day of strain and distress, Margaret reacted with relief. 'Well, what was all the fuss about?' A club foot was nothing new to her. She'd seen the condition before, and knew it could be rectified. The main thing was, her child was alive and, as for his eye – 'Well,' I says, 'if you've only got one eye, you've only got one eye. We'll take it from there.'

She wanted to get to know him. Gently, Margaret unwrapped her baby from the folds of blanket that enclosed his little body. Under the swaddling, someone had done their best to dress him in a back-fastening hospital nightie, but whoever it was had incompetently neglected to poke his hands through the flapping, empty sleeves. What a bundle of rags, she thought, feeling beneath the garment for his arms.

She couldn't find them. With a lurch of anxiety she opened up the nightie. Her baby had no proper arms. Two short stumps ended on each side in a clutch of just three curled-in fingers. His tiny torso was contorted by hips that had dislocated from their sockets.

And I thought, now I know what they were talking about. Now I knew what the doctor meant when he said phocomelia. This was it. And I thought, 'This poor little scrap of humanity, what am I going to do with him?'

But as I looked at Baby, it went through my mind, 'Well, you've only got little arms. How are you going to cope? How are you going to eat? And how will you go to school?'

And I said to myself, 'Well, Margaret, your mother always told you that God never gives you anything you can't deal with.' That was always a saying of Mother's.

So I just thought, 'Well, here goes. He's yours. Now get on wi' it.' And I loved him. Oh, aye, I loved him.

But from that first day I saw David I found my inner courage. Before that I wouldn't have challenged anyone. But I think it's something that all mothers find, that have a baby that is nae normal, that is nae perfectly formed – they get a fighting spirit inside them telling them, 'You've got to do it, because nobody else will.' And in those days nobody else would.

Phocomelia, the word that Margaret Hogg failed to understand, means a birth deformity in which the hands or feet are attached close to the torso, with the limbs being underdeveloped or absent. As a diagnosis of David's condition, it described, but it did not explain. And in 1960, it couldn't – because nobody at that time knew enough about the 'wonder drug' thalidomide. Nobody had done the relevant tests on the drug, developed in Germany and marketed as a safe treatment for anxiety, insomnia and gastritis. And nobody in the UK saw any connection between Distaval, which contained thalidomide, and the estimated two thousand babies born in this country, the majority of whose impairments meant that they did not live to tell the tale. So when Margaret turned to the professionals and said to them, 'Why is he like that?' the only answer they could give was, 'Well, Mrs Hogg, it's just one of those things. It's what we call an act of God.' And Margaret was left with no choice but to say, 'Well, if that's it, then I don't think much of Him.'

Coping with some of the hardest demands motherhood could impose has been Margaret Hogg's lot in life, and one that was dealt to her with no warning or preparation, and very little professional support. Many of the defining freedoms enjoyed by young women of her age would be denied her. Instead, she herself believes that that terrible night in 1960, when she cried herself to sleep in a maternity ward in Leith, was the time she grew up, and went from being a teenage mother to being an adult with responsibilities.

That maturity had crushing costs, but also extraordinary rewards.

*

Today, Baroness Benjamin has not a single doubt that the bad times she too endured were worth it:

'Adversity could break my spirit or make me strong.'

The words appear quoted on the cover of her second book of memoirs, *The Arms of Britannia* (2010), published after she had become a successful singer, actress, television personality, public figure and eventually, life peer. Floella Benjamin has come a long way from the little white clapboard house in Pointe-à-Pierre, Trinidad, where she lived till the age of eleven.

I knew we were getting closer to England because the weather started to get much, much colder and the sun seemed to disappear under the low clouds . . .

It was September 1960. That year 57,700 immigrants – nearly 50,000 from the West Indies – arrived on these shores seeking a better life and new opportunities.

Floella's experiences at this time mirror those of many black migrants to Britain. The terrible unthinking racism that she was about to encounter would put iron in her soul. But the 1960s was also a time when to be black was to be exotic, glamorous and desirable. When Floella eventually wrote her memoirs, she did so deliberately in order to reach out to those who felt discouraged and embittered by their experiences. But she also felt able to offer solace and inspiration.

After a separation of over a year, the Benjamin parents ('Marmie' and 'Dardie') sent for Floella and her elder sister and two little brothers to join them and the two younger children in the Mother Country. Dardie was now working as a garage mechanic during the day, but nursed dreams of breaking through as a jazz musician. Their island home, with its gaudy garden blazing with hibiscus, hummingbirds and butterflies, was a faraway memory.

In Trinidad, the Benjamin children had been educated to feel pride at being British. Every day at the start of school the classes assembled to sing 'God Save the Queen', 'Rule Britannia' and 'Land of Hope and Glory'. Lord Nelson, Queen Victoria and Alfred, Lord Tennyson inhabited the young Floella's imagination. Would the English streets be paved with gold? Now, as she rushed down the gangplank onto the dock, the dreamed-of moment of reunion coincided with the start of a new life. Overwhelmed as she was by the joy of being back in Marmie's loving embrace, Floella was almost as elated to receive her first English present. 'I thought you might be a little cold . . .' said Marmie, opening her bag, and presenting her daughter with a powder-blue Marks & Spencer's cardigan, embellished with pink and yellow flowers. 'I felt I had been sprinkled with magic dust and that all my dreams were coming true.'

The journey to London by train left Floella drunk on a cocktail of new sights and sounds: the hissing locomotive that carried them, the bright green grass, the swarming rush-hour crowds, moving staircases, automatic doors, roaring traffic. And staring people. Floella and her sister had dressed in their best for this important day. Were the colourless, funereal-looking passers-by staring at them because of their joyous parrot-hued outfits? 'I didn't realise . . . that staring was something I was going to have to get used to.' Marmie led her brood up a side street, to the down-at-heel Edwardian semi that was now the family home. Weary and drained with new experiences, the children tailed her up the steep flight of stairs and across a landing, where she unlocked a door. Here it was. One dark, cluttered room, furnished with a large bed, table, couch, chairs, cupboards, for a family of eight. Was this the better life that had been promised? The land of hope and glory? Surely not.

I hadn't considered the fact that it was all my parents could afford, that they had saved every penny to send for us to be together . . . My dreams were shattered and scattered. I suddenly burst into hysterical tears, Sandra started to cry too, then the boys joined in. [Marmie] started to cry as well, and began to prepare a meal. At least that was the one thing that hadn't changed – Marmie and her cooking.

Growing up in 1960s Britain, Floella Benjamin had a long road to travel. There would be deprivation, abuse, discrimination, betrayal and horrible violence. But there would also be the dawning of confidence and ambition born of a rooted self-belief. She knew, deep down, that the colour of her skin was no cause for shame. And by the age of twenty, she was to discover that her own sense of black dignity – along with her wide smile, curly hair, rich voice, expressive body, her defiance and her fighting spirit – was part of something bigger. For this young woman, pride was on the march.

Forecast for a Future

Racial identity, rights and the validity of strongly held beliefs were ideas that would gather momentum over the coming decade. For the younger generation they were ideas that were worth shouting about, worth waving banners for.

Thousands of people marching, jazz bands – why aren't I there?

wrote diarist Kate Paul on 16 April 1960. Passionate, starry-eyed, defiant and questioning, twenty-year-old Kate kept her diary in the pages of an old ledger she'd found discarded in a cupboard at her art school in Somerset. That day, she had heard radio reports of the 100,000 protesters who were gathering in Trafalgar Square at the end of the third annual Aldermaston march by the Campaign for Nuclear Disarmament, to protest against the atom bomb. These were mainly peaceable men and women of the left; idealistic students, and mothers afraid for their children. Though stuck in provincial Somerset, Kate was one among many who felt she had no future:

We're a sitting target, it's absolutely futile – radiation is inescapable. I
suppose it won't be long now.

I'll probably die before I've lived, before I'm thirty. And all my
friends and contemporaries.

With what seemed malignant intent, the last world war had
extended its claws beyond the confines of the battlefield. Within
three months of VE Day, the dropping of two atom bombs on Japanese cities cast a curse of fear over the entire world that has never
since lifted.

On 17 May, the fear was worse than ever before:

I'm depressed and worried . . .

wrote Kate. Now, the news was carrying reports that a Paris summit,
called to bring about a rapprochement between the Big Four nuclear
powers (the USA, USSR, Britain and France), had fallen apart in
tatters after Russians shot down an American spy plane over the
Urals. As a result, talks between the four heads of state had descended
into hostile recriminations.

That evening Kate and her fellow students were drinking in the
Compass, Taunton:

There was a woman talking as people do in pubs. She said: 'I haven't
been so frightened since just before the Second World War.' People
were coming in and their first words were: 'Any news?' or 'Heard
anything yet?'

'What right have these four men got to just press a button and get
rid of us just like that?' said another woman . . .

I want to grip these maniacs by the shoulders and shout: 'Don't
you dare destroy me!'

The prospect of nuclear annihilation blackened the future, but for
many, another terrifying tomorrow seemed just as ominous. High on
the post-war list of doom-laden terrors came the threat of population
explosion. Ninety thousand people were being born every day, and
commentators predicted that humankind would double in fifty years
if unchecked. The planet would starve. For many, the only hope of

avoiding calamity lay in birth control. 'Are we really to go on bringing fresh individuals into the world until we have to put up the notice
"Standing Room Only"?' asked Sir Russell Brain, head of a special
medical advisory committee appointed by the Family Planning
Association, which was spearheading research into new methods of
contraception. Early in 1960, tests were being conducted among
women volunteers in Birmingham, London and Devon of Enavid
and Primolut N, hormonal compounds developed in the United
States, designed to regulate fertility. Though side effects were still a
worry, the doctors and scientists conducting the tests were optimistic. 'I think we have reached a stage in this hormonal business which
is quite remarkable,' said Dr Margaret Jackson. 'It is demonstrated
without doubt that a hormone is practically 100 per cent effective.'
The momentum that would bring in the Pill was now unstoppable.
Meanwhile, increased use of penicillin to treat sexually transmitted
diseases reduced the morbid fear of consequences that throughout
history had been connected with promiscuity.

For Kate Paul, and many young women like her, boxed in by the
palpable destruction of the past, and the probable annihilation that
lay in the future, there seemed little point in living whatever life was
left to them by the dying rules of their parents' generation. From
music to morals, clothes to sex, the time had come to start living for
the moment. And now it seemed that pharmaceuticals could save the
world, it was also, perhaps, possible to live differently.

*

Fashion was on the front line in declaring your allegiances.

Sitting in the bus station café in Taunton, Kate Paul was picked on
by the old 'witch' who ran it, and told that she must leave. She was
running a respectable café for respectable people, and Kate's skirt
was too short to answer to that description.

Undeterred, Kate Paul recorded later that summer that she was
making herself 'a very short tight skirt . . . in pink and white check.
It sounds revolting.'

By today's standards most women's garments in 1960 were uncon-
troversial and homogeneous. Dior's 1947 New Look had left its
mark in the bell-like shape of skirts. These, though shorter by the

year, still had to amply cover an area of thigh from knicker to reinforced stocking top, thus concealing the complicated panoply of
wired suspender attachments that upheld one's hosiery. Tights weren't
readily available until 1968, and didn't overtake stockings until the
1970s. Meanwhile, on any weekday lunch hour, there was barely a
trouser to be seen clothing the legs of the average female office
worker. Felicity Green, later a celebrated fashion journalist, began
work at the *Daily Mirror* in 1960, and straight away ran up against an
editor who pleaded with her not to wear trousers in the office, in case
she was unexpectedly sent to interview the Queen. Indeed, Royalty
was a byword for conservatism, in modest pleated skirts, matching
hats, gloves and handbags, and an enduring love affair with the silk
headscarf, demurely knotted under the chin. The Queen's sturdy
tweed suits (which had been made to last for ever) reappeared annu-
ally from their mothballs, as they still do. Her look had little to do
with fashion.

But that phenomenon, too, was starting to realign and, along with
so many other aspects of popular culture, it reflected the generational
tug of war now mobilising. In 1955 Mary Quant had made fashion
history by opening her first shop, Bazaar, in Chelsea, followed soon
after by a second in Knightsbridge. Here she sold liberating chemises
with kick-flared skirts that were 'short, short, short . . .' Quant's
ultra-modern silhouette was quickly taken up by the teen élite, while
her extraordinary entrepreneurial flair conferred a new, edgy identity on bohemian Chelsea. This was, as Felicity Green later described
it, 'way-out, with-it fashion . . .' It was London-centric too. And
whereas in the past Dior, Molyneux, Jacques Fath, Schiaparelli and
Chanel had ordained what women wore, by the end of the 1950s
young women like Kate Paul were simply deciding what they liked
to wear, running it up on their sewing machines, and wearing it. For
the first time, Teddy girls, beatniks and art students found they could
influence how their contemporaries dressed. The pavement became a
catwalk for a generation of youthful self-created models.

One of these was Mavis Wilson. Today, Mavis is a soignée elderly
woman with a shapely bob, taut skin and dangly earrings, who
lives in a modest cottage in London's westerly suburbs. In 1960 she
was growing up in a working-class family not far away in leafy

Wimbledon. Having failed the eleven-plus exam, Mavis knew that her face – with its huge round blue eyes and curtains of hair – was her fortune. Certainly, her Saturday job at Morden Co-op didn't go far towards financing her teenage longings. Nonetheless, she dyed her hair red, and saved for a pair of high-heeled bronze mock-croc winkle-pickers. Tottering down the arterial road from Raynes Park to Kingston-upon-Thames, she and her friend Cherry would sing along to their favourite Ronettes numbers playing at top volume on Cherry's portable tape recorder: 'Be my, be my baby . . .' 'We were hoping for boys! That's what we were hoping for.' If they didn't find any by the time they got to Kingston, they just turned round and walked back.

The journalist Mary Ingham's portrait of her adolescence in the Midlands also points to the emergence of a new kind of female effrontery in the first years of the new decade. On Saturday nights the 'council estate girls' milled around the local coffee bar, with their beehive hairdos, natty suits, pink lipstick and stockings. Mary and her friends from the high school straightened their curls, coated their faces with pale powder and defined their eyes with the blackest of eyeliner. Fake snakeskin boots and box-pleated low-waisted dresses completed this edgy, brazen, sexualised look. Pubescent fantasies also fed on romantic comics such as *Roxy*, *Mirabelle* and *Romeo* ('banned at home as "common trash" and at school as an insult to our intelligence'). For no prohibition could suppress the 'base bodily undertow' and 'forbidden thoughts' which accompanied the journey towards the adult world.

The Sexual Supermarket

After *Lady Chatterley* the unspoken was starting to become the spoken.

In 1960, sex was getting ever harder to ignore. Lady Chatterley's class status played a part in this, for the book's acquittal was a recognition that 'posh' girls could enjoy sex, as much as 'bad' girls. And from now on, the class disparity which the guardians of this nation's morality found so unpalatable was on course to be paraded as never before, with sexual double standards dragged protesting and denying from the closet. Titillation was going public.

Marilyn Rice-Davies was fourteen in 1958, so didn't have the chance, at that time, to read the unexpurgated *Lady Chatterley's Lover*, which was still under a ban.* Instead, she got her teenage information about sex from another 'contraband' bestseller, *Forever Amber*, the spicy historical romance by American author Kathleen Winsor, set in seventeenth-century England; fourteen US states banned it as pornographic. The story, set in a seamy, noisy, colourful London of bordellos and coffee houses, is the reverse of 'Lady C' and its bucolic 'slumming-with-a-gamekeeper' theme. Winsor's heroine, Amber St Clare, headstrong, beautiful and adventurous, is a rags-to-riches courtesan who sleeps her way to the top, taking in bubonic plague, civil war and the court of Charles II along the way.

Marilyn Rice-Davies seems not only to have internalised the social messages of *Forever Amber* undiluted, but also to have shared a number of characteristics with Amber St Clare herself: her resourcefulness, independence and sexual allure. Certainly, on a romantic level, Marilyn 'believed fervently in the agony and the ecstasy of love – red, violent and blood-splashed'. But this was lower middleclass Solihull. And as the pretty daughter of a tyre-factory employee, Marilyn felt trapped in its prosaic, suburban streets. She started to plan a way out, left school and took a post in the china department of a Birmingham fashion store at £3 a week. It didn't take long before she discovered that becoming a catwalk mannequin in a shop was more fun, if you had what it took: charm and sex appeal.

> I have never done anything to encourage a pass, I have never been a great beauty, at best passingly pretty, yet all my adult life I have fended off men.

Handsome Robin was the first to penetrate the barriers. Marilyn liked him, but was mildly unimpressed by the experience. Soon after, a man stopped her in the street and asked her whether she would like

---

* When she started her modelling career in early 1961, Marilyn Rice-Davies's agent told her that her name was too middle-aged, so she adopted the stage name 'Mandy', by which she was always subsequently known.

to model at the Earl's Court Motor Show. In 1959 the brand-new car that was hitting the headlines was BMC's Mark I Mini, designed by Alec Issigonis. 'The car . . . was young in spirit, the girl had to be young too.' Marilyn packed her high heels and launched herself on London. After a week of swish hotel bathrooms, glittery receptions and launches, and posing for photo sessions, she was hooked. 'I was leading a glamorous life and I loved it.' She had earned £80, and was dead set on trying her luck in the city on a permanent basis. The suggestion was met by her parents with horror. Nevertheless, undeterred, and without telling anyone, she gave in her notice at the fashion store, and wrote a note to her mother and father telling them not to worry. One Monday morning in the autumn of 1960 she picked up her suitcase containing three pairs of shoes, a cocktail dress and a leather-bound copy of *The Canterbury Tales*, left the house unseen and headed for the station. 'I said no goodbyes . . .' Marilyn was sixteen.

In 1960 three and a quarter million people lived in inner London. And everywhere, there were bulldozers. Road-widening schemes were wiping out Victorian terraces to make way for cars. New buildings were springing from the bomb sites, with flats, shops and concrete tower blocks replacing slums and changing the skyline. A new Hilton hotel was in the offing in Park Lane. The city was in flux, and for the young and adventurous it was a magnet: a tatty, squalid, vulgar, wealthy, foul-aired, pervasively grey, neon-lit, star-studded metropolis, where red-painted pillar-boxes and telephone booths furnished the streets, and muddy city sparrows pecked among wilted cabbage leaves in Covent Garden's market halls. Tobacconists, fishmongers and dairies existed next door to Italian coffee bars and American-style Wimpy bars. The crumbling stuccoed porches of Notting Hill Gate gave onto the dingy basements and warrens of tiny rooms that now accommodated families of immigrant Caribbeans, while nearby Portobello Road was a colourful mix of cauliflower stalls and fruit barrows, side by side with poky junk shops and alleyways of stolen goods. Queensway after dark was the haunt of insomniacs, hookers and assorted people of the night who clustered around the stalls to drink coffee and eat hot dogs. By day, gloved and hatted débutantes congregated at their favoured teatime rendezvous in Piccadilly,

Fortnum and Mason's. Later, such aristocrats and sophisticates headed with their escorts for a cellar in Leicester Square, the 400 Club, where Princess Margaret might be seen. In this London, Islington, Clerkenwell and Fulham were down-at-heel working-class districts, home to grimy pubs; Fleet Street still meant newspapers, Chelsea meant arty bohemia, and – in among its bookies, pubs, cheap trattorias and tailors' workshops – Soho meant sleaze.

In 1959 the Street Offences Act had cleared prostitution off the streets and sent the women and their haggling pimps underground. But in the Soho of 1960 it was as easy as ever to get whatever kind of value you wanted for your money, whether that meant between the sheets, or something more imaginative. The coded adverts pasted to the interior of telephone booths ('Rubber and rainwear made to measure . . .'; 'Young lady gives Swedish lessons . . .' and so on) were to be found in every city in the land. The upper crust spent their money on call girls – hotel porters could usually be trusted to outsource the visiting businessman's needs – while clients prepared to risk it could still pick up women on the streets. But West End strip clubs and night spots were generally the first stop for the lonely and lust-driven. In 1960 it was estimated that there were two hundred strip clubs in London, many of them liberally scattered among Soho's network of cobbled alleyways, street markets and grubby thoroughfares.

A guide to the capital's sexual supermarket in the early years of the decade describes the strange ritual of club opening time, which was often lunchtime.* Clusters of businessmen are to be seen on the pavement outside such establishments, shuffling in as the doors are unbolted, with many a furtive glance and muttered apology to the other bowler hats in the queue: 'Oh, er, hello old man. Just thought I'd look in for a lunchtime drink. As good a place as any, don't you think?' A pink gin at the bar is pushed aside as the men make for the darkened auditorium, where no one speaks or makes eye contact.

Walker's Court, an alley just off Brewer Street, was the location for the most famous of these clubs; in 1960 Marjorie Davis was one of the dancers there. Now seventy-five and the owner of a picturesque

---

* *The New London Spy: A Discreet Guide to the City's Pleasures* (1966), edited by Margaret Forster's husband, journalist Hunter Davies.

flint-cobbled pub in a north Norfolk fishing village, she spoke with nostalgia of the excitement and glamour of her days at the Raymond Revuebar.*

The Revuebar was first opened by Paul Raymond in 1958. Marjorie explained to me that, for female employees like her, their place of work had a hierarchy. Dancers like her were at the top of the tree – above (in this order) showgirls, hostesses and strippers.

> The place was very glamorous, very plush, with bars and tables and restaurants – and there might have been gambling tables. And the men's wives came too, all dolled up.
>
> As dancers, we had the most wonderful costumes. Money was no object. It was all sparkling high-cut leotards and beautiful headdresses. We did sometimes have a midriff – but we were fully clothed over our bosoms and our nether regions.

The showgirls, however, were selected with toplessness in mind:

> They were semi-nude: naked on the top but not on the bottom. They had G-strings on, and stickers on their boobs. Then as well, there were half a dozen of what were called hostesses: very glamorous women in low-cut evening dresses. And when two or three men came in, they were offered one of these hostesses to sit with them, talk to them, entertain them, and drink with them – and encourage them to spend their money.

Hostesses took commission on drinks, and did well out of this. At some clubs they used their flirtatious skills to persuade the customers to buy them cuddly toys and floral bouquets – generally recycled through new customers the very next day. More vulnerable to sexual entanglements than the dancers, the hostesses also provided many a lonely man with a sympathetic ear and a shoulder to cry on.

> As for the strippers, a lot of them were foreign girls. Some of them hardly spoke English. Paul Raymond brought them over from Scandinavia and so on. One was a doctor, with a degree, from Sweden. It's

* Thanks are due here to Paul Willetts, author of *Members Only: The Life and Times of Paul Raymond, Soho's Billionaire King of Burlesque* (2010), for taking the trouble to put me in touch with ex-club dancer Marjorie Davis.

actually quite a skill, stripping. It's very choreographed. You can't just go on and take your knickers off, you have to know how to stand on one leg.

And Raymond was always getting into trouble with the Lord Chamberlain, because in those days there was a law set by his office, that a complete nude wasn't allowed to move (except in private members' clubs).* She was allowed to strip off at the end of her act, completely naked. But she had to stand stock still till the music finished and the curtain closed.

And us dancers were mostly clad apart from our arms and legs, and we could dance our heads off!

'By no means all club hostesses take men back to their own flats after the club or drinking dive where they supposedly work has closed. But there are not many who will say "no", if the offered payment is high enough,' reported *The New London Spy*.

On the face of it, the club culture of the 1950s and 60s played on the male fantasy of women as delectable forbidden fruit, with much of the attendant shame. Vice and depravity in dark hideaways. Look, but don't touch. By the same token, women like Marjorie Davis working in these glamour palaces traded the supra-feminine projections of bodily perfection and eroticism for money. This mirrored the conventional sexual status quo, in which the bond between a man and a woman was all too often a transaction: security in return for subjection. For the club's owner, a beautiful woman was an important commercial product, and was treated as such. A girl with chipped nail polish or ungroomed hair would have her pay docked. At the time, Marjorie Davis didn't question the rules of this game:

> I remember one man saying to me, 'You can always tell the character of a man by looking at his wife,' – meaning, was she overdressed, or was she subtly dressed, or understated? Was the ring on her finger a real diamond? That was how you told whether he was generous, and whether he was rich.

* The Royal Household encompasses the Lord Chamberlain's Office; prior to 1968 the Office licensed all public performances, was responsible for theatre censorship, and was regarded by many playwrights and theatregoers as a killjoy agent of puritanism.

Marjorie herself had a full-blown romance with a wealthy book-maker with whom she made flirtatious eye contact across the auditorium. He looked like the movie actor Montgomery Clift, ran a big flashy car and wore shiny mohair suits. It took two years for her to discover that he was married.

She finds it heart-warming to recall how supportive her fellow glamour girls were to her at this time, sharing the fun as well as the fallout. Some of the girls were respectably engaged or married, set-ting up home and choosing curtains. These were the friends whose shoulders she cried on, whose clothes she borrowed. They held her hand and kept her secrets.

This, then, was the world that Marilyn Rice-Davies entered that Monday afternoon in 1960. From the Raymond Revuebar, a five-minute walk through Golden Square and past the end of Carnaby Street leads to Beak Street, which runs east–west off Regent Street, and here, at number 16, was Murray's: a night club whose boast was that it catered to the élite. Unlike the Revuebar, Murray's didn't present strippers. But in other respects – the 'boarding-school atmosphere', the hierarchies, and the strict rules so easily bent – Marilyn's working life would be the same as Marjorie's.

When, at 4 p.m. on the same day as her arrival in London, Marilyn presented herself for audition as a dancer, she was one among thirty hopefuls who lined up obediently in the gaudy, airless surroundings of the cabaret, all flocked wallpaper and potted palms. Having checked that she *could* dance, the middle-aged owner, Percy Murray, sent her off to change into a skimpy leotard and then requested her to perform a simple routine. Her abilities and figure were to his taste. By the end of the session, the job was hers, at £25 a week. Murray asked her age. ' "Eighteen," I lied blithely.' It didn't seem to matter, any more than her obviously baseless promise to supply a guarantee from her parents, something she easily forged.

Marilyn Rice-Davies was happy at Murray's. It was fun, and it was very glamorous. King Hussein of Jordan was a regular there and was known to fill his car with girls and drive at top speed to Brighton, sirens blaring. Also, she could now afford an expensive pair of green velvet trousers from Mary Quant, a pair of high black leather boots and a batch of hit-parade records, as well as a flat with a film-star-style bathroom in Swiss Cottage. But despite the backstage companion-ship, Marilyn felt lonely. A few weeks into her job at the nightclub, she made a new friend. This stunning nineteen-year-old was another dancer, a sleek, feline beauty – vulnerable, susceptible, extravagant, flippant and infuriating. The name of the young woman who would become her flatmate, make her famous, and change her life was Christine Keeler.

1961

Bobby's Girl

In 1961 my grandmother, the Bloomsbury group artist Vanessa Bell, was eighty-one years old. She had been born in the nineteenth century, when Queen Victoria was on the throne. Creatively, and as a woman, Vanessa had been ahead of her time in many ways. But tragedy and war had quenched the volcanic passions of her youth. In old age my grandmother retreated into a detached and gentle routine, painting, sketching and watching the seasons pass from the attic studio window of her Sussex home, Charleston. Its isolation made the house seem timeless and other-worldly; a place largely forgotten by post-war modernity. It was there, one night in April 1961, that Vanessa quietly and painlessly died.

I was five years old. Later in the year my family decamped to Charleston for the summer, as we always did. I guess standards had been slipping for some time, since in 1953 Grace Higgens, Vanessa's devoted housekeeper, had acquired a television to watch the Coronation. My brother and I were sometimes allowed to watch it in her little sitting room. Under-exposed as we were to popular media, it seems ironic now that it was under Charleston's culturally elevated roof that he and I got our first taste of *Popeye*, *The Flintstones* and *Juke Box Jury*. So, when I think back to my childhood days at Charleston, it is not just the freedom of the South Downs, the smell of oil paint and old books along with the visual riches of the house itself that I remember. It is also the small-screen vision of a smiling teenager in a full frock with a brittle, lacquered hairdo, jigging to an irrepressibly catchy tune, and – with the surprisingly smoky contralto that had won her a capti-vated following, including me – belting out those indelible lyrics:

> *Walking back to happiness, woopah oh yeah yeah*
> *Said goodbye to loneliness, woopah oh yeah yeah . . .*

What was it about Helen Shapiro that was so 'of the moment'?

Helen had been born into a Ukrainian Jewish family in London's East End. Like all the teenagers in her Clapton gang, she was 'into the beatniky look . . .': stiletto winkle-pickers, box pleats, eyeliner and hairspray. But already Helen had found her direction in life and nothing would persuade her out of it. Aged fourteen, schoolgirl Helen was 'discovered' and signed up by a Columbia Records producer, who traded on her extreme youth and extraordinary vocal power. Both were to prove chart-topping attributes. Her first record got to number 28. Her second, 'You Don't Know', made it to number 1. She was Schoolgirl Star of the Year, with three hit records to her name before she even left school.

Helen's management quickly realised that their new artist had a special talent, but they failed to embrace the sass and swagger of this Cockney teenager, bursting with confidence, cool and unwavering ambition. Instead, for lack of alternative role models, they unimaginatively modelled her on Alma Cogan, a traditional pop singer of thirty whose career was now on the wane. Cogan (also Jewish) had been famous for her figure-hugging feminine frocks. Helen was dressed up as a stagy middle-aged Jewish princess in elaborate costumes with beaded, heavily structured bodices and gold satin skirts, matching shoes and frou-frou petticoats made from hundreds of yards of tulle. Each one cost £80.*

Helen Shapiro sold over a million copies of 'Walking Back to Happiness'. But her success was short lived. Columbia Records had locked her into an early sixties moment. And maybe that's why I remember her so vividly. The girly innocence of those trite 'Yeah-yeah' lyrics were as much a throwback as the inappropriately elaborate frocks encasing her adolescent body. In that short period Shapiro was unnaturally frozen in time, as rigidly presented as her bouffant lacquered hair, a child-woman caught between the old world and the new. The pop-music scene was on the cusp of change. Left to herself, Helen's instincts and incredible talent might have allowed her to adapt to that change, to be the feisty fashion-conscious beatnik and jazz soloist she felt herself to be. But trussed up in whalebone, she was parked in the past, out of date when she was barely mature enough even to need a

---

* Worth nearly £1,700 today.

foundation garment. In 1961 Helen had a lot of growing up still to do – but, while she developed into a woman, her career would have difficulty progressing beyond 'girl-next-door'. One day, a year after her hit record, she opened a copy of *Melody Maker*, and read the head-line 'Is Helen Shapiro a "has-been" at 16?'

*

In the early sixties a vibrant, unruly teenage culture was struggling to break free from the chains of the past. But the chains were strong.

It was tough, in the fifties. Girls wore white gloves . . .

remembered the novelist Angela Carter.

White gloves were the visible badges of female bondage – and chastity. The wearer of white gloves could not risk contamination with dirt, stain or pollution; purity was paramount. Encased within their snowy sheaths, a woman's fingers remained as unsullied as her virtue.

This was the world of the 'perfect wife', with her matching hat, handbag and vanity case, backcombed and lacquered, poised and radiant. Her world embraced femininity, man-made fibres, punctual meals and mended socks. The 1950s stereotype was alive and well in 1961 and, as we have seen, it would take some shifting.

But women's fetters also took the shape of deep-rooted assumptions, for example the widespread belief among parents, teachers and self-appointed elders and betters that it was unnecessary for women to be properly educated. Even where schools offered vocational courses for girls, these had a strongly gendered slant, towards house-craft, retail, clerical and secretarial work, cookery and nursing. Right into the 1960s – and despite a recognised lack of 'trained brains' in the professional marketplace – it continued to be claimed that higher education for women was of limited value, because the average woman's career spanned barely seven years, from twenty-one to twenty-eight. Early marriage and 'marriage wastage' were the cause. Bright girls were discouraged by their teachers from applying to top universities, medical schools, architectural colleges and law schools where quotas would make it hard for them to obtain places. It was thought that 'normal' young women should go to teacher-training college or sec-retarial school, have 'a little job', and then get married.

As so often, pop lyrics reflect majority sentiments. Susan Maughan's bouncy little hit 'Bobby's Girl' spelled out the prospects for many an unambitious young woman:

> *When people ask of me*
> *What would you like to be*
> *Now that you're not a kid any more?*
> *I know just what to say,*
> *I answer right away*
> *There's just one thing*
> *I've been wishing for.*
> *I wanna be Bobby's girl,*
> *I wanna be Bobby's girl . . .*
> *That's the most important thing to me!*

And sooner rather than later Bobby's girl would become Bobby's wife.

But others had visions of fulfilment beyond getting Bobby's tea on the table. The problem was persuading those authority figures that there could be more to life.

Margaret Forster encountered uncomprehending hostility at her decision to pursue further education. She was 'daft', according to her father. 'I was a girl, I'd just get married.' In her curious and unsparing memoir *An Education*,* the journalist Lynn Barber tells the story of how in the early sixties she was courted, while studying for her A levels, by Simon, a much older married conman. On the day of her last exam he proposed marriage. To her horror, Lynn's parents urged her to accept Simon and drop all thoughts of going to Oxford. 'You don't need to go to university if you've got a good husband . . . Why go to university if you don't need to?' Never mind the fact that Simon was obviously a bad apple. She wasn't even pregnant, they insisted, and good husbands didn't grow on trees.

Even after she'd graduated, one young woman was firmly told by a grumpy aunt: 'If you hadn't've gone to that university, you'd've been married by now!'

But things were starting to change and, inexorably, the challenging of values had begun. Unreasonable, prudish and rigid, the older generation

* Published in 2009, and later adapted as a film starring Carey Mulligan.

already seemed to be on a collision course with the young. The penny-pinching, frugal wartime values of our grandparents were beginning to seem old-fashioned and irrelevant in the 'never-had-it-so-good' years.

★

At the dawn of the 1960s consumerism exploded with a bang. Women, more than men, took the hit, because shopping was what women did. In some respects, it was who they were. In the 1950s a survey reckoned that the average working-class woman spent around one hour every day shopping. In 1961 shopping was still an almost exclusively female pursuit, whether for potatoes and bacon or knickers and nail lacquer. (As Lilian Forster told her daughter, 'A man shouldn't be shopping . . .') And the nation's circuitous economy relied on promoting desirable consumer goods to susceptible (female) customers. Thus, women working in the factories were producing goods to earn money that would enable them to purchase the wish-list of those same dream appliances, clothes and homewares, without which they felt deprived of identity and status in the ranks of womankind. By the 1960s, the product choices on offer were becoming ever more exciting. Shopping was already moving away from its associations with the daily grind and becoming something a woman did for leisure and self-indulgence.

Enter Vivian Nicholson, the twenty-five-year-old Yorkshire-woman who came into £152,319 after her husband Keith won the pools, and originator of the catch-phrase 'Spend, spend, spend!'★ Viv's rags-to-riches story exactly caught the spirit of the times.

Viv, born Vivian Asprey in 1936, had grown up in abject poverty in Castleford, not far from Leeds, first of five children, the daughter of a coal miner. Debt and deprivation dominated Viv's early years, there were never any Christmas presents, and the family survived by fiddling their National Assistance allowance. Nevertheless, Wallington Street, Castleford was a friendly place to grow up. Nineteenth-century back-to-backs, soon to be condemned as slums, bred a special kind of neighbourliness. Anyone poorly who lived here could depend on a helping hand, and the children could be sure of playmates. There were no cars. On summer evenings Castleford families sat on their

★ Their winnings would be worth around £3.2 million today.

doorsteps sharing beer and a packet of Woodbines. If somebody died, the whole street went into mourning.

Viv's schoolteacher suggested that she should try for a place at art school, but the family needed her to work. So she left school at the age of fourteen and found employment in a sweet factory, making liquorice allsorts, before moving on to a job in the local cinema. The only thing that lifted Viv's humdrum, skint existence was her ability to attract the local boys. 'My breasts were developing, it seemed, faster than time itself. I thought, God, they're never going to stop! And all the other girls were flat in front, flat!'

This was power, but it was also a trap. At sixteen, Viv was pregnant. There was nothing for it but to get married:

> Oh hell fire, I thought, a mother at seventeen. It wouldn't sink in. I didn't want to look after any kids, I wanted to be a roamer, I wanted to be off. I would have been too if I had been a man . . .
>
> At seventeen, stuck in that bleeding house baby-minding . . .

Marriage to Matt Johnson had nothing going for it. Keith Nicholson was her mischievously attractive young neighbour; with him, 'everything was stardusty'. Sexually infatuated with each other, Viv and Keith were soon clawing, biting and undressing at every opportunity; on freezing evenings by the canal, down on the towpath, in the lee of a hedge, four times a night; they were like addicts. By 1961 Viv was twenty-four and divorced with four children, three of them Keith's. He became husband number two, the one she would always swear she loved the most. He called her Goldie. But dumping Matt wasn't a soft option.

> Life was a terrible struggle. Keith only earned seven pounds a week as a trainee miner . . .*

Somehow, the children got fed, but Viv herself lived off bones and mashed-potato sandwiches. On Saturday 30 September 1961, sick and bad tempered with money worries, Viv had a row with her mother and stormed home, to find the Rentaset man on her doorstep waiting for the TV rental money. She paid up, and after he'd left Viv put her hair in rollers, bribed her reluctant father to babysit (another ten

---

* About £145 in 2017 (to support a family of six).

shillings . . .), and said to Keith, ' "Does tha know what I think we'll do, lad? We've two pounds left. Shall we blow it in?" "Those are the best words I've heard for bleeding months," he said. "We'll get drunk." '

While Viv got the kids washed and brushed, Keith started getting ready to go out, shaving in the living room with the TV on. The announcer was broadcasting the football results.

> Then he calls, 'Hey, Viv, I've got a draw there,' shaving away.
>
> I says, 'Has tha?' I never bothered to take much notice.
>
> Then he shouted, 'That's two.'

By the time the children were in bed Keith had clocked up four draws. Then five, then six. Oblivious to what he was doing, Keith was rasping at his skin with the razor, and blood was pouring from his throat. With seven draws Keith was bleeding down his shirt front, frantic to find his pools coupon, turning the house upside down. At last, it showed up in Keith's trouser pocket. And they had the full complement: eight draws. Viv felt dizzy. They said in the paper that could mean £75,000.

The Littlewoods representatives took them down to London. At King's Cross station they were mobbed. A reporter asked Viv what she was going to do with the money.

> And I said, 'I'm going to spend, spend, spend, that's what I'm going to do.'

As if by a fairy godmother, she was whisked round a dress shop, and kitted out with outfits, expensive nylons, underwear and a pink-rinse hairdo, with the press wolfpack in hot pursuit. Two days of shows and champagne followed; there was steak too. Viv's stomach was too tight with excitement to eat it, but she could drink. In the hotel she and Keith poured champagne, brandy and Dubonnet over each other, licked it off and made love. When the cheque from Littlewoods came, it was for £152,300 18s 8d. The spending could begin.

Back in Castleford it started with a £200 booze-up for Keith's work-mates, after which the drink never ran dry. Viv moved from beer to gin. Then came the dream car: a top-of-the-range silver Chevrolet Impala, 'that big, [it was] like a bloody bus . . .', and the dream house: a ranch-style bungalow with picture windows on a posh estate outside Leeds, ten miles from the back-to-back hovels where she'd started out.

In Grange Avenue, Garforth, nobody spoke to the Nicholsons.

Goldie hits the goldmine. Viv Nicholson's stratospheric pools win catapulted her into the high life. There was no way but down.

Most days now, Viv sailed out at about eleven in her stretch motor, to spend a few hours buying clothes, £100 or £150 at a time. The children were packed off to expensive boarding schools. Time passed with shopping and hair appointments; Viv's candyfloss platinum do went from pale pink, to mauve, to green, yellow and blue. She partied till the early hours.

To begin with, Viv couldn't understand the headaches, the prickly rash, the failure to focus, the depression, the fear of death and the uncontrollable shaking. And the loneliness.

> I was walking round the house, I couldn't sit, I'd put records on, television, sing to myself. 'Oh hurry up phone, ring, ring, ring, ring, do something.' I'd sit in kitchen, keep splashing my face, wondering what it was all about . . .

And the money was trickling through their fingers.

She is Having Fun

The press beat a path to Viv Nicholson's door. The interest in her was insatiable, from her cars to the colour of her hair, but perhaps above all in her irrepressible personality. Later, like hyenas, they would feast greedily on her remains, when the big win disastrously failed to buy friends, love, health or happiness. But as the possessor of a windfall, who had been catapulted overnight from breadline to big spender, Viv Nicholson embodied a post-war fulfilment fantasy. Here was the recipient of every dreamed-of dissipation, drowning in a vulgarian cocktail of consumer excess, suffocating under a superfluity of Cadillacs, couture clothes, swimming pools, exotic holidays, silk underwear, jewellery, movie-star make-up, pink champagne and pink rinses, cosmetics, furs, racehorses, gold watches, brandy and sex.

Miners expected their women to stay in the kitchen. 'A woman's only good for two things – looking after the house and lying on the bed,' one of them was quoted by a social survey, and Castleford wives were no exception. But Viv broke the mould. Life for her was about more than being Bobby's girl. And when fate blitzed her narrow, hard-up world, she jubilantly stepped out, unapologetically, reck-lessly raised a glass to Wealth and stood isolated under the wreckage as it cascaded down around her, against a landscape of destruction. 'It is my life,' she told a reporter, 'and I won't be told how to live it.'

Consumerism was taking off. Viv Nicholson wasn't the only one who dreamed of new shoes, sitting-room suites, and the good things that money could buy. For if education was denied young women, paid work was not. And though not everyone could win the pools, earning your own money entitled you to Fun.

To generalise, women's jobs were largely routine, low-status and unskilled, and many of them, especially those with young children, worked part-time. It didn't take education to pack liquorice allsorts. Nevertheless the statistics showed the numbers of women in the work-force steadily rising, up 2 per cent between 1951 and 1961, from 31 per cent to 33 per cent. And though equal pay across the board was still a long way off, in 1961 half a million women were awarded parity with men for equal work. Any school-leaver could earn enough to look 'with-it', buy records and go to the cinema. Affluence fed back into popular culture. Like clothes, music was central to the sixties. Between 1955 and 1960 the market for 45-rpm vinyl singles leapt from 4 million records sold each year, to 52 million, with the boom in sales powered by teenage crazes. Rock'n'roll peaked around 1961, and the volatile, high-spending pop economy was hungry for new talent.

And here was another root cause behind the attack on the Establishment by the young of the 1960s. Unwittingly, the old had cleared the decks for mutiny by advancing the cause of post-war capitalism. The baby-boomers were encouraged by politicians to believe that they were growing up in an age of unequalled prosperity. Inevitably, cars, holidays and television were broadening horizons. These, and an easy-come, easy-go approach to the plethora of available jobs, were to a high degree what gave the young the freedom to indulge and explore their aspirations, and to attack their elders for that very materialism.

It felt like luxury:

– I started work [in the bank] at £350 a year, £6 a week, which was an amazing amount of money. I could do anything I wanted on that amount, living at home . . .

– In 1961 I earned 9 guineas a week and I had a bedsitter in Hyde Park Gate that cost 3 guineas a week . . .

– I was earning nearly twice as much as my dad . . .

– I was sent to some publishing companies, and they all gave me interviews, and they all offered me jobs. Full employment, or virtually full employment, had a very big impact.

I mean, to come out of some ordinary little secretarial college and just walk into a job in the area of your choice was what we took for granted.

Magic!

Undoubtedly, the economic prosperity of the late fifties and early sixties would help detonate the explosion that was to come. For young women like these with cash jingling in their purses, and the sound of rock'n'roll ringing in their ears, nothing seemed out of reach. Journalist Sara Maitland came to see the sixties as an historic turning point:

> Far from silent, but with 'wild surmise' we stood there and saw the infinite possibility of a huge new world – a vast ocean waiting for our exploration.

*

A huge new world. And when nineteen-year-old Rosalyn Palmer took the train to Liverpool in 1961 she couldn't wait to leave the old world behind her.

Rosalyn had grown up in the Surrey hills, in Oxshott, the daughter of quietly oppressive Catholic parents (an Irish mother and an English father), who sent her to be half-educated by some 'appalling, rigid, unhappy' nuns in a convent in nearby Leatherhead. The Palmers' home environment was equally stultifying and prohibitive. Her mother and father had no aspirations for her while, at that time, Oxshott was changing from a rural village into a bastion of nouveaux riches, who clung to the English class system and its rigid ordinances of wealth, accent and suitability.

But Rosalyn was unsquashable. Though the convent was dire, she managed to pass four O levels, which qualified her for a place at Guildford Technical School. Despite her parents' rooted belief that she was stupid, she firmly pressed ahead and enrolled for an A-level course. Rosalyn recalls her everyday journey down to Guildford as symbolic of the new direction that her life was now taking:

> I would walk down to that suburban Surrey station – and there would be a parade of the British class system in microcosm lined up along the platform. And the first-class commuters, all the stockbrokers, men with bowler hats and furled umbrellas, were up at the top end of the platform, heading for Waterloo. And then you gradually worked your way down the social line till you got to the people at the bottom end, possibly heading for Surbiton. And I would be sitting there opposite them, on the down side, in the sun, looking at all those people travelling in the opposite direction.
>
> And that, to me, has been my life. I've always gone against the flow.

Arriving at the technical school was more than an affirmation. It was a declaration of war against nuns, bowler hats, ignorance, snobbery, stratification, neglect and conventionality. On her first day Rosalyn stood speechless, taking in the dynamic mix of girls and boys, long hair and jeans, sloppy pullovers and black eyeliner. 'And I just thought, Wow!'

Without further ado Rosalyn adopted the accepted slouchy student look, started to grow her hair long and lost weight. The Student Union was the heart of the school. It galvanised the students into joining political groups and campaigns, and laid on jazz evenings. 'I learnt to jive in the most slinky, slidey way!' With her dark hair and china-blue eyes she was outstandingly attractive. And – for a repressed convent girl – the new-found accessibility of the opposite sex was like a drug. Furtively, so as not to bring her parents' wrath down on her, Rosalyn started going out with one of the more 'way-out' members of her group, a bearded, long-haired painter who played in a jazz band. Sexual ignorance, plus fear of hellfire and pregnancy, prevented her from going the whole way. Also, as Rosalyn now points out, with contraception still hard to obtain, many of the boyfriends felt inhibited from taking the ultimate risk. Abortions were illegal except in cases where it could be proved that a woman's mental or physical health was in danger, though everybody, including her, knew somebody who had come to grief. But overall, both socially and academically, life for Rosalyn was starting to become a whole lot more fun.

Soon she discovered that it was not only possible, but likely that she could gain a place at university. In the early 1960s the selection process began and ended with an interview. Aspiring students sent letters to the admissions departments of their choice, and trekked across country to be interviewed, which cost money. But Rosalyn had no support from her parents. Being of the persuasion that women's education was a pointless pre-marital pastime, they weren't prepared to pay for her to be different. So she hitch-hiked to Exeter and Nottingham. Then, somehow, she scraped together the fare to Liverpool.

Rosalyn stepped off the train at Lime Street, to be hit by the salty, smoky air of Britain's grand old port, with its history of slavery, commerce, cotton and transatlantic culture.

I don't know how I got the fare together – and I remember walking out of Lime Street. It was very grimy and dirty and grubby. But there was just a vibrancy about the place. It felt completely different – with that wonderful view of the great buildings on the Mersey. Even the air was different. And I fell in love with it. I just thought, 'This is Paradise. This is the place for me!'

The distance to the university was little over half a mile, and she had to ask for directions from passers-by – only to be instantly disarmed by the energetic warmth and willingness with which they were supplied. Her interview went well. The professor of Political Theory and Institutions had written a seminal book, which Rosalyn had read and admired. That, and her exam record, were sufficient to gain her a place.

'Then I had to tell my father.' Her elder brother had failed to get into university, which made it even harder to persuade this short-sighted and unbending man to accept that his clever daughter might do so. But the course was free and most of her maintenance grant would be paid by Surrey County Council. Reluctantly, he agreed to top it up, but not to pay a penny more. For the remainder of that year, while studying and awaiting the start of her course, Rosalyn spent the holidays waitressing and sorting mail, knowing she had only herself to rely on.

But now, a door stood open. Her confidence rocketed. She could be a journalist, a teacher, maybe even a politician? She could dance differently, dress differently, expand her mind, fight injustice, fall in love. And Liverpool beckoned, like the promised land.

*

It is striking to witness how many of the sixties generation of young women, faced – like Rosalyn Palmer – with bias, bigotry and sheer misogyny, reacted with drive, determination and self-belief. New forces were propelling them. This age group had been reading *On the Road* (1957), Jack Kerouac's cult chronicle of hedonism and disaffection, which had given form to the seismic instability boiling beneath the surface of American society. The novel offered the vision

of a life rich with unorthodox possibilities. But they also had opportunities of a kind denied to their elders.

That generation, who had lived through the war, seemed locked
into a cycle of self-sacrifice, thrift, stoicism, and self-denial. But for
their daughters, the war was little more than a mythic memory; they
were starting to swim against the tide, in many cases flinging out the
white gloves that their own mothers had destined for them.

Turning their backs on their parents' values demanded strength of
mind, fearlessness and a thirst for adventure. For example, nineteen-
year-old Doreen Hall paid no attention when her father, a cotton-mill
worker from Darwen near Blackburn, told her: 'Our type don't go to
university: it's too uppity and grand.' Instead, she got a place at
Birmingham University to read French, became vice-president of the
Student Union, graduated in 1961, applied for the new Graduate
Service Overseas scheme and – to her mother's utter horror – was
sent for a year to teach black children in Gabon, West Africa. That
same year, intrepid débutante Harriet Debenham threw in her 'little
job' in a London photographic studio and joined the crew of a 100-
foot yacht making the transatlantic journey to the West Indies. 'And
having got across the Atlantic it seemed *stupid* to come home
again . . . ! ' So she worked in a Californian ski resort for the rest of
the winter, revelling in the snow, solitude and freedom of Squaw
Valley's empty early morning trails.

Pat Quinn, the daughter of a Belfast bookie, sailed in the opposite direction. In her own words, she 'got on the water' to England
in 1961, at the age of seventeen, to seek her fortune as an actress
in London. Living hand to mouth in a bedsit in the Caledonian
Road may not have felt like the big time. But, with help, she found
temporary work at a bookie's and got fixed up with a singing in-
structor. Pat's long-term showbiz aim was starting to take chaotic
shape.

Above all, London seemed touched with stardust, and ambitious
young women like Pat no longer felt there was anything to stop them
buying one-way tickets to the capital. Kathleen Etchingham was
typical of many who prefigured the Beatles' 1967 song 'She's Leaving
Home':

> At sixteen I realised I no longer had to put up with anything if I
> didn't want to . . . Like thousands of other teenagers, I believed that
> London was waiting with open arms. All I had to do was turn up and
> the adventures would begin.

Kathy's destiny would eventually draw her into the web of the 1960s'
most glamorous pop aristocracy. It was a destiny she created herself,
in 1961, simply by walking out of the Derby shoe shop where she
worked for £3 6s a week, and which she could easily see held no
future for her.

We have already heard how Marilyn Rice-Davies picked up her suitcase and headed for Soho. And so far, the plan was working. 'London
was my village.' The string of wealthy and titled followers she now
attracted were held at bay: 'lunches only'. The dancing work at Murray's
gave way to modelling – which was more flexible and lucrative – and the
new work brought with it a new, sexier name: Mandy. Early in 1961
Mandy and Christine Keeler upsized to a two-bedroom flat in Fulham.
The girls celebrated by getting in a bottle of whisky, a bottle of sherry
and some peanuts, and inviting a motley crew of admirers round for a
housewarming. These included the well-connected osteopath Stephen
Ward: 'a good conversationalist, quite charming'. But more to Mandy's
taste was 'a plump middle-aged property speculator', Peter Rachman,
perma-tanned and groomed, in cashmere and crocodile. Over that
year, both friendships developed, and it was at this time that Mandy first
visited Ward's rented cottage on the Cliveden estate, and met his landlord, Bill Astor. Meanwhile, Rachman and she grew closer. He started
giving her £80 a week in cash, more money than she knew how to
spend. Welcome as it was, Mandy actually liked being with Peter: 'I
knew that whether I went to bed with him or not I could keep him as a
friend.' And for her birthday in October that year he handed Mandy the
keys to a white 3.2-litre Jaguar.

'She . . . is Having . . . Fun . . .' (as Lennon and McCartney sang).
Women like these believed that pleasure, fulfilment and adventure
were their due in the post-war world. In a sense, they were pioneers,
blazing a gutsy, unrepentant trail, as they rejected provincial tedium,
matching accessories and perfect wifedom.

Cool

Liverpool, the huge new world that Rosalyn Palmer was discovering, was familiar home to Beryl Marsden.*

In 1961 it was a city of Irish, Welsh, Africans and Chinese; a city of football, steeplechasing and green double-deckers, flaunting its mighty warehouses, its ocean-going ships, its opulent palaces of commerce and art, its granite Merseyside magnificence, alongside back-to-backs, bomb sites and ragged children. A melting pot of Catholics, Protestants and Americans; of dance halls, jazz clubs, poetry readings, jive competitions and sailors arriving from the New World with Rhythm and Blues records in their knapsacks and burnished guitars slung across their shoulders. Little Richard, the Platters, Jerry Lee Lewis, the Shirelles, the Miracles . . . the Americans brought with them, too, the wind of the prairies, the heartache of soul, the intoxication of blues, a casual turn of phrase and a winning way with a cigarette. In a word, cool.

The raw air of those northern docks seemed charged with electricity. The Mersey generation had found its mojo.

> I just had this thing inside of me, which – no matter what – I'd decided was what I was going to do.

The 'thing inside' Beryl Marsden was music.

As we saw earlier, Beryl had a tough start in life. Born Beryl Hogg in Liverpool in 1947, she never knew who her real father was, and the family – her mother, a series of intermittent men friends of varied nationalities, and ten children – lived in poverty in a slum area of the city. Growing up in the heart of Liverpool in the late 1950s, she was immersed in its sounds. The background music to Beryl's childhood was the pop ballads of the 1950s. Elvis Presley's rebellious rock and outrageously sexual performing style were a wake-up call which coincided with her adolescence. An extraordinary makeover of Liverpudlian music-making accompanied her childhood and teens, and Beryl was determined to be part of it. 'From the age of nine or

* Marsden replaced Hogg as Beryl's stage name.

ten it was just: "I'm going to sing . . ." ' As with Helen Shapiro, that ambition was unshakeable. Both were astonishingly young when they achieved it. But though she never had a number 1 hit, Beryl was in some ways luckier than Helen.

At secondary school, Beryl seized every opportunity to sing, whether in the school choir, or doing Shirelles-style synchronised dancing and harmonies with a small band of girls in the playground. Most of those mates were heading for shop work, factory work, or – if they were lucky – the typing pool. But for Beryl, there was never any question in her mind about her future.

In 1961 Liverpool's most popular beat group was the Undertakers, a five-man band who pulled in an adoring local crowd for their appearances at the city centre Cavern Club and, thrice-weekly, at the Orrell Park Ballroom in Bootle. At the age of fourteen, Beryl was a devotee. The Undertakers were local lads, so when her friend called up to the vocalist and said, 'Hey, mate, she's driving us mad, she wants to sing with you,' she didn't think twice about jumping on to the stage. 'Boys' was the Shirelles' big hit from the previous year. Beryl knew its energetic melody and lyrics by heart.

> So that was it – I just went on the stage and belted it out. And my heart was exploding. And the audience looked at me, listened, and clapped. And I thought, I was right – this is what I should be doing with my life. And Brian Jones, who did tenor sax and vocals, said, 'Can you stay behind till we finish and have a little talk?' And then he said, 'Would you like a trial?'
>
> And that was it – I never looked back.

Beryl joined the band, and walked away from her education. The Mersey Beat was calling, and she was one of the faithful. That meant putting the music she loved first. The ripe, upbeat, gutsy timbre of her voice quickly earned her a following. Money started to roll in, but for her that wasn't a motive. The plus was that her mother could finally see why she didn't need to work in a shop. Being a teenager – going on dates, hanging out with friends – no longer interested her. 'My life was with bands, music . . . Just put me on the stage and I'm as happy as anything.' Even then, Beryl was foremost a singer, who would try to avoid the audience banter expected of stage performers.

When it was my turn to do my lead vocal, Brian would go, 'Beryl, take your chewing gum out,' and I'd stick it on the mike and do my song. Then after, he'd say 'Do you want to say something to the audience?' And I'd say, 'No.'

And then as often as not I'd take the chewing gum off the mike and put it back in again.

Though it may have cost her a fast track to stardom, Beryl refused to be controlled. For, as Helen Shapiro had found out, the male manager class had little imagination when it came to producing teenage girl singers. For them, there was one way to do things, and that was the way they had always been done. In Beryl Marsden's case, her first manager, Joe Flannery, modelled her on the glamorous female vocalist Susan Maughan, who was ten years her senior, and tried to gift wrap his latest acquisition in pretty pastel-blue net and nylon. The monstrosity got a couple of outings before it was put away, never to be seen again. ' "That's it," I said. It felt so wrong and so uncomfortable . . .' From then on Beryl's look was her own: leather jeans, straight short hair, a sloppy pullover or polo neck, and pin-toed boots. It was unstructured, young, 'beatniky' and androgynous. And it was, of course, cool.

There was no dogma behind Beryl's rejection of chocolate-boxy fifties femininity. If anything, the edgy tomboy garb underlined this young woman's anxiety not to pose a threat or set herself apart from her older male accomplices. 'I wanted to be like one of the guys.' Less cynically, perhaps, Beryl was genuinely committed to the group who had given her her break. She wanted to belong, and she wanted to be taken seriously as a singer. Above all she wanted to honour the music, follow her star and be true to herself.

Beryl Marsden's Liverpool club audience could identify with the casual, unfrilly fifteen-year-old belting out 'Everything is gonna be all right, all right, all right . . .' from the platform, because she was just like them. She wore leather and cut her hair short. Her voice, like Helen Shapiro's, was strident and sexy, with an 'only young once' urgency to it that reached out to the free and daring. It said: 'I decide how to live my life, what road to travel, and what adventures to have along the way.'

And this was rebellion. Just ten years earlier, an adolescent would have had her clothes chosen for her by her mum, and dressed as a younger copy. By the time Beryl was past puberty, the teenager had been born: defiant, irresponsible and modern; chewing-gum, rock'n'roll, leather jeans and all. In the early nineteen-sixties, it wasn't enough for teenagers seeking role models to identify with their heroes. The code of conduct also demanded rejection of the older generation. Parents were square. Teachers were square. Authority was square. The teenager did not want to look like her mother, did not want to listen to her music, live her life, or obey her rules.

A crack was forming in the social cement, with youth defying age to cross the line, not just in Liverpool and London, but in small ways across the entire country.

★

One of the chief battlegrounds was clothes. Just sixteen years after the end of hostilities, the 1960s still defined itself against a backdrop of wartime rigidities: discipline, short-back-and-sides, battledress. In the female domain, uniformity – being *the same* as everybody else – was beginning to seem craven and repulsive. Emma Codrington's experience in the early 1960s reveals the fissures that were beginning to show at this time.

Emma's father was an army administrator. Born in 1930, and brought up in a handsome country house in beautiful Wiltshire parkland, she was familiar with the world of double-barrelled names and social rules. Today she is in her late eighties, living alone in a spick-and-span modern cottage on the banks of the sparkling River Wylye. Since the early 1950s, the Girl Guide movement has been her life. After boarding school Emma went home to live with her parents, and started up a Guide company from public-spirited motives, because in 1950 there was nothing else for her – or for the girls in her rural village – to do. Back then, her Girl Guides were happy, biddable and outdoorsy. It was an innocent age. Emma spent hours with them devising treasure hunts, climbing trees, constructing rope ladders, and singing 'Ging Gang Goolie' round campfires while roasting sausages. She trained them to acquire the badges – Cook, Homemaker, First Aid – that qualified them to pursue their natural female destiny. But by 1958, aged twenty-eight and single, Emma was looking for change in her own life, and discovered that she too had an intrepid streak. 'I needed to get away and *be myself*, not just be my parents' daughter . . .' She decided to go to Australia. The World Association of Girl Guides was her passport to the Antipodes.

When she arrived in Melbourne there were eight letters of welcome from Guide organisations awaiting her. Emma paid her way, spending five months in Melbourne working as pantrymaid in a boys' school to cover the cost of her onward flight to Tasmania. There she spent nearly a year helping to run a company with another guide, Meg.

In 1961 she and Meg returned to England and set up house together in the sleepy, quintessentially English market town of Wilton near Salisbury. Emma decided to relaunch her Girl Guide company in the nearby village of Winterslow, expecting to pick up where she had left off. But by 1961 the tranquil, traffic-free, obedient 1950s world that she had said goodbye to just three years ago had become unrecognisable:

> In the fifties, Mother was always there, and she did the shopping, the cooking, the washing while everybody else was at school or at work. But in the sixties many more mothers were working, and that made a big difference to family life. Also, many more families had telephones and cars. So when I had something planned for a Saturday – a treasure hunt, or tent-pitching or something – quite a number of them couldn't come. It would be: 'Oh, I have to go and see me Gran . . .' and so on.
>
> Also, supermarkets were starting, and the whole family would pile into the car on a Saturday to go shopping at the supermarket – so weekend arrangements were problematic. Holidays too . . . In the fifties, literally the only holiday the girls got was Guide camp. But in the sixties, they started going on holiday in their cars. Even abroad – very exciting! But that made it hard to organise a camp.

Attitudes, too, had shifted dramatically. Individualism, and guardedness towards the older generation, were making inroads into the friendly team spirit of the Girl Guide movement. Emma was now thirty-one and, in the eyes of her teenage charges, well over the hill:

> The girls were emerging, finding their own levels. But overall, they were becoming harder to get through to; harder to, well, manipulate. You had to be more careful how you said things. You couldn't preach

at them. Bolshie is too strong a word, but it wasn't 'cool' to be seen chatting and laughing with an adult as the fifties lot did. Yes, they were definitely becoming – what's the word? – anti-adult.

For the Winterslow guides, their conformist blue attire – complete with berets, neckties, badges, whistles, lanyards and leather belts – was attracting the wrong kind of attention.

I noticed that on outings the girls didn't like being seen in uniform – they'd cover themselves up with coats or jackets. You had to look 'right', you know? And that didn't mean Guide uniform. The association was that being a Guide was goody-goody and '*uncool*', and I suspect they didn't like the boys saying, 'Coo, she's a *Guide*!'

For now the tremors of Mary Quant's fashion earthquake were starting to be felt even in the shires, and for teenage girls to appear on the streets in mannish blouses, knee-length gored skirts, ankle socks and flat lace-ups was far from desirable. Instead, the 'Chelsea girl', leather-booted and black-stockinged, was starting to be seen from Chester to Chelmsford.

'It was [the Chelsea Girl],' recalled Quant herself, 'who established that this latter half of the twentieth century belongs to Youth . . . Never before have the young set the pace as they do now.' But Mary Quant's rule-breaking, experimental vision deserves the credit for reimagining fashion at this time. It is hard today to appreciate the revolution that she spearheaded. Women's aspirations were being remoulded, quite literally. Post-war, their rigid foundation garments had been the sculptural armature for elaborately draped masses of satin and net, from ballgowns to wedding dresses. They had been expected to appear stately, serene and dignified: shapely goddesses in pearls, court shoes, and matching gloves and vanity cases. Quant threw that out of the window. Females were to be long-legged, streamlined, slender and, above all, sexy: 'I am sure all switched-on girls will agree with me – that sex appeal has absolutely number one priority,' she declared. The look was classless, androgynous, wild and fun. Trimmings, florals and taffeta gowns were replaced by shrieking synthetic colour, PVC and op geometry. Quant's perfect model would have no curves to interrupt the linear cut of those bright and simple shift dresses. Her hair would be short: no more overnight curlers. She would be a nubile, pubescent teenager, gamine and fawn-like.

Though they hadn't yet met, that teenager, Lesley Hornby – later universally known as Twiggy – was on course to embody Quant's vision: a case of a concept finding its perfect incarnation. In 1961 skinny Lesley Hornby, the daughter of a Neasden carpenter, was just twelve – but already 'into fashion'. Practising on her mother's old Singer sewing machine, she learnt to do skilful dressmaking, and could soon follow a pattern and run up copies of the latest styles. With material at 2s 11d a yard, it was much cheaper to make clothes than to buy them, and anyway, street fashion was so volatile that it was the only way to keep up. Suburbia had its own fashion rules. While Mavis Wilson and her friend Cherry were wearing their mock-croc winkle-pickers out west, Helen Shapiro was going for the beatniky look in Clapton. Meanwhile, Lesley and her chums in Neasden, Brondesbury, Kingsbury and Kilburn had their own brand of chic. They lengthened their skirts almost to the floor, wearing them with 'granny' blouses in chiffon and cropped hair. And you had to have a nylon mac. 'I drove my mum insane to get a nylon mac.'

The Yellow Peril

Mums were being driven insane across the country.

Increasingly, youth was being viewed as a problem, and its swaggering visibility didn't help. Embattled, frightened, and dismayed by their inability to control the younger generation, the old started to fight back.

Correspondents to newspaper editors voiced concerns about truancy, immorality, the disappearance of notions of right and wrong, jazz, the use and abuse of 'Indian hemp' at parties, stiletto heels ruining girls' feet, early smoking and drinking habits, the crumbling of social norms and waves of 'senselessly destructive hooliganism'. 'Teenage wreckers' were behind two deplorable attacks on an old folks' club in Streatham, in which lipstick was scrawled across the walls and soap powder strewn around the premises. 'We think the culprits should be birched,' said the club's chairman. In Stevenage a cinema proprietor banned all teenagers from his establishment for a month after they ripped seats, smashed lavatory fittings and let off fireworks during performances. The blame was repeatedly laid at the door of inadequate teachers and working mothers.

In the autumn of 1961 Home Secretary R. A. Butler launched a campaign to combat juvenile delinquency. But beneath all the outrage lay fear of teenage sexual licence:

Some parents would be horrified . . .

wrote a *Daily Mail* journalist outlining a report on sexual health in Newcastle-upon-Tyne:

. . . if they knew of their daughter's sexual escapades. Teenagers of the lower age group are causing a great deal of concern. Their sexual immorality is noticeable where there is a lack of parental supervision due to both parents working.

And, as shown by a 'bombshell report' published in spring 1961, the number of illegitimacies as a percentage of total births had risen steadily from 4.8 per cent to 5.1 per cent over the previous three years. Underlying that statistic were thousands of case histories involving misery, guilt, betrayal and stigma; of women relinquishing their babies for adoption, of shotgun weddings, of illegal abortion, of poverty, heartbreak and scandal.* In her bestselling novel *The L-Shaped Room* (1960) Lynne Reid Banks had brought the predicament of the single mother to vivid life. Jane, the central character, becomes pregnant after her very first sexual experience with an ex-boyfriend and decides to have the baby; her father throws her out. She then visits a doctor who leaps to the conclusion that she has come to him for a sixty-guinea abortion. In due course, despite strenuous efforts to hide her pregnancy, she is sacked from her job, told by her boss that 'my staff must be . . . one hundred per cent' and forced to lie her way past potential landladies. When she moves into the bug-infested L-shaped room of the title she finds herself in company with a miscellany of 1960s misfits, including two prostitutes, a gay man and an immigrant.

---

* Jane Robinson is the author of an excellent, compassionate social history of this subject, *In the Family Way: Illegitimacy between the Great War and the Swinging Sixties* (2015).

Jane is brave and clever, and for her the fiction resolves. She inherits a cottage; she will have her baby and find stability. But for the young, confused mothers of 50,000 illegitimate babies born in England and Wales in 1961, the adversity and prejudice were a reality. Social policy stigmatised the unmarried, who were constructively regarded as 'guilty', and were not permitted to make any claim on the fathers.

Eirlys Ellis, who had grown up in rural Wales, told her distressing story in a collection of oral histories; it's a tale of trauma, racism and denial. Eirlys was in Leeds studying to be a dietitian in 1961, when she got pregnant by Hassan, a Sudanese British Council student. Hassan, disgraced, abandoned her and returned to his homeland. Confessing to her father was agony:

> The poor man was so upset. I will never forget the look on his face.
> He must have thought, Not just in the club but a black man as well.
> [He] was horrified and went straight to bed . . .

After that the subject was off limits within her family. In great secrecy Eirlys was admitted to a home for unmarried mothers run by the Church of England Adoption Society. But because her baby would be mixed race, he would not qualify to be adopted by white parents, and would be accepted only by a children's home. Eirlys made up her mind to keep him. But sermons came with the package. The vicar would stop by to tell the girls the error of their ways – 'We were all, according to him . . . terrible sinners.' Six weeks before the baby's birth her mother and father finally visited; the family had decided that her child would be taken back to Wales and brought up by Eirlys's sister and brother-in-law. Eirlys grieved, but endured. She completed her studies, and followed her chosen career – 'but I was not allowed to talk about [David] . . . I am sure that quite a few people knew of his existence but nobody said a word.'

Commenting on the rising illegitimacy figures in the *Daily Mail*, columnist Anne Scott-James wrote,

> There is a widespread new attitude among the young to marriage and motherhood . . .
>
> The Christian idea of the family has broken to pieces . . . The new attitude is not positive in any way. It is merely slap-happy.

Illegitimacy inevitably featured in the generalised outcry against collapsing morals. In 1960 the Catholic Archbishop of Westminster was to be heard lamenting Britain's sliding standards. Pictures, literature, advertising and entertainment, he railed, were displaying sordid indecency and licence at a level which 'defiles the dignity of the human person'. Meanwhile a Committee of the Free Church of Scotland spoke out specifically against

> the gratuitous exhibition of the female form . . .
>
> Much that passes today for outdoor dress ought never to have left the house, nor even come down the stairs. Much of it, as it canvasses the eye, is too painstakingly frank, some of it recognisably vulgar.

In September 1961 the retired theologian and Methodist minister Dr Leslie Weatherhead launched what was to become a prolonged correspondence in the pages of *The Times*, under the heading 'A Nation in Danger'. From where he stood, Britain appeared to be standing precariously on the verge of a slippery slope of 'dire moral peril', evidenced by the 'sinister' statistics for homosexuality, marital infidelity, pre-marital sex and pregnant brides. Weatherhead cited the headmistress of a London grammar school who 'recently stated that not one girl in her sixth form was a virgin . . .' and invoked the racist media legend that such girls proudly wore 'yellow golliwog' badges to advertise their carnal knowledge. (Had he been watching the film *The Pure Hell of St Trinian's* (1960), with its sexualised schoolgirl delinquents in revealingly laddered stockings and blackened devil eyes?) Weatherhead called on Christians to wake up to the peril:

> the decline of Rome and of other empires began with sexual depravity . . .

and to stand shoulder to shoulder as a nation to bring about a religious revival. Within days the leader of the Salvation Army weighed into the debate. The evils referred to were 'the symptoms of a nation's sickness'. Catastrophe was nigh. The master of an Oxford College agreed with him – 'For God's sake let us wake up before it is too late . . .' – while another vicar opined that the sale of contraceptives to under-18s should be a punishable offence. Other correspondents

Diabolical Delilahs: Ronald Searle's depraved schoolgirls tapped into a fear that the female sex was running out of control.

(mainly male) added their voices to comment on the rise in venereal disease, now steadily climbing after a post-war dip, the need for improved sex education and the earlier physical maturity of girls. Weatherhead himself rounded off a fortnight's worth of correspondence with an impassioned plea for moral guidance for the young. Without it, he lamented, society would be deluged with 'Teddy boys and girls', and our Christian homes would be submerged beneath a tide of pornography unleashed by the *Lady Chatterley* verdict:

> I blame the homes and the mothers who are content to tie a latch-key round a child's neck while they themselves go out to work for a 'telly', meanwhile refusing the child love and adequate care and guidance.

Not long after, the novelist and social commentator Ruth Adam was given two successive double-page spreads in the *Sunday Times* to tell the other side of the story. Her reportage into teenage morality offers a more nuanced picture of the young woman of 1961. In week one she gives us a portrait of the street-smart working-class school-girl, fashion-conscious, free and in control. As a teen, she feels she is a leader not a follower, part of a community – 'with its own privileges and customs, its own songs and dances, and its own secrets'. Home, and her parents, have become alien, and powerless in their deterrents. The old admonition to turn her out of the house if she steps out of line has become meaningless:

> 'I'll run away,' is not the hollow threat it once was. 'We could keep ourselves, you see,' the girls explain. 'We know how to get work, because we do Saturday-morning jobs. Anyway, you can always get a boy to keep you.'

Where sex is concerned, Ruth Adam stresses that these teenagers are primarily out to get married.

> And if their dominating interest, during these nubile years, was not the boys, there would be something the matter with them.

In week two, Adam turns her focus on the middle-class grammar-school or boarding-school girl. Here again, we encounter a cohort of young women who have matured early, and whose stock riposte to a fatherly or motherly rebuke is, 'What's it got to do with you?' These girls are living their own lives, going to their own parties and dating the boys they prefer without reference to parents. The old vetoes are losing their power in the face of simple desire. 'If I love someone enough, I'm entitled to go as far as I like. *They* live by one standard themselves, and expect us to live by a stricter one.' Adam also draws attention to the new permeability of class boundaries – soon to become a tendency of the times – whereby middle-class girls opted to go out with working-class boyfriends. These attractive lads with good jobs were more fun, and more trendy than the tweedy nerds of their social peer group. They had motorbikes, and money to spend. As Ruth Adam's public-school interviewee put it:

> These boys are on top of the world. They're having themselves a ball every night, as we say. I always meet mine at the pub. Mummy thinks I'm at a party in someone's house.

This was a polarised world of 'them' (parents and authorities) and 'us' (the young); of fear and outrage, audacity and entitlement. Above all, what surfaces from the panicky coverage is the width of what had now become known as 'the generation gap'.

But if this was moral laxity, society's guardians were going to have to fasten their seat belts for a turbulent ride. It was going to get a whole lot laxer.

Off the Deep End

I kind of went looking for wildness . . .

In 1961, Melissa North started her own small rebellion. Her origins were privileged. The family money – 'We weren't massively rich,' she insists – came from her American mother. Through her father she inherited class: 'He had a couple of earls for uncles.'

Today, Melissa is known as a distinctive interior designer who shares a dazzling apartment in west London with her husband, the architect Tchaik Chassay. The wildness began when she was sixteen, and had just emerged from her so-called education at Downham, a horsey and fashionable girls' boarding school in Essex, where learning was frowned on and snobbery was all. At Downham, your social standing depended on a subtle signifier: the postmark on the envelopes that lay waiting for you on the hall table, sent by boyfriends at high-ranking public schools. So if your letters were stamped Eton, Winchester or – at a pinch – Harrow, you were all right. Any lower down the order and you took the hit. This extended to the mothers. Melissa's mother would extract the names of her daughter's correspondents from her, then go straight off and look up their breeding in the aristocrats' stud book, *Debrett's*, and produce comments such as, 'Oh yes, your great-aunt was best friends with the grandmother of . . .'

That was quite claustrophobic. So by the time I went to the deb dances I was sort of looking for someone who wasn't in the stud book . . .

Melissa started to rebel – if going out with an attractive and amusing young man three years older than her who hadn't attended the approved list of schools counts as rebellion. The relationship was chaste – though Melissa was better-versed in the facts of life than many of her generation, having both grown up on a farm and read *Lolita*. But there were murmurings from the mothers when it was discovered that not only had The Boyfriend been merely to Sherborne, but that, notwithstanding his 'drawly upper-class voice', Nigel Dempster was Australian by birth.* All of this, and the fact that he had been expelled with only three O levels, meant he was looked down on for being dodgy, unsafe and 'not quite top drawer'.

Meanwhile, Melissa was being prepared for her social debut, so promptly after leaving Downham she was packed off to be 'finished' in Paris, to lodge with a respectable admiral's widow and attend a school run by nuns, who took the girls to the Louvre and taught them the rudiments of French philosophy. But there was no latitude when it came to admirers and curfews, and the presence of two fun-loving titled young men dressed in velvet hanging around the widow's town house was regarded as iniquitous. As a result, Melissa was quickly expelled for being wild and dangerous. Back home, her parents faced the problem of what to do with her, and it was decided to send her to London.

In 1961 the débutante season was still going strong.

> No amount of information on the deb routine can in itself be a complete guide to the complex etiquette of the British tribal dance known as launching a débutante.

Those words were written as late as 1969 by the doyenne of etiquette writers, Drusilla Beyfus, who then proceeded to sketch in the priorities of the socially ambitious mother, from tea parties to fork buffets, Ascot to Henley, dress shows to coming-out dances. Melissa North's American mother was a sophisticated and well-read New Yorker, who trusted to her daughter's common sense and yet bought into the old-fashioned mores of her adopted social set. It was fixed that, while awaiting the start of the deb dances, Melissa would stay in a house in Montpelier Square owned by the parents of one of her school friends. In this world, many of the more moneyed families whose regular

---

* Nigel Dempster, *Daily Mail* gossip columnist, 1941–2007.

bases were in the shires also owned grand town houses in Knights-bridge and Hyde Park, and kept them fully running with a staff of cooks and housekeepers. That made it easy for the girls to move in and be cared for by the retainers – though the mother, popping up to town for a spot of shopping, might appear at any time and say, 'Oh dear, girls, do tidy your rooms . . .'

But the assumption was that these debs would be looked after, hand and foot. Melissa's mother made it clear to her daughter that she expected her to be ladylike and well groomed, and told her to book in to have her nails manicured at Rose Laird's beauty parlour on the top floor of Harrods. All the mothers had accounts there, and under-wrote the girls' expenditure on underwear, nylons, make-up, packets of custard creams and just about anything else. Of course, what Melissa really wanted was records. Lots of these were put down to Mrs North's account. 'You just signed . . .'

'Well, so there we were, running around London, going to cocktail parties and tea parties . . .' remembers Melissa. At this time, despite her 'wild' reputation, she hadn't broken any fundamental rules.

We were very pure! We didn't drink, we didn't have sex. I think we were just very old-fashioned . . .

and, echoing Angela Carter:

We still wore white gloves.

But the strictures of the older generation were starting to seem ever more irrelevant.

That summer, at the end of our deb year, I was with my gang, who were my four great cronies, at a party in the Isle of Wight. And one of us said, 'It's nearly the end of the season, and we're seventeen. I think we should all have sex with our boyfriends now, don't you?' And we all agreed. And the boyfriends adored us, so we all went off and lost our virginity in a pack, and there was a lot of chortling about that.

And the boys were thrilled. And mine was Nigel.

If there was any guiding principle for Melissa North, it was Fun. Aged seventeen, she jumped headlong off the diving board into the bubbling, churning, kaleidoscopic waters of the 1960s without a backward glance. There was so much in life to relish: beautiful dresses, pop and parties, friendship, jokes, books and sex. When I asked Melissa what advice she would give a young woman today, starting out on life, her reply was: 'I would tell anyone like me, try to have as much fun as possible. Because what they don't tell you is, you're old so much longer than you're young. You should do what you enjoy. And if it makes you miserable, well, just don't do it.'

*

Melissa's privileged social scene nurtured her untroubled creed of pleasure. Freedom of the mind, the nurture of dreams, freewheeling spirituality, 'doing your own thing' and the gratification of the body become intertwined as the sixties progress. They all depended on one pivotal milestone.

In early December 1961, with the year drawing to a close, the key was provided to unlock a new gateway to freedom, as the pharmaceutical revolution that was the birth-control pill finally got the go-ahead and it was announced in Parliament that doctors were permitted to prescribe this wonder hormonal contraceptive – to married women – at a subsidised price of two shillings a month.* After centuries of bodily captivity, women were provided with the means to separate sex from conception, with momentous consequences. And these women rejoiced:

– The most fundamental thing that happened was the Pill. It was the most wonderfully liberating thing that ever happened to femalekind because it meant you could behave like a man if you wanted to and I'm eternally grateful for that.

– It was completely wonderful. It changed my life . . . I felt in control, I felt free . . .

Women say now that the Pill was just a man's plot so that women would be more available, but they can't be serious. They would have to be women who can't remember what it was like before: worrying all the time and all that messing about.

Sex belonged to me.

* Now valued at a little over £2.

Maids and Models

'The Pill had to be the best thing ever, *ever*, <u>ever</u>. My mother'd had four children. And I remember her saying to me, "Don't you think if I could have done something about it, I *would* have done?" It was <u>so</u> important that women took charge of their own lives.'

Veronica MacNab, tasteful, smart and smiley, is remembering her mother. But Veronica herself was an innocent when it came to sex and contraception. 'I'd read about the Pill. But it wasn't relevant to me. There was no question that I was going to need it, because it didn't happen.'

Veronica MacNab's teenage years are a necessary reminder that not everybody in the early 1960s was swinging, promiscuous, permissive or angry with the Establishment. On the contrary, her early story gives a picture of that Establishment: a society frozen in time, where manners, culture and above all class remained fossilised in the face of the prevailing currents of change.

Today Veronica is in her early seventies, comfortably settled in a Victorian semi in the respectable market town of Peebles, on the Scottish borders. Her bay windows permit a view onto the rolling hills and woodland of the Tweed valley. 'I never lived in a street until recently, but I can still look straight up to the hills in any direction.' The sense of space is as vital to Veronica as the air she breathes, because she grew up in one of the wildest, most isolated glens in the Highlands. It was immortalised by Sir Walter Scott, who wrote of 'lone Glenartney's hazel shade' in *The Lady of the Lake*. Veronica comes from generations of Scottish hill shepherds; her grandparents, who spoke only Gaelic, guarded their flocks on the island of Eigg, but later transferred to Perthshire, where the glen was kept as a shooting playground by English aristocrats. Shortly before the Second World War her father, Padraic, was sent for a spell to work as gamekeeper on the south of England estate that they also owned. There he courted the pretty parlourmaid who worked for the neighbouring land-owners, brought her back to Glen Artney, and raised a family.

So young Veronica grew up beneath open skies, in a timeless land-scape of heather, deer, wheeling buzzards and trickling burns. Every day she walked two miles down the glen to her school, which had only six pupils. But this unalloyed childhood came to an abrupt end when her uncompromising parents sent her to a huge, noisy, sprawl-ing grammar school in Lanark, where she was expected to get good results. Here, Veronica felt shipwrecked; her only consolation was books, which she devoured voraciously. 'They didn't see that I was shell-shocked, suffocated. I just hated it beyond anything.' With-drawn and de-socialised by her isolated upbringing, she failed to engage with her contemporaries. The teenage revolution passed her by. Scottish country dance music, the contralto ballads of Kathleen Ferrier, and Handel's *Messiah* were the soundtracks to her youth. 'And my mother was a wonderful needlewoman . . . there were no idle hands in our house!' That meant wearing hand-stitched shirt-waisters and home-made cardigans. Her stern and dominant father frowned on vanities. There would be no make-up on his daughter's scrubbed Highland complexion – 'though maybe I wore Pond's cold cream?' – and certainly no jewellery.

Where her physical development was concerned, Veronica was '*absolutely* green as grass'. When puberty kicked in, her mother gave her a well-intentioned manual about fruit flies. She was none the wiser. Next to her streetwise contemporaries, she felt alone, ignorant and detached. As for the future, there was never any doubt in her mind that her mother's career would be hers: menial work, followed by marriage. Vaguely, she considered trying for nursing. But she felt herself to be struggling through a swamp. School was that swamp, and she was sinking.

In 1962, with her O-level results looming, Veronica took drastic action.

> I knew I had failed the exams, and I knew that there was going to be one hell of a row coming up. So I bought a copy of *The Nursery World* maga-zine, and there was an advert for a job in Sussex, which I applied for, privately, in my best handwriting: 'Dear Madam . . .' and so on. The first

thing my parents knew about it was when I got a letter asking me for an interview to be a junior nursery maid. And I was offered the job.

By chance, her new employers, Jeremy and Rona Smith, moved in the same elevated circles as the family who had once employed Veronica's mother as parlourmaid. It turned out that Rona Smith wasn't any old Smith, she was the daughter of a baronet who lived in a castle. Suddenly, everything was all right, and Veronica flunking her O levels was clearly 'meant to be'. In July 1962, just weeks before her sixteenth birthday, and never having gone further than the English border counties in her life – 'I still had heather in my hair!' – she packed her trunk and took a train to London.

Veronica travelled out of one time warp, and straight into another. At Euston station she was met by the Smiths' chauffeur, who explained that he would drive her directly to the Earls Court arena, where the family were attending the Royal Tournament. For a wide-eyed lass from the glens, nothing could be more bewildering, exciting or intense than the military tattoo she now witnessed. Ushered to her seat in the vast auditorium, a cacophony of brass bands and gun salutes greeted her: the whole fandango of the British Empire, from RAF athletes to Ghurkha formations. There were march pasts, gymnastic displays, uniformed pageantry and horseback parades, all in the presence of Her Majesty the Queen. And there was to be no let-up in the sensory overload. Later, having been introduced to her young charges, Dione, Julian and Hugo (aged eight, six and four), she was driven down to the Smiths' capacious Sussex seat and given scrambled eggs and potted shrimps for supper. 'It was the first time I'd ever had potted shrimps!'

In 1962, 90 per cent of this nation's wealth was owned by just 19 per cent of the population. Britain's country houses and the inherited money that maintained them are indelibly pinned to our national psyche through the fictions of Brideshead and Downton Abbey, and romance still lingered around the turrets, terraces and minstrels' galleries of countless decaying ancestral piles. Though the war had played its part in equalising mistress and maid, the chatelaines clung tenaciously to their rules, rituals and privileges. Here too, nannies and nurserymaids were indispensable in upholding the leisured lifestyle of their employers. This was the once-upon-a-time world that Veronica MacNab now entered, a

world she had only ever imagined in the pages of books. In this household she was inevitably the most junior member, whose work was to
care for another woman's three offspring, with a fourth on the way. No
concern here with reproductive controls; Rona Smith could afford the
best in medical care, and her decorous life would barely be interrupted
by the seamless arrival of an additional baby. Meanwhile, bombarded
by unfamiliar experiences, Mrs Smith's new nursery maid gratefully
welcomed all that the post had to offer, below and above stairs. She
learnt to swim in the family's pool. She wandered in the manicured gardens. On Sundays she had lunch with the children at the big family
dining table, to be served with fresh peaches from the hothouse, each
one presented on a porcelain platter decorated in the deepest blue pig-
ment and figured with exquisite gold and polychrome ornamentation.
Much later she learnt that this ware was known as Sèvres. As for the
peach – she had never had a fresh one before, and had to watch others
carefully to discover how such a superior fruit should be eaten.

Summer turned to winter, and the family decamped for Christmas to
Rona Smith's family home, Knepp Castle in Sussex, where two butlers,
Mr Pink and Mr Hack, premeditated the household's every need. On
Boxing Day morning, abiding by long-established tradition, the Craw-
ley and Horsham Hunt met in front of the castle, providing an obsolescent
spectacle of pink coats, majestic hunters groomed and braided, hatted
and habited ladies side-saddle on their mounts, milling and munching
Madeira cake and quaffing stirrup-cups to the echoing bay of the fox
hounds resounding across Knepp's icy lake and frosted woodland.

> There was always a big, big turnout. It was just extraordinary. There
> were Mr Pink and Mr Hack handing round the cake, and me trying
> to keep the children away from the horses' hooves. It was fairy-tale
> stuff, it really was. It was the stuff of magic.

★

Knepp embodied an entrenched way of life in which a Scottish nursery maid not only knew her place, but embraced it.

But the Knepp model was itself in the process of change, heralding an
era in which stirrup-cups and Sèvres porcelain dinner services were
consigned to the museum of history. The young female products of

the system – debs in search of a country landowner to marry – were (like Melissa North in the last chapter) reinventing the rules. And importantly, the embalmed hierarchy itself was losing legitimacy, as new money gained entry to such revered temples as the Ascot enclosure, Queen Charlotte's Ball and the pages of *Tatler*, all for the price of a posh frock and a swanky hairdo. Royal presentations – those arcane yearly rites of passage in which upper-class virgins were paraded before the monarch in order to qualify them for the marriage market – had finally ended in 1958. By 1962 it was noticeable that jaded partygoers were starting to modernise the time-honoured rituals of the London season. Ball-gown designer Belinda Bellville was heard lamenting the downbeat chic of a new generation of debs in their 'black stockings and a rather Chelsea-look and much more fashion conscious . . . not nearly as worried about waists and full skirts as they used to be'. The roll call of guests at these parties – once programmed by the debs' mums around the match-making potential of the high-society invitee, each and every one of them carefully vetted against the stud book – was becoming a lucky dip of playboys, the upper classes and new money. You could get in if you could pay. A new terror loomed for the mothers of the well-bred virgins: interbreeding. Where formerly, dynasties had been secured and protected through prudent and reputable marriages, that exclusivity was now threatened, with a new front opening on the class war.

The culture of the late 1950s had already championed fluidity. Shelagh Delaney's 1958 play *A Taste of Honey* put gender, class and race relations under the spotlight, while the 'rough diamond' working-class hero was glamorised on screen in *Room at the Top* (1959), *Saturday Night and Sunday Morning* (1960), *The Loneliness of the Long Distance Runner* (1962) and *A Kind of Loving* (1962). A certain type of middle- or upper-middle-class girl – as Ruth Adam had pointed out in the *Sunday Times* – preferred her boyfriends gritty and proletarian. Compared to the chinless Hooray Henrys favoured by their mothers, these likely lads appeared to have more freedom, more ready cash, more sex appeal and more talent. And the boys were equally eager.

'All us working-class lads love a posh girl.' The words were photographer David Bailey's, spoken in 1996 at the funeral of his old comrade Terence Donovan. Along with a third photographer, Brian

Duffy, these three (usually known only by their surnames) were the hub of a new London-based cultural meritocracy: edgy, mongrel and transgressive. They mixed easily with gangsters, artists, film stars and fashionistas. 'Before 1960, a fashion photographer was tall, thin and camp,' explained Duffy later. 'But we three are different: short, fat and heterosexual!' Their raw material was beautiful, posh women.

The story is well known of fashion model Jean Shrimpton's affair with Bailey: their princess-and-frog myth is part of our cultural history. 'I was a naive girl from the country and he was the streetwise Cockney,' she recalled in a 1990 memoir. In his fashion photographs for *Vogue*, Bailey captured the essence of 'the Shrimp's' breathtaking beauty. 1962 was the year when 1950s sex symbol Marilyn Monroe met a tragic death caused by a drug overdose. And now here to take her place was a new siren for a new decade. Supermodel Shrimpton substituted Monroe's sultry, studied, voluminous womanliness with something different: a breath of fresh air. Every girl who saw Bailey's images envied Shrimpton's outdoorsy girlish allure, unkempt brunette waves, unaffected femininity and huge blue eyes. Men too were mesmerised:

> There's a hardness to her forehead and cheekbones only just mollified
> by that soft, lush mock-innocent mouth, the kind every man would
> like to have nuzzling the back of his neck from the pillion seat . . .

wrote Hunter Davies in the *Sunday Times*. But it was Bailey who found the way to Shrimpton's heart, and bed. In part, he seduced her with his world. ' "Wanna come down the East End?" he would say casually.' He would drive her up Brick Lane in his Morgan sports car, past the hangouts of razor gangs and thieves, or take her to visit his parents, Glad and Bert, in their fusty semi in East Ham. They didn't go to fancy West End restaurants, because Bailey didn't know how to order. Instead, they ate chicken chow mein at Chang's in East Ham High Street. Jean was captivated.

But though Bailey's Cockney world, with its noisome buildings, crooks and poverty, fascinated her, there was a side to it which was less welcome, if unsurprising. Evidently Bailey's mum, Glad, like many working-class matriarchs, ruled the roost. But the expectation was that she had to know her place, and not rock the domestic boat.

Sexism came with the territory. In East Ham and Poplar, men did as they pleased, and despite his 'effeminate' interests in fashion and art movies, Bailey was no exception. He pestered Jean for sex until she finally succumbed, one unromantic evening, on a piece of public grass in the dark. '[It was] quite awful. I was miserable, protesting all the time that I did not want to do it, and complaining that he was pressuring me.' Though married, he – like all his group of cool East End photographers – saw no contradiction in infidelity.

> None of the photographers went home to their wives. One . . . kept his wife safely tucked away at home by making sure she was constantly pregnant. It was said he used to push a pin gently through her Dutch cap.

In her memoirs Jean is largely resigned to the incessant backchat, making of passes, innuendo and macho posturing endured by the model girls. In the early sixties, she explains, nobody saw anything wrong with such behaviour, and 'generally speaking, the girls could look after themselves'. So while Bailey and his mates felt free to take what liberties they liked – a tickle or a squeeze, a derisive or bawdy comment – the models kept working. Just once, Jean's sense of sisterly grievance got the better of her. One evening after a shoot Bailey, Jean and the crew were drinking in the pub. Usually, Janet, the girlfriend of Bailey's young assistant, hung around with them, but that evening she was absent. Jean asked him why. 'She's waiting for me in the car,' was the reply.

> I didn't understand. 'You mean she doesn't want a drink?'
> He looked at me as if I were stupid. 'I don't know. She's waiting for me in the car,' he repeated.
> It dawned. I gave him a dirty look and, without asking for his yea or nay, went out and brought her in to join us.

★

Pattie Boyd's early experiences with the photo pack mirrored those of the Shrimp. Pattie was a young blonde model of limpid loveliness, porcelain-skinned, with cornflower-blue eyes, aged eighteen in 1962. Like Jean, her background was relatively privileged; she spent her

formative years on her grandparents' Kenyan estate, and was convent-
educated in Nairobi until the age of nine, when – her parents'
marriage having disintegrated – she found herself back in England
with a new stepfather and a new family. Pattie was packed off to an
inadequate Catholic boarding school. At seventeen, utterly unquali-
fied for anything except marriage, she left. Strings were pulled, and
Pattie was manoeuvred into an apprenticeship at Elizabeth Arden's
beauty salon in Mayfair. At last, flat-sharing with three other girls in
South Kensington, life's feast lay on a plate. 'I was young, nubile and
had everything in front of me . . .'

Work at the salon was undemanding, but it opened doors to the
imagination. Leafing through the once-prohibited pages of *Vogue*,
Tatler and *Queen*, she saw glossy spreads of the latest celebrity models:
Shrimpton, and Celia Hammond.

These girls were young, fresh and different. I wanted to be like them.

Agent Cherry Marshall spotted Pattie's potential within minutes of
meeting her. 'She was clean, fresh and bubbly . . . With her coltish
quality, beautiful legs and hands, she was the new contemporary girl,
and she looked fantastic in all the way-out clothes of her generation.'
It was a look that needed little intervention, though Cherry had to
impose a confectionery ban when Pattie gigglingly confessed that she
had an insatiable appetite for sweets. Pattie was sent off, clutching her
portfolio, '– and soon my diary was full of jobs'.

At this time there were no stylists. A model was expected to cart
her necessities with her to every shoot, in a capacious bag. These
included stockings in various shades, costume jewellery, a choice of
shoes and boots, underwear, hair accessories including wigs and hair-
pieces, and a full supply of make-up and false eyelashes. A hairdresser
would probably style her hair, but she would be expected to do her
own face. Pattie's life was disorganised but fun. She moved into a new
flat off Cromwell Road with four other models, lived off sweets and
Bird's Eye frozen chicken pies, and broke all her stepfather's injunc-
tions. There was no shortage of boyfriends, and one of the earliest was
the self-taught photographer Eric Swayne, an acolyte and fellow East-
Ender friend of Bailey's. Plebeian Swayne adored posh Pattie, but also
saw her as the Shrimp to his Bailey: a passport to success. Seven years

her senior, he felt entitled to mould her, telling her how to do her hair and make-up, telling her to smile, controlling her image.

> Eric and I didn't sleep together for quite a while. He kept asking and I kept refusing. Eventually I felt pressured and knew I'd have to give in, so although I didn't really want to, I agreed. He was kind and sweet, but it wasn't the big deal I had imagined. In fact, it was pretty painful and I regretted it . . .

Grace Coddington was another classically beautiful model who stepped over the class lines. From where she stood, going out with East End boys was the equivalent of a fashion statement. They were cool, fun, cheeky, drove Rolls-Royces and looked up to women. Terence Donovan's adventurous artsy take on his home patch – industrial chic, blondes on bomb sites – earned him the street credibility to photograph and be seen with this flame-haired, polished *Vogue* cover girl. Coddington (inevitably known as 'the Cod') also patronised the hippest of hairdressers, Vidal Sassoon, another self-made working-class success story. The hugely talented and original Sassoon worked his way up from extreme poverty and recruited an elocution teacher to help rid him of his incomprehensible Cockney; Vidal's Mayfair salon soon became a magnet for the fashion élite who came for his famous 'five-point cut', and repositioned hairstyling as heterosexual. Here, according to Coddington, the juniors tended to be raunchy boys, 'who, after cutting the customers' hair, took them upstairs and attempted to shag them'.

The combination of sophisticated beauty and raw unvarnished sex, the 'bit of rough' having it off with the fairy-tale princess, was a potent one. In an era of fast-changing fashion and the expansion of aspirational colour magazines, photography made it even more so. The glottal accent, the interrogating eye, the explosive finger – ever ready to probe, detonate or combust – was explicit, exploratory and erotic.

> The photographer must have absolute control over you . . .

wrote Jean Shrimpton in *The Truth About Modelling*.

> You must trust his judgement and his eyesight . . . You must be a blank sheet upon which he can create.

Note the pronoun. In 1962, though class barriers were starting to crumble, gender stereotypes were still deeply rooted.

Is Chastity Outmoded?

Nevertheless, in the early 1960s the British intelligentsia was starting to interrogate the sexual status quo. In 1962 the BBC commissioned Professor G. M. Carstairs to deliver a kind of state-of-the-nation address entitled *This Island Now*, via their flagship series of broadcasts, the Reith Lectures. The learned and liberal-minded professor incited controversy by questioning whether chastity was a supreme virtue in an age when women were moving closer to social and economic equality with men. 'Women are taking the lead in re-exploring and rediscovering their own nature,' he told his Home Service listeners, 'and, in so doing, [are] modifying our concept of man's nature also.' Another highly popular, if notorious, academic author who challenged conventions was the psychiatrist Dr Eustace Chesser. Where sexual behaviour was concerned, public opinion was shifting, and the old, Victorian conventions were no longer relevant, Chesser insisted (in *Is Chastity Outmoded?* (1960)). Even if pre-marital sex remained unacceptable in society, it was time for the notions of sin and guilt to be pensioned off, along with sexual fear and the resulting neuroses.

But outside chattering circles, the orthodox narrative held good. Even Chesser conceded that –

> . . . no matter what stage of equality is arrived at between the sexes, the tendency will continue for man to *insist*, and woman to *resist* . . .

– as Jean Shrimpton and Pattie Boyd found out.

When the sociologist Michael Schofield conducted his most famous survey among young people in the early sixties, it appeared that conventional attitudes persisted.* Schofield's interviewers asked nearly 2,000 fifteen- to nineteen-year-olds of both sexes, from all sectors of society, about their attitudes to sex before marriage. The responses

---

* Michael Schofield, *The Sexual Behaviour of Young People* (1965). The research was carried out in 1963/4.

his interviewees gave were not altogether surprising. Asked, why did they first have sex? the boys were – typically – motivated by sexual desire, and the girls by a belief that they were in love:

Boy, aged sixteen:
I felt like it. I felt I was entitled to it after four months.

Boy, aged nineteen:
You just get tired of kissing and that.

Girl, aged eighteen:
He kept on telling me that this sort of thing is all right for two people who are in love and plan to get married.

Girl, aged seventeen:
He wanted to. It wasn't rape or anything. Just that I was in love with him.

More surprisingly perhaps, in the context of all the wringing of hands by Dr Leslie Weatherhead and his ilk, Schofield's statistics revealed that most seventeen- to nineteen-year-olds, boys and girls, were virgins. Of the boys in that age group, one in three had had sex; of the girls, just one in six.

However, the fear of sexual licence felt by the older generation, and the threat, were real enough. Schofield demonstrated that there was a correlation between levels of sexual experience and disrespect for adults. An oppositional culture was growing up around the generation divide, and the smashing up of Christian morals. The flip side of Dr Weatherhead's catastrophe scenario, in which the nation would be consumed by biblical plagues of rampant underage brides and Teddy boys riddled with gonorrhoea, was an intense and widespread anger and antipathy, sometimes verging on phobia, on the part of the young towards the old. As one oral history respondent told the interviewer:

Our elders and betters do not inspire us, do not give us the slightest incentive to be as they are . . . We see the death of life in the terrible faces of our elected ministers and pundits and judges . . .

Sometimes I positively hate these people.

Anyone over twenty is past it. The most terrible thing on earth would be to be drawn into the adult world.

Nineteen-year-old Kate Paul was more succinct:

> Why can't oldish women *walk*?

she begged –

> They really annoy me, they're so grey and stiff and *unnecessarily*
> old . . .

while, echoing the Who, pop star Cilla Black told the *Daily Express* –

> I would never want to grow old. I've always said I would shoot myself
> when I'm 50.

Two other writers with their fingers on the pulse of the younger generation were the journalists Charles Hamblett and Jane Deverson,
who brought the voices of 'Generation X' before the public, in their
book of that name. Hamblett and Deverson's aim was 'to get young
people talking'. The multiplicity of voices that speak out from their
pages testify to a generation of surprisingly honest, confident, entitled young men, and young women still wrestling with the
imperatives of their 1950s upbringing:

> *Richard, 24:*
>
> If you go to a party and have a few beers, bed is the main thing you
> think about, then you don't care how rough the girl looks . . .

> *Alan, 22:*
>
> I find girls are usually willing to sleep with me . . . But I don't see
> them regularly. I smooth them over the first date. I take her out and
> we neck and I judge what she's like, whether she's hot stuff. If she is I
> take her out again and sleep with her . . . If I got a girl pregnant I
> wouldn't marry her . . .

> *'June', 16:*
>
> You're annoyed if a boy tries to make you on the first date because
> it shows he thinks you're easy, and you're annoyed if he *doesn't* try to
> make you because it shows he doesn't fancy you . . .

> *'Annie', 17:*
>
> Mother says never give in to a boy because he won't respect you,
> you'll only go on from one lover to another and end up a tart . . .

Of course, she's right. But Sheila at school slept with her boyfriend and everyone looked up to her, there's a sort of mystique about it. You feel you're missing out on something and you're not a real woman until you've slept with a boy . . .

First sex is abominable . . . But you feel great once it's over and you want to go off and tell all your girlfriends.

Pain, humiliation, pride, regret, liberation, confusion: for women they were all part of the package, at a time when the sands were shifting fast, and a tide of sexual change was threatening to submerge the familiar moral landscape.

And – here too – bias, intolerance, hatred, exclusion and injustice came with the deal. It wasn't till later in the decade that somebody found a word that summed up these attitudes: sexism.*

*

Since 1975, the Sex Discrimination Act has protected both men and women from discrimination on the grounds of sex or marital status. It is no longer lawful to treat someone unfavourably because of their sex, to abuse or harass them, or to pay them differently solely on the basis of their gender. Until that Act became law, you could abuse and discriminate with impunity. Women were generally on the receiving end, and never more so than when they attempted to 'trespass' on territory men regarded as their own.

Valerie Gisborn, uneducated and unconfident, worked for years in a Leicester textile factory before taking the controversial step of enrolling in the police force at the age of twenty-four. The probationary period, which she completed in 1961, called on all Valerie's strength of mind in dealing with sexism in an almost all-male world. Physical harassment was the norm.

One officer was a sergeant who earned himself the nickname 'Titter Fox'. No woman was safe in his presence. He thought it extremely funny to creep up to the girls . . . and touch them on their breasts. Often he

---

* The vocabulary of feminism still had no dedicated terminology. Pauline M. Leet, who contributed a paper entitled 'Women and the Undergraduate' to a student forum held in a Pennsylvania college, appears to have originated the word 'sexism', in November 1965.

approached them from the rear while they were on the telephone and slid his hand underneath their armpit, giving their breast a slight squeeze. Sometimes, as the girls walked along a corridor in the police station, he would stop them for conversation, then quickly touch them on the breast before parting. Most of us were wary of him and steered clear . . .

Threats to report the sergeant were dismissed as hearsay. The women had to cope alone.

After her probationary period, which she passed through with flying colours, Valerie was given a two-year trial in CID as a fully fledged detective officer, which she expected would lead straight into a criminal investigation qualification. To her astonishment, Valerie's name did not go forward; instead she was put back into uniform. 'The reason, only male detectives were allowed to attend the special course, because they were able to stay over the two-year attachment. Women were not allowed this privilege, and therefore not the special course.'

Or take the experience of Ann Leslie. In the face of blatant hostility and prejudice, she was outspoken and combative compared to the downtrodden Valerie Gisborn. But that was, and still is, her job.

Dame Ann Leslie is one of the foremost journalists of her generation, an award-winning star of the *Daily Mail*, who has covered entertainment, war and politics over a kaleidoscopic career. In 1962, fresh from a private education and with an Oxford degree, Leslie found herself posted to her first job working on the news desk of the *Daily Express* in Manchester. Here, her boss was the news editor Tom Campbell, a drunk and malevolent Scot, who was consumed with fury and resentment at having 'a bloody intellectual' from the south foisted on him. But his rage stemmed as much from the feeling that this young female had torn up the class rule book by mincing into a northern male powerhouse with her airs and graces.

I was everything he hated . . . upper middle-class, an Oxford graduate, privately educated, and thus someone who was ipso facto a 'stuck-up snob' . . .

What did a young woman with her lah-di-dah accent, who should have been on débutante duty, think she was doing in his down-to-earth proletarian office? When she arrived at work on day one, neatly turned out in an inexpensive knock-off Chanel suit, Campbell swore at her that she was 'not at the bloody Savoy today!' From then on, spitting with anger, he took every opportunity to point out to her that she was 'keeping a good man out of a job'. The other bully who made her life a misery was Campbell's deputy, Bob Blake. Blake's famously discriminatory remarks were circulated among his underlings: 'I have no objection to women on newspapers. I think women on newspapers can be a good thing for us. Just so long as they are on other newspapers.' Or, 'Bottle-washing, that's what you university graduates have got to do here! And I'll certainly see that you get a few dirty bottles to wash! Especially you *women* graduates!'

Together, Blake and Campbell allied in a power struggle to drive her out. Every morning Ann would choke down the watery fried eggs and fatty bacon provided by her landlady and force herself into work. Every evening she pushed pennies into the slot of a malodorous call-box, phoned her boyfriend, Michael Fletcher, in London and wailed: 'I hate this job, this job hates me, I'm chucking it in!' Frequently, Campbell dumped her on the 'dog-watch'. She'd be 'on' from 4.30 p.m. till the small hours, and was required to trek out to far-flung police stations in toxic slums in search of 'stories'. But as it was the norm for desk sergeants to sell any fruity tip-offs straight to their chums on the newspaper's Crime Desk, Ann rarely came back with anything substantial. And it wasn't until a colleague advised her to join the journalism union that Campbell was forced to concede her right to claim late-night taxis home against expenses.

At twenty-one, Ann was the youngest journalist working for the *Express* in Manchester. Halfway into her year there, the northern editor ambled across to her desk and told her to put together a column aimed at teenagers, about pop music and fashion. Ann did not feel suited for this; her own musical tastes veered towards Sibelius and light opera. But it wasn't optional. The brief was to give column space to youthful trends south of the border and north of Nottingham. So she attempted to woo the younger generation by dutifully plugging a number of ill-favoured, tongue-tied Lancashire skiffle groups.

Ann's lack of knowledge blinded her to the gathering momentum of the Liverpool music scene, which was now bubbling over with a new energy. At the start of 1962 the Beatles were still little-known outside their home town, but in January that year they had taken the important step of signing Brian Epstein as their manager, in August Ringo Starr joined the group as drummer, and in the north-west Beatle-idolatry was a growing phenomenon. Unaware of all this, Ann kept dialling around. Finally, she lucked into a funny, sardonic Scouser with a nasal voice, who told her jokes and provided her with observations for her column. His name was John Lennon. Ann Leslie had great instincts, and the Lennon wit and wisdom made fabulous copy. For several months she pulled off a series of interviews with him and his little-known band. Then the editor called her in and said she was overdoing it. 'Too many of these "Insects", or whatever they call themselves, on your page . . . sounds as if you're in their pay,' he complained. Soon after, Epstein invited her to hear the band play a gig in Liverpool. Apologising, Ann explained that she couldn't; she'd been barred from running any more Beatles features.

Barely eighteen months later the Beatles became the biggest pop group in the world, and Epstein never took my calls again.

Back in Manchester, Ann Leslie infuriated her unreconstructed bosses by neglecting to play by their unscrupulous rules. For example, an assortment of ruthless male hacks from the *Express* had, one after another, failed to get a female crime victim to tell her story despite infiltrating her hospital ward in disguise as doctors, sending bouquets and the like. Ann tried approaching the woman through official channels, via the hospital secretary, with gratifyingly immediate results. 'Mrs A says you sound like a nice, polite young woman, and certainly she'll talk to you.'

'How did you get the bloody story?' barked Campbell the next day.
'I asked the Hospital Secretary . . .'
'You did *what*?' His moustache bristled with rage. 'That's no way to get a story!'
'But,' I pointed out coolly, 'I did get it. And no one else did.'

In vengeance, Campbell plotted her downfall, by sending her on the worst, most preposterous assignment he could dream up. There was, it seemed, a dwarf somewhere in Oldham claiming to have memories of his schooldays with the film star Cary Grant. Nothing else was known, and Campbell packed her off to track down the dwarf. 'And, while you're about it, lassie, there's a flock of sheep frozen to death on the moors . . . You'll find them by looking for hooves sticking up over the snow. And you know what? You're keeping a good man out of a job!' Ann struggled through a blizzard, located the dwarf, shared a few whiskies with him, and (omitting to cover the dead sheep) scooped the story.

Campbell and I were locked in a deadly battle,

recalled Ann Leslie in her memoirs,

> . . . about class, education and above all gender – and I was damned if I was going to lose it to this ghastly, failed, fraudulent old drunk. I fully intended to leave – but on my terms. Modern feminism hadn't been invented then, but I was innately feminist enough to know that I wouldn't be driven out of a job – even one I hated – merely because of the genital arrangements I was born with.

Satire and Street Cred

'Ann Leslie – yes, I remember her well. I can see her now, blue mascara and pale pink lipstick, always full make-up even then . . . She was a real dauntless journalist in a way I never was.'

Anne Chisholm was Ann Leslie's exact contemporary at Lady Margaret Hall, Oxford. Anne – 'Chiz' to her friends – graduated in History in the summer of 1962. Sharp-witted, gorgeous and confident, her education had endowed her with the knowing, faux-sophisticated and ironical mindset of her mostly male Oxbridge college generation. These were the affiliates of the Angry Young Men – like John Osborne and Kingsley Amis – who, according to the journalist Christopher Booker, had gone rogue in the mid-1950s, turned on the Establishment, and bitten the hand that fed them.* The anger may have seemed indiscriminate, but it was very much alive, directed against the military, the bomb, complacency, royalty, the Church, sexual hypocrisy and the class divide. Booker identified 1956 as a

---

* Booker explored the root causes of the 60s spirit of liberation in *The Neophiliacs: A Study of the Revolution in English Life in the Fifties and Sixties* (1969).

turning point: 'A new spirit was unleashed – a new wind of essentially youthful hostility to every kind of established convention and traditional authority, a wind of moral freedom and rebellion . . .' For these clever young men, the waning of empire and all its ponderous values felt like a letting-go, a deliverance. The party could begin.

This was the zeitgeist when Anne and her contemporaries were at Oxford.

My earliest boyfriend was the son of a Hampstead Socialist MP. So though I came from a naturally Tory background I never voted Tory.

I was caught up in the whole anti-Establishment mood of the time. The prime minister, Harold Macmillan, seemed like an old, walrus-faced figure of fun. He just seemed ridiculous, out-of-date and stuffy, a man whose time had been and gone.

It was while at Oxford that Anne first tried her hand at journalism, writing for the university paper *Isis*, edited by Paul Foot. Soon she was bitten by the idea of pursuing a career in newspapers. So when her Oxford contemporary, a Balliol graduate called Peter Usborne, phoned her the autumn after she came down and said, 'Hello, Chis, do you want to come and work for the *Eye*?' she didn't hesitate.

I simply said 'Yes . . .' thinking, while I look for a proper job, this will do, and it sounds like fun.

Private Eye was, and continues to be, the court jester of the Establishment – half in, but mainly out: needling, funny, and risk-taking. Like the all-male fun-poking hit show *Beyond the Fringe*, the magazine, founded in 1961, grew out of Oxbridge. Usborne and his college contemporaries were all public-school, all in love with their own brand of irreverent, anarchic undergraduate humour. By the time Anne Chisholm came on board the magazine had a cult following under the editorship of another talented fellow student, Richard Ingrams. Anne's rather sketchy role was that of editorial assistant and office help, the office in question being a cramped, chaotic space up a grimy staircase above a striptease joint and a betting shop in Greek Street, Soho.

Everybody did a bit of everything. People would wander in and out with drinks or cups of coffee. We all sat around making jokes and reading the papers and thinking how clever we were . . . And they'd ask you to think up an idea for a caption or a cover or something. I just thought of it as an extension of student life. It was great fun.

This was Satire Central. A couple of doors down was the short-lived but hugely in-demand Establishment Club, a Mecca for hip metropolitans who didn't want to miss out on the craze for puncturing pretensions. Here you could catch a glimpse of Alan Bennett hot from ridiculing the Royals in his *Beyond the Fringe* New York transfer, John Wells sending up John Betjeman's Victorian-Gothic lavatory fetish, or über-camp comedian Frankie Howerd lasciviously comparing a sausage to a lamb chop. The *Private Eye* team had a free pass for the Establishment. Willie Rushton, one of *Private Eye*'s founders, also

'Wasn't it superb when he said "?*★!", and when he said "‡¶†§" I thought I'd die laughing.'
Punch (September 1962) mocks the smug subversives.

gained them entry to the live broadcasts of the BBC's cutting-edge comedy current affairs show *That Was the Week That Was* (aka *TW3*), which drew television audiences of up to 13 million.

So Anne Chisholm felt that she was right where it was at. 'Sitting in the audience at the BBC I felt I was in the forefront of all the most amusing, entertaining, different, subversive, naughty, rude stuff, you know? I remember my father shaking his head, bemused, and saying, "I knew you quite fancied journalism. But I hadn't quite realised it would be *this* kind of journalism!"'

Like the satire craze in general, *Private Eye*, the Establishment and *TW3* were male-dominated. 'One of the reasons I knew I wouldn't stay long-term was that it did feel very much like a boys' club, and the humour was also very much public-schoolboy kind of humour,' says Anne. 'It all felt a bit misogynistic. You had to be "one of the lads". Women weren't taken awfully seriously, and I suppose I played along with it. But it wasn't somewhere I wanted to get stuck.' Though *Private Eye*'s inner circle were eager to ridicule most conventions, they suffered from a collective sense-of-humour failure when it came to entrenched

Anne Chisholm joins the boys' club: *Private Eye*. An affectionate caricature by one of her many admirers (and co-founder of the magazine), Willie Rushton.

female inequality, and as a mere office girl it was clear to Anne Chisholm that she wasn't ever going to be asked to write anything.

There were exceptions to this. The Establishment gave a platform to the talented actress and comedian Eleanor Bron. Bron starred in one of the club's favourite sketches, which shone a squirming, painful light on sexual embarrassment: this two-hander had an intellectually earnest boy navigating the vacuous shallows of intellectual pseudery to get his equally intellectually earnest girlfriend into bed. The sophisticated metropolitan audience recognised themselves, and loved it. On *TW3*, Millicent Martin deployed a pitch-perfect combination of wide-eyed sex-kitten and ice-maiden – both earthy and untouchable – to launch each week's show with her brassy vocals. Martin's class act made it all the more shocking when she stepped over the line with scripts alluding to sex before marriage, illegitimacy or – and this provoked unparalleled hysteria alongside alarmed accusations of smut-peddling – a sketch of a couple in a café, in which Martin's character informed Roy Kinnear's character in ringing tones, 'YOUR FLY'S OPEN!'

My own family didn't possess a television set in 1962, but such was *TW3*'s compelling attraction when I was a child that my parents would organise a babysitter every week in order to spend the evening watching it in company with a group of like-minded friends. Saturday nights didn't get any more fun than this.

*

My brother, sister and I were children in Leeds in the early sixties. And, though our parents were middle-class southerners, we unthinkingly adopted a posture of scorn and derision towards those we termed 'Snobs Down South'. We unlearned our long vowels, and took on the protective colouring of the Yorkshire accent. An unformulated but powerful instinct told us that the north, with its tough moors and sooty back-to-backs, was more gritty and authentic than the soft-bellied south – all dreaming Downland and pampered city commuters. Leeds was energised, and friendly too. 'Down South' seemed sleepy, subdued. In an infantile way, we were pro-proletarian, and anti-posh. The pop culture of the time endorsed those instincts.

It was the same for Rosalyn Palmer. In September 1962 Rosalyn packed her trunk with books and black jeans, said goodbye to Surrey, took the train to grimy, salty, vibrant Liverpool – and fell in love with the city at first sight. The University had offered her a place to study Political Theory and Institutions. But first, she was going to have fun. So she showed up at the freshers' dance at the Student Union, where an excited flock of fledgling students, girls in full skirts, boys in suits and ties, were milling and shuffling to the lush, polished, swooping rhythms of the star turn, celebrity bandleader Victor Sylvester and his Silver Strings. No music more perfectly represented the sound of the 1950s, conjuring a world of potted palms and tea for two.

Halfway through, Sylvester finished his first set and took a break. He was replaced on the platform by a local pop group with a rather different sound. They were called the Beatles.

> And when they'd finished, the audience didn't want Victor Sylvester to come back. And I can remember the impact of hearing their music: it was just amazing! And they were very tuneful . . . their singing was so good. I thought they were wonderful, and I just fell instantly in love with them. We all did – with their mop tops, and their collarless suits. They were just such beautiful young men!
>
> You know, I never knew which one I really loved the most . . . George Harrison? Paul? John?

Rosalyn was hooked by the Mersey scene. Though the place was heaving, hot and sweaty, there was always great music to be heard at the Cavern: the Hollies, Wayne Fontana, the Big Three, Freddie and the Dreamers. Another popular Merseybeat haunt was the Casbah Coffee Club, a damp cellar in an outlying area of the city, where Cilla Black and the Beatles often performed. Lennon and his mates had painted the Casbah's walls themselves, with spiders, rainbows and stars. But Rosalyn's favourite was Liverpool's big dance hall, the Rialto: the venue for Gerry and the Pacemakers, the Remo Four, the Searchers and the Swinging Blue Jeans. In the early days of the Mersey Sound all the Liverpool bands were exciting, and it was a matter of showing up at your preferred venue and dancing to whatever music happened to be playing that night. Audiences were from across the city, not just students. Rosalyn now worked on her street credentials, proudly acquiring a Scouse accent, cultivating her hip, edgy appearance, and relishing the wit and sociability of the Liverpudlians she met in bus queues. 'There was loads and loads of laughter. People in the south *never* talk to each other at bus stops.'

The important thing was to be seen as a child of the sixties – not the fifties. To be fifties was to be a loser. To be fifties was to be old, not young. The fifties girls were still wearing the obligatory middle-aged uniform of twinset and pearls. But the fifties boys in particular were easily identifiable among the students. Victor Sylvester's world was their spiritual home. They were neat, wore ties, liked ballroom dancing, had usually been to public schools, and their views on women were ineradicably snobbish.

> I can remember one chap I dated casually, and he said, 'I'm proud to say I've never been out with a girl that's been to a secondary modern school, and I promised my mother I would never do it.' To which I said, 'Well, actually, *I* did!'
>
> And he more or less got up and left the table. What a pompous little git!

The sixties boys, however – with their long scruffy sweaters, jeans, duffel coats, androgyny and centre-left political mindset – were different. Rosalyn's Surrey upbringing – the nuns and crushing snobbery of her early years – fuelled her determination to identify with the new decade. Here again, posh met pleb. She hastened to make friends with the cool crowd, like Roger McGough, uncrowned king of the Liverpool poetry scene, a regular at the same drinking hole, whose irreverent and romantic verse inspired a generation. Being young in Liverpool in the early sixties felt like being at the centre of the universe, a vigorous, vibrant nerve centre of creativity. At this time Rosalyn and her friends regarded London with contempt. 'We used to say, what we do in Liverpool gets picked up in London about six months later. All the energy was coming from Liverpool, all the dynamics were coming from Liverpool. And London was just where you go to make money – *after* you've done the exciting things.'

*

Like Rosalyn Palmer, teenage vocalist Beryl Marsden was anti-pomposity, a star of street cred. Her style was sloppy joes, jeans and winkle-picker boots, though the beautiful full-length leather coat she

craved was beyond her budget. Her friend Ida Holly had one, and she
looked on in envy. Ida, who was seeing John Lennon, was a double for
Cleopatra, with long, straight jet-black hair and black-lined cat eyes,
and would show up at the Cavern in her magnificent leathers.

The vaulted basement space of the Cavern was small, dark and
smelly, and there wasn't space to execute the extravagant moves of a
jive. On the dance floor everyone had to get up close and personal,
and a dance evolved known as the Cavern Stomp, with funky, precise, skipping moves which sexily echoed those of your partner.
There was no alcohol – the club sold only soft drinks – 'so you just
took off on your own adrenalin, and the excitement of the music . . .'
At this time the Beatles were still unknown outside a small north-of-
England circuit – and Hamburg. But Brian Epstein was managing
them now, and that included a makeover. He'd de-scruffed them,
taken away the leather jackets, put them in matching suits and ties,
and had their hair restyled. De-loused, de-contaminated, 'embour-
geoised', they could now have national appeal. The working class
was being mainstreamed.

Liverpool itself was a small city. According to Beryl, in 1962 everyone who was involved in contemporary music, poetry or art knew
everyone else. When the Beatles played the Cavern, and provided
John had his glasses on ('he couldn't recognise anybody when he took
them off . . .'), they knew all the audience by their first names. 'So
there was all this banter – you know, "What are you up to today?
And how're you doing?"' For Beryl, their on-stage relationship, the
intimacy and the backchat, was almost as good as the music.

But already there was a dark side to the pungent, wisecracking
front that would bring the Beatles so many fans. Much of their clean-
living, wholesome appeal was a façade, for Epstein was a master
image creator. John Lennon may have been dating Beryl Marsden's
beautiful black-haired friend Ida, but in reality he had been married
for less than a year to a clever, classy, reserved twenty-two-year-old
named Cynthia Powell. John and Cynthia had met at art school in
1958; she was blown away by his scruffy, rough-diamond sex appeal
and, besotted, had started a passionate relationship with him. In
thrall to John's arty preferences, she jettisoned her middle-class
'secretary-bird' look and morphed into a black-clad bohemian with

fishnet stockings. In the summer of 1962 Cynthia found herself pregnant. 'Sick and faint . . . I broke the news to John . . .' 'There's only one thing for it, Cyn, we'll have to get married.'

The Lennons' wedding took place on 23 August 1962 at the Mount Pleasant register office in Liverpool. Six weeks later, the Beatles released their first single, 'Love Me Do'. It reached number 17 in the charts.

Under Epstein's orders the marriage was to be secret, and the new Mrs Lennon was now firmly advised not to wear her wedding ring in public, and to keep a low profile. Behind the pretence was a concern that a married Beatle would alienate the fans and jeopardise the group's growing popularity. It was true that, even in the days when she was just John's girlfriend, Cynthia had lived in terror of some of John's more fanatical followers. Accompanying him to performances, she didn't feel safe:

> I was a threat to their fantasies and dreams. The most dangerous place for me in those days was the ladies' loo . . . I was definitely no match at all for those girls. They could have killed me as soon as look at me.

Now, awaiting the birth of their baby, it was a case of 'Love Me Don't'. Cynthia found herself virtually under house arrest and, enveloped in billowing shirt-dresses to disguise her expanding bump, John's new bride was literally under wraps. With an unacknowledged wife, and an unacknowledged child on the way, John was as free to chase women as he had been prior to his shotgun marriage. Soon the beautiful Ida Holly was on his radar. Though Ida herself seems to have been unaware that he was married, John's public flirtation with the brunette in the fabulous leather coat helped put his ever-growing army of fans off the scent. And Cynthia was trapped.

In her memoir *A Twist of Lennon* (1978), Cynthia recalled:

> The group was a marriage of four minds, three guitars and a drum, and the girls in the main tagged along and moved in whichever direction they were pointed by their men. The Beatles were very happy to have their women subservient in the background. It made life easier for them. The northern male chauvinism was quite strong within the group and independence was a bit of a dirty word . . .
>
> It was a question of 'don't do as I do but do as I say', and we did.

Alarm

The Lennons were long parted when John wrote one of the songs most powerfully associated with him: 'Give Peace a Chance' – it would become the slogan for a generation. But Lennon's pacifist lyric is the outward expression of a movement mainly created by and for women. For more than a century, women had worked together against male militarism.* And women were at the heart of the anti-H-bomb movement.

In 1958 the Campaign for Nuclear Disarmament had been born – the brainchild of a conglomeration of north London women's groups. In 1962 the word peace belonged with hearth and home, with domesticity, with the gentle, feminine virtues of healing, caring and nurturing. And many a woman born before war broke out in 1939 had reason to recognise the latent bellicosity and fieriness of their menfolk, their love of fists and firearms. 'Men are brought up from early childhood to admire those who fight to destroy enemies,' declared the author of a peace campaign newsletter. But post-1945, men's appetite for war was being re-evaluated. 'We were the first generation not to be conscripted,' the film-maker Jo Durden-Smith told an interviewer. 'Maleness was becoming peripheralised, there was no real function for maleness.' A cohort of men was growing up without a war to fight.

But if they couldn't have a hot one, they would have a cold one. Over the previous fifteen years of Soviet–NATO hostility, international tensions had been escalating. In the autumn of 1962, the temperature rose to an acutely alarming degree when an American spy plane confirmed that President Khrushchev and Fidel Castro were collaborating in constructing nuclear-missile launch facilities in Cuba. The resulting stand-off would bring the world to the brink of nuclear war.

*

We thought we would never grow up. That was our great fear really . . .

---

* See Jill Liddington, *The Road to Greenham Common: Feminism and Anti-Militarism in Britain since 1820* (1989).

Sophie Jenkins, the bright daughter of lower-middle-class parents, was an eager Ban-the-Bomber. Sophie, who spent her teenage years in Abingdon, near Oxford, was appalled and terrified when she learnt at her school how the government planned to protect civilians. Towards the end of the 1950s, it had been explained to Sophie and her class that in the event of a nuclear attack the population would have just four minutes in which to gather together the necessities of life beneath a table – because the table would protect them from the house falling down. These necessities were: carrots, whitewash, flower pots and candles. The whitewash was to coat the windows in order to lessen the heat of the nuclear blast. The carrots were because they were the most complete form of nutrition. They could be cooked by placing the candle underneath the flower pot to make a primitive stove. 'And you did this all underneath the table. Apparently you can survive for a very long time on just carrots.'

Sophie and her fellow pupils were utterly terrified. She and her best friend Cathy – the daughter of a well-established left-wing family – decided to join the Campaign for Nuclear Disarmament and, in their O-level summer of 1962, they set out with a crowd of beatnik students taking their anti-nuclear protest to the American air base at Greenham Common. The march was organised by the Committee of 100, yet another group which had been formed in 1960 to campaign for non-violent unilateral nuclear disarmament.

> I can remember sitting on the hot tarmac, and you could smell the creosote – and I was reading *De Bello Gallico*, studiously trying to swot it up for my O levels . . .

The demonstration was good-humoured, exhilarating, spontaneous and youthful, all wholesome sandwiches, baggy shirts and bare feet. From time to time it swelled with the singing of a rousing CND anthem:

> *Don't you hear the H-bomb's thunder*
> *Echo like the crack of doom?*
> *While they rend the skies asunder*
> *Fallout makes the earth a tomb . . .*

('And I'd think, yes, *yes* I can hear them!'). In due course, after a few hours sitting peacefully on the tarmac, Sophie and Cathy and some of their new-found CND friends were arrested in a friendly but businesslike way by the attendant policemen, put into a furniture van which served as prisoner transport, and driven to a makeshift magistrates' court that had been set up in the vicinity. The students were asked whether they had anything to say. With all the certainty of a righteous cause, the majority made passionate pacifist declarations, and were each fined £5. But when her moment came in the dock sixteen-year-old Sophie was lost for words. So she just replied 'No', and somewhat to her surprise was let off with a £3 fine for obstruction.

Undeterred, Sophie and Cathy were among many thousands of women, young and old, who continued to march and wave banners whenever they could. But in mid-October the newspaper headlines started to proclaim Sophie's worst Cold War fears.

On Tuesday 23 October *The Guardian*'s US correspondent reported that all American TV stations were being disrupted by newsflashes, confirming that President Kennedy would be speaking to the nation on a matter of 'the highest national urgency'. In the Atlantic, Soviet and US ships were moving closer, while US military flights monitored their movements. Diplomacy had stalled. On 26 October the Pope appealed to the world to pray for peace. There were multiple arrests in British cities as peace protesters marched shouting 'Hands Off Cuba'. *The Guardian*'s editorial that day stated unambiguously that, were the crisis to be mishandled by either side, a major war might ensue, which could 'mean death or slow extinction for millions of people'. On Saturday the 27th the secretary of the Committee of 100 declared that they planned to go ahead with a Cuba crisis demonstration in Trafalgar Square, despite their application to hold it being rejected by the Ministry of Works. On the 28th, 623 British academics wrote to the prime minister in alarm at the 'imminent threat of global nuclear war over Cuba', and threatened mass demonstrations.

I have no memory of the crisis. 28 October 1962 was my seventh birthday. My parents, almost out of their minds with existential worry, had the unfortunate task of preparing a party for a dozen overexcited small children, organising pass the parcel, a treasure hunt and a birthday tea. Despite being oppressed with the near certainty of imminent oblivion, I suppose they must have put on a good face as they helped me blow out my candles while thinking, 'Was it for the last time?' (It was in fact on that very day that Kennedy and Khrushchev reached the understanding that would end the stand-off).

> During the Cuba missile crisis I was convinced we were going to die . . .

remembered Sophie Jenkins.

> We didn't have a television, and I recall going to watch the news with our neighbour at the end of the road, who had one. And I can remember the background – very grainy pictures, of the grey sea, and these two grey battleships laden with missiles in conjunction with each other. And I can remember watching that and thinking, it's the end of the world.
>
> Because, it wasn't just the fear of being dead oneself, but of one's whole planet being dead – the whole human race being wiped out. That is what we believed.

Sophie's sense of apocalyptic helplessness is echoed in many other accounts, such as that by Zena, a Cardiff schoolgirl:

> I was 14 at the time . . . Someone burst into the classroom, exclaiming, 'Russia and America are at nuclear war!' In the hubbub that followed, I sat silent, and can now recall the desolation I experienced: that my family and friends (and I) would perish, with lives unlived and words unexpressed . . .

The writer Jenny Diski* was another:

> I . . . waited, along with the rest of the world, to be blown to pieces [in] October 1962. While I sat on the snowy pebble beach watching the grim-grey sea in Brighton, America and Russia played chicken in what became known as the Cuban Missile Crisis . . . It was perfectly

---

* Jenny Diski (1947–2016) was born Jenny Simmonds. After a troubled childhood she lodged in the home of the novelist Doris Lessing, who became an important influence. She later moved into a squat, became a teacher, and in 1976 married fellow counterculturalist Roger Marks, with whom she invented their joint surname. Her prolific writings include a standout memoir, *The Sixties* (2009).

clear to me, and to others, that my world was very likely to end within forty-eight hours . . .

– while the broadcaster Joan Bakewell, having landed her first BBC appearance on a current-affairs chat show called *Table Talk*, expressed the opinion that President Kennedy 'should act with extreme caution'.

For several days people lived in raw terror, expecting the flash in the sky at any minute. We tended our children with extra care . . .

In the case of fifteen-year-old Mary Ingham, whose recent under-the-desk discovery of D. H. Lawrence's *Lady Chatterley* had awakened forbidden adolescent appetites, the crisis made her curiosity ever more urgent:

The question was what to do with your last four minutes on earth, and the consensus of opinion was to rush out into the street and grab a man . . . Please God, don't let me die a virgin.

But Sophie Jenkins and her friends were in less of a hurry:

I can remember young lads – undergraduates I knew in Oxford – saying 'Yes, now's our chance – we can't die without having "had it"' (as they put it).

Though of course *we* didn't think that was a good enough reason.

*

'Ban the Bomb!' 'A future for our children!' In the early 1960s many women who were unaccustomed to being listened to were learning to shout louder. One of these was Margaret Hogg.

Shortly after the birth of Margaret's first child, David – born on 24 October 1960 with one eye, a club foot, and shortened fingered appendages instead of arms – Billy, her soldier husband, was sent a telegram in Germany where he was stationed. It read, 'Mother and baby doing well. Baby deformed.' Billy was allowed home on com-passionate leave and arrived in Edinburgh. He came to the hospital and found his young wife. Margaret called the nurse and asked for the baby to be brought in, but was met with refusal. No, he couldn't be released, it wasn't feeding time. But this time Margaret wasn't tak-ing no for an answer. ' "I don't care. My husband has just come home from Germany," I says, "I want him now." That was when I learnt to make myself heard.'

After ten days, Margaret was allowed to go home. But baby David had to stay. Every day she phoned the hospital, and every day she was told, 'Oh, no, he's not ready to come home yet.' After a week of this, she protested.

And the doctor was blunt. He says, 'Well, Mrs Hogg, we really think it would be better if you left Baby here, and went home and just forgot that you had him, and just carry on and have another baby.'

And I looked at him. And I says, 'You *what*?' You see, at that point they were only expected to live till they were five!

And he says, 'Well, Mrs Hogg, he'll never do anything, he won't live a normal life, or a very long life,' he says. 'Why don't you just make the break now?'

And I says, 'Well, where's he going to go?'

He says, 'Oh, don't worry, he'll be well looked after.'

And I says, 'Where, in a <u>home</u>?' I says, 'NO,' I says, 'he's got a home – and that's with ME!'

Margaret Hogg took her son back to her mother's house when he was five weeks old. His twisted feet were in plaster; special toeless bootees had to be made for him. The family were matter-of-fact about his disabilities, though Margaret's little sister was a bit glum when she realised that all David's hand-knitted cardigans would now have to be altered. By and large, Margaret's close working-class community were accepting, though sixty years ago society was less educated in reacting to disability than today. There were times when Margaret wheeled David down to the shops in his pram, when people would stare and whisper. The first time she braved the outing, it was a freezing Edinburgh winter day, and she had her baby swaddled in wraps. On her way back from the shops she encountered a provoking neighbour who greeted her with, 'Oh, you've got your baby home, can I have a little look?' while starting immediately to pull at the covers. Tact was not this woman's strong point. 'Oh!' she exclaimed, as the side of David's face was revealed, 'he's got TWO eyes! I thought he only had ONE eye!' Margaret was contemptuous. 'Well, yes, he's only got one eye. But what did you expect? Did you think it would be in the middle of his head like Cyclops?' Then she walked off home, smarting with anger.

But Margaret herself has always been completely without self-pity. 'David thrived,' she remembers, 'and he was the most easiest, lovable baby to bring up. We never had any complaints, any bother or anything with him until he started to walk' – though when asked how she and Billy coped in those early days there is a long hesitation before she points out that it was easier for her husband than it was for her, once he had been released from the army on compassionate grounds, and got a job locally. 'He didn't have to deal with David's difficulties day in, day out,' is all she will concede.

The first the Hoggs heard about thalidomide was in the late summer of 1962. Unknown to them, news was creeping out that there might be a link between thalidomide, an ingredient in Distaval, often prescribed as a sedative or analgesic, and birth defects. In November 1961 British chemists were asked to withdraw the drug, though only as a precaution. The chairman of the British company that distributed the tablets was quoted by the *Sunday Times* as saying that there was 'not the slightest risk' associated with them. But by May 1962 the link appeared incontestably established, and questions were being asked in Parliament about how to alert the public to the danger that might be lurking, unacknowledged, in their medicine cabinets. *The Lancet* meanwhile estimated that a possible 500 babies had been born in the UK with thalidomide-related abnormalities, but the *British Medical Journal* thought the number was nearer 800.*

Meanwhile Margaret – along with her mother, her two sisters, her auntie and uncle and their five children, and David of course – went for a week to a Butlin's holiday camp, that magic, welcoming seaside dream of escape so loved by the half million-odd British holidaymakers who flocked there every year throughout the 1950s and 60s for an annual release from the daily grind. Butlin's was all about

---

* The Thalidomide Society now estimates there were at least 2,000 live births of thalidomide-affected babies in the UK, with a possible further 10,000 or more who were stillborn, miscarried and occasionally aborted. These figures may not include the babies born alive, but who were soon after 'allowed to die' in hospital: the so-called 'mercy killings' which most living thalidomide survivors are painfully aware of.

joining in. So Margaret entered a smiling curly haired David, eighteen months old, for the Bonny Baby contest – 'but only because everybody else was doing it'. For his thrilled and exultant mum, the moment of triumph when she heard that David had won second prize was a high spot that challenged and confounded the craven bullies who had told her that he would never amount to anything. Her baby was beautiful. She knew it, and the judge had told her so. Even better, the judge took Margaret's mother aside, and made a point of telling her, 'If he'd opened his other eye he would have got first prize.' 'Och,' said her mum, matter-of-fact as ever, 'he hasn't got another eye.' But to this day, Margaret is almost speechless with pride at the memory.

It was at this time that the story behind David's distressing condition started to hit headlines. In June *The Observer* ran an investigation into the drug testing failures that had led to the thalidomide babies' tragedy. 'No one . . . had ever thought of testing drugs for their effects on the foetus . . .' wrote their correspondent. In July, the *News of the World* announced, 'These are Thalidomide babies', alongside touching photographs of some of the affected children. 'For pity's sake let us look after them.' In August *The Guardian* reported that an appeal was being launched to fund research into birth abnormalities and to develop technologies 'to help those born cripples'.

The autumn that David was two, Margaret Hogg visited her general practitioner and asked him point blank, 'Did I have Distaval?' 'No,' came the answer. He had never prescribed it. Not only that, but the GP insisted that she couldn't ever have had Distaval, because it was a sleeping tablet, and, knowing his patients as he did, he was well aware that Margaret had never had sleeping tablets during her pregnancy.

But Margaret's doctor must have been alarmed. Though she had had a straightforward pregnancy, there were records in his surgery files of her early bout of bronchitis, and of the medicine he had prescribed for her – in good faith at that time – to alleviate a racking cough. What did that medicine contain? If it was Distaval – and therefore contained thalidomide – Margaret would need proof. And that might not look good for him. Given what emerged later about those medical records, this appears to be something he anticipated. What he did not anticipate was that, in Margaret Hogg, he had a young mother who was loving, determined, indefatigable and a believer.

> They said David wouldnae live till he were five. He wouldnae see his teenage years. He wouldnae see twenty. Well, he's fifty-six this year.
>
> I'm well-known now, for saying how proud I am of *him* – of all of them – for what *they've* achieved. And after we were told they would be nothing.

And what about her own achievement?

> I'm just a mum, I got on wi' it. That's all. You're a mum and you do it.

1963

Climate Change

The winter of 1962–3 was the coldest for over two hundred years. Across the British Isles, snow lay on the ground for two months. The sea froze; there were icebergs in the Thames and icicles hung from every gutter. I have a memory of my father supine on the snow, below the chassis of our old Austin, trying to get it to start with a crank. We'd be late to school that morning. Those were the days when every schoolchild was provided with one third of a pint of milk. But nothing could be more disgusting than full-cream milk partially defrosted on the radiator, clogged with shards of ice. Ugh! The teachers stood over us to ensure we drank every drop. At playtime we muffled up and raced out to the school yard, where certain eager fourth-form boys had buffed and polished the snow to ribbons of mirror-glass. We lined up, one after the other, to experience the hectic, delirious, scary joy of a perfect headlong chute down its slithery surface. Two months of sheer heaven – until the awful day came when the school caretaker sprinkled every single slide in the playground with grit. He was acting under orders, but I still find it hard to forgive him.

*

Floella Benjamin was eleven when she first saw snow –

> – a whiteness I had never seen before . . . everything was covered in it. I gasped with wonderment. The landscape looked so beautiful, it took my breath away . . . I had fallen in love with snow.

Loving the weather was one thing. But acclimatising to the people of her new homeland was harder. There could be no going back to Trinidad now. Nevertheless there were times when Floella and her older sister, Sandra, talked of running away, home to the beloved sunny

Caribbean island of their birth. Night after night, in the years after she and her siblings arrived in London, Floella sobbed into her pillow. In the mornings, setting out to school, the tension built inside her, her fists clenched, her heart lurched in her chest. Fear stalked her. Which bully would appear from the shadows, lift her skirt and demand, 'Where's your tail then, monkey?' One day, as Sandra and Floella stood side by side on a railway platform, the train approached and some men on board pulled down the window, unbuttoned their flies, and took aim at the girls. Just in time, they evaded the shower of urine. On another occasion Floella intervened when a gang of bullies viciously beat up her younger brother. She could run fast, and soon it was their turn to be terrified, as an aggressive fourteen-year-old girl thumped and bashed them to the ground.

Bullying wasn't the only form of attack that Floella endured. In shops, the assistants ignored her. Her teacher stripped her of her lilting Trinidadian accent: 'Stop, you guttersnipe! If you want to stay in my class and be understood by everyone you will learn to speak the Queen's English!' Floella quickly adapted, understanding that it was the best way to get educated. But she felt devalued and deprived of her identity.

Experiences like this put iron in her soul. But Floella's self-respect had its roots in her mother's steadfast love and belief. 'Marmie always tried her best to make us forget the outside world.' A matriarch of unshakeable morality and conviction, Mrs Benjamin gave her daughters goals and pride, escorting them to museums, dressing them immaculately and telling them every day that education was their passport to life. 'Wherever we went people would stop and look with great admiration at my mother.' In the early 1960s Floella learnt to be competitive, angry, physically confident and proud.

*

Following the record low temperatures of that winter, there was a mild spring. But in the early months of 1963 the British press started to boil with a story that had been on the slow burner since 1961, but would come to dominate the year with scalding headlines. Two very young women were the key ingredients in this toxic brew: Mandy Rice-Davies and Christine Keeler. Their names have become synonymous with sexual scandal.

What was it about the behaviour of these attractive girls-about-town that so gripped the nation? Titillating headlines have always attracted readers, so there was nothing new about that. But the Profumo case stirred up a hornets' nest of enraged righteousness. How are we to explain the hate, the extreme demonisation, the excessive vilification and persecution launched at two confused and powerless young women? Christine and Mandy would be branded drabs, common tarts, nymphomaniacs and monsters of depravity. The judge in the Stephen Ward case defined them both as prostitutes – which they were not – but the label stuck when Lord Denning conducted his inquiry into the Profumo Affair. For, worst of all, Christine Keeler and Mandy Rice-Davies had gone public. Their punishment for this would be implacable – the last flare-up, perhaps, of an angry male Establishment. Never again would women in this country be pilloried as Mandy and Christine were in 1963. A generation had liberation in their sights.

So how bad were they? Mandy Rice-Davies, like innumerable girls her age, was a romantic, a reader of spicy bodice-rippers. And she had a dream. 'I need romance: the food, the music, the soft lights, getting to know someone really well. I want to be courted before I will share a bed.' Christine Keeler had started out with bad prospects in impoverished circumstances, but – looks apart – nothing else made her or her aspirations any different from those of thousands of her contemporaries: 'I always wanted a man around. I thought life was all about couples, being together; it was the way everybody was and I wanted to be the same as everybody else. The sex side of the relationship seemed part of that.' Christine Keeler was a damaged person, who had had a limited education. She was naive, needy, indiscreet and spent periods in a fog of marijuana. But, like Mandy, she also believed that life owed her more fun than it had offered. 'I wanted a lark. I felt I deserved it . . .' Arriving in London, she was like a kid in a candy shop. 'One evening we put on our best dresses and went to an expensive restaurant. We ordered champagne and acted like duchesses . . . We stuffed our faces with goodies from the dessert trolley, giggling madly from all the champagne.' Like a million other teenagers Mandy and Christine were silly, giddy and irresponsible. But wicked? Iniquitous? Depraved? As we will see, the labels attached to them tell us much more about the fears, vanities, vulnerabilities and vindictiveness of the men themselves than they do about the women they so casually stigmatised.

In 1961 both the girls had left Murray's night club and found work, vaguely, as models. Christine had moved in with their new friend, the top-drawer osteopath Stephen Ward, in his Wimpole Mews flat in Marylebone, regularly weekending with him at his cottage retreat on the Cliveden estate owned by Lord (Bill) Astor. This was a platonic relationship. Meanwhile, Mandy's new daddy-figure, the Polish-Jewish slum landlord Peter Rachman, was keeping her in the lap of luxury in his flat near Marble Arch.

For her part, Christine was now on course to play the role of nemesis to a very different kind of man, an Establishment Tory to the core, proud recipient of wartime medals, Member of Parliament for Stratford-on-Avon and, since 1960, Secretary of State for War: John (Jack) Profumo. He was married to a poised woman who exuded breeding, the actress Valerie Hobson; like the good on-the-pedestal wife that she was, Valerie had put her career behind her after their marriage, and was occupied doing her dutiful share of charitable works and ribbon-cutting. The only thing that Profumo and Rachman had in common was that they were both middle-aged womanisers. Profumo, aged forty-six, was captivated by Christine, who radiated the feline beauty of an Egyptian deity. She was just nineteen.

Mandy tells in her memoirs that she found out about her friend's affair with the government minister when the pair of girls had gone for a fun jaunt to London Zoo. Against a backdrop of giraffes and monkeys, Christine blurted out her secret 'with barely suppressed excitement'. Christine later claimed this was pure invention. Whatever the case, the story soon emerged about the June night at Cliveden, when Profumo first encountered a curvaceous, giggling Christine, splashing naked in the Astors' swimming pool. From then on, the waters get progressively murkier.

Accounts vary, but they are all consistent in asserting that Christine slept with Profumo on a number of occasions. Later, Profumo said of her, 'I simply thought that she was a very beautiful little girl who seemed to like sexual intercourse . . .' Mandy, in her memoir, agreed: 'she enjoyed [sex] in a way that if it suited her, she was not too fussy who the other person was'.

Whatever the case, Profumo seems to have split up with Christine after, at most, a few months. He had been warned off spending too much time with Stephen Ward and his circle. This could have been a security risk, for Ward was known to be close friends with the Soviet naval attaché Yevgeny Ivanov. It cannot be known for sure whether Christine Keeler also slept with Ivanov.* Nevertheless, in her own careless, impulsive way, she – and Mandy – were now wandering into a swamp, and by the end of 1962 both girls were up to their necks in the kind of mud that sticks. Christine had become embroiled with two West Indians who were themselves in trouble with the law. The press started to take an interest when one of them tried to shoot his way into the flat and threatened to kill her. Meanwhile, Mandy's wealthy protector died of a heart attack, and not long after, or so she claimed, Bill Astor dropped by for a drink and she ended up in bed with him.

Christine drifted around the London party scene. By early 1963 she had divulged enough information about her unconventional sex life to enough prurient ears for the wires to start up a low but persistent hum. Her revelations helped to intensify activity among a network of behind-the-scenes score-settlers. And the Fleet Street editors had every motive to persuade an inexperienced girl to ginger up her story with espionage, sex and depravity in high places. It was

---

* In June 1963 Christine Keeler's lurid and sensational account of her passionate encounter with Ivanov was published in the *News of the World*. In *An English Affair: Sex, Class and Power in the Age of Profumo* (2013) Richard Davenport-Hines observes that 'although sexual discretion was not her métier, no one could recall her mentioning her night with Ivanov before January 1963, when journalists first saw their chance to run stories pretending that official secrets had been jeopardised by her multiple affairs . . . [and] there is every reason to discount Keeler's memory . . .' But Keeler's lawyer, who knew his client personally for forty-seven years, takes a different view: 'In his autobiography, *The Naked Spy* (1992), Ivanov says that he and Christine had sexual relations at 17 Wimpole Mews on 9 July 1961. The only two people who were present on that occasion say that they had sexual intercourse. There is no doubt that he was a heterosexual man and that she was an attractive woman and that they had the opportunity to have sex, so why should anyone with an open mind doubt that they are telling the truth about this?'

starting to seem inevitable that the scandal would detonate. The Establishment was closing ranks, the girls were getting in way out of their depth, and nobody ever seems to have regarded them as other than expendable.

On 22 March, spurred by the press furore, the Leader of the House, Iain Macleod, summoned Profumo to the Chief Whip's room at three in the morning and brazened it out with him: 'Look, Jack,' he is reported to have said, 'the basic question is: did you fuck her?'

Beside such a key factor, a trumped-up fable about high treason was secondary. The world of powerful men regarded it as vital to shore up appearances. Profumo stood in the House of Commons and lied to his fellow members:

> There was no impropriety whatsoever in my acquaintanceship with Miss Keeler.

With the scandal ratcheting up several notches, it was now becoming urgent to find a scapegoat. Together, Chief Inspector Samuel Herbert and his associates in the Metropolitan Police constructed an elaborate perversion of justice. Christine Keeler would have to lie. She would have to make a court believe that Stephen Ward was a pimp, even if it meant smearing her own name. Over the next three months Christine was interviewed thirty-eight times by police officers. Only slowly did she begin to realise that she was being remorselessly used.

> I did not understand what they were doing. What were all these questions about? But they persisted with them. Who visited Wimpole Mews? How many men? How often? Who paid the rent? . . . The question sessions sometimes went on for more than eight hours . . .

For the press, however, these were electrifying, joyous times. In *Private Eye*'s editorial office in Greek Street Anne Chisholm and her colleagues followed the affair avidly:

> The whole thing, I have to say, was just the most wonderful subject for satire.
>
> Macmillan, and the old-fashioned Tories, did seem ridiculous. Nobody believed Profumo when he made his famous statement – and we all assumed he was lying.

But even then there was already a feeling that Stephen Ward, although a dodgy character, was being railroaded.

Anne had little fellow feeling for the women in the case. Their virtue was easy, their demi-monde was far from her own, and the notion of female solidarity, insofar as it existed at all, did not yet extend to low-life adventuresses:

> To be honest I do remember being slightly amazed that they could have been cavorting with politicians in the swimming pool at Cliveden. Yes, I did feel a certain amount of sympathy with them . . . I certainly don't remember feeling 'shock, horror!'
>
> But nor did I feel any sense of outrage or sisterhood, or any sense that, isn't it awful that these girls were being so exploited? For example, I had no idea what a rotten background Christine Keeler had come from.

Mostly, for a knowing twenty-two-year-old Oxford graduate, the scandal was just great fun. Anne's finest hour at the *Eye* came after she was despatched to a picture library to hunt through all the visual cuttings featuring John Profumo, and returned triumphant with the image for one of the magazine's most famous covers:

> The photographer had caught the unfortunate man going round some sort of army barracks – and he was bouncing on a bed, you know – sort of trying out a bed. Well, this was a gift! So I came back proudly saying, 'Perhaps you could do something with this?'

The *Eye*'s cover for 5 April 1963 duly had Profumo perched ludicrously on the opposite side of a mattress from smiling fellow Minister Geoffrey Rippon, with Profumo's speech bubble reading '– if Private Eye prints a picture of me on a bed – I'LL SUE THEM!'

> The Profumo Affair gave us the feeling that we were in the forefront of something . . .

remembered Anne –

> . . . that we were part of this move that was going to take the lid off everything, that the *ancien régime* was corrupt and hypocritical, and that everything would be different.

As spring turned to summer, Profumo's story stuck, but it was open season on Christine and Mandy. They were mobbed wherever they went. Stolen secrets, poolside capers, black lovers, aristocrats, sugar daddies, slum landlords, drugs, gun crimes, whores, common tarts: this was the hall of mirrors to be navigated daily, the backdrop not only to police intimidation but also to a barrage of press bullying that reduced Christine to abject powerlessness: '[The *Daily Express* men] wanted to manipulate my every move, my thoughts, what I wore, what I ate and drank; they even escorted me to the bathroom . . .'

Stephen Ward was under relentless pressure too, and in June, in an attempt to save himself, he decided he couldn't continue to cover up for Profumo. He passed the true story to the prime minister's private secretary, exposed Profumo's lie to Parliament, and on 5 June forced a spectacular U-turn resignation. More guilty of a sin against the House of Commons than a sin against morality, Profumo was disgraced and finished.

The day after the resignation the *News of the World* published 'Confessions of Christine (by the Girl who is Rocking the Government)', paying her £24,000 for page after page of scurrilous fabrication.* Meanwhile, Profumo's deceived wife, ex-actress Valerie Hobson, who had played by the rules, got the full 'stand-by-your-man' treatment from the *Daily Express*'s star writer Anne Edwards:

> She earned top marks as housewife, hostess, social asset, bazaar and fête opener, listener to speeches in the House of Commons, faithful sitter on platforms at political meetings, and companion on political tours . . .
>
> How can anyone imagine a woman like this letting even this crushing blow get her down for good?
>
> I predict she'll go on looking cool, aloof [and] fastidiously elegant . . .

The Profumos went to ground. When they returned to London to run the gauntlet of the press Valerie Profumo was seen to be queenly and dignified in headscarf and the inevitable white gloves. She made no mention of the scandal.

Three days after Profumo's resignation, Stephen Ward was arrested and charged with living wholly or partly on the earnings of prostitution.

* Around £500,000 today.

How to sell newspapers: Christine Keeler, the woman at the heart of the Profumo Affair.

At the magistrate's hearing, Mandy secured her place in history with an audacious jibe at Bill Astor, who, it was put to her, denied that they had had a sexual relationship. Mandy had her pride. She wasn't going to be treated as a liar. Her response – 'Well, he would, wouldn't he?' – was taken as brazen cheek, and the court burst into laughter. But Mandy felt cheapened and belittled. 'I said it in all seriousness,' she wrote in her memoir.

Six weeks later Ward's travesty of a trial opened. As Christine Keeler entered the court the crowd screamed abuse at her. Once in the witness box, her character was shredded. The *Daily Mirror*'s Donald Zec drooled helplessly over her appearance and testimony:

> The voluptuous lips, slightly parted over protruding teeth, extend from high cheekbones, a slash of red against the sallow skin.
>
> Names, and yet more names. Sexual intercourse with this man, that man, here, there, at such a time and such a place . . .

But when counsel and judge [asked] whether she was a prostitute or not – the lips sagged open and her tongue slid across the whiteness of her teeth.

'I am not a prostitute. I never have been,' she said angrily.

Under oath, Christine reluctantly spun the story that Chief Inspector Samuel Herbert had coached her in. 'I had not wanted to do that despite everything,' she later recalled. 'Stephen had never had to live off women.'

Mandy arrived at the Old Bailey wearing an astonishing outfit: a soberly elegant grey wrapover dress with a hint of a split skirt, topped with a preposterously frivolous petalled pink hat reminiscent of a retro swim cap. What kind of woman was this? Bluestocking, dizzy doll, demi-mondaine or respectable bachelor girl? 'I wore it to boost my confidence,' was her version. In court, the prosecutor was Mervyn Griffith-Jones: that same censorious, self-appointed custodian of public morals who had pursued Penguin Books over their publication of *Lady Chatterley's Lover* in 1960. Thin-lipped and pompous, Griffith-Jones behaved throughout the proceedings like a man holding his nose beside a bad smell, doing nothing to conceal his disgust. Mandy described the judge, Sir Archibald Marshall, as 'a wrathful figure from another century'. In his summing-up Marshall advised the Old Bailey jury that Christine and Mandy could be defined as prostitutes. It amounted to a condemnation of thousands of women who did not share his out-of-touch notions of morality.

After they were sent off to deliberate, Stephen Ward went to a friend's flat and took an overdose of barbiturates; as he hung between life and death, the jury convicted him of living off immoral earnings. 'GUILTY' shouted the *Daily Mirror* front page. Three days later he died. It was a perversion of justice that penalised the living as much as the dead. Mandy realised that her reputation was sealed. Christine collapsed in uncontrollable sobs. 'It was as much for me as for Stephen. I had been robbed of the truth.'

Harold Macmillan called on Lord Denning, a man of impeccable Establishment credentials, to conduct an inquiry into the Profumo Affair. Its point of departure was unquestioning acceptance of the lies told in court. Mandy and Christine were assumed to be prostitutes, and

Ward a procurer. Macmillan's government was capsizing, and in October he resigned. For Christine Keeler, there was a different price to pay. Having been used by the police to incriminate her protector and friend, she was lethally soiled by the connection, and branded 'slut', 'trollop', 'scrubber' and a lexicon of other defamatory terms. She was then arrested, charged with perjury for the lies she had been forced to tell, tried and sentenced to nine months in Holloway prison. Used, and binned. When she came out, a newspaper published her telephone number.

However you describe them (Mandy preferred the word 'courtesan'), there have always been women like Mandy Rice-Davies and Christine Keeler, but their world, and their sexual role, had been clandestine. In 1963 the Profumo Affair turned sex from a topic of furtive tittle-tattle, into one of tell-all revelation. Now cheap infidelities, blackmail, vice, betrayal and lurid rumours about two-way mirrors, whips, masks and orgies became the subject matter of chequebook journalism, wholesale lies, public voyeurism and mob morality. And to the horror of their high-rolling escorts the girls themselves seemed only too willing to collaborate with the exposés, kissing, screwing – and telling the tabloids. Where was their sense of shame? Mandy Rice-Davies had a matter-of-fact attitude to sex. What was the big deal, she asked, in Profumo's infidelity? All men played around, cheated on their wives. These were 'minor indiscretions, surely'.

The rules had changed. Christine and Mandy were clear that they were not earning money from having sex with grandees – but if the world wanted to judge them for having sex simply because they liked it, well, that was fine by them.

'I still cannot understand why I was ever called a "call girl",' wrote Mandy in her co-authored memoir:

> Promiscuous, perhaps, but not a call girl. I was Rachman's mistress, that doesn't make me a call girl. I had men friends I went to bed with, but they were friends. A call girl goes to bed with strangers . . .
>
> I tried to express myself to the judge, but every time I went to open my mouth he would say: 'Stick to the questions, or I'll have you for contempt of court.'

After the trial was over, the columnist 'Cassandra' (in reality, William Connor) told his *Sunday Mirror* readers that Christine Keeler had 'showed a catholicity of undiscriminating sexual taste that makes all-in wrestling seem like a monastic pursuit . . .', and described Mandy Rice-Davies as 'a pert slut, who for fun, gain, or God knows what, had slept with [Stephen Ward]'. This was untrue. But Connor's denunciation continued: '[The] female sexual monsters who gave evidence against Ward did so with an amoral candour that has a blood-chilling quality . . .' As for Lord Denning's report, Christine wrote later that she felt hung out to dry: 'the attitude was simply: let's blame Christine Keeler for everything'.

In Act 4 of *King Lear*, Shakespeare articulated 'the great image of authority':

> *Thou rascal beadle, hold thy bloody hand.*
> *Why dost thou lash that whore? Strip thine own back.*
> *Thou hotly lust'st to use her in that kind*
> *For which thou whipp'st her . . .*

More than three centuries later, the rascal beadles were still lashing out, not at whores, but at women who for the first time felt no shame about their own desires. The Profumo scandal gave a couple of 'good-time girls' and 'common tarts' column inches, and placed them in the witness box. Now they could be heard.

But what their voices were saying was unacceptable. In the eyes of complacent men, the lower ranks appeared to be mutinying. Here were less-educated women voluntarily having sexual affairs with their social superiors. Here were women having sex with men they didn't love, who weren't their husbands and who would not be the fathers of their children. Here were promiscuous women – who sometimes had sex with black men. They might have had 'kinky' sex, or 'deviant' sex. And these women were not only experienced at sex, they actually enjoyed it.

In 1963, mighty men quaked in their boots in fear of the ungoverned power of women's sexuality: a weapon stripped of its guard. For centuries, in the continuing war of the sexes, men had won, and dictated the peace agreement. Women's libido had come with terms and conditions attached, both moral and financial. But that transaction put no price on women's pleasure. Moreover, the generally accepted narrative had been controlled by men. In that narrative, women were either nice or naughty, ladies or tramps, and whichever they were, they didn't like sex – not in the way men did, since for men to want sexual enjoyment was understood to be a law of nature. But that story didn't hold up any more. A fiction that for years had been constructed by and for the male sex was exposed and laid bare by the tawdry tale of a politician, a spy and two showgirls. The threat to male ascendancy was such that Christine and Mandy had to be torn to pieces.

As for Valerie Profumo, never again would she sit on the political platform beside her husband. Never again would she be invited to open fêtes or bazaars, entertain or appear immaculately groomed at meetings and hustings. For this was also the year when the edifice of white gloves, poise, passivity and perfection rocked precariously, tottered dangerously, swayed – and never quite recovered its balance.

Problems with No Name

In 1963 the voice of female sexuality was getting louder, braver and more insistent. America, home of everything modern, heralded progressive ways of thinking about pleasure, fulfilment and relationships.

The two Kinsey Reports had shown the way, encouraging women to believe that the bedroom was a place where exciting things happened.[*] And that year two recently published books which had also been making waves across the States were beginning to rock the boat in Britain. Helen Gurley Brown's *Sex and the Single Girl* was a how-to manual aimed at the unmarried. Its author, a happily married high-flyer with a job in advertising, understood her readership – and took it for granted that what most single career women wanted was Mr Right. But it also braved it out on the sex front:

> *Should a Man Think You Are a Virgin?*
>   I can't imagine why, if you aren't. Is he?
>   Is there anything particularly attractive about a thirty-four-year-old virgin?

[*] *Sexual Behavior in the Human Male* (1948), and *Sexual Behavior in the Human Female* (1953), by Alfred Kinsey.

> Once in bed, it's kind of silly to fake inexperience . . . If he is the
> kind of man who is only interested in deflowering virtue, he should
> stick to unraveling chrysanthemums!

Sex and the Single Girl was a bestseller for over a year, and was first
published in Britain in spring 1963, prompting a similar scramble to
the bookshops, despite some po-faced reviews sneering at the 'wom-
en's magazine style' of the writing and the author's relentless go-getting
attitude to eligible men. For, refreshingly, Helen Gurley Brown lived
in the real world. From sex to money, from dieting to home entertaining, from where to meet men to what to do with them between the
sheets, her book concerned itself with practicalities, which she spelled
out in frank and frisky prose. Gurley Brown was no prude, and her
book was on the side of women. She saw herself as having got lucky,
and she wanted others to have what she had got. But though some
commentators have claimed that *Sex and the Single Girl* was a fore-
runner of second-wave feminism, this was a book more about making
the most of opportunities than about the oppression of women.

That accolade should go to Betty Friedan, author of *The Feminine
Mystique* (billed in America as 'the book that's causing all the talk'),
which equally got people chattering when it was published in Britain in
May 1963. Friedan, a university-educated mother of three, had surveyed
a number of her Smith College contemporaries about their education
and subsequent experiences. Her book was based on their responses, and
probed to identify what she called 'the problem that has no name':

> It was a strange stirring, a sense of dissatisfaction, a yearning that
> women suffered in the middle of the twentieth century in the United
> States. Each suburban wife struggled with it alone. As she made the
> beds, shopped for groceries, matched slip-cover material . . . lay
> beside her husband at night, she was afraid to ask even of herself the
> silent question: 'Is this all?'

Friedan's premise was that these problems particularly afflicted educated women – her sample came from that category. Her book also
explored the fantasy promise of sexual satisfaction, which conventional marriage seemed to dull and deaden. 'Even when they
experience orgasm, they feel unfulfilled . . .' And she had a larger

aim: that American women might give more to society, and achieve greater fulfilment for themselves outside the home than in it. She urged a solution that optimised women's education by bringing them back into the working world after they were no longer essential to their families.* In Britain, where fewer school leavers went to university than in the USA, the problem seems to have been less acute. Critics, however, pigeonholed *The Feminine Mystique* as shouty and censorious. In 1963, many people still took it for granted that the post-war era was also a post-feminist era. Mrs Pankhurst and her window-smashing militants had served their purpose and were consigned to history. 'The pendulum was bound to swing away from the suffragettes,' wrote Anthony Storr, reviewing Friedan's book for the *Sunday Times*. And he chided the author for her stridency: 'The lady doth protest too much, like all feminists.' *The Guardian*'s (female) reviewer didn't quarrel with Friedan's premise, but – despite wringing her hands at the lack of university places or entry into professions for British women – she was resigned to society's intractability. If women were to break out of their prison, they had an uphill task ahead of them. But Joan Bakewell described reading *The Feminine Mystique* as 'a moment of epiphany . . . From now on I was alert to the snares and delusions of male values; I was eager to see change and improvement for women.'

Through Gurley Brown and Friedan the seedling notion had been planted – and was germinating – that there could be more to life than babies, barbecues and bridge parties. 'Who knows what women can be when they are finally free to become themselves?' was Betty Friedan's challenge, while the ever-shrewd and canny Helen Gurley Brown simply reminded her readers, 'Career girls are sexy. A man likes to sleep with a brainy girl.'

*

* Friedan's more influential work had been pre-empted in the UK by two lesser-known studies: Alva Myrdal and Viola Klein, *Women's Two Roles: Home and Work* (1956), and Judith Hubback's *Wives Who Went to College* (1957). A hands-on approach to helping intellectually frustrated housewives was also initiated in Britain in 1959 by Maureen Nicol, who founded the self-help network which was to become the National Women's Register.

Giving 'problems' a name was also a priority in 1963 for the lesbian community. Recognition and acceptance were still a long way off for women who preferred women. The conventional view was that lesbian women were dangerous. A female teacher might be afraid to confess her lesbian orientation for fear of jeopardising her job: '[the parents'] immediate reaction would be one of disgust ... [They] would believe that I would "contaminate" their children, or teach them "dirty habits", or educate them to be "not nice"', recalled one. A lesbian civil servant told how she owned up to a colleague about her sexuality, and was soon after asked to resign. Another woman, Sharley McLean (cited in a history of gay women in post-war Britain), later identified as lesbian – but felt impelled by overwhelming social pressure to marry and have children. Sharley attempted suicide. A contemporary in the same situation explained: 'They kept on so! They say the day a girl marries is the happiest day in her life. I can tell you it was the unhappiest in mine.'

In *The New London Spy*, his unconventional 1960s guide to London's pleasures, Hunter Davies commissioned the author Maureen Duffy to give an insider's view of the difficulties faced by lesbian women finding love in the capital:

> Pubs are ... risky places for unaccompanied women, youth clubs are impossible. Dining out with the girlfriend is an expensive business and few women earn as much as men. Restaurants often bar women in slacks but a great number of homosexual women feel uncomfortable in anything else.
>
> From time to time girls are beaten up but they don't as a rule complain to the police. They know that in a sense they are guilty of provocation simply by being themselves and they don't expect anyone else to sympathise.

So where could you go? Duffy pinpointed a couple of pubs, one in Battersea, another in Notting Hill Gate, which had a gay clientele. Westbourne Park was also known to have a club that welcomed transvestites; otherwise, if you weren't too fussy, you might try one or two other late-night clubs in the same part of town, known to be frequented by drug-pushers and sex professionals. The desperate might resort to the pop-up private drinking venues in people's houses, which manoeuvred around the licensing laws and charged high prices for a gin and tonic. Or, eventually, there were always suburban bottle parties, where women danced with women. But inevitably, Duffy was left having to recommend the only real option, the famous Gateways Club at 239 King's Road, which for much of the mid-twentieth century was *the* underground sanctuary (and pick-up venue) for the self-described 'gay girls'. Here, squashed between the bar and the juke box, the fruit machine and the dance floor, a crew-cut bohemian crowd in fly front trousers, with 'femmes' in shapely cocktail dresses, milled, drank, twisted to the 'Brontosaurus Stomp', and flirted. If you were lucky you might even see Dusty Springfield.

Which was all very well for those who lived in relatively tolerant communities like London or Brighton. But Gateways and the south coast aside, the scenery was bleak for women looking for companionship or love, if their orientation did not conform to sexual norms. Loneliness and isolation, secrecy and guilt were to be endured daily. As permissiveness crept up the heterosexual agenda, lesbian freedoms failed to keep pace.

But from 1963 the literature of lesbianism would find a new voice. That year, a remarkably intelligent, well-read, and unconventional middle-aged single mother named Esmé Langley sat down to read a correspondence about lesbianism in the pages of the sociological journal *Twentieth Century*. The first writer had put the case that women became lesbian mainly because of failed relationships with their fathers. The piece was suffused with notes of pity and disgust, describing lesbians as tea-shop dames with an unhealthy love of dogs. In response came back a strongly worded speech for the defence: sexual self-expression was not to be dismissed as neurosis. Esmé, herself homosexual, had been trying for some time to launch an organisation that would bring sexual minorities together. Now she felt she might have an ally who could help. She made contact, and in the summer of 1963, along with a number of like-minded confederates, Esmé held the first meeting of the Minorities Research Group. One of its supporters remembers it as 'a sort of lesbian club based in London . . . They met monthly just behind Liberty's off Regent Street at the Shakespeare's Head . . . They were quite literary people, who really knew what they were doing.' Today, the MRG would

probably have a less euphemistic title, but in 1963 anything racier
would have invited prurience and controversy. The group's stated
aim was to 'collaborate in research into the homosexual condition,
especially as it concerns women; and to disseminate information to
those genuinely in the quest of enlightenment'.

And so, at last, thanks to Esmé Langley, lesbianism started to come
in from the cold, as for the first time a vital support system emerged,
offering gay women understanding, the feeling that they were no
longer alone, and the freedom to be who they truly were.

Hessle Road

The cultural historian Robert Hewison buys into the popular understanding of the decade as defined by personal liberation, when he
writes, 'the Sixties did not really begin until about 1963'. Philip Larkin's poem 'Annus Mirabilis' is also proof that poetry can recast our
understanding of history.

> *Sexual intercourse began*
> *In nineteen sixty-three*
> *(which was rather late for me) –*
> *Between the end of the Chatterley ban*
> *And the Beatles' first LP.*

Of course, it didn't begin in 1963, but the landmarks Larkin planted
are as good as any in shaping and delimiting the three transitional
years that bridged the 1950s and the so-called Swinging Sixties (Larkin might have chosen the Profumo Affair, but perhaps it didn't scan
so well). In the time he was writing about, the poet was a forty-year-
old librarian, bespectacled, bald, awkward and sensitive, observing a
changing world from the upper-floor windows of his flat in a leafy
area of Hull.

Badly bombed in the Second World War, the early 1960s saw Hull
recovering some of its civic and industrial prowess, much of it built
on the docks and the trawling industry. Its heart was Hessle Road,
whose four-mile length, running parallel to the north shore of the
Humber, housed Hull's fishing community. Here the scream of gulls

competed with the clatter of steel-studded clogs. The smell of tar, beer and above all fish hung on the wind. The fishing industry employed thousands in skilful but perilous work, with a trawlerman seventeen times more likely to die at sea than a coal miner down a pit. The women had low-paid jobs in the fish houses skinning cod and haddock, or in the subsidiary industries like crate-making, processing or packing.

This was the world Mary Denness grew up in, born in 1937, the daughter of a trawlerman. By 1963, twenty-six-year-old Mary had achieved her early ambition. She had married a skipper.

We met Mary earlier, telling her story fifty years on, in her comfortable but rather airless little sitting room in a north Lincolnshire village. She started life in Hessle Road as Robina Mary Taylor, the fourth child and only girl in a large and impoverished family. Eventually there were eight brothers, all of whom followed in their father's footsteps. Her mother had been a fish worker at the docks. The Taylors' marriage was a travesty – though of a type not uncommon in working-class industrial communities, where many men regarded their wives as no more than providers of meals and an orderly home. Mr Taylor got drunk and regularly beat his wife black and blue while the children cowered, terrified, behind the furniture. 'I grew up thinking there was no such thing as a happy marriage.' Her mother had brought her up to confront a future without prospects: ' "Don't think you'll ever amount to much," she told me, "and *don't* expect too much of life, 'cos you *won't get it*!" And those words stuck in me like a knife.'

But a girl could dream, and Mary did.

There was a posh clothes shop on Hessle Road called the Clothing Shop, and of course I couldn't afford it, because I was only a teenager. But my friends and I used to look in the windows with our noses pressed up, and say, 'Ah, look at THAT coat! Oh, just *look* at that dress!'

And then you'd see some woman out in that same gear. And we knew that these women decked out in their finery were all married to skippers. So that's who I wanted to be! You see, on a trawler the top post is the skipper. And they had the money.

So I was very sceptical, very mercenary, very much: 'I've had enough of poverty, I want something a bit better in life materialistically.' My idea of 'better' was not really all that much – I'd no idea what real luxury was. For me it would have been a neat little sitting room. Or just going into a shop and buying something new. That was my ideal life.

Mary Taylor left school when she was fifteen. Her face, her figure, and her brains were her fortune. In the 1950s there was no shortage of factory jobs for young women, so to start off with she worked in a box mill making fish crates a few blocks down from her Hessle Road front door. But it was poorly paid, menial work. Poverty and want were teaching Mary that the only way to acquire finery and comfort was to get a well-off husband, and she was determined not to settle for less. She was an unashamed gold-digger, and that meant being clever and playing the field. But the dating game in working-class Hull had rules, and Mary got some sour looks from the neighbours when she demonstrated that she had no intention of observing them. Her bloom and her curves got her a barrage of offers from potential boyfriends, but instead of settling for one, she cast her net wide.

Having a regular boyfriend was a signal to the world that you were going steady, and wanted to get tied down. But I didn't want that! And my mother's neighbours would say, 'Oh she's a right little hussy that one, you see her with a different boy every night!' They were right too!

Mary's watery old eyes are still full of mischief and delight recalling her teenage years:

We used to go to the Scala. That was where you really escaped. There was a mirror ball hung over the middle of the floor. It was wonderful! I'd wear my hair curled under, but fuller at the top, all backcombed, and skirts halfway up the thigh. Fortunately I had good legs in those days. And oh, I was quite a jiver!

Getting multiple dates may not have boosted her standing among the Hessle Road matrons, but the pulling power of her good looks gave Mary a different kind of status. For a young girl who had been put down since childhood, there was the confidence of knowing you were pretty, and the power that knowledge delivered into your supposedly fragile female hands. She entered adulthood with a new boldness, and a new sense of self-worth.

Mary had spirit and ambition. By the time she was eighteen the dreariness of working-class life had become unbearable. With two friends she took off for London: 'A lot of us girls from the north did that. We wanted to get away before we were caught getting pregnant to a boyfriend, which would have put an end to that plan. I'd had enough of making boxes in factories, and we all thought the streets were paved with gold . . .'

For a year she was a shop assistant in a jeweller's in Edgware Road. Then the opportunity arose to join the merchant navy as a ship stewardess; two years working for the Wilson Line opened her eyes to distant horizons in Canada and North America. She was a different person when she returned to Hull and met the man who would become her husband.

Barry Denness was a Brixham man from Devon . . .

It was 1959. Barry had come up from the West Country to Hull in search of bigger fish and better money. The relationship started well. 'He was charming. Like they all are at the beginning. And anything I wanted that he could afford, he would get me.' But with her parents' example before her, Mary didn't want to risk marriage too quickly. For a while she and Barry cohabited, keeping up the social pretence that it was a conjugal arrangement in order to suppress gossip. So long as the world believed you had a document, nobody would ask to see it. 'My parents could always say to their neighbours, "They got married in Scotland!"' More importantly, for Mary, not marrying was a way to keep her options open. 'I'd have been off with the next one if somebody better came along!' But when the question of having babies arose it seemed better to officialise things. It helped, too, that Barry Denness had now got his skipper's ticket. They married in December 1959. In 1960 a boy was born, followed by a girl in 1962.

And all too soon, Mary discovered that she had signed up for a role that put the lid on her freedom. She saw Barry Denness as replicating some of the same defects of her own father, who had been cruel, unjust, jealous and a drinker. But worse than that, Mary found she'd traded creature comforts and skipper's wife status for captivity. This was a community that imposed male and female apartheid, and there was a reason for it. On the trawlers, the men lived with the fear of what their wives might be doing. Were they being cheated on when their backs were turned? While the men were at sea – which they were for weeks at a time – there was the expectation that their wives would remain within their domestic boundaries. So, though it was acceptable to take a child to visit a relative, it was not acceptable for a wife to seek adult companionship, of either sex, outside the home. Once you were married, your dancing days were over. A man could go out for a drink with his friends. A woman couldn't. If she insisted, the segregation continued, with most Hull pubs providing a 'Gentlemen's Bar Only', right through the 1960s.

Jealousy and suspicion were built into the lives of the trawler families. Even on board ship, the onshore fishermen would inform on the wives by radio, letting the husband know that his woman was not playing by the rules. 'What have you been up to while I've been away? One of my shipmates told me he saw you out with somebody . . .' 'Nobody in their right mind got up to anything in the trawling industry,' remembered Mary, 'because if you did the radio waves would be sizzling with it.'

It was: 'I go to sea, you stay indoors.' Back on shore, according to Mary, her jealous husband would walk in the door and head straight upstairs to ransack the wardrobe for clues, turning pockets inside out for anything that was there that shouldn't have been. 'He never did find anything.' Anybody who looked at his gorgeous wife was a threat. 'Who's he? Why are you being secretive?'

But though it wasn't worth risking a beating for, constancy had never been Mary's strong point. She craved admiration. 'I was a redhead. People used to tell me I looked like Christine Keeler. When people saw her picture in the papers they'd say, "Oh, she looks ever so much like you, Mary!" And, well, I know I'm vain, but there were far too many that said it!' Bright-haired and buxom, plastered in eyeliner, shapely legs encased in tight boots, headscarf firmly anchoring her bouffant hairdo from the city's raw onshore gales, she'd set out with the pushchair making sure to pass construction sites on her way to the shops, where the overalled workers would let rip with a 'WOOooow, love *them*, Ginger!!' After years of being crushed by her parents, years of being told she would never amount to anything, how could she not respond to the feeling of being desired? 'It was so morale-boosting. I felt wanted. And it was the opposite of what my parents had done to me.' How could she resist if someone offered to buy her a shandy? But tongues would wag – 'Oh look at *her*, her husband's away at sea slogging his guts out – and who the hell is *she* with?'

Mary Denness had travelled, and lived. She'd felt her own power, and she knew that the world held more than four walls. But this was a cage.

> It was the dominance of men. They just expected it. No different to the Indian woman throwing herself on the funeral pyre when her man died. It was that kind of thinking, that kind of conditioning. I felt completely trapped.

Mary Denness had dreamed of materialistic betterment and upward mobility. She had those. But by 1963, that dream had begun to seem ever more illusory.

Twist and Shout

The cool, cloudy summer weather of 1963 failed to compensate for the grim winter and, aside from the Profumo scandal, summer was a slow news season. Newspaper reports from July that year offer up the usual lucky dip of the prosaic, the droll and the bizarre. The Transport Union voted to recruit more women officers, with a London bus driver commenting that a man could persuade a woman to do almost anything, but only if it was something the woman wanted to do in the first place. The House of Lords debated whether housewives could be seen as profiteering if they were allowed to keep savings on their housekeeping money – which, as Lord Boothby said, would surely tempt them to skimp on meals for their husbands; and at the Newcastle Assizes an all-male jury was unable to agree whether the thirty-four-year-old vicar of Cassop-cum-Quarrington was guilty of charges of gross indecency. Meanwhile, negotiations inched forward for Britain to join the Common Market, and Pat Smythe looked set to win a hat trick at the Hickstead Ladies' European Championship after Flanagan jumped two clear rounds. Business as usual.

But the incidence of 'beatnik girl' runaways was so commonplace that, although a missing teenager made the front page of the *Manchester Evening News* on 17 July 1963, this one didn't make the nationals until almost two years later. Under a smiling head-shot, the column read:

Girl, 16, vanishes on way to jive club

Pauline Reade put on her new figure-hugging Twist dress, said goodbye to her mother, and went off to a teenage jive club. To-day, five days later, Pretty Pauline, aged 16, had still not returned to her home in Wiles-street, Gorton, Manchester.

Her mother, Mrs. Joan Reade, aged 35, said: 'It is a complete mystery. She had no boy friends and we had no rows at home.

'She was making her way towards the dance, but apparently she never arrived there.

'Her father and I are worried sick about it. I fear she may have done something and decided not to tell us about it.

'I would rather know that she is safe and have her back home no matter what she has done.'

Pauline disappeared wearing a powder blue coat, square-necked pink dance dress and high heeled shoes. She is about five feet four, blue-eyed, and dark-haired. She had 10 shillings with her.

Mrs Reade's pretty daughter hadn't run away. She would never return home. The sixteen-year-old had been taken by her killers to Saddleworth Moor, raped, strangled, and a large knife used to cut her throat with such gruesome savagery as almost to decapitate her. Her brutalised body, buried three feet below the rolling sedge and heather, would remain unfound for another twenty-four years.

*

The moral panic allied to 'Stranger Danger' can trace much of its momentum back to the Moors Murders. In 1963 the perpetrators

PAULINE READE

Girl, 16, vanishes on way to jive club

PAULINE READE put on her new figure-hugging Twist dress, said goodbye to her mother, and went off to a teenage jive club. To-day, five days later, Pretty Pauline, aged 16, had still not returned to her home in Wiles-street, Gorton, Manchester.

Her mother, Mrs. Joan Reade, aged 35, said : " It is a complete

Pauline Reade from Gorton, Manchester: just another teenage runaway?

were still at large, and between then and 1965 would torture and kill another four children. But in 1963, when Pauline Reade went missing, her mystified parents' primary concern was that their daughter, who had no boyfriend, might have 'done something . . .' A sixteen year-old could be supposed to have a secret, private life.

For girls were noticeably insisting on their independence in a way not seen before; buying one-way tickets to adventure, fobbing their parents off with, 'Mummy thinks I'm at a party in someone's house . . .' or hanging around late listening to the juke box in the kind of coffee bars that conferred status, identity and 'cool'.

The periphery of London was Modland. Elizabeth Woodcraft, who grew up in Chelmsford, Essex, recently published a novel, *The Saturday Girls* (2018), about being a teenage Mod. But this was truly her own story:

> I wrote it simply because we had such a good time in the sixties – the music, the clothes, the coffee bars . . .
>
> I wanted to recreate the excitement of going to Southend or Romford or even Oxford Street, to Martin Ford or C&A, to buy mod clothes. The boys were buying parkas and the scooters to go with them, but girls were buying straight skirts, that we wore below the knee, and twinsets in deep mod colours – bottle green, navy blue or maroon. For some of the more well-off mods, fashions came and went quite quickly, but people like me and my friend Christine had to save up for weeks.

Twiggy's territory in Neasden was also situated in the suburban hinterland of London. 'I liked all modern things,' insisted the former Lesley Hornby:

> Anything modern was wonderful, and anything old was terrible. It has a lot to do with the middle-class, suburban way of thinking, to revere new things, everything up to date, up to the minute, brand new and streamlined and contemporary – that's what everything has to be – houses, home décor, ornaments, clothes! I'm sure it has a lot to do with post-war consumerism . . . In the sixties . . . everything had to be in fashion instantly and then out again, constantly changing.

For now, in 1963, when the Mod phenomenon peaked, the look was, as Elizabeth Woodcraft described, a precise, soberly coloured uniform of pinstripes, herringbones, tweeds and flannels. Working-class girls like her made their own fashion, from the street up. Till now the only slacks available to women were bottom-hugging and side-zippered, so they shopped in men's stores for floppy-legged fly-buttoned trousers. Before the mini came in, Mod teenagers like Elizabeth and Twiggy often sewed their own long pencil or A-line skirts with box or kick pleats, tailored blouses or polo-neck sweaters, to be worn with square-toed 'granny' shoes. Shift dresses with cut-away armholes were the thing for dancing. Lace had a moment. Elizabeth had a brown suedette jacket, Twiggy a nylon mac. Hair had to be boyish and sleek; it could take hours to flatten it to the right degree before lacquering it into glossy submission. Make-up was important, the face and lips whitened to corpse-like paleness, the eyes obliterated with heavy mascara and eyeliner. It was cool to be thin, flat-chested and androgynous.

Mod girls were defiantly anti-feminine, anti-curves, anti-romantic. As their male counterparts fussed and prinked for hours getting ready, obsessing about the perfect parka, the softest desert boots, or the most immaculate Italian mohair suit, these young women edged closer to a look that would later be described as unisex. Was it a desire for autonomy and freedom that made them cross into boy territory? Or was it envy – wanting to look like a boy, be like a boy, join the boy-gang? One writer on the short-lived Mod phenomenon captures the sexual politics of their teen subculture:

> Mods were more interested in themselves and each other than in girls . . . One female Mod from the time, Sara Brown from Kensington, remembers some of the frustration girls felt: 'The guys were so preoccupied with their clothes. It got to be a big deal to have a conversation with a guy and we thought we were very lucky if one of these gorgeous creatures actually *danced* with us.'*

Girl Mods were adjuncts, camp followers, hero-worshippers, hangers-on – the precursors of the sexually active groupies. Girls acquired attitude, jettisoning womanliness in favour of asexuality. But this made them all the more oddly robotic, anonymous and objectified. They were numbers on scorecards, there to supply and service: this facet of the sexual free-for-all, later to become a full-on sixties trend, was already gaining ground. Back in the world of Mod, young men were the embodiments of a renascent vainglory, posturing and dandyism. In that world, women were secondary. Self-adornment was a male preoccupation – done to impress other blokes, not girls. Chasing 'birds' was seen as weedy, not cool. Girlfriends were expensive too, and with the amount these lads were spending on Fred Perrys and two-tone mohair, there wasn't a lot to spare on taking them out. The typical dance date would be, 'See you in there at 8.30.' That way, she would pay for her own ticket and bus fare.

For Elizabeth Woodcraft the Chelmsford Corn Exchange on a Saturday night was the arena for throbbing music, impeccably ironed pleats, boyfriends in pork-pie hats and Hush Puppies; there was a hint of violence, and more than a hint of sex. The true Mod adopted a vacant expression and danced with rigid angularity. Jive had now given way to the twist – the first dance in which partners went free form, liberating both sexes from the inequality embedded in formal dances in which the man 'led', and the woman followed.† And that year *Ready Steady Go!* debuted, co-hosted – from 1964 – by 'Queen of Mod' Cathy McGowan. Getting on to this was the holiest of grails.

---

* *Mods!* compiled by Richard Barnes (1979).
† Though a nice corrective to the male dance-domination model is the often-quoted line by cartoonist Bob Thaves, describing power tap-dance couple Fred Astaire and Ginger Rogers: 'Don't forget that Ginger Rogers did everything he did: backwards and in high heels.'

McGowan, a nineteen-year-old ex-secretary from Streatham, hit the modernistic, lower-middle-class, suburban button to perfection. 'She was a heroine to us because she was one of us,' recalled Twiggy. Girls wanted to *be* Cathy, and started cutting their hair in boxy fringes. Casual, creative and hip, she got people dancing, dressing and talking differently. The music was 'fab', the gear was 'smashing'. Television brought her look and her choice of pop into homes across the country, and for millions of teenagers at six o'clock on a Friday night, its slogan 'the weekend starts here . . .' was a feel-good promise. Twiggy again: 'It was our bible. This was the TV programme that you would *not* miss. You just did not miss it.' *Ready Steady Go!* was go-to TV for the young, about the young, by the young. It set trends overnight, and teens from Dundee to Dover could pick up the latest in Cuban heels, hairstyles and skirt fashions.

At the beginning of 1963 the world had not caught on to the Beatles. But there were signs that this was changing. Maureen Cleave, a wised-up pop journalist on the London *Evening Standard*, had spotted their following in Liverpool, clocked their Liverpudlian lack of affectation, and drawn attention to their hairstyles. In February the band was booked onto a national tour, packaged as Helen Shapiro's support group. But as the Profumo scandal started to lose traction, the Beatles phenomenon began to take over the front pages. On 4 October 1963 they appeared on *Ready Steady Go*, where they were interviewed by Dusty Springfield, who read out letters from their besotted fans: 'John, tell me, how did the Beatles get their name? John, do you have false teeth, as they always look so even? Hello, gorgeous Paul . . . please ask [him] if he plucks his well-shaped eyebrows? They're absolutely beautiful . . . [And] do you mind girls screaming all the way through your act?' The fame, and the fetishisation, of the Fab Four had begun.

★

With five chart-topping singles in 1963, and the release of their first album, *Please Please Me*, the Beatles' Liverpudlian pop sound had moved beyond the confines of the Mersey. Mary Ingham recalled: '1963 was the year the pop music scene burst into raw life . . .'

John, Paul, George and Ringo.

They're on stage, and they're singing 'She Loves You'. A blonde teen-ager with black eyeliner stares glassily at her idols, her lips dropping open with awestruck adulation. Another, about fifteen years old, dishev-elled, weeps uncontrollably. A sweaty, plump-faced girl pushes her knuckles into her mouth in an unsuccessful attempt to suppress her own frenzied screams. Some are transfixed with ecstasy. Some collapse or faint, some shout deliriously, hold their hands over their ears, tremble, pant and shudder convulsively. They scream and scream and scream. They scream loudest of all when George and Paul spasmodically shake their unruly collar-length mops. But though the mop tops were a defi-ant departure from the short-back-and-sides wartime proprieties, the Beatlemania phenomenon wasn't really about a talented long-haired rock band from Merseyside. It was about girls. And it was about girls losing it.

Beatlemania was public misrule and tumult on an unprecedented scale. Girls in their thousands took to the streets and screamed with all the lung-power they had. Law-abiding schoolgirls in cardigans morphed into huge crowds of disorderly, dishevelled adolescents stampeding police and overturning crash barriers. Some wet them-selves. They hurled jelly babies (rumoured to be the Beatles' favourite sweets), disobeyed uniformed authorities, and lost control. The parental generation looked on in horror. There was bewilderment, and hostility. Writing in the *New Statesman*, the patrician journalist Paul Johnson delivered a diatribe against the female fans:

> Those who flock round the Beatles, who scream themselves into hys-teria, whose vacant faces flicker over the TV screen, are the least fortunate of their generation, the dull, the idle, the failures.

Johnson was a cultural snob who couldn't countenance anyone pre-ferring pop to Wagner. An amateur psychologist writing for the *News of the World* was more forgiving, attempting to understand the young people's state of abandon in terms of womankind's 'natu-ral' proclivities:

> The girls are subconsciously preparing for motherhood. Their fren-zied screams are a rehearsal for that moment. Even the jelly babies are symbolic.

But such a contorted argument serves only to highlight how difficult the older generation found it, when confronted by Beatlemania, to uproot their fixed ideas of young women as docile, deferential, charming, chaste and good, with an unambitious future limited to the 'little job', followed inevitably by the cages of marriage and motherhood. When Beatlemania happened, it was as if the massed multitudes of projected wives-and-mothers of the world had screamed out, with one voice, 'We have been held captive too long, and WE WANT TO BE FREE!'

Though everyone agrees that 1963 was the year it took off, nobody can determine how the term Beatlemania originated, or where the phenomenon began. Was it at the London Palladium, the Glasgow Odeon, or the Odeon, Guildford on 21 June? That night the queue to get in stretched a quarter of a mile down the street. A girl got injured trying to climb a wall to catch a glimpse of her idols. Fifteen hundred frantic teenagers made it into the Surrey venue, but nobody could hear the music. After that, screaming at Beatles concerts became the norm.

In a small town in the Midlands, Mary Ingham's pubescent daydreams – like those of thousands of other sixteen-year-olds – were fuelled by grainy-coloured teen magazine pin-ups in *Fabulous* of George Harrison or Paul McCartney – 'the face contorted by the middle fold and pockmarked with staple holes'. Everybody had their favourite Beatle, and everybody could say in which order they loved them.

'Mine was George. My friend Sheila's was Paul . . .' Jessica Chappell tells me, sitting in her front room in leafy Dulwich, remembering her adolescence in Sheffield. Jessica and Sheila managed to get tickets to see them on a double bill with Helen Shapiro at City Hall. (At my primary school, everyone in the playground had their favourites. 'Mine' was George too, even at the age of eight. Today I am gnawed with retrospective envy of Jessica, less than ten years my senior, for having been part of those teenage audiences.) 'They had navy-blue Beatle suits on. And they were suddenly there! I couldn't believe it, you know, looking down on them.' They played 'From Me to You' and 'All My Loving'. Jessica has difficulty putting the emotions into words, but her voice becomes breathless at the memory. 'The songs were somehow so moving. It was wonderful. I didn't scream. I just loved them, I was "Beatle barmy". We fancied them like mad, and, I don't know, we just thought they were amazing.'

In July the Beatles played the Odeon in Weston-super-Mare for a week, and there was more Beatle-barminess. Bus conductors sang along to 'She Loves You, Yeah, Yeah, Yeah', hairdressers treasured sweepings from the floor after the lads had been in for a trim, autographs were signed, jelly babies sold out. Kristina Reed was in the audience at Weston. She tagged along with a boyfriend, and was staggered by the sight of 'lots of lunatic girls screaming'. Her own buttoned-up upbringing also meant that she didn't join the screamers. But this was her kind of music.

The screamers saw no reason to suppress their vocal urges. In November the band were in sedate Cheltenham. They played 'Twist and Shout'.

> I don't remember much about the concert, just the noise. Everyone screamed. It was rather like being on the Big Wheel. When that goes hurtling down, you have to scream to release yourself . . .

'It was what you did,' recalled the novelist Linda Grant. 'It was mandatory.' And drowning out the music was part of it. At venue after venue, the virtually all-girl fans were in the spotlight. As much as the performers on the platform, they were the act. Three years on, Bobby's Girl had put docile passivity behind her, and chaotically discovered her own power to take centre-stage and go completely berserk. Beatlemania gave the baby-boomers permission not to be good any more. This was freedom. It was release. It was bad behaviour. And it was girl-power. What's more, as one feminist writer points out, adoring a Beatle didn't have consequences – it was a fanfantasy.[*] You were never going to have to get John Lennon's dinner on the table for him. Nor was Paul McCartney threateningly hypersexual, like the gyrating Elvis Presley. The Beatles were playful, cute, cheeky and funny; dressed in their party-best buttoned-up fawn suits they were more cuddly than sexy: lads, not men.

But these young women were starting to sense their power. The

---

[*] Barbara Ehrenreich's essay, 'Screams Heard Around the World', in *Re-Making Love* (1986), is an intelligent analysis of the Beatlemania phenomenon.

gloves were really off now, and as a generation flexed its newly discovered muscles, the battle lines began to form.

Bye Bye Johnny

In 1963 John Lennon and Paul McCartney sat down and wrote a
short, stompy song with a heavy dance beat called 'I Wanna Be Your
Man'. The lyrics were nothing special. They were liberally infused
with repetitions of the infantilising motif 'baby', that conditioned
reflex, so common in 60s pop, and indiscriminately applied to
'woman', 'girlfriend' or 'lover'. But the sound was punchy and commercial, and the Beatles song-writing duo were riding such a wave in
late 1963 that they could afford to give it away. Which they did, to the
young Mick Jagger and his up-and-coming group the Rolling Stones,
who happened to overlap in a Soho studio space at the time. The
Stones performed it, and recorded it as a single.★ Later, the Beatles
themselves recorded 'I Wanna Be Your Man', and it's striking to see
how differently the two bands delivered the same material. Ringo
Starr on vocals is like a dog wagging his tail, beaming and relaxed,
shaking his tousled locks in time to his own thumping drumbeats.
George and Paul provide energetic accompaniment, skipping around
the stage with enthusiasm. By contrast, Mick Jagger is an impatient
stallion, snarling and grimacing, acidic and unsmiling, occasionally
pawing the platform with his Cuban heels. His posture is pent-up,
fidgety and rigid – and when he spits out his desire it's a threat not a
plea. The word *'man . . .'* is saturated with cocksure anger. Brian
Jones's slide guitar adds notes of fire and ice. The Stones endowed an
innocuous lyric with unambiguous edge, sexuality and danger.

The following year, Jagger began writing his own songs with
Keith Richards. Their language was different. Altars, wedding rings
and eternal devotion were supplanted by devils, spiders, wild horses
and howling hounds. 'Don't play with me, 'cause you're playing

---

★ At this time the Stones were only performing covers. Their version of 'I Wanna
Be Your Man' made the Top 20 in 1963, and paved the way for their first EP, with
its opening track 'Bye Bye Johnny', first written and recorded by Chuck Berry.

with fire . . .' The themes were punishment, betrayal, break-up, night-time, darkness and shadows, lust, satiety, sex with a capital S – and above all, male dominance: 'Tables turn – and now her turn to cry.'

Rock 'n' roll was a gladiatorial arena, a skewed pitch; in some cases an unequal fight to the death. We've already watched as Cynthia Lennon fell victim to her faithless husband. She felt helpless. But Chrissie Shrimpton, model Jean's younger sister, entered her relationship with Mick Jagger in 1963 armed with an untamed temperament and a reputation as something of a hellcat. 'My sister was truly naughty and rebellious at school,' recalled Jean, '[and] didn't give a damn for authority.' Dating Jagger would call on all of Chrissie's instincts of resistance and self-preservation.

She was seventeen when their relationship began; he was nineteen. One of Jagger's biographers reports that their first dramatic encounter was when Chrissie took on a dare during a Stones gig, by climbing into the decorative fish nets looped above the stage.* They gave way under her weight and she apparently landed unhurt on top of Brian Jones. But it was Jagger who was in her sights. The band was up-and-coming, while part of Chrissie's desirability for him came from her hip connections to the world of fashion and photography. As well as this, she was the epitome of the pretty Mod, Cathy McGowan-style, groomed, groovy and up-to-the-minute with her sleek 'big' hair, pasted-on make-up and false eyelashes. One of the many women who later competed for Jagger's favours would describe Chrissie as 'very put together . . . It took her simply ages to get ready. She could never spend the night anywhere because she might fall apart.' By the spring of 1963 she and Jagger were an item.

Mick and Chrissie's relationship would hold up, shakily, for three years. But from the outset it was characterised by shouting, high emotion and jealousy. There were explosive rows. Andrew Oldham, manager of the Stones, had much to gain by promoting the group as 'bad boys', so perhaps a pinch of salt needs to be added to his account of the flaming exchange between the couple just forty-eight hours after their first meeting, when Chrissie slapped Mick violently across the

* Laura Jackson, *Heart of Stone, The Unauthorized Life of Mick Jagger* (1997).

face in retaliation at his suggestion that they have sex. But it's credible, and Jagger's later track record makes it even easier to believe that he was not only hugely ambitious, charismatic and sexy, but also had a strong selfish and narcissistic streak: Chrissie and he would compete for the mirror. Female adoration fuelled his self-absorption, and though Chrissie was intermittently sharing his flat in Hampstead he appears to have had few qualms about two-timing her with his ex, Cleo Sylvestre.* By November 1963 the Stones had become hot property, with a single in the charts and a national tour slated. They were regulars at Studio 51, a sweaty cellar off Charing Cross Road. One sixteen-year-old who went on her first date here recalled: 'The venue was stifling with condensation and we drew CND signs in it on the low ceiling. The Stones looked like cavemen . . .'

As with Lennon, it was becoming imperative that any girlfriends should be kept in the shadows. Chrissie wasn't allowed to go to the Stones' recording sessions. As Jagger's visibility increased, hers had to be reduced, and when fans recognised him in the street he would hurriedly drop her hand, cross the road and pretend not to be with her. The rows escalated.

Chrissie Shrimpton appears to have been more than equal to her boyfriend's game. Nothing provoked him like jealousy. She needled him by going on dates with other men, and got him crawling back to her that way. Their relationship was a crockery-smashing, crying, screaming power struggle, riddled with contempt, manipulation and double standards. 'Mick doesn't really respect women,' Chrissie was heard to say. 'Mick doesn't like women. He never has.' But, as all too often in the giddy, unequal world of rock'n'roll, it would be the man who had the last laugh – for Chrissie's legacy would not be her soigné beauty, her feisty rebelliousness, her daring or her cool milieu. It would be in Jagger's lyrics, and the sound of the Stones: great to dance to, with misogyny calling the tune.

*

The news burst upon a scene of unwary female domesticity. Floella Benjamin and her sister Sandra were washing up. Marmie was

---

* Cleo Sylvestre (born 1945) was and is a talented singer and actress in her own right. In 1964 she recorded 'To Know Him Is to Love Him' with the Rolling Stones.

seated at her sewing machine, and the television was on.* Suddenly a wail of horror was heard from the front room, as Marmie cried out, 'They've killed a great man, they've killed a great man!' To Floella's parents, John F. Kennedy had been a champion of the civil rights struggle. For seventeen-year-old Beatle fan and party girl Kristina Reed the news came through on the Home Service while she was ironing her best dress for a Chelsea soirée:

> But the party ended early 'cos everyone was devastated. We'd had such a safe life. The post-war world was founded on things going on being the same. And one had always thought – things like that don't happen.
>
> And actually, it felt like the beginning of slightly losing the solidity of the ground beneath your feet . . .

Ann Leslie's boyfriend had taken her that night to see Nureyev and Fonteyn dance in *Marguerite and Armand*, in an attempt to cure her obstinate resistance to the classical canon. As the curtain fell, the audience was flooded with emotion; but instead of a curtain call there was a formal announcement. Horror replaced catharsis, and Ann dashed for her newsroom.

That day had been unseasonably warm and sunny, and President John F. Kennedy's visit to Dallas had showcased his First Lady, at her most visibly elegant and gracious, waving and smiling beside her husband. It was said that JFK himself had joked that morning that she got more attention than he did and, as events unrolled, interest in the beautiful, tragically bereaved wife was not set to wane. Tapes recorded when she was still newly widowed reveal an intelligent and cultured woman, deliberately, if unconvincingly, projecting the acceptable version of a 1963 political helpmeet.† 'I get all my

---

* A nice detail: in the days before colour television it was possible to buy a sheet of multi-coloured transparent plastic – banded blue for sky, reddish in the middle, and green for grass – which you stuck over the black-and-white screen to pretend it was colour. The Benjamins had one of these; it was satisfactory over landscape photography, but made the studio announcers look quite odd.

† Recorded in 1964, released in 2011, and published as *Jacqueline Kennedy: Historic Conversations on Life with John F. Kennedy*, by Caroline Kennedy and Michael Beschloss.

opinions from my husband,' she told the interviewer. 'How could I have political opinions? His were going to be the best . . . I think women should never be in politics. We're just not suited for it.' This was barely a year after *The Feminine Mystique*.

On 22 November 1963 Jacqueline Kennedy played her part to perfection. Like Valerie Profumo, she was indeed the personification of that particular mystique which accompanies the traditional, supportive political wife-and-mother, ever the loyal companion and social asset. Mrs Kennedy's look was gleaming, groomed, big-haired, tailored and – inevitably – white-gloved. That day in the Texan sunshine she was a dazzling fashion plate at the President's side, dressed in a candy-coloured Chanel-style wool bouclé suit with dark blue trim and trademark pillbox hat, an armful of intensely crimson roses making her the focus of all eyes as the presidential motorcade rolled through the crowd-lined streets. After the bullets hit, she was spattered with his blood and fragments of bone and brain. For the rest of her life she herself would be stained and defined by his tragedy.

The Kennedy killing propelled Jacqueline Kennedy, in her now gruesomely daubed clothes, into the spotlight. At the time of the assassination, the contemporary commentary deferred, awestruck, to the First Lady's dignity. This widow would not throw herself on her husband's funeral pyre, but she would orchestrate its realisation, and devote many years to fuelling the flame of his legacy. Coming from a world where the magnitude of women's fulfilment was measured by wifehood, history trapped Jacqueline Kennedy – the sugar-pink, deferential and adoring consort – in a time-warp of loss, grief, satin bows, pearl earrings and high-profile marriages. What did it take for her to tell a friend, as she apparently did many years later, that 'she had come to realise she could not expect to live primarily through a husband'?

1964

Whitehouse-land

For a fifty-three-year-old Art teacher from the Midlands, the BBC's coverage of ministerial high jinks was the last straw:

> Homosexuality, prostitution and sexual intercourse became the routine accompaniment of the evening meal . . . as night after night, the Profumo Affair unfolded before our eyes . . .
>
> A totally different way of life became accessible to all of us, including children, via the television screen.

Mary Whitehouse felt embattled. As an observant Christian, much influenced by the Moral Re-Armament movement, the unshakeable principles that she had taken for granted all her life felt threatened, not just by badly behaved teenagers, but by the professional and religious Establishment. First it had been Professor Carstairs defending pre-marital sex in his BBC Radio Reith Lectures, followed soon after by Dr Chesser's *Is Chastity Outmoded?* Then the clergy themselves had begun to unpick the Church's doctrines. In 1963 John Robinson, the Anglican Bishop of Woolwich (a prominent defence witness at the *Lady Chatterley* trial) published a controversial bestseller, *Honest to God*, in which he pointed the way to a 'new morality', and offered up a transcendent vision of personal freedom and sexual love. That was followed by *No New Morality: Christian Personal Values and Sexual Morality*, a book written by another 'South Bank theologian', Canon Douglas Rhymes, who aired his view that contemporary codes of behaviour were outdated.

But Mrs Whitehouse was even more offended by what she saw on the television. By 1963, the small screen was in 82 per cent of homes, and there was no avoiding its cultural impact. It was utterly dismaying to her to be invaded by the suggestively sexual tone and content of *That Was the Week That Was*, hugely popular as it was. She also took particular exception to the BBC's flagship religious discussion programme, *Meeting Point*, which had promoted the acceptability of pre-marital sex. One of her teenage pupils watched this programme, and came to her saying, 'Well, I know now that I must not have intercourse – until I am engaged.' Mrs Whitehouse was appalled; she felt the girl had been 'won over to a sub-Christian concept of living'.

The post-war world order had been based on the idea of the wife surrounded by four walls. The female ruled her fortress. It was clean, domestic, impregnable and familial. Now, the baleful piece of technology in every living room threatened to reshape and denature family life. Meals were eaten on the knees, from trays, with all eyes refocussed on the pundits, actors and advertisers drowning out family discourse from the corner. Television threatened to poison and corrupt woman's sanctified domain, releasing – as if from Pandora's box – a swarm of malignant and noxious pests into the very heart of the home, uninvited. Mrs Whitehouse, and thousands like her, were seeking for ways to pull up the drawbridge.

Early in 1964 she sought out her friend Norah Buckland, a vicar's wife and leading light of the Mothers' Union, to join her in a fight-back. Mrs Buckland was only too willing to come on board. Women in her parish had already been talking to her about their concerns. One of them said that she had persuaded her teenage daughter not to give way to her boyfriend's pressures to have pre-marital sex, only for the girl to change her mind after seeing a programme broadcasting the opposite view. 'You see, the BBC say it is all right,' the girl told her parents. Another mother was very distressed because a television programme had shown a man unbuttoning his trousers before getting into bed with a woman who was not his wife. 'There was not the slightest suggestion that it was wrong, and it came straight into our family circle.' Soon after, Mrs Buckland rented a television to see for herself, and was equally disgusted.

Both women firmly believed that there was a causal link between what young people saw on television and what they did; their virtue was consequently at risk of corruption. 'Cannot something be done about the demoralising effects on our children?' Equally, Mrs Whitehouse believed that a majority of British people, particularly women, agreed with her that society was on a slippery slope to perdition. So when, on 27 January 1964, the pair launched their manifesto for the Clean-Up TV campaign, it was to 'The Women of Britain' that it principally spoke:

- We women of Britain believe in a Christian way of life.
- We want it for our children and our country.
- We object to the propaganda of disbelief, doubt and dirt that the BBC projects into millions of homes through the television screen.
- We call upon the BBC for a radical change of policy and demand programmes which build character instead of destroying it, and encourage and sustain faith in God and bring Him back to the heart of the family and national life.

Over the next three months, leaflets were distributed and journalists invited to report on the growing campaign. Through the channel of the *Birmingham Evening Mail* Mrs Whitehouse urged those who supported her to join a rally in Birmingham Town Hall planned for 5 May. She thought a couple of hundred might show up, but the response exceeded her wildest expectations.

It was so fantastic . . . We were absolutely petrified, and then to see that great town hall absolutely packed. Thirty-seven coach loads . . .

Mrs Whitehouse kept her nerve and, conspicuously authoritative in a dark suit and fancy pillbox hat, put her case from the platform:

We recognise that the period between 6 and 9.15 is a period for family viewing. Well, I think we're being palmed off! Because last Thursday evening, we sat as a family, and we saw a programme that started at 6.35, and it was the dirtiest programme that I have seen for a very long time . . .*

The roots of our democratic way of life are set deep in our Christian faith . . . Do we want a materialistic philosophy to control our country and have power over the minds of our children?

---

* The programme was the satirical Scottish comedy series *Between the Lines*, starring Tom Conti and Fulton Mackay. The BBC billed it as 'an enquiry in depth . . . And there is no limit to the depth to which we may sink . . .'. One critic described *Between the Lines* as 'TW3 in kilts'.

It was fighting talk, and the press, local and national, caught on quickly. *The Times* reported, 'Perhaps never in the history of Birmingham Town Hall has such a successful meeting been sponsored by such a flimsy organisation,' describing the attendees as mostly middle-aged women from as far afield as Wales and Devon. By August the Clean-Up TV campaign had collected 235,000 signatures endorsing its manifesto, and 7,000 letters of support. For though Mrs Whitehouse and her campaign often came across as sanctimonious and ridiculous, her cause nevertheless tapped into something deeper than just puritanical moralising. There was a sense among Mrs Whitehouse's many correspondents that female self-respect was at stake. 'The women of Britain need to give their all to ensure an end to this portrayal of them as a sex symbol,' wrote one signatory to her manifesto. 'My experience is that the men seem very reluctant to sign. The women do so willingly. I think that this is another "battle of the sexes".' As Middle England stood on the brink of a national sea-change, the fortress of home, femininity and family looked as if it was in danger of being swept away. And a lot of women like Mary Whitehouse and Norah Buckland felt fearful, vulnerable and defensive. If women were knocked off their pedestals, cheapened and degraded, where would it all lead? Would male idolatry of the fair sex turn to violation and misuse?

Mary Whitehouse looked like everybody's respectable aunt. Her image, with heavy-rimmed glasses and helmet of elaborately permed grey hair, would soon come to embody the guardianship of a particular set of values. To many those values were dated and disapproving; but few could deny her sincerity, her unclouded certainty and her single-minded determination in the face of derision and abuse. There was, too, more than a touch of sexism in the vilification levelled at her. Soon after her campaign launched, Mrs Whitehouse had to defend herself in court against a TV producer who commented in a press interview that she was a member of the lunatic fringe who had given up her job to monitor late-night TV programmes. What could that job possibly have been? – he asked. 'I suppose she must have been on the streets.' And her principal adversary, the director general of the BBC Sir Hugh Greene, purchased a cruelly scurrilous caricature of her, naked with six breasts, hung it on his office wall, and amused himself by throwing darts at it.

★

Mrs Whitehouse made many enemies. But throughout a campaign which would last the best part of thirty years she continued to claim that she had the grass roots support of a silent majority in Britain:

> People say this isn't a Christian country, but if you move among the rank and file, as I do, you know it is.

The 1960s are often portrayed as an extravaganza of colour and permissiveness. For a significant minority this would become their reality. But Whitehouse-land was real too. Though church attendance in Britain was steadily declining – the membership of major Christian denominations had halved since the start of the century and, overall, only one in ten people were regular Sunday worshippers – nevertheless a surprising number of young people were churchgoers.

> I go to church nearly every Sunday . . .

an eighteen-year-old deb told one of the *Generation X* interviewers:

> and I try to listen to the sermon and concentrate but it's awfully hard sometimes, and I don't think about it much between Sundays. I definitely believe in God, though, and I pray like billy-o when I want something . . .

One survey carried out among fifteen- to twenty-year-olds in Preston showed 45 per cent attending a religious service once a week. Religious education and daily assembly were compulsory. At my own primary school we gathered each morning, hymn books in hand, in the echoing hall. Mrs Mason, our headmistress (who could have been Mrs Whitehouse's double), intoned the Lord's Prayer and the Blessing, and read a passage from the King James Bible, so that I grew up well-versed in Testaments Old and New. Day in, day out, we sang such time-honoured favourite hymns as Bunyan's 'He Who Would Valiant Be', or a lugubrious setting of 'The Lord's My Shepherd', with the result that, despite my irreligious upbringing I – like many of my generation – still know all the words by heart, their

tunes as indelibly associated with my sixties childhood as those of
Helen Shapiro or the Beatles.

Whitehouse-land coalesced around observance of the Sabbath. On
Sundays in Middle England there was nothing to do. It was illegal for
shops, theatres or cinemas to trade. Pubs could open for only five
hours, and not at all in Scotland, while in Northern Ireland some
councils even chained up the children's swings in parks. Despite there
being no legal requirement for them to do so, restaurants often
remained closed. In villages and towns across the land the shutters
were down, and only the churches kept their doors unlocked.

Coffee bars, *Ready Steady Go!*, *TW3* and the Profumo Affair
co-existed with a nation that seemed to become ever more static and
backward-looking. When Geoffrey Moorhouse anatomised the
nation as he saw it in 1964 (in *Britain in the Sixties: The Other England*)
he singled out Chipping Campden – '[it] still feels and looks like a
fifteenth-century wool town . . .' – and cited the poet Housman's
eulogy to Shropshire for being as true as when it was first written
nearly seventy years earlier:

> *Clunton and Clunbury*
> *Clungunford and Clun*
> *Are the quietest places*
> *Under the sun.*

England was still 'wallowing in the past'. This was the world of
Sunday lunch, prayer books and retired gentlewomen: an ineradicable vision of Britain that, even thirty years later, would move Prime
Minister John Major to eulogise 'the country of long shadows on
county grounds, warm beer, invincible green suburbs, dog lovers and
pools fillers and, as George Orwell said, "Old maids bicycling to holy
communion through the morning mist" '.* Ann Gurney's world, for
example:

I have lived within a tradition of the past . . .

---

* John Major misquoted Orwell. The passage (in *The Lion and the Unicorn: Socialism and the English Genius* (1941)) reads: '. . . old maids hiking to Holy Communion
through the mists of the autumn morning . . . solid breakfasts and gloomy Sundays, smoky towns and winding roads, green fields and red pillar-boxes . . .'

As a deaconess, Ann was the nearest the Church of England could offer religious women short of priestly ordination, which for the next thirty years would remain barred to them. A deaconess was a sort of auxiliary vicar; her responsibilities were greater than those of a lay parish worker, but though it meant making a lifetime commitment, she had none of the power of a priest in holy orders. Ann Gurney had a vocation, and she gave herself up willingly to a life serving her Church by teaching other deaconesses. In 1964 she was in her mid-thirties, working as principal of a training college in south London. But while red buses rolled past the front windows on their way to the swinging West End, inside all was stained glass, prayer and austerity. Ann's yearly remuneration was £210 – worth about £4,000 today. No television disturbed the pious atmosphere of her adoptive home; she hand-washed all her clothes, and barely travelled. The modern world and the increasingly vociferous challenge to the values of the older generation were muffled, and Ann was only scantily aware of them, while the religion that guided her life made no demands on her to meet that dissident sector halfway. 'I think there were two separate worlds. There was no meeting point. One never felt threatened. One just felt they were totally on the wrong course. To tell the truth, I just couldn't understand what they were getting at.'

This Britain, Ann Gurney's Britain, Whitehouse-land, was bourgeois, unfashionable and conformist, but it exercised moralistic power over the wayward fringe, particularly in institutions. In 1964 Angela Patrick, pregnant aged twenty, spent four months at Loreto Convent in Theydon Bois, Essex, where the nuns told her, 'You will be expected to work just as hard as we do; to rise early and use the day productively just as we do; to attend Mass and to ask the Lord's forgiveness.' ('I noticed she didn't tag "just as we do" on the end of that last one,' commented Angela.) The führer class could be depressingly petty. As the Mod, 'swinging' look infiltrated cities and shires, school authorities kept a beady eye on third-year fashion rebels, like those who attended Holton Park Grammar in Oxfordshire. There were penalties for girls who didn't tie their hair back, or backcombed it. And here, at the end of the school day, the headmistress stood by the gate checking the length of skirts lest the young ladies be seen in the town indecently dressed, while bus prefects were charged with policing the school's reputation on public transport: no pupil should be seen removing her regulation velour hat.* 'We felt honour-bound to keep up appearances,' remembered one.

Female students were still expected to adhere to rigid regulations, with many women's colleges resembling nunneries. Until 1975 the age of majority was twenty-one, so universities were *in loco parentis*. When the former MP Ann Widdecombe was a fresher at Birmingham University, her hall of residence had a female wing and a male wing. There were strict rules as to when the inhabitants of one wing might visit the inhabitants of the other, and there was no mixed dining. All-girls suited Ann just fine, and she sought out companions who shared her views and joined the same clubs. She hosted a weekly Bible study and prayer group in her room, and belonged to the Conservative Association and the Christian Union.

> I think that's quite normal? Birds of a feather flock together. We forget how conservative society was. People like me who were children in the 1950s just assumed the normal established order of everything. Outwardly, anyway, people all signed up to the same set of rules. There was an enormous social consensus at the time about what was right and what was wrong, and what we fought the war for.

Ann Widdecombe was indeed far from alone, and cases like hers abound. But her subsequent career tells a more complex story, for – though the 'normal established order' regarded women as stay-at-homes – she was one of a breed of women who directed enormous energy into standing on platforms, and combating permissiveness. 'This was the age of socialism, of student unrest and of sit-ins and it was against this background that my political views and ambitions were crystallising.'

Julia Cumberlege, now Baroness Cumberlege, is another example of a young woman who combined conservatism with drive. The daughter of a village doctor in the rural south-east of England, Julia shared Ann Widdecombe's deeply rooted values. Her upbringing had

---

* The girls' grammar school I attended in Sussex from 1967 also appointed bus prefects to enforce this miserable rule.

instilled into her a strong, observant Catholicism, as well as an unquestioning acceptance of a woman's role – 'There was no expectation in those days that you would do other than be a housewife.' But unlike Ann Widdecombe, and despite an offer from a nursing college, Julia stepped off the career ladder at the first opportunity. At seventeen she was married; by the age of twenty she had two small children. Nevertheless, passion and enterprise prevailed, and soon Julia Cumberlege found a new channel for her energies, first on the parish council, and soon after on the rural district council, which she was chairing by the age of twenty-two. Most of its members were men, naval and military types, lawyers and professionals, all at least forty years older than her.

But I never ever had any feeling that women weren't as good as men. Being elected made all the difference.

The fact was, being with all these older people all the time, I became *part* of the Establishment . . . I didn't have time to be caught up in youth movements, and fashion rather passed me by, though I do remember suddenly these things called the Beatles turned up . . .

I was very, very busy, and loving it . . .

*

Earlier in this book, we met Anthea, a student studying English Literature and Language at Reading University, who later married a clergyman. Anthea Martinsmith's mother had been a high-flying girl in the 1930s, who had been removed from school because her parents could only afford to educate the boy of the family. Anthea would be the gainer. An only child, she was encouraged to star at her (single-sex) school, and never doubted that girls were as able as boys. She sailed into university without difficulty, and enrolled there in the Michaelmas term of 1963. At Reading, social life revolved around the Saturday night 'hops', held in the Great Hall. 'One put on a pretty frock, and one stood round the wall hoping that a nice bloke would come and ask you to dance. And we would dance the foxtrot, the Gay Gordons, the waltz, the quickstep – and I had a lovely time . . .'

But when Anthea met the nice bloke who would become the love of her life, it wasn't at a hop. At the end of her first year, she spent a week on the coast of north Devon.

I went on holiday to Lee Abbey with my recently widowed mother. It was a beautiful Christian place.

And when we got there, there was this lovely curate, Anthony Millican. He had come with his youth group. Well, we had a brief conversation, and later I saw him walking below, outside. And I thought, 'Blow it – there's this lovely guy.' So – well, I pursued him . . . And to cut a long story short, within the week, we both fell deeply in love.

The sheer happiness that began then . . . On September 29th, St Michael and all Angels Day, Anthony asked me to come to the coast with him on his day off, so I did. And we were walking along at Rottingdean, on the front by the sea, at a good, brisk pace, in the sunshine, with a lovely breeze blowing, and we were holding hands. And he suddenly gripped my hand extra tightly, and he turned, and he looked at me, and he said, 'My wife!'

And I whispered back, 'My husband!'

So a term later I went back to Reading University, wearing an engagement ring. A beautiful topaz engagement ring with rose diamonds around it.

Anthea had grown up a dedicated Christian, and now she had even less interest in finding someone to pair up with at the college dances. But she had no intention of abandoning her studies, so marriage – and all that went with it – would have to wait until she graduated.

I had always had a very strong personal resolve, that I was going to be a virgin when I married. But that didn't mean that Anthony and I didn't have a good cuddle when we were engaged, because we did . . . We adored each other. But we kept ourselves until we were married. That is a Christian tenet. It did make me look forward to my wedding day though. And poor Anthony – I do remember he almost cried one evening with sheer frustration.

Darling man! The father of my children . . . But we didn't and I think that was the right thing to do. It was lovely. I've been so blessed.

Anthea Martinsmith's bred-in-the-bone Anglican beliefs have been a lifelong support. 'We're all wasting our time if Christ be not risen.' She often attended church three times a day on Sundays; as a teenager she went to Bible study groups and bonded with other like-minded Christians whose faith illuminated her own. Reading from scripture has been a daily habit – 'as a basis for my prayer'. Picture Anthea in 1964, beaming for the camera, her side-parted wavy hair framing open, clean features that radiate conviction and hope. She is wearing a simple, gathered, printed cotton frock; modestly girlish, knee-length and sleeved, with a wide Peter Pan collar and a sash tied in a bow at the waist. Anthea's was a timeless, gently feminine look, a million miles from the Mod phenomenon which in 1964 was bringing cutaway shift dresses, geometrics and sepulchrally made-up faces to high streets and dance halls across the country. But her artless demeanour masks a steely determination and analytical intelligence. At nineteen, Anthea Martinsmith was her own woman, determined to be herself and pursue her chosen course, and even more intent on staying true to her beliefs in a fast-changing society.

> I had a very strong inner resolve, which had grown in my teens. That resolve had been informed by my father's early death. I felt that the bottom of my world had fallen out, and therefore I was going to swim not sink. I was quite determined that I was going to be a virgin when I married, but I also had a personal resolve that I was going to do my utmost academically. And I was going to fight this one, and I was going to win through, both personally and academically. I was going to keep *me* intact.

Anthea maintained her inner self-belief. But arriving when she did at university, she encountered attitudes and mores that tested it. As at many other universities and colleges, large numbers of the student population at Reading University were starting to challenge, to make demands, to find their voice, to experiment sexually. The overt love-play between students took Anthea aback. 'I'd never seen that done before.' She began to recognise that not everybody shared her sense of physical integrity. Returning after the 1964 Christmas vacation, Anthea found the hops had completely changed their character:

> It was a different world. The social committee had changed, and there was no more waltz and quickstep and a pretty frock. Instead it was the Beatles, 'Twist and Shout', flashing lights, 'I wanna hold your

haa – aa – and . . .', you know? And here I was, doing the twist, subdued lights. And being innocent I thought, this is fantastic!

But I did observe then how some people comported themselves,
and I thought, well, I'm not going to do that. They were getting up
pretty close to their partners, snogging – you know? I thought, I
don't want to snog with anybody. There was sleeping around too . . .

And I didn't want to because I was *me*.

Then there was an incorrigible wing of the English faculty, where
she encountered a strain of anti-Establishment sophistry that clashed
with her deeply felt brand of Christianity; for example, Anthea was
resistant to the way that specious, phallic interpretations of towers
and turrets seemed, all too often, to find their way into poetry tutorials. And on one occasion, having divulged her intention to marry an
Anglican curate, she was infuriated to be told dismissively, 'Oh, the
Church of England's _finished_ . . .!' and that she would be wasting her
life. Anthea had to restrain herself, and leave the room. But this was
an attitude she was by now growing accustomed to.

Much around her in the university world spoke to Anthea of hostility to tradition, of cynicism and the sway of fashionable ideas, of blind
dissent and reflex protest, of the sexualisation of behaviour and cultural
references – and of certain men's rapacious tendencies. But she felt protected by her faith, depending on its power to preserve all women:

> There's an element of self-preservation in my beliefs, as well as moral
> conviction. Men were getting off scot-free and leaving the damage
> behind. I wasn't going to wreck my life!

Anthea Martinsmith did not feel imprisoned. Her self-respect drew
not only on religious certainty but also on the unshakeable sense that,
as a woman, she was every bit as good as a man.

> I'm not a femin*ist* – *vive la différence!*
>
> But people tell me I have a fairly strong personality. And I inher-
> ited from my father his belief in equality, whether of class or gender:
> in the integrity and validity of the human individual. I have never
> really minded whether one was male or female.

These are not the words of a passive and docile woman. The idiom is modern, progressive and emancipated. But there is no contradiction in them being the words of a committed Christian, whose faith – like that of Mary Whitehouse – energised her life. Anthea too had certainty, and courage to swim against the stream. When the student magazine, *Shell*, ran favourable coverage of Eustace Chesser's books advocating free love and criticising the Church, nineteen-year-old Anthea jumped straight in with a rebuttal: 'Dr Chesser's attitude is built upon the sand,' she wrote. And she was quick, too, to pick holes in the student end-of-term revue for its lavatorial humour and depressing lack of zest. From where she stood, the prevailing current of sexual freedom, liberal philosophies, fashion, music and rebellion against the older generation was running too fast to stop:

> Of course it was nonsense. How can we completely ignore our well-springs, and our history, and break up our family lives, and snub our parents? I mean, I could see it all happening . . .

Her public stance quickly had her labelled as a square. Anthea Martinsmith had arrived at a point where she felt discounted and misrepresented for her own views. So when Mrs Whitehouse's Clean-Up TV crusade came to Reading, she made sure to go along. Afterwards, they spoke, and it was a meeting of minds:

> A more lovely, warm-hearted, articulate, intelligent, perspicacious, perceptive woman I have seldom met.

*

This glimpse into the world view of the 'moral majority' gives a snapshot of a less familiar, less mythic 1960s than the phantasmagorical one rooted in our collective imagination. It is socially conservative, chaste, conventional, patriotic, law-abiding and God-fearing. But it also places the women of that era centre-stage. Fearless, ambitious women like Mary Whitehouse, Norah Buckland, Julia Cumberlege, Ann Widdecombe and Anthea Martinsmith found a voice in the 1960s. They were no longer inhibited by a culture that suppressed their sex. The unstoppable Ann Widdecombe, for example, was simply amused by her father's reaction to the role reversal she represented: '[He] shook his head in bewilderment and observed to my mother that "Ann should have been the boy"!' Ann's ethic, and that of women like her, was one of work. And they chose to speak out – not as feminists, anti-Establishment activists, or student radicals – but on behalf of their country's Christian tradition.

In 1964 there were already many signs that the 1960s were going to be a scary and bumpy ride for women. The attacks on moral certainty had begun. The satirists, iconoclasts, insurgents and despots were emerging into the open. In this climate, it is hardly surprising to see women pulling up the drawbridges of their fortresses, waving the flags of family and home, as Christianity became yet another front on the sex war.

Rockers

I was sent to a mother-and-baby home in Aylesbury. It was all very hush-hush. It was run by religious women, and they were very cruel with me. They said, 'You've sinned against Jesus,' and I said, 'I did what?' And I said, 'I have done no such thing.'

Kimberley Saunders was fourteen. Attempts to disguise her advancing pregnancy had become ineffectual. Her headmistress in Harlow was told that she had gone to get a job in London, and she spent the next six months off her school's radar.

Since the 1920s, mother-and-baby homes had replaced the workhouse as a refuge for 'fallen women'. Though the institutions had a benevolent and religious purpose, and were generally run by well-meaning and righteous-minded women, the stigma often remained. There was a strong culture of rules. Kimberley had broken them, and was punished. But she was an unmitigated rebel.

They tried to make me write an essay about being a sinner, and I wouldn't, so they made my life hell – absolute hell. They threatened me and gave me extra duties to do. They told me I was sinful. Oh, it makes me shudder to think of it – and I could NOT wait to get away.

Six weeks after the birth of her daughter, the baby was removed for adoption, and Kimberley, now fifteen, went back to school 'as though nothing had happened'.

'In those days you got a lot of stick for being on your own without a man, you know what I mean – one-parent families . . . ?' Kimberley Saunders knows what she's talking about. Now in her late sixties, Kimberley has pitched up in a flat a minute from the Hastings sea-front, where she spoke to me about her memories, wearing a bright floor-length caftan and smoking. Seagulls scream in the background. Her story provides a colourful counterpoint to the events that took place on that nearby shingled beach when she was a teenager, more than fifty years ago.

In the spring of 1964, hostilities erupted in a number of seaside towns across the country. There were renewed lamentations about the decline in public morality, and calls for the birch, compulsory hard labour and a reinstatement of national service. Beaches – at Clacton-on-Sea, Margate, Hastings, Brighton, Bournemouth – were the arena for rampageous collisions between gangs of Mods on two-stroke scooters and their arch-enemies the Rockers, who had arrived on custom twin-cylinder motorbikes, and immediately the news-papers spilled over with denunciations of 'vermin', 'thugs' and 'grubby hordes'. But reports of the violence were probably exaggerated. What had started as a style statement had become another excuse to demon-ise the scary, freewheeling power of the young, and to reproach their mothers for bringing them up badly. Under the headline 'Jolt for Complacent Parents', *The Times* wagged its magisterial finger at 'mothers [who] were out to work' for spending too little time with their delinquent sons, and for being too lenient:

> A mother trying to rear her family single handed said: 'Sometimes my boy doesn't get in till 3 a.m., but I've never asked him where he has been. He wouldn't like that.'

Kimberley was another child who effectively made up her own rules. She had started life in Hayes Town, north-west London. Like those cradles of Mod culture where Twiggy and Elizabeth Wood-craft grew up – nearby Neasden and Chelmsford in Essex – it was another 'invincible green suburb' disturbed only by the revving of Lambrettas. Outer-city council estates were fertile soil for the edgy, asexual attitudinising of Mod. But Kimberley had a hard-up, messed-up, working-class upbringing. Her father was afflicted with a mental disorder. Her mother, suffering from post-natal depression and emotional repression, put Kimberley, her first baby, in a children's home when she was ten months old. Effectively single in the post-war austerity years, Mrs Saunders struggled to bring up three small children in overcrowded conditions, her scant income topped up through the National Assistance scheme.* When Kimberley was six, the family were rehoused in Bracknell New Town, a utopian developers' dream superimposed on an area of fields thirty miles to the west of London. Now the family had space, big rooms, big windows, a garden and modern shopping facilities. But for a precocious teenager, there was nothing to do.

> I went to a youth club – but I wasn't going to sit there playing Ludo! I was out looking for blokes!

School had little to offer. As we have seen, Kimberley hated authority. She dug her heels in, and refused to attend any classes apart from Art. 'I just didn't like being told what to do.' From early on, she identified as a Rocker. The bikers in black had what she wanted. Rebellious, stroppy, and starved of affection, Kimberley built a world around her rock music idols – P. J. Proby, Billy Fury,† Jerry Lee Lewis, Chubby Checker – and any available good-looking leather-jacketed males she could attract, in possession of a motorcycle. At fourteen, wearing a provocatively short and shiny 'Maid Marian' dress with criss-cross lacing up her bust, diamond-design stockings and kitten heels, this wasn't difficult. But like most of her generation, Kimberley had the vaguest notions about sex –

> We had the usual biology lesson, with rabbits and all that. It was, like, 'this goes there, and that goes there, and out pops a baby!' So I

---

* National Assistance was introduced by the Labour government of Prime Minister Clement Attlee in 1948 to replace the Poor Law, and provide a safety net for the homeless, the physically disabled and unmarried mothers, among others. It is now known as Income Support.

† Proby and Fury are good examples of the tendency among male rock stars and bands in the late 1950s and right through the 60s to choose aggressive, arousing stage names. Others are Marty Wilde, Tommy Steele, Cream and the Animals.

> thought, well, I think I know now what happens. So I tried it out one
> day, with some gorgeous fellow that lived in Enfield . . .

That one lasted a few weeks, and it was better than Ludo.

But sex was only part of the thrill that Kimberley was now discovering. Rocker culture – music, men, and bikes – hit all her buttons. And most weekends the tribe would gather in their statement uniforms: black, Brylcreemed and studded, bikes fuelled and ready to hit the arterial roads to the coast. Kimberley rode pillion, astride, wearing her kitten heels but no crash helmet, gripping on for dear life with her thighs as, exhausts roaring, twenty gleaming black and chrome Tritons ripped up the tarmac at 100 miles an hour. This was 'doing a ton'. On a bike you were queen of the road. 'I love speed – I thought it was fantastic . . . The adrenalin buzz, the excitement of it – it was like a fantasy come true . . . It was a real ego thing as well I suppose. You felt that you'd made it . . .' Bikes were about masculinity and machismo, down and dirty. They roared, they thrusted; they were hard, dynamic, dangerous and also – as the lyrics of a whole genre of pop songs prove – intensely romantic.

This was the peak of the so-called 'teenage tragedy' song in which, to the accompaniment of revving throttles and grinding gearboxes, singers poured out tear-jerking melodramas of fatal skids and twisted metal. The Shangri-Las' 1964 doo-wop classic 'Leader of the Pack' is probably the most famous, with its Romeo and Juliet themes of love at first sight, parental disapproval and violent death – though the BBC refused it airplay probably because it was thought to encourage Mod-versus-Rocker violence. Another home-grown, chart-topping version of the theme was written by a well-bred blonde, Lynn Annette Ripley, aka Twinkle, when she herself was just fourteen, and also released in 1964. At the age of nine I developed a morbid adoration for this singer with her straight hair, blackened eyes, peaked PVC 'Lennon' cap and her bewitchingly tragic song, 'Terry'. The heart-rending tale of the girlfriend who quarrels with her beloved before he rides off into the night, 'accelerating his motorbi-ike . . .', had me close to tears and choked with emotion by the time the short ballad reached its beseeching climax: 'Please wait at the gate of heaven for me, Te – e – erry!'

In other words, bike culture, whether Rocker or Mod, had it all. Freedom and fantasy were enhanced inside these revved-up, supra-masculine fraternities; but femininity too, for how could a blonde in kitten heels look anything but vulnerable and sweet sitting pillion behind that hot-headed, hairy, animal he-man with his fenders and his handlebars? In her dreams, one day, through a woman's love, she would tame him – ('They told me he was bad – but I knew he was sad / That's why I fell for – the Leader of the Pack – *Vroooom, Vroooom*'). But at fourteen Kimberley Saunders hadn't joined their club because she wanted a wedding ring:

> Obviously, there was another side of it: and it'd all get pretty steamy and sexual by the time you got down to Hastings! Ah, there's a whole lot you can get down to on beaches, you know? – not just frightening the Mods . . .

To Rockers, Mods were the objects of scorn. Kimberley and the gang ridiculed them for their taste in music, their affected clothes and per-ceived effeminacy, but above all for their impotent scooters, the Toytown-style Vespas and Lambrettas that seemed like playthings beside their own monster motorcycles – ' "Get off that spin dryer and milk it!" we used to say. We just saw their scooters as no better than a spin dryer . . .' – and as domesticated, meek and feebly ruminative as a cow.

> They were weak, they couldn't stand up and fight or nothing – and they were tested out on the beach down there!

When fists started to fly, Kimberley stayed at a safe distance. The girls watched from the parade, and had a drink afterwards with the victors, listening to the juke box.

She is unapologetic about her casual, thrill-seeking attitude to life, while admitting that she paid a price. She'd got involved with a sexy-eyed, square-jawed guy with a mop of dark hair – 'he looked like P. J. Proby!' What was the attraction?

> Well, looking back, that's how music got to you, it was in your soul, it was in the air – and it was part of your everyday life . . . And I thought oh, he's groovy! He had great big Chelsea boots on – and his

hair was like P. J. Proby's, and he had on this great big swanky jacket.
I fell in love with him because of that. I mean how shallow is that?
But I thought he was the business, you know?

So I was running risks . . .

Before her fifteenth birthday, Kimberley discovered she was pregnant.

My daughter was conceived with 'P. J. Proby' on the train from Victoria to Hastings, in a carriage with the shutters down. We had a really great time for that journey!

And that's how she came along.

Becoming a mother was not part of the plan. Abortion was illegal, but plentiful folk wisdom about abortifacients was exchanged between women, and Kimberley's mum – who was still unattached but who now had a new baby ('my little sister . . .') – having tried and failed to terminate that pregnancy using the hot-mustard-bath-and-quinine method, now passed on the tip to her elder daughter. 'Sometimes it worked, and sometimes it didn't.' In Kimberley's case, it didn't. For a few months she continued to attend school in her own haphazard way, wearing a stretchy hold-in corset, but getting bigger and bigger. 'P. J. Proby' denied he was the father, and distanced himself by finding a new teenage girlfriend. And so she found herself in Aylesbury.

After that I didn't want nothing to do with men . . .

But within a year, Kimberley would be engaged to be married.

Happenings

'I'm a real sixties woman,' Kimberley told me. But she admits now that being stuck in Bracknell (and six months in Aylesbury) excluded her from some of the decade's key experiences:

What they used to call 'Swinging London' – that was the bit I missed out on: all those clubs with the live bands, and Carnaby Street and all that. I've tried to make up for it ever since, believe me!

In 1964, 'Swinging London' didn't have a name. That would come later. But from 1963 people were starting to talk about the electricity, the new pulse of life being generated in Britain's capital. Listen to what they were saying:

> The young have taken over the London scene in a way that almost no generation has done before . . .
>
> Janey Ironside

> There was energy then, and if you had an idea, however silly, you could get it on the road . . . It was a terribly naive period . . . it was like falling in love.
>
> Jean Shrimpton

> [It was] a time when ordinary people could do extraordinary things . . .
>
> Twiggy

> There was a yeastiness in the air that was due to a great deal of unrestrained and irreverent frivolity . . .
>
> Angela Carter

> We used to drink and dance till dawn in those early days . . .
>
> Grace Coddington

> It was the women of Chelsea who fascinated me . . . not the men. They wore big floppy hats, skinny ribbed sweaters, key-hole dresses, wide hipster belts and, I believed, paper knickers. They had white lipsticked lips and thick black eyeliner, hair cut at alarming angles, op-art earrings and ankle-length white boots . . . They had confidence and, it seemed, no parents . . .
>
> Alexandra Pringle

Well, five of us girls shared a flat in Gunter Grove in World's End, Chelsea; one was studying cello, another was learning to be an opera singer, and I was at the Drama Centre, and there was another girl called Melissa, and she had a rolled purple umbrella, and always a velvet ribbon round her neck, and a Vidal Sassoon haircut. Well, Melissa was so <u>WITH IT</u>! And then just across the road were these artists' studios, all lived in by journalists and painters. And us five

girls gave a *lot* of parties, you know? And that's really where the
sixties began for me . . .

Patricia Quinn

You spoke to strangers and invited them back to your flat without
thinking twice. The King's Road was like an exclusive school playground. Everyone went to the same parties, the same shops, the same
coffee bars, bistros and pubs. And on Saturdays, if you weren't parading up and down the King's Road, you would migrate to Portobello
Road, in Notting Hill, to meander up and down looking at the market stalls and people strutting their stuff . . . Everyone looked glorious
and was so relaxed and friendly . . .

London belonged to the young. All the old class structures of our
parents' generation were breaking down. All the old social mores
were swept away. No one cared where you came from or what school
you'd gone to, what accent you spoke with or how much money you
had. All that mattered was what you could do, what you could
create . . .

We were breaking new ground in every area, embracing everything that presented itself and, I suppose, living without a care for
tomorrow.

Pattie Boyd

Pattie was surely wrong in declaring that class was dead. The
working-class-boy/posh-girl dynamic we've already encountered in
the magazine and modelling world served only to underline differences between the genuine *riches* and the *nouveaux*. But it is true that
fashion models, fashion designers, style icons, advertisers, publishers,
broadcasters, actors, artists, musicians, journalists and writers defined
this excitingly meritocratic era. In 1964 TV audiences saw the first
broadcasts of the BBC's *Wednesday Play* and *Top of the Pops*. The latter
triumphantly pulled off the trick of becoming required Thursday-
evening viewing for every self-respecting chart-following teenager.
This was also the heyday of the maverick pirate station Radio Caroline, hippest listening for pop fans. After dark, the Ad Lib club was a
melting pot – 'Where else can you find Lord Plunkett, Lord Blandford, Diana Dors, James Ormsby-Gore, a pool of typists, fashion

models and fashion photographers and the occasional highly paid young docker all dancing together?' asked its PR. The Cromwellian (patronised by the Beatles) and Annabel's were less democratic, but equally chic. The same year also saw the arrival of a new female daydream in London: Marianne Faithfull. Huge-eyed, motionless, passive, she sang her haunting, ethereal hit 'As Tears Go By' with a heart-rending, breathy intensity. Exposed, vulnerable, it was her very stillness that made her so sexy, so available.

This was a world in which women could make their mark. The lists of invitees to the annual Woman of the Year lunch give an indication of the range of female achievement, from sports to showbiz, publishing to diplomacy; in 1963 Mary Quant was asked to speak at the lunch, following in the footsteps of Janey Ironside, head of Fashion at the Royal College of Art. But the question *du jour* for modern women was still, 'To trouser, or not to trouser?' A Pathé Cinemagazine feature in 1964 aired the controversy: 'What was once strictly for the beatniks, is now accepted at the best-dressed functions,' purred the commentator, over footage of a woman in a very posh pink trouser ensemble and matching hat.

Meanwhile on TV's *Late Night Line-Up*, Joan Bakewell chaired the nation's intellectual and cultural debating forum. Barbara Hulanicki (Biba) started her first Kensington shop on the proceeds of selling 17,000 sugar-pink gingham dresses mail order via the *Daily Mirror*'s fashion pages. In the art world Bridget Riley's eye-popping aesthetic was the newest must-see – plagiarised as 'Op' on everything from tea towels to biscuit boxes – and Pauline Boty's sexy, experimental collages gained her a meteoric reputation among the cognoscenti.* Meanwhile Boty and Riley's male contemporaries started to construct random events known as 'Happenings' – usually an excuse to project an image of the Pope onto a naked woman's bottom, push a naked woman around a stage in a wheelbarrow, or paint her (naked) with red dye – and Allen Jones was starting to explore the violated, plasticised female body, using a visual language drawn from movies, superhero comics and pornography.

---

* Tragically, it was short lived. Boty died from an incurable tumour at the age of twenty-eight; her work was forgotten until the 1990s.

Chelsea was buzzing with the opening of the first Habitat in Fulham Road. There you could buy cheap pasta storage jars, tubular frame furniture and stripy butchers' aprons. At this time an area of central London became a forest of scaffolding and cranes, as workmen erected sixties London's most confident landmark, the Post Office Tower.

In 1964 Pattie Boyd was twenty. She had now crossed over from mute modelling to small speaking parts in adverts, such as the 'Smith's Crisps girl', which led to a day's shoot playing one of four scatty schoolgirls in the planned Beatles film, *A Hard Day's Night*. The location was a train. The 'schoolgirls' spent the whole journey collapsing with laughter at the Beatles' cute quick-wittedness, infectious humour and Scouse accents. 'And George . . . was the best-looking man I'd ever seen.' Pattie was smitten, on fire, high on laughter, craziness and the unmistakable aura of creative energy that emanated from the four. 'It was amazing, very powerful . . .' At the end of the day the train drew into Paddington. 'Will you marry me?' said George, adding, as she giggled helplessly, 'Well, if you won't marry me, will you have dinner with me tonight?' Within ten days she had dumped her photographer boyfriend Eric Swayne and they were going out together. Life with the Beatles' lead guitarist now became a giddy fairground of experiences. There were holidays in Tahiti, Paris, Monte Carlo and the south of France. Private planes alternated with skirmishes with the fans and reporters who besieged them. Pattie and George were like children, shepherded from airports to vehicles to hotels by Auntie Epstein. George didn't rate her cramped apartment near the Chelsea embankment, so he moved her and her flatmate into a bijou mews house in stylish Knightsbridge. Their relationship boosted Pattie's modelling career and, while the Beatles were touring, she was kept busy by *Vogue*, *Tatler* and *Vanity Fair*. 'I counted the days until George was due back . . .' In August 1964 the band set off on a month-long, twenty-three-city tour of America, ending in New York, where Bob Dylan spent an evening introducing them to marijuana. 'Somehow George managed to get hold of some . . . while he was away and brought it back for us to try . . . All of a sudden we were roaring with laughter and realised we were stoned . . . Everything seemed hilarious.'

Pattie Boyd, twenty years old, beautiful, successful, famous, and dating a Beatle, was living every girl's stardust fantasy.

*

But for the Highlands-raised nursery maid Veronica MacNab, Pattie's life was beyond her wildest dreams.

Until 1963 Veronica had no taste of teenage culture. Her preferred music was Scottish reels, and her first childcare post in an isolated Sussex mansion had brought her into contact with nothing more colourful than hunting pink or blue Sèvres porcelain. But that year Veronica gave in her notice to Mrs Smith and landed herself – via an agency – a new, city-based post as nursery maid to Charlotte, Henrietta, Alexandra and Philippa, the four little daughters of Count Joseph Czernin and his wife Hazel.* The Czernins, who owned one of the most valuable family estates in London and a racing property near Newbury, lived in Chelsea Square, just a few minutes' walk from the very heart of London hip, King's Road. But 54 Chelsea Square was not hip. This timeless oasis was beautified with old masters, silver and antique furniture, and the household showed no sign of class breakdown or the sweeping away of social mores. Veronica now found herself one of three live-in staff along with Angelina the Spanish cook and Jean the qualified Norland nanny. The chauffeur lived out. Veronica took the job at four pounds a week,† plus board. She was enchanted to find that her windows overlooked the square's gardens, and that her tiny room was decorated in floral Colefax and Fowler fabrics:

> It was so pretty – and it was *mine*!
>
> I had my own uniform too: a green checked gingham dress with white collar and cuffs, covered with a white apron, green tweed coat, brown gloves, brown brogues and thirty-denier lisle stockings. My hair had to be kept short and tidy, and on top of that I wore a green velour hat.

---

* Mary Hazel Czernin was the daughter of the ninth Baron Howard de Walden; on her father's death (in 1999), and as the oldest of four sisters with no male in the family, she gained the right to become Baroness Howard de Walden. Count Joseph Czernin did not use his Czech title.

† Nearly £80 today.

Thus clad, it was Veronica's job to take her privileged little charges – aged four, three, two and nought – to attend a children's party in some equally sumptuous residence, to their lessons at Madame Vacani's dancing school in Brompton Road, or for an airing by the Round Pond in Kensington Gardens, *the* select rendezvous for socially elevated babies. There you might meet David and Sarah, children of Princess Margaret, also accompanied by the nanny and their nursery maid Jenny, who was daughter to the Sandringham grocer. The little Czernin girls were accommodated in two magnificent, carriage-built twin perambulators. Veronica was required to polish up the chrome brake levers and handles on these conveyances ('they had to be just so . . .'), as well as to goffer iron the children's hand-smocked and puffed-sleeved frilly frocks. 'I felt I was just a little person – but I was looking after some very important children!' Then home for lunch: shepherd's pie, rice pudding, and fish on Fridays.

Looking at the London social scene in 1964 through the eyes of a Scottish nursery maid from the glens is like observing a distant planet through a telescope. Mr Czernin leaves each morning for his office in the City. The Hon. Mrs Czernin has breakfast in bed before ascending to the day nursery to discuss with Nanny the routine for the day, the allocation of duties, and what errands need to be run.

Mrs Czernin did not have a job, but she had a full diary of lunches, shopping and appointments. Aged thirty, she dressed conservatively in twinsets and pearls. During the day she was not often to be seen, though at teatime she might join the children for Fuller's walnut cake and egg-and-cress sandwiches. But after tea, the little girls were generally brought washed and brushed to visit their mother in the drawing room. 'Daddy' sometimes joined them for half an hour. Often, the Czernins dined out or attended society occasions that demanded all the trappings; then, Mrs Czernin would wish the children goodnight resplendent in evening dress and 'sparkly bits'.

By comparison, Veronica's social life was almost absurdly humble. Despite transferring from the Highlands to London, she was still wrapped up in 'a safe cocoon'. She had every Monday off, but with a curfew imposed for 9.30 p.m. (10 in exceptional circumstances) there was little opportunity for adventure:

> My big excitement was going to St Columba's, the Church of Scot-
> land in Pont Street, where they had Scottish country dancing
> evenings on a Monday* – and that was my connection with home . . .

Still, those evenings off sometimes offered tantalising tastes of a forbidden world:

> My dancing partner was a very nice young Scottish policeman called
> Norman. He was Gaelic-speaking, and he would walk me home and
> I remember going to a coffee bar with him in Knightsbridge, where
> trendy people were smoking Gauloises and Peter Stuyvesant ciga-
> rettes, and you could drink <u>coffee</u>. Which I had never done before!

The coffee bar had a juke box too. To ears attuned to eightsome reels
and Gay Gordons, 'Carol' and 'Can't Buy Me Love' were alien
sounds – but she loved them.

Veronica began to feel like a member of the audience at an extravagant pageant. If she stepped out of her new front door in Chelsea she
might encounter a host of leggy and beautiful young women her age,
heavily made-up with dark eyeliner and pale lipstick, parading past in
leather jackets, Courrèges trouser suits, or A-line Mary Quant dresses,
with black-and-white PVC boots and sleek Sassoon bobs. Sometimes,
she found herself in Harrods, where the upper crust bought their linen,
longingly fingering the fashions on the hangers. 'But I could only stand
and look . . .' Glamorous couples roared around the Chelsea streets in
Jaguars or cute Mini Clubmans. To an utterly sheltered, sensible, 'do-
as-I'm-told, put-on-the-uniform, do-my-job, goody-goody' virgin,
these beings seemed like extra-terrestrials. Especially memorable was
the sight of two long-haired Chelsea dandies, 'one in a purple velvet
suit, and his friend in a bottle-green velvet suit, both smoking cigarettes'. For decadence, there had never in her experience been anything
like it. 'It was like going to the movies!' Their plushy swagger and
bravado sent out an unmistakably licentious message – 'but it was much
too dangerous for a nice girl like me to even think about'.

Could Veronica ever be more than a spectator? Around her, people
seemed to be living in a world of adventure, excitement, wonderful
fun and magic freedom, where anything was possible.

* They still do.

There I was in the middle of Chelsea. Part of me was a little bit envious, in fact quite a lot envious I guess. I would have liked to have had the freedom to go and play . . . And, of course, I didn't have any money – and one had to have money to dress appropriately to go to night clubs. And anyway, who was going to take *me* to a night club?

I was like a child looking into a picture book, and seeing the pictures, and not being part of it.

At the same time, I disapproved, because, gosh, weren't they naughty? And I was a goody two-shoes. So I kept my knees together.

Behind the day nursery windows in Chelsea Square, Veronica Mac-Nab felt protected from the naughtiness and risk of the big bad city with its brash modernity and alarming hairstyles. Instead, a different city laid out its treasures for her: its music, its museums, its traditions, its polish and privilege.

It was an education. Two years later, Veronica would return to Scotland. And when she did, she carried with her a passionate taste for art, antiques, beautiful objects and gracious living that would stay with her for the rest of her life.

'You don't need a gymslip to be with it.' Though still modest and ladylike, in 1964 the fashion emphasis was moving inexorably towards girliness.

Dreaming of Houses

There was King's Road, with its Spanish bistros, Habitat and PVC-clad dolly birds. There was 54 Chelsea Square, with its Georgian silver teapots and Colefax and Fowler curtains.

And there was Lambeth. And in boroughs like this in London, and across the country, there was a very different story to be told. It was a story that counteracted the prevailing narrative of the affluent society, with money jingling in teenagers' pockets to be spent on vinyl singles, make-up and motorbikes. In the autumn of 1964, as the Conservative government under Alec Douglas-Home geared up for a general election, the energised Labour Party led by Harold Wilson went out to campaign against the Tories' record on homelessness. 'Thirteen years of Tory rule,' Wilson told his supporters, 'have left Britain with a million families without houses of their own, at least a million slums and two and a half million other houses lacking fixed baths, piped water, or indoor sanitation.' The desperation arising from accommodation shortages would become a refrain of the 1960s, with hardship, eviction, exploitation and council-house waiting lists becoming familiar headlines in the press.

In the 1960s the significance, to women, of house and home remained primary. One writer who fully recognised this was the sociologist Hannah Gavron, much praised for her study *The Captive Wife* (1966), a ground-breaking analysis of the female dilemma. When Gavron lifted the lid on the 'captive wife', she uncovered a self-referential, introverted state of affairs. Young wives had few friends, but turned instead to their own mothers for support. Family and four walls had replaced community.

> The nuclear family was clearly the focus of the wife's attentions and interests . . . [This] was an inward looking unit, from which contact with the outside world was [in]frequent.

Home was a refuge. But it could also be a prison.

And yet for many a walled-in wife, old or young, the limits of her imagined happiness were a spick-and-span new-build with picture windows, a kitchen with wall cupboards and wipe-clean tops, and a plastic bathroom suite. The imagery beckoned to her from cereal packets, hoardings and TV. 'Every couple who have ever set up a home have had a vision in their minds of their dream house,' proclaimed the *News of the World*. 'Win a £10,000 Dream House – a new, modern house sitting in its own grounds. A warm and cosy house, furnished and decorated smart as a new pin, all the cupboards full.' Here was something for everyone to aspire to – like these women:

– I'd live in the future. I'd have it all modern. Nothing old in it. You know, all the buildings and everything. Not old and horrible like Balsall Heath. The people would all be happy, not miserable and fed-up.

– I'd just like to, you know, have a big place and everything in it, a swimming pool and all that type of thing.

– We lived in a completely broken down house . . . we had practically nothing, a mattress on the floor . . . And I did suddenly feel that I wanted something better.

There was no carpet on the floor, I couldn't lie down on the floor and play with the child, and build bricks, and I suddenly saw myself with a carpet and a warm room in a sort of television advertisement world . . .

And yet, as Hannah Gavron spelled out, the dream was elusive, particularly for working-class wives and mothers like those quoted above. Families, particularly large ones, were unfairly disadvantaged. Gavron cited statistics showing that, whereas 50 per cent of childless couples owned their own homes, only 6 per cent of families with four children were home-owners; moreover, the younger the children, the worse the conditions they had to put up with. For low earners, children complicated everything. She gave instances in which mothers living in cramped rented rooms with active small children were tormented by the lack of play space, and by the complaints provoked by their noise. Stress and isolation were the result.

The worst case in this sample was a family of six . . .

A detached dwelling with clean geometry, plate-glass windows and up-and-over
garage doors summed up 1960s aspirations for many women.

wrote Gavron:

> The husband was a plumber's mate. They lived in one room and a
> small kitchen in which the wife and her husband slept on a mattress on
> the floor. Repeated attempts by the doctor to get them rehoused on
> medical grounds failed, and as the wife said, 'There was only one
> thing left for me to do' – she had made an attempt at suicide.

In 1964 a young woman named Pauline O'Mahony found herself
in the distressing and daunting position of assessing the housing needs
of many hundreds of such unlucky or dispossessed families in south
London.

> The numbers of them: the volume, the vastness – it felt like a huge
> problem! And I sometimes wonder how we ever coped with this vol-
> ume of tragedy.

Pauline was born in 1948, in a Belfast slum. Homelessness played a role
in her life almost immediately, as the family decamped to England to
reunite with her father who, following his discharge from the army,
had found a job as a removals driver. The O'Mahonys were lucky, and

were provided with a council house in the London suburb of Brent-wood. But their good fortune stopped there. There was never much money, and Mrs O'Mahony supplemented the family income by cleaning in a hospital. Pauline grew up feeling stigmatised and short-changed by life, with a determination to distance herself from her roots, and become self-sufficient. She loved reading, but was low-achieving at school. A talent for sport came to her rescue, but at the age of thirteen she was awarded a prize for public service, and soon after joined the Young Socialists and CND. Pauline O'Mahony – like many of her generation – was gripped by a growing conviction that young people, whether male or female, had something to contribute to running the world. 'I did feel that both individually and collectively we had power, and we *could* make a difference.'

Her chance came in 1964. The family were in financial straits; following an episode of ill health, Pauline's father was put on half pay and it became imperative for her to start earning.

> So I wrote a letter to the Town Clerk at Lambeth Borough Council explaining that I'd won a school prize for public service, and that I was in the netball team! And I said, 'Is there anything I can do? Could you take me on?' And I got an interview, and he gave me a job as junior tea-maker in the Housing Department.

To start with, this job wasn't going to change the world. Pauline made tea for over twenty men – architects, engineers, planners, welfare officers and housing officers – but there were also two other women in the department, and they were the housing manager and her deputy. In 1964 slum clearance was ongoing; the borough's strategy was discussed around tables spread with paper plans and layouts. Pauline provided tea and biscuits to the officials, and would linger, fascinated to see the intricate drawings.

> And one day the senior architect, Deirdre Haines, noticed me. And she said, 'Do you want to learn to look at plans?' And I said, 'Yes.' And she said, 'Come back later, and I'll teach you . . .'

After that, Pauline progressed quickly. In turn, she was seconded to the architecture and engineering departments. Before the year was out, and armed with her new-found training, she was given the dual job of housing visitor and housing interviewer, assessing families on the council's waiting list, or whose homes were due for demolition, and interviewing evicted tenants with more immediate housing needs.

What Pauline now encountered was shocking and harrowing. On visiting days, she was given a caseload of up to a dozen households to assess. In theory, she was supposed to knock on doors when least expected, so that the owner or tenant was unprepared. There were risks to this. On one occasion a schizophrenic locked her in a cupboard, and on another she walked unsuspectingly into a south London brothel, innocently inquiring where the ladies' husbands were. But before long she was known locally and, seeing her coming, somebody was bound to shout out, 'Oh Gawd, it's the welfare lady . . .' Once inside, it was her task to review conditions and fill in a registration form: number of children, their ages, their state of health et cetera.

But in addition the officer was expected to make judgements regarding the applicants' standards of cleanliness and tidiness. So a dirty floor, dishes piled up in the sink, or a baby's nappy lying unwashed would all be logged; and then the accommodation had to be checked over for bug infestation – the bugs were often to be found by scratching under the wallpaper. All such factors affected the allocation: clean hygienic families got nice new houses. Dirty slovenly families didn't. There was also embedded racism. The large immigrant population in south London was badmouthed and discriminated against. No law existed to prevent this so, no matter what their needs, white families would be pushed up the queue ahead of black families. Pauline found this dismaying. The black families she met were generally warm-hearted and welcomed her with cups of tea and condensed milk.

Temperamentally, Pauline was on the side of her 'clients'. So when she filled in her case notes, she often found herself giving the immigrants, and the 'dirty' families, the benefit of the doubt. She could see how hard it was for them to do battle with rising damp, peeling walls, mouldy woodwork, leaky roofs and crumbling plaster, 'and the children getting chest infection after chest infection . . .' Many of the homes lacked indoor sanitation, electricity, gas or hot water. Some even lacked a floor: one elderly woman sat in her basement on a dirt foundation.

We were supposed not to show we cared. But I couldn't ignore their plight. I couldn't not be sympathetic . . .

On Christmas Eve, Pauline was in tears.

It was snowing, it was 7 o'clock at night, and it was dark. I was trudging through the snow, on the very last of my ten cases, and I was desperate to start out on my long journey back home to Brentwood. I knocked on the door, and it was an immigrant family and they had *so* many children – and they had literally <u>nothing</u> for Christmas. The youngest baby was lying in a bottom drawer. And I sat there, and I just put my head in my hands and wept with them . . .

But Pauline found the other side of her job equally pitiable. Home visits took up three or four days a week. The remainder of the week Pauline was an interviewer, installed in a tiny cubicle, hearing the grievous tales of evicted tenants who arrived in desperation at the doors of the Housing Department, because they had nowhere else to go. Outside her little space, the waiting room was thronged with these refugees from the rental market, mostly families, with numerous babies in creaky pushchairs and ill-favoured, sick toddlers. Most of them had been tenants of houses 'in multiple occupation', often entire families living in just one or two rooms, with access to an outdoor toilet. Their landlords (like the notorious Peter Rachman) were allowed, within the law, to buy up semi-derelict terraces, fill them with families, charge them uncontrolled rents and serve them with notice to quit at any time when there was a prospect of selling the property. It was a charter for intimidation, and in her time in the Housing Department Pauline witnessed the reign of terror exercised by merciless landlords who had the doors broken down and terrorised their tenants with dangerous dogs to compel them to leave. Fearful and miserable, the destitute families arrived in Kennington with their 'Notices to Quit'. Time and again, Pauline heard the plea, 'We've nowhere to go . . .'

I remember going to my male manager and saying, 'I have a family . . .' I can remember the family, I can see the man now with his trilby hat on, and the woman, very round faced, very warm, motherly, lovely, with the children at her skirts – and my manager showing no compassion or interest or care. And I thought, 'I just *can't* do this . . .'

Time and again, her seniors would say to her, 'Send them away. There's nothing we can do. We can't produce accommodation out of nowhere . . .' The only provision in such cases was the local authority hostel. Women and children were bundled into transport and taken to prison-like dormitory accommodation in Southwark. The husbands were prohibited from joining them.

Every so often this vast caseload of human misery was alleviated, when Pauline was able to inform some patient family whose slum home was threatened with demolition that the council was proposing to rehouse them. For many, that was cause to rejoice. But mixed reactions might greet the announcement that their new home would be an eighth-floor flat, or a low-rise in Bognor Regis. However unhealthy and wretched their slum houses, people were being forcibly removed from all that was familiar and sociable.

For Pauline O'Mahony, the work was gruelling, numbing and exhausting. But she was never in any doubt about her own motivation:

> I learnt how to work the system in their interests, and if that meant stretching the story on occasion, I thought that was an OK thing to do – because it was about access to resources. Being in the position of a gatekeeper, it was my duty to get the most out of the system for the individual or household that I possibly could . . .

Unavoidably, in this context, we return to the vision that so dominated post-war social aspirations, in which every woman was goddess of her home, and that home was her temple, her refuge and her source of identity. But for thousands of unlucky women, the brutal, shameful, 1960s homelessness crisis, with all its attendant dispossession and exile, ate away at the very foundations of family and femininity, denying them status, sense of self and even a reason for living. For what was a woman without her dream? As Hannah Gavron's desperate young wife declared: 'There was only one thing left for me to do.' Even worse off was the single mother, excessively vulnerable to exploitation by private landlords. In *Mothers Alone: Poverty and the Fatherless Family* (1969) the sociologist Dennis Marsden demonstrated that unmarried mothers were at the bottom of the pile in terms of housing deprivation. They lacked furniture and basic household equipment, suffered most from overcrowding, and were least likely to be rehoused by local authorities. For hundreds of Pauline O'Mahony's supplicants, where dream homes were concerned, well, they could dream on.

Maybe – along with country dancing and church on Sundays – women's exclusive self-identification with interior spaces needed to slip gently into the past. Of course, everyone required a roof over their head. But homelessness, and the sense of annihilation and negation that went with it, meant different things to women than to men. If you took a man's home away, he remained an effective human being, but if you took a woman's home away, she was nobody. More than that: all around them in 1964, women were being led to believe that their worth was enhanced through domestic acquisitions. Advertisers and journalists targeted them with the message that the secret of happiness lay in abundance, modernity and possessions; in vacuum cleaners, kidney-shaped dressing tables and covetable three-piece suites. The dream was legitimate – but did it have to be the only dream? Maybe there was another way to be a woman in the modern world?

Pauline O'Mahony wouldn't describe herself as a goddess, and women do not have a monopoly on empathy and compassion. But in 1964, they felt more permitted to expose those qualities than men did. Society expected its women to be healers, givers and nurturers. Pauline was just sixteen, and she had little power, struggling with the contradictions of her position. But for many a hopeless and dispossessed mother, the friendly, bespectacled features and gladdening personage of 'the Welfare Lady' represented the chance of a future for her family, and the chance to rejoin the ranks of womankind. In a dingy cubicle located in a Kennington office building, humanity was conspicuous, and it had a female face.

1965

Not Quite the Same as Before

In October 1964 the Labour Party under Harold Wilson won the general election with a tiny majority of four seats; two years later Wilson was to gamble on a second election, bringing him a workable majority. Labour would stay in power for the remainder of the decade.

In the run-up to the 1964 election my parents campaigned for the Labour candidate in Leeds North-West, against the incumbent, Sir Donald Kaberry, a Tory backbencher who was chairman of the Association of Conservative Clubs. Generally, the world of art, literature and media was pro-Labour. That autumn, duplicated leaflets littered our kitchen dresser, and the talk was all of majorities and getting out the vote. All day on 15 October my father and mother took it in turns to collect Labour voters and drive them in our unreliable Austin A40 to the polling station in Moortown. (Conservatives were more likely to be car owners, so this service was essential if the Labour candidate was to stand a chance.) Sir Donald won the seat, but with a reduced majority, and my parents celebrated a Labour victory that to them, in their middle years, seemed like a rejuvenating breath of fresh air.

Doreen Hall from Darwen in Lancashire was of the same persuasion. At twenty-four, she was a first-time voter,[*] and a year spent teaching in colonial Africa had heightened her awareness of social injustice:

> I got a sense that people were reacting to toffs in government – and that Wilson was something else. Wilson was forward-looking about technology, and he had a northern accent like me. So I thought, things are actually going to change. And I thought this is really, really exciting . . .

[*] In 1964 the voting age was twenty-one. It was lowered to eighteen in 1970.

Wilson had grown up on the Wirral and represented the Merseyside constituency of Huyton. Pretty west-London teenager Mavis Wilson's working-class background also instinctively drew her to the Labour Party. At sixteen, though she was too young to vote, she felt Harold Wilson's Merseyside affiliations gave him credibility. 'The Beatles thought Wilson was good. That helped . . . And he smoked a pipe and he looked like your uncle. It did seem as if the world was opening up, and this was quite a changing moment.'

At Liverpool University, where she was studying Political Theory and Institutions, twenty-two-year-old Rosalyn Palmer could hardly believe her luck. Earlier in the autumn term she and her fellow Labour Party members in the Student Union had invited Wilson to speak at the University on 16 October. Although it was home territory, 'we didn't realise it was going to be the day after the election . . .'

And we said, 'Are you still coming?' And he said, 'Yes'. He said, 'The Queen can wait, but you can't!' Lovely man!

As part of the student committee, Rosalyn joined the new prime minister on the platform and had the opportunity to talk to him after he had given his speech – 'which was amazing, and I just thought he was wonderful. I always thought he was the most brilliant prime minister we've ever had. And I still do actually.' For Rosalyn, a Wilson-led Labour government was the clincher to her new Liverpool life of poetry, pop and politics.

It only remained to fall in love and lose her virginity, which she did, in her second year at the university. Paul was 'the love of my life', a year older than her, talented, clever and dangerous: an actor, a musician and a renegade. They became a couple, and hung out in a circle of artsy, political, pot-smoking partygoers, listening to music and philosophising. But where sex – and contraception – were concerned, Rosalyn's ignorance remained profound. And in her final year, with her all-important degree exams looming, she became pregnant.

To put it mildly, holy shit. My mother went ballistic.

And to start with, the university said that I would have to leave, because they couldn't have unmarried mothers. Well, I challenged them. I said, 'Would you have unmarried <u>fathers</u>?' At that time if girls got pregnant they would throw them out. So I said, 'Well, what about the boys?' And they kind of said, 'Huh, it's different for them. You know, the boys can't help themselves.' My professor was among them. He said, 'Oh, so you're pregnant – you're going to have to leave.' And I said, 'Don't be stupid – I'm not going to leave, who's going to make me leave?' I wasn't going back to Surrey and my mother's house!

So I got together with a whole load of girls and we fought it.

And eventually my professor recognised I had a point. And he said, 'Yeah, why should you?'

But Paul said, 'It means we can get married. It'll be wonderful.' I didn't really know that I wanted to be tied down, but to cut a long story short we got married in February 1965 . . .

Rosalyn and Paul moved into a shabby flat in the run-down Georgian area of Liverpool. The baby was due in July. As her finals approached, Rosalyn took little time out from her books to think about the birth. A friend accompanied her to buy clothes, nappies and various unfathomable necessities. The impending physical ordeal had no reality for her. Her evasive and disapproving mother had merely told her that having a baby was mildly 'discomforting'. When people inquired apprehensively whether she would hold out during the exams, Rosalyn's ignorance made her unafraid. ' "Oh it's all right," I said, "it's not due for another three or four days, I'll be fine." I just thought, oh, I'll face all that when my exams are over. So of course having the baby was a huge shock.'

My finals finished on July the second. Graduation was on the twentieth, and on the twenty-fifth I had Alex.

The hospital, bless them, kept me in for ten days, not because of any complications, but because they realised I didn't know which way up was this baby!

Ambitions, goals, the result of her bachelor's degree now receded before the unforeseen and bewildering demands of looking after a new baby in a one-room flat in a Liverpool slum. But one absolute dividend derived from Rosalyn's shaky, clueless propulsion out of higher education and into motherhood: there was no going back to Surrey.

★

Labour won its slender majority in the 1964 election. But from Surrey to Southampton, Basingstoke to Basildon, England's heartland would remain a sea of undeviating blue. At its centre, the quiet commuter town of Andover was home to teenage socialite Kristina Reed's well-heeled parents. Conservatism defined who they were. Kristina herself had always felt as comfortable with the Tory status quo as she did with her pearls and her white gloves.

Three years earlier, in 1960, Kristina had been a reluctant pupil at Queen's Gate School for Girls in South Kensington. She did not excel academically, and in 1964, having effectively been told by her school that she might as well give up on education, Kristina settled for two O levels, and left without regret. 'I was fifteen, sixteen . . . and the old social life had taken off . . .' A photograph of Kristina, taken at her first 'grown-up' party in 1962 shows her posed, seated in somebody's front hall, in a full-length white gown and pearls, looking closer to thirty-five than fifteen. Apprehensively, eyes downcast, she clutches a thimble-sized glass of sherry. 'I was on my way to the Sandhurst Summer Ball, made to go by my parents with some boy I didn't know, and I can feel it now, the terror of it!'

In 1965 she made her entrée to the London season. Though court presentations had been consigned to history by 1965, Kristina's mother jumped through the expected hoops of lunching and taking tea with the mothers of her peers, making social arrangements with the mothers of suitably vetted young men, and acquiring a table for Queen Charlotte's Ball.

But Kristina's assumptions were about to be reset. 'The post-war era, for me, had been founded on things going on being the same. I didn't know anything about Wilson, but I just knew he wasn't Conservative. I mean, the prime minister had always been Alec Douglas-Home or some similar Old-School bod . . .' On the evening of 15 October 1964 Kristina scrubbed up and stepped out to a swanky party in a Kensington mansion, where a crowd of debs and their delights were watching the election results on television:

And Harold Wilson got in.
    And I remember thinking, 'This is the end of life as we know it. It's going to be like Russia here now!'

> And I just thought, 'He's a *Socialist*!! Gulp!' And this was a <u>whole new thing</u>! I thought the working classes would rise up or something, and our houses would be bugged – well, that's an exaggeration. But I kind of worked out, this is *not* going to be beneficial to people like us.
>
> And it was just another shift under one's feet, of things being, well, how can I put it? – not quite the same as before . . .

The Kennedy assassination and the Wilson election were bringing home to Kristina that she lived in a changing world. But as the only child of model high-bracket parents, those assumptions weren't just political. Girls like her did certain things, and they didn't do certain other things. Careers didn't figure. Marriage was the goal. With this in mind, boyfriends were tolerated. At sixteen Kristina started going out with James, an 'adorable' Etonian two years her senior, whom she'd met at the Windsor Horse Show. 'It was a real little love affair.'

However the boyfriend-tolerance didn't extend to sex: 'Nothing below the neck!' Kristina had grown up in a don't-talk-about-it culture where the physical realities of birth and death were suppressed and denied.

> Anyway, I was much too frightened. There was no pill. I didn't know what penetration was. I didn't know what a willy did . . . And I couldn't ask my mother – she was completely dippy about sex.
>
> So I didn't *do* anything . . .

Nevertheless, her appearance sent out erotic messages. For even London's socialites were in love with Mod: Mod music and Mod fashion. Mod was what set you apart from the older generation. In 1961 Kristina had looked like a mini version of her mother, coiffed, gloved and hatted: an unlikely candidate for the role of teenage tearaway. But by the age of eighteen the persona had changed. It was 1965. Gone were the pearls. She acquired a short skirt and a silver leather jacket designed for her by an art-school friend. Small of stature, her petite features were framed with a backcombed do and a stylish fringe *à la* Cathy McGowan, her lids defined with black eyeliner and her lips with ashy white. The look was – albeit unintentionally – kittenish and provocative. Now, when she joined the parade of Saturday-morning followers of fashion flaunting up and down King's Road, she no longer looked like a posh deb. She fitted in.

> We felt we were at the centre of the world . . .
>
> At that time the first Wimpy Bar had opened, and it was a place where you could meet people and just have a cup of coffee. And there was Mary Quant – so we'd go and have a rifle through the rails. And sometimes you went to a scruffy little cinema called The Classic, because it was a jolly good opportunity to sit in the dark . . .

The love affair with James the adorable Etonian ran its course. 'I got to a point where I did get a bit bored with all my sort of people . . .' As Kristina herself took on a new, classless camouflage, the A-list public schoolboys of her milieu began to seem starchy and Bertie Wooster-ish. It was time to find a new boyfriend: preferably one with Mod credentials from a somewhat lower social drawer. So without more ado she went to a party at the Ritz and promptly made a successful play for Alan Buck, drummer of a band called the Four Pennies, who had made the charts with their harmonious 1964 chart-topper 'Juliet'. It was quite a coup. 'That song was all over everywhere . . .'

> He was from Manchester and he spoke with a Mancunian accent. Well, I went out with him for about six months. And I guess I thought I was being incredibly rebellious, because I must have thought, 'This'll piss my parents off!' And actually, my mother was having an absolute heart attack about him . . .

But there was nothing for Mrs Reed to have a heart attack about. Though she pushed at the boundaries, and was regularly grounded for not observing a 10 p.m. curfew, the relationship with Mancunian Alan had little staying power.

Nevertheless, it was a matter of treading water until Mr Right came along, so Kristina did what so many girls like her did, and got a basic secretarial training. 'The people at the college told me "You'll never make a second-rate copy typist", which was probably the worst insult I've ever been given!' These were the glory years of the office temp. As *The New London Spy* pointed out, 'If you are reasonably intelligent and able to type you need never be out of a job typing someone's letters and answering *his* telephone . . .' (my italics). In 1965 Margery Hurst, self-made founder of the Brook Street Bureau, floated her highly profitable employment agency on the London Stock Exchange, having tapped into the swing towards female independence. As Hurst herself put it:

> The women who came to my bureau for jobs wanted to earn money, of course. But the job was also a passport to new friends, romance, and a means of filling in the day.

Kristina's qualifications in the basics of paperwork and filing were enough to get her employment as a temp in a variety of offices, from the Sudanese embassy to a showbiz accountancy firm. It filled her day. But her nights were not filled.

At nineteen, Kristina Reed was still a virgin. Times had truly changed. Five or ten years earlier, that fact would have been not only unremarkable but unimpeachable. But for a very pretty débutante in 1965 it was beginning to verge on the freakish.

> I hadn't done it, and I guess most people of my type had by then. I think I was terrified of getting pregnant, or something awful happening. But I was beginning to think, I really don't like this any more, people are beginning to say, 'She's frigid.' I don't think they quite said, 'She's gay,' but it was slightly that way – kind of: 'Oh, she doesn't like boys . . .' The problem was, I looked as though I did. You know, I had the bedroom eyes . . .
>
> Anyway, I thought, this can't go on . . .

The question was, how to go about things? As a first-timer, she didn't want to launch into a one-night stand, or take risks with some sadistic seducer. Coincidence came to Kristina's aid; the circles in which she moved guaranteed that, sooner or later, she would bump into James, her adorable Etonian ex. Though they'd parted, their reunion was delightfully pally and civilised, and he invited her to visit his parents. Following a cosy evening, it now struck Kristina that James was the perfect bet.

And now Kristina demonstrated, if only to herself, and if only in London SW3, how far women had come. Her decision was driven by curiosity, not love, and by a wish to fit in, and it was one that she took confidently, unashamedly and without guilt. She knew when she decided to have sex with James that it wasn't going to reignite their relationship. Nor, when she took that decision, did she calculate any risks to her reputation, marriageability, class cachet, or eternal soul. Gone were the days when loss of chastity meant a girl was damaged goods. The world order that ordained that an impure woman must be shunned, disowned and sent abroad held no more sway. Lady Chatterley had shown the way: sex was supposed to be soft flames, feathers, and rippling bells. And Kristina Reed saw no reason to be left out of the fun.

> 'Cos it was a big thing! Well, it was to me . . . And I can't imagine five years earlier making that kind of decision on my own. At that time Women's lib, Feminism, whatever you want to call it – wasn't a factor.
>
> But by then women like me did feel we were part of a changing world – and that made one feel more independent and capable of making such decisions.
>
> Anyway, I thought, 'James is the guy to do it. This is the guy to whom I would like to lose my by now rather irritating virginity. And he won't hurt me, and he'll be kind.'

And so it proved when James helpfully obliged.

But what about the flames and feathers? And the bells?

> Well, I thought it was <u>quite</u> nice. I didn't think it was absolutely wonderful!
>
> But it was *such* a relief to have got rid of it.

Nonetheless, having joined the human race, Kristina was absolutely determined to make up for lost time. Somewhere, despite her lack of information, and despite not reading D. H. Lawrence, she had picked up the idea that sex was supposed to be overwhelmingly fantastic. Girlfriends had told her, 'If you don't faint it hasn't worked!' Naturally, that wasn't going to happen the first time, but perhaps if you kept trying it with different people, you'd get lucky. Kristina had no difficulty in finding willing accomplices: 'I think there are certain physical aspects about women that men like very much, and I suppose I was blessed with them . . .' In addition, her well-bred upbringing had programmed her to believe that, when a man took you out to dinner, it was rude not to say thank you nicely. And now that there were no social penalties attached to the practice of post-prandial fornication, it was hard to think of a reason to say no. So – as often as not out of pure politeness – she said yes.

What's New, Pussycat?

One case history doesn't make a sexual revolution. But Kristina's story paints in some nuances of a broad-brush perception, that the traditional understanding of sin and virtue was on the wane. The rising notion was that centuries of guilt, repression, shame, prohibition, stuffiness and double standards were being replaced by a new age of honesty, openness, spontaneity, empowerment and sexual freedom. In the era of op art, and the Wilson government's 'white heat' of technology from which would emerge a newly forged Britain, the new freedoms appeared to be correspondingly black, white and streamlined.

In 1964 Bob Dylan told the world, 'The times they are a-changin'.' It was impossible to ignore his message: 'Your sons and your daughters / Are beyond your command.' And in 1965 the Who stuttered out a defiant, half-coherent, exhilarating challenge to the squares in 'My Generation'. Meanwhile, the marriage motif that had so saturated pop ballads just a few years earlier was stealthily overtaken mid-decade by the lyrics of desire. In 1965 the charts sent the Rolling Stones' '(I Can't Get No) Satisfaction' to number 1. The narrative that sex was available and pleasurable was gaining ground.

In 1965 we are entering a 'live now, pay later' mindset: an era of abandonment. Libido was out of the box, with confused women – and men – unsure how to play by the new rules.

We are in a state of flux . . .

wrote the *Daily Mail* columnist Anne Scott-James in September 1965 –

The male is no longer dominant, women are restless and resentful and are fighting for a new role.

Hostilities were breaking out in the sex war, with the opening salvos of the conflict fired on stages and stadiums, on the street and on cat-walks. The skirmishes were channelled through the pages of books and glossy magazines, and depicted on screens large and small. Amid the crossfire, the distinction between pornography and permissive-ness was blurred. Never mind the fallout, never mind the losers: questioning laxity placed you in the intolerant camp.

For the most part, TV viewers were bombarded with an armoury of crudely glamorised, trivialised females.* In television comedy for example, women provided glamour and the opportunity for innu-endo, or else were conspicuous by their absence: *Steptoe and Son*, *Hancock's Half Hour* and *Dad's Army* featured almost no female char-acters. In action drama, *Doctor Who*'s young lady assistants were damsels in distress, while 1965 saw the suave dominatrix Diana Rigg playing *The Avengers*' Emma Peel on ITV wearing a kinky zip-up bodysuit, in which she appeared both unassailably feminine and mouth-wateringly sexual. But Johnny Speight's immortal *Till Death Us Do Part* was more nuanced. Though Alf Garnett's long-suffering nag of a wife Else (played by Dandy Nichols) was characterised as unfathomably stupid, the helpless witness of his ranting sexism and racism, she was often given the last laugh, while their daughter Rita (Una Stubbs) was portrayed as an effervescent, feisty Mod. At the age of nine, my own favourite television programme was the American fantasy sitcom *Bewitched* (starring Elizabeth Montgomery), which also resisted the stereotype by having a suburban, 'Feminine Mys-tique' housewife turn out to be a clever witch, married to a gullible mortal man.† I loved watching smart Samantha run rings round goofy Darren.

Cinema, however, offered little to comfort the woman fighting for a new role. *Thunderball* (1965) projected the passionate/aggressive/ compliant Bond girl specimen: all mink gloves, bikinis and power

* For giving me a steer on this topic, I am extremely grateful to my friend and neighbour, the comedy writer Kim Fuller, who has drawn on his encyclopaedic knowledge of 1960s broadcast media.
† It wasn't until 1967 that my parents finally gave in and acquired a television. Until then I watched these programmes at the home of a schoolmate who lived in a modern semi on the nearby Wimpey estate.

play. *The Knack*, also 1965, starring Rita Tushingham, was the tawdry, slapstick tale of Nancy, an out-of-town ingénue who becomes an
object of desire for three misogynistic flatmates. The film ends with
a disturbing sequence in which Nancy is portrayed as an unhinged
simpleton having rape delusions; the blokes, of course, are merely
having 'a bit of fun'. 'Girls don't get raped unless they want it,' says
one of them. *The Knack*'s director won the 1965 Palme d'Or at
Cannes. The year's classiest hit film, *Darling*, starred Julie Christie at
her most photogenic: a toy for men, playing into the fantasies of
beauty, wealth, fame, love and high society. At the opposite end of
the scale, Woody Allen's hugely successful male wish-fulfilment
screenplay for *What's New, Pussycat?* – a fantasy about a man besieged
by lust-crazed females who all want to trap him into marriage –
could have won an Oscar for its commodification of women. In one
scene a beautiful parachutist (Ursula Andress) falls from the sky into
Peter O'Toole's lap and unzips her snakeskin catsuit. Looking back, it
is hard to imagine how such films were considered palatable, but the
foolproof, formulaic *Carry On . . .* series (fifteen films, from *Carry on
Constable* to *Carry On Up the Jungle*, were made between 1960 and
1970) proves that the public lapped up this sexist, innuendo-heavy
stuff.

More than ever, clothes were *the* combat zone, *the* sensation, *the*
controversy. The *Daily Express* told its readers that Cilla Black spent
£100 a week on clothes. Fashion was the meteoric medium. Up and
up it went. Up with it went the erotic barometer. In 1964 there had
been a short-lived craze for topless 'shock frocks'. 'Where's it all leading, this mania for sexy clothes?' asked the doyenne of dress codes,
Felicity Green.

It is intriguing to uncover at least three quite separate origin myths
for the miniskirt. Did Mary Quant invent it? Whether she did or
didn't, she was gracious enough to give the credit to 'the girls on the
King's Road'. But Barbara Hulanicki ('Biba') had her own theory. In
1965 a factory failure meant that a whole batch of temperamental
jersey-fabric skirts arrived in the store shrunk to half the desired
length. 'That little fluted skirt walked out on customers as fast as we
could get it onto the hatstands.' Jean Shrimpton, however, had a quite
different account of its genesis. The synthetic fibre company Orlon

had hired her to promote their product on a trip to Australia, but had been stingy with the fabric for her outfits. 'It doesn't matter,' the Shrimp told the designer. 'Make them a bit shorter. No one's going to notice . . . He did. And that was how the mini was born.' But Shrimpton's public appearance at the Melbourne Races, bare-legged in a mini-dress with no hat or gloves, provoked a press furore down under. Meanwhile, back in Britain, American visitors such as the journalist John Crosby were frothing uncontrollably over the sexuality of the London streets. The *Sunday Telegraph* printed Crosby's drooling description of the miniskirt phenomenon:

> . . . a frenzy of the prettiest legs in the whole world belonging to models, au pair girls or just ordinary English girls, a gleam of pure joy on their pretty faces . . . all vibrating with youth . . .
>
> They're more than pretty; they're young, appreciative, sharp-tongued, glowingly alive . . . Young English girls take to sex as if it's candy and it's delicious.

'They're getting shorter, shorter and shorter,' headlined the *News of the World*'s fashion page in March 1965. 'All eyes will be riveted on the legs and feet.' Not just there. One young woman referred to her mini as a 'helicopter skirt'. Why? she was asked – 'Because you can see into the cockpit.' Michael Caine's mother, a charlady, didn't believe in the mini until her son took her to King's Road, where she reacted with repugnance: 'If it's not for sale you shouldn't put it in the window!' Many eyes now swivelled towards the upper thighs and crotch area revealed whenever a fashion-conscious young woman climbed upstairs on a double-decker bus. 'There is only one solution,' wrote Felicity Green. 'Tights. Not longer stockings. Not panty-girdles. Just tights.'

Inevitably, the mini was tough on the heavy-busted, the thick-ankled, or the plain fat. Advertisements for slimming aids multiplied. This was extreme fashion that disenfranchised those over twenty-four. Hips, bosoms and all they symbolised – motherhood, milk and honey, ample home-cooked meals – were inappropriate for a new age of contraception and long-legged youthfulness. The 'dolly bird', in all her nubile, compliant, Lolita-like immaturity, was in the spotlight.

Mary Quant spelled it out: 'Every girl with a hope of getting away with it is aiming to look not only under voting age but under the age of consent.' In 'Mrs Albion You've Got a Lovely Daughter' (1965), the Liverpool poet Adrian Henri (who was in his thirties) indulged his babe-fantasies around 'navy-blue schooldrawers' and 'old men looking up their skirts', and allowed his thoughts to wander upstairs, as they . . .

> *comb their darkblonde hair in suburban bedrooms*
> *powder their delicate little nipples*
> *wondering if tonight will be the night*

The message that attached to many of these ductile, doe-eyed, dewy little damsels with their angular figures, minimal crocheted cover-ups and pigeon toes was: bring on the lollipops, and welcome the stranger who offers you sweets.

Where the print media were concerned, an irreconcilable polarity was taking shape. Since 1964, Hugh Hefner's *Playboy* magazine had declared itself 'the largest-selling men's magazine of all time', having

The discreet, lace-trimmed dolly-bird look referenced maidenly Victoriana, while putting the emphasis on wide-eyed immaturity and availability. Designs by Barbara Hulanicki for the Biba catalogue, 1965.

hit on a winning combination of cultural heft and titillating arousal: über-reputable writers such as Harold Pinter and Jean-Paul Sartre were juxtaposed with alluring centrefolds of 'playmates' baring refulgent, gravity-defying breasts. But particularly indigestible were '*Playboy*'s Party Jokes':

'There's nothing like a girl with a plunging neckline to keep a man on his toes . . .'

'Then there was the girl who didn't know she'd been raped until the check bounced . . .'

Playboy's cartoons meanwhile paraded a regiment of pneumatic pink plasticised totty across its pages, and the adverts sold deodorants, slimline slacks and car coats with the aid of simpering females gazing in adoration at the proud possessors of the relevant merchandise.

However, 1965 also heralded a refreshingly brazen stance in the written and published word. The inexpensive paperback had democratised reading – although escapist titles such as Mills and Boon's *Inherit My Heart* and *Beloved Tyrant* still dominated the market. By 1965 women were also spending approaching £80 million a year on weekly and monthly magazines. But the time had come for a new tone of voice. Since the 1920s, magazines like *Woman*, *Woman's Realm*, *Good Housekeeping* and *Woman's Own* had been addressed to housewives. Their pages opened onto a world of knitting patterns, batch-baking and fancy garnishes. Magazines like this were read by over 80 per cent of women. *Woman's Own* told the housewife how to homemake. *Honey* (launched in 1960) told the teenager what to buy; its typical reader loved clothes, travel and boys, wanted to get married at twenty-five and earned £10 a week. For younger girls *Jackie* (from 1964) provided prim fantasy fodder. But there had been little on offer for women who looked beyond home, shopping and romance. Now, at last, editors and writers were stepping out of line, agitating to be heard by intelligent and grown-up readers.

'It makes me hopping mad when I hear of any man who regards a woman, especially his wife, as less than an adult human being . . .' wrote Mary Stott in *The Guardian* in 1965, commenting on the case of a reader whose husband had finally granted her a personal allowance of five shillings a week. Under Stott's editorship her page, 'Mainly for Women', had grown to become a security zone for its readers, where they could share thoughts about relationships, morals and manners. Another ground-breaking publication was *Nova*: 'a New Kind of Magazine for a New Kind of Woman'. *Nova*, launched in March 1965, was for adults: women who had 'more to think about than what to do about dinner'. That year it ran features on New Wave cinema, venereal disease, racism, contraception, impotence, abortion, logical positivism, female sterilisation and childbirth. Its cover images of gingered-up, supercharged, unsmiling women became legendary, and its distinctive typography and layouts instantly made the fancy-garnish brigade look obsolete. Elizabeth David wrote the cookery column, and the fashion pages featured black models.

In *Nova*'s September '65 issue their star reporter, American journalist Ruth Inglis, explored the female zeitgeist through fiction. She identified the cream of the crop of London's literary women – Doris Lessing, Brigid Brophy and Iris Murdoch – and argued that there was a prevailing mood of sexual abandonment running through their writings. 'Sex is great . . .', proclaimed Inglis. Her article exactly caught the spirit of the times and the spirit of *Nova*'s readership – while *Nova* itself hacked a path through the chauvinist thorns and briars which for decades had kept thousands of Sleeping Beauties eloquently confined and intact in their sugarplum castles, frozen in time.

In *1965: The Year Modern Britain was Born* (2014), the journalist Christopher Bray makes the claim that not only was '65 a year of defining impact culturally, ethically, politically and technologically, but it was also 'the year feminism went mainstream'. His claim is premature. *Nova* (which doesn't get a mention in his appraisal of the year) barely uses the word 'feminism'. Juliet Mitchell had yet to write *Women: The Longest Revolution*, her ground-breaking discussion of male oppression, which would pave the way for a genuine new-wave of feminism. But in 1965 there were dawning signs of a female fightback, with women talking, writing, being heard and being read in a way that was different.

Christopher Bray's book rightly makes reference to a TV drama screened that year, Nell Dunn's *Up the Junction*. The play was based on Dunn's book of the same name, published two years earlier: a series of vignettes of working-class women's lives south of the river, faithfully portraying all their foul-mouthed, poverty-stricken, carnal realities.

The book of *Up the Junction* had shocked, but the drama shocked more (unsurprisingly, it was one of Mrs Whitehouse's targets). Set in the lee of Battersea Power Station's steaming towers, Dunn's documentary-style script caught the voices of a female community, with the volume turned up to loud:

'I never once lay down with him. I used to meet him in a back alley off the Latchmere. I didn't really know what he was at – I never got no pleasure out of it.'

'Do you like 'em fair or dark?'
  'It's not their 'air I'm interested in!'

'When you love a boy, you want to give him the best thing in the world, and there is only one thing, isn't there?'

'They say it's marvellous when yer naked . . .'

The director (Ken Loach) was equally unsparing in filming a harrowing scene in which one of the girls, seventeen-year-old Rube, miscarries and nearly dies after a botched backstreet abortion, cost: £4. Barely two miles from the peacock paradise of King's Road, a London of debt, deprivation and slum demolition was a sooty, grimy contrast to the boutiques and bright lights of Swinging London.

The two worlds shared little in common, beyond the new norm of sexual laxity, for which women were still expected to pay a heavy price.

Paying For It

It was quite a lot of money – round about £100* I think. Which was why people who couldn't afford it drank bottles of gin and stuck knitting needles up their bottoms.
  Getting a safe abortion was a rich person's sport. There was a guy in Harley Street who had a very good trade in women like me . . .

* Getting on for £2,000 today.

As she put it, Kristina Reed had 'fallen on her face'.

Having got rid of her virginity, Kristina discovered that it was easy to include a busy sex life in her round of social activities. She rarely stayed the night with any of her lovers, and her parents were left in the dark. But the sex wasn't all that much fun.

> Each time I thought, well maybe *this* will be the time when I'll discover exactly what it's all supposed to be about. Because I can't see the point of someone just humping you, unless you want a baby . . .

And that was something she emphatically didn't want. Where contraception was concerned, Kristina relied on her partners to take care of things. On this occasion, the man in question was older than her, and she expected him to know what he was doing, but something went wrong. She remembers feeling 'terror, horror, shock . . .' on realising her situation.

> I couldn't even think past today. And all I wanted was for this mess to be over. It's a bit like having a migraine 'cos you've drunk too much the night before. And when you've got the migraine you feel guilty, because you know you inflicted it on yourself, and all you can think about is getting rid of it, whatever it takes. I just wanted to paste a nice clean sheet over this horrible messy page, and go back to what I'd been before.

In the event, she was relatively lucky, and not even out of pocket. Her lover, who was wealthy enough to pay for his pleasures, took the inglorious blunder in his stride. He made arrangements with a clean clinic, and signed the cheque. The staff were kind and non-judgemental. She stayed overnight, went home, and never told her parents a thing. But within a year, Kristina was caught a second time. This time her boyfriend was, ironically, Roman Catholic, but neither of them hesitated in taking what seemed the essential step of a second abortion.

> I didn't ever countenance the thought of having the baby. So it was straight to the clinic – and I was not alone. There really were a LOT of girls this happened to . . .

Across the social spectrum, both married and unmarried, there were a LOT of women breaking the law. A minority of women wanting abortions could seek help, legally, through the National Health Service, but only provided they could demonstrate conclusively that their mental health was at risk. Until 1967 (when the Act was passed that – under certain highly defined circumstances – legalised abortion by registered doctors who could be accessed through the National Health Service) approximately 10,000 abortions were carried out yearly in private clinics across the country, few of them legal, while estimates of illegal 'backstreet' abortions ranged from 15,000 to 100,000 a year. With unwanted pregnancy still a source of shame and family conflict, many a desperate young woman found her way from the provinces to London in hope of a secret termination.

The New London Spy explained that abortions were available in London to anyone who wanted one, at a cost 'from £20 to £300 plus . . .' (Rube's £4 abortion in *Up the Junction* was outside *The Spy*'s experience).

> There must be at least thirty practising abortionists in London, including one who offers a special students' rate. Most of them do it simply for the money, but there are a few who risk their livelihood occasionally in the belief that no woman should be obliged to bear a child which she does not want and which she has conceived involuntarily.

Behind the figures are some harrowing stories. When I started making a wishlist of the kind of women I wanted to interview for this book, I didn't include on it 'Woman willing to talk about having abortion' – and that was because I didn't have to. A surprising number of women I contacted for other reasons, Kristina Reed being one, volunteered the fact that they had 'fallen on their faces' in the pre-Abortion Act era. Another was Carmen Callil, who told me with horror that 'this was one of the worst things that ever happened to me in my life'. Carmen got pregnant despite being sensibly equipped with a Dutch cap. At this time she was an anxious, fragile and unstable young woman who had already made a suicide attempt. 'I really wanted to die.' Her wealthy married boyfriend would never permit her to go ahead with a baby. Instead, he set her up with a therapist, who was able to arrange a National Health abortion by claiming that Carmen suffered from 'mental instability'. But the interrogation process put her through hell, and caused excruciating delays. The procedure was performed five months into her pregnancy, and she was exceedingly ill as a result. 'And you know, what I think about "women's right to choose", and all that, is that an abortion is the most <u>unspeakable</u> experience you can have in your life, and you don't need anybody else telling you what to do. It's just *shocking* to have to do it –'cos you *know* it's a living creature.'

A third woman who told me about her experiences was Sophie Jenkins, who, at the age of seventeen, had what she described as 'a DIY abortion'. She and her boyfriend, Jeremy – who at that time was working as a part-time auxiliary in a mental hospital – had gone 75 per cent of the way; their petting sessions were non-penetrative. But rumours abounded about the risks, 'and I didn't know enough about sex to know what could make you pregnant and what couldn't'. So when Sophie missed a period, she panicked. No way could she have a baby. 'It was the most terrible thing. And I only considered going through an abortion because I had seen, through the example of a girl at my school, how much shame there was attached to being an unmarried mother. Another girl at my school gassed herself because she was pregnant.' It never occurred to Sophie to tell her parents. Instead, she confided straight away in Jeremy, who spoke privately to a medical friend at the hospital. There was, it appeared, a combination of abortifacient drugs that could do the trick. So he stole them from the hospital dispensary. Sophie went to his tiny bedsit on a Saturday afternoon and took a dose of the tablets, followed by an injection administered by an inexperienced student friend of Jeremy's, and then spent the next two hours vomiting, convulsing and having extreme diarrhoea. 'It was frightening and disgusting, and a terrible risk. Those two hours count among the most horrible of my life.' A couple of days later she had her period. 'And I never even knew whether I *was* pregnant . . .'

Amanda Brooke-Dales was another woman who needed little encouragement to talk about the circumstances of having an abortion in the 1960s. Born into a military family in 1941, Amanda's teens were a time of court shoes, cocktail suits and properly 'done' hair. By 1965 she was a sophisticated, trendy twenty-four-year-old graduate working in the social secretariat of the American embassy and enjoying all that Swinging London had to offer. Her mother, as she explained, was clear-sighted, but nevertheless baulked at confronting the implications of her daughter's sex life. Instead, she enlisted a worldly family friend to talk to Amanda about sex and contraception, which she did, over a gin and tonic, before producing a Dutch cap in a box and packing her off to consult her own gynaecologist. Despite this, something went wrong. 'I was having an on-off fling with somebody, and managed to get pregnant . . .' There was no question of marrying the father, 'and I did feel very much that women should be allowed to choose whether or not they went through with a pregnancy'.

> I just knew immediately that it was a mistake. He didn't want it, and I didn't want it, and it had to be dealt with.

So it was back to the gynaecologist – who had a network of colleagues prepared to perform the operation. Amanda was passed first to a 'celebrity' abortionist in Mayfair,* whom she found slimy, patronising and loathsome. She then transferred to a clinic in Wimbledon, where the Belgian immigrant doctor treated her in a matter-of-fact, human way. 'He made me feel that this was just something unfortunate that was now going to be sorted out.' Though Amanda's father was never told, her mother went with her to hold her hand. 'It was manageable. But it was all deeply unpleasant. Everything about it was horrible. It was over quite quickly, and I was stuffed full of gauze and told to go home and lie down.' What did it cost? 'About £150, I think. The guy paid.'

> Actually, it was more physically than emotionally unpleasant. I've not been tormented by it – though it did come back to haunt me, when it turned out, much later, that I couldn't have children. And I did rather wonder whether I'd done something horrible to myself.

---

* The celebrity abortionist was Edward ('Teddy') Sugden, known as the Deb's Delight, a favourite consultant to society women from his practice in Half Moon Street off Piccadilly. Sugden had a dubious reputation as a womaniser and participant in orgiastic parties. He had also performed a murky legal balancing act by procuring the lethal tablets with which Stephen Ward committed suicide. Ward's death might have come as a relief to Sugden, since the police may have been intending to implicate him together with Ward on charges of procuring abortion.

Meanwhile 'Marion', a London art student, told her story to Charles Hamblett and Jane Deverson, the authors of *Generation X*. After failing to induce her period using pills, Marion asked around and was recommended an abortionist, who met her and her boyfriend in a pub and charged £50. He told her he 'did' a lot of celebrities. On the appointed day he turned up, gave her a douche and went away. Hours later she started to abort.

> There was a lot of blood. It was agony, as though my whole inside was being ripped out. I was screaming and screaming. It lasted six hours and I really thought I wouldn't live through it . . .
>
> I haven't slept with a boy since . . .

We have already seen how, the previous year, Kimberley Saunders became one of the many women who attempted – and failed – to self-abort, hoping that her unwanted pregnancy could be curtailed by taking a hot mustard bath and administering quinine. Home abortions were common, and older women in the know passed on recipes to unwilling expectant mothers. Jumping down stairs was often recommended, or violent skipping. Another method was to mix up a solution of soap and boiling water, which was then pumped into the uterus. One woman who didn't realise the mixture had to be cooled first died from internal burns.

It should not be forgotten that married women, often in impoverished circumstances and with large families, bore the brunt when it came to getting rid of an unwanted infant. Few such mothers could find the wherewithal for a safe termination in a clean clinic. Instead, they turned in desperation to home abortifacients, coat hangers and knitting needles, or an amateur with a kitchen table. All too often these operations ended at the mortuary.

Even of those women I spoke to who didn't personally endure the distress of invasive and horrible interventions, a high proportion had friends or acquaintances who did. The experience of 1960s débutante Melissa North echoes those of Kristina Reed and Amanda Brooke-Dales, with the exception that most of the men who impregnated Melissa's friends didn't seem to accept any liability:

> Lots of people got pregnant, the entire time. The girls usually paid. Most people had allowances. It didn't cost that much – though I suppose a bit more than a pair of shoes.

> There was an anaesthetist in Harley Street who must have made a fortune, because posh girls were going there every week . . .

The inner circle knew who to turn to.

> There was one girl who became a very, very posh soubrette, and she was always going off to see whatever-he-was-called. She had about three abortions! I didn't have one. But I went with friends sometimes.
>
> It was a bit like going to the dentist, and people would say, oh dear, I mustn't let that happen again.

Maybe for some it was, indeed, as trivial a matter as having a tooth pulled. But Melissa North's airy manner is untypical – and she herself hadn't undergone the experience. Most of the evidence suggests that having an abortion was a terrifying last resort, whose criminality raised the stakes for women in the unhappy position of wishing to terminate a pregnancy.

As the twentieth century progressed, the gap between statute and social practice continued to widen. By 1965, doing the womanly thing and having a baby was no longer always an inevitability. For Kristina, Melissa, Marion, Kimberley, Amanda, Carmen, Sophie and many thousands more, sex had become detached from reproduction and all that went with it: prams, aprons and a husband to provide them. Instead, the advance of female emancipation brought with it a natural wish to participate in the privileges previously reserved for the non-childbearing half of the population, men. Women wanted access to fulfilling education, to political power, to economic independence, careers, self-realisation, creativity and self-expression – things that, as every mother knows, are far harder to accomplish alongside the demands of motherhood. They wanted equality. And as well as that, they wanted sex – without consequences, and without punishment.

The Abortion Law Reform Association, which had commenced its lobbying campaign in 1936, found new momentum in the revved-up post-war world. By 1965 demands for a change in the law were becoming increasingly vocal, and that year the Labour MP Renée Short introduced a bill outlining provisions for legal terminations. The relatively smooth passage of reform is probably attributable to the self-evidently lamentable status quo. For law-makers and politicians, it was a matter of defining parameters and eliminating abuse, and public opinion was approximately three-to-one in favour of reform.

But for some, it remained a matter of absolute morality. The temperature of any debate about the destruction of human life was always going to be heated. 'How', asked one lady correspondent to *The Times*, 'could abortion ever be seen as liberal and humane?' She claimed that the argument that defective infants, babies conceived by a mother with mental health problems, or by a raped mother should be aborted did not hold good; the children should be adopted. 'Do disabled people really wish they had never been born?' asked another, questioning the eugenics dimension of the debate. 'Let us call a spade a spade,' wrote a (male) Cambridge don, asserting that it was arrant hypocrisy to assert the human rights of the mother while killing the live organism in her womb – for any human being was surely created nine months prior to its birth.

Ann Widdecombe was another who argued then, and over the years to follow, that it was wrong to take life in any circumstances other than when it was necessary in order to save life. As a convinced Christian at Birmingham University in the mid-sixties, she cut her debating teeth on the issue, when it was proposed, as part of a provocative motion, that abortion was one of the signs of a civilised society. In such strongly left-wing student circles, her outspoken anti-abortion views couldn't have been less popular. Nevertheless, they twice won her the debating cup.

Belinda Mitchell, a trainee nurse in the first half of the sixties, was shocked when she realised that her hospital had a semi-secret ward where women who were having abortions were looked after. Belinda and her fellow trainees were deliberately kept blinkered from certain facts of hospital life deemed unsavoury for young women; for example, they were prevented from watching deliveries in the maternity ward, and during Belinda's brief nursing career she never saw any male genitals. But the young nurses were also steered away from that particular 'shady little ward' whose true function was never specified, separate from the main gynaecological wards and containing just six beds. Belinda heard whispered accounts that its occupants were there because they were having terminations under the NHS 'mental health' criteria.

But had having an abortion become just too easy? This young woman, interviewed by an oral historian, was comfortable with the step she had just taken:

> As I left the abortion ward the doctor said, 'Take the Pill and don't come back.' I got back into the swing of life. There was no grief, nothing.

Nurse Mitchell was sceptical about what she saw as a loophole. 'Being pregnant was inconvenient. You might just want to go on a skiing holiday – so you simply said, "My mental health's at risk . . ."' She brooded and worried:

> I wanted to know the truth of things. Other people didn't seem to be like that. But when a person acts, they need to know what exactly they are doing. So I made myself pretty unpopular by asking people, 'Do you know what abortion actually *is*?'

She procured leaflets that included unsparing images of aborted foetuses, and from then on seized whatever opportunity came her way to inform acquaintances, strangers and anyone who would listen about the realities of abortion.

> What the leaflets were about was, these are the facts. I said, if you're pro-abortion, you need to know the facts. This is actually what is being done. I wanted people to know the facts about foetal development – that, you know, a foetus isn't just a bundle of cells.
>
> I wasn't 100 per cent anti-abortion in all circumstances. I do think there are awful things that have to happen sometimes. But it was the idea that people would choose to undergo abortions for trivial reasons that bothered me.
>
> And it's all very well, you know, as T. S. Eliot said, 'Mankind cannot bear too much reality.' And yes, sometimes, terrible decisions have to be made. But, well – just don't trivialise them.

*

The arguments of those who supported abortion law reform in the mid-1960s were strengthened by the growing scandal of thalidomide. At its height in 1962, a poll showed 73 per cent of the public to be in favour of legal abortion where a child might be born with physical impairments. Between 1963 and 1965 membership of the Abortion Law Reform Association doubled, while its officials also claimed support from over 200 MPs, attributing both factors to the all-too-visible tragedy of hundreds of deformed babies born to mothers who had unwittingly taken Distaval.

1965 was the year that Margaret and Billy Hogg finally got confirmation of the fact they had long suspected – despite the assurance given to Margaret by her GP that he had not given her Distaval – that their son David was indeed a thalidomide child. The Hoggs' conviction sent them to see specialists at a hospital in Stirling in search of medical proof for the cause of David's condition.

> And the doctor examined him and that, and he turned to the other doctor and he says, 'Well, this little lad is a typical thalidomide person. You just have to look at his eyes to find out. He has the standard Columbine eye of a thalidomide.'
>
> That's the iris. It's pear-shaped and it's down in the bottom of the pupil. He says, 'David is thalidomide.' He says, 'There is no doubt about it,' he says. 'Apart from that, he has the same arms, same hands and, unfortunately, the same nose.'

David's arms and hands were little fingered appendages. The bridge of his nose was flat.

And so began a story, for Margaret Hogg, that to this day has still not ended: a daily test of patience and resilience, a growing anger at those responsible, a solidarity with other women also struggling to mother their impaired children, a fight for justice. A story of learning, day after day, what David could and couldn't do. Of discovering that her GP, fearful of exposure, had destroyed her medical records. Of pride, morale and determination. There were days when there wasn't enough money, when support systems failed, days when Margaret – who had left school at the age of fifteen – felt swamped by complicated red tape.

But Margaret has never felt personal guilt. And she maintains to this day that she wouldn't have had things any different.

> No. Somebody once said to me, 'If this happened now, where you have scans and everything else, would you have went through wi' that pregnancy?' And I said, 'Yes'. And they said, 'Why?'

I says, 'Well: one,' I says, 'David was a baby. And two,' I says, 'I cannot agree wi' abortions.' I says, 'I would never have had an abortion.' I says, 'What other people do is up to them. For me, the taking of life is just – well, it's wrong.'

I would never say I'd change things. I used to say to Billy over the years, 'By God, I've got a broad back and He keeps giving me it . . .' And as my mother always instilled in me, 'You are never given more than you could bear.'

It happened for a reason, and that was that.

And what was that reason? Margaret Hogg's eloquence, strength, courage and principles testify to a life well lived. Born in wartime into a low-income household, she grew up with limited horizons. Her twice-widowed mother slaved in factories to get food on the table. Margaret herself, like the majority of her generation, didn't look for a future beyond humble work, marriage – and motherhood. But it was this last that catapulted her into unimagined territory. It helped her grow up, and grow as a woman. Since its foundation, Margaret Hogg has been an active trustee of the Thalidomide Society, in due course becoming vice-chair and chair. More recently she has been awarded the status of honorary trustee of the society. These posts have brought her a wealth of enriching experience and friendships. She has triumphantly conquered a fear of standing on a platform, speaking from the heart about her son and his fellow-thalidomiders in front of a packed audience at the Wellcome Trust in London. Afterwards, one of the listeners told her, 'When you started, there was a hush – you could have heard a pin drop,' and for months afterwards, there were requests for transcripts of her talk. Over the years Margaret has given numerous interviews to reporters for press and television, and recently, after years of self-denial provoked a debilitating crisis of confidence, she took the decision to enrol on a rewarding college course in Women and Health, proving to herself yet again that she had staying power and ability. 'I had a fantastic tutor, and she says, "You'd lost yourself" – She said, "You've needed this time to pull yourself back, to remind yourself who *you* are."' Her life has been one of love, endurance and reward.

Today, Margaret Hogg might agree that thalidomide, though she didn't choose it, chose her.

What to Do About Dinner

In 1965, family life was making unprecedented demands on Margaret
Hogg. But from time to time she opened a newspaper. And what she
saw there made her angry. The press had appropriated a term first
used by American *Vogue* editor Diana Vreeland to describe the dizzy-
ing upheavals in fashion, pop culture and music that were putting
youth in the forefront of change. This 'Youthquake' was beginning
to change the scenery of the nation that Margaret had grown up in:

> It would come out in the papers, all that 'the youth of today' had been
> up to. And I used to say, 'They need a good damn smack on the back-
> side!' To me they didnae seem to have any values, they didnae seem
> to have any respect for their elders.
>
> And I used to think to myself, looking at them with their dirty
> long hair, Good God, where's your self respect? Go and wash your
> face and brush your hair!

Margaret was not in a minority. It helps to understand the new
topography if the Youthquake's highly coloured and vivid eruptions
are projected against the respectable, class-ridden, boring, at times
eccentric screen of our national daily life.

For Harold Wilson's Britain remained a land of gentility, stoicism,
sobriety, rigidity and tedium; of freezing houses, of Tudor coaching
inns converted into steak houses, of silver that needed polishing, of
navy-blue houndstooth, drip-dry shirts, coal tar soap, peppermint
creams and potted calceolarias. A land of bingo halls, budgerigars
and hairdressing salons. A land, too, of women whose primary concern was – as *Nova* had described it – 'what to do about dinner'.

Through the decade, fanned by Betty Friedan's portrayal of neurosis in the domestic doll's house (and by the *News of the World*), the
presumption gained currency that such women were martyrs to
motherhood and homemaking. 'I wonder if people realise how easy it
is to become a drug addict these days,' wrote one, under the headline
'Anguish of a Pep-Pill Wife'. 'I went to the family doctor two years
ago because I felt tired. How I wished to God I hadn't . . .' 'Doctor
please, some more of these . . .' ran the Jagger/Richards lyric to

'Mother's Little Helper', written in 1965. The politician Edith Summerskill had described the London suburban housewife as 'one of the loneliest people in the country'; her only regular point of contact being the doctor's waiting room, where she patiently waited to pick up her prescription for phenobarbitone tablets, to ward off 'nerves'; while a mid-century overview of the 'permissive morality' presented a portrait of 'Mrs Jones', a daydreaming, enervated, sensation-hungry housewife, who found stimulus in her daily life only through the 'telly', and 'pep tablets'.* 'She exists in an almost incessant round of titillation, leading inevitably to emotional exhaustion.'†

Nevertheless, there is plenty of evidence that dinner, children and knitting patterns were meaningful pursuits for enormous numbers of women. Here are some glimpses.

Harriet Debenham's adventurous spirit had been fed by a year spent crewing on a transatlantic yacht, bumming in a Californian ski resort, and then rejoining her crew to sail the Pacific. In 1964 she had come back to England and taken a stiflingly dull job as a receptionist in a London advertising agency. When I pressed her: 'But surely London was the centre of the universe at that time?' she replied:

> *Was* it? Swinging London? I don't think I even noticed it. People talked about Mods and Rockers, but I never came across any.
>
> Yes, I did wear short skirts, because they were practical for bicycling, but you know, I'm not interested in fashion and clothes. Or having my hair done, or shopping.

Bred in rural Sussex, Harriet's country soul yearned for fresh air, home-made jam, ponies and furrows. Her first sight of Nick Lear was one winter's day on a ploughed field, dressed in white knee breeches

---

* *The Permissive Morality* (1964), by C. J. and Winifred M. Whiteley.
† In 1959 my own mother found herself fainting with the pressures of running a home and looking after three very young children. She turned to her GP for help, and the locum on duty prescribed a course of tablets which were a revelation. 'Suddenly I was bursting with energy, and managing on four hours' sleep without batting an eyelid!' When they ran out she returned for a top-up prescription, only to be told by her regular doctor that he could not recommend her continuing with the amphetamines, since they were highly addictive. To her astonishment she realised that for three weeks she'd been on speed.

and a green coat, whipping in the beagle pack with her father and brothers. In 1965 Nick proposed, and they arranged a spring wedding. Nick would continue to earn his living as a solicitor, they would settle into a farmhouse, Harriet would cook and care for hearth and home, and then there would be babies: lots of them.

A glance through almost any generic women's magazine mid-decade reveals the social aspirations of the mainstream middle-class wife. In this world dinner parties were a minefield of taste and taxonomy: what cutlery to use for your avocado vinaigrette, which glass to drink your whisky from, what to talk about; how to serve *coq au vin*, trifle or Camembert with crackers. Sixties Britain may have been a hybrid of posh and proletarian – but the social rigidities were as coagulated as the chocolate mousse. Belinda Mitchell regarded dinner parties as a non-negotiable aspect of her role as a newlywed. She married her husband in 1965, and they honeymooned in a bed-and-breakfast lodging in Scotland, where they were told, '"It's single rooms you'll be wanting . . ." – until we could prove that we were married.' As a young wife (when she could spare time from her personal mission to inform anyone who would listen about abortion) there were social imperatives: playing house, tending your yoghurt plant ('we all had them . . .'), going to dressmaking classes and entertaining; Belinda quickly learnt to whip up delicacies with her Kenwood Chef. Kitchen gadgets had status. Since it was first introduced into the UK in 1961, the Tupperware party had been a fixture on the young-wife circuit. Imported from America, these highly successful receptions were dreamed up as a sociable way to sell airtight plastic boxes under cover of a girly gathering with dips and drinks. The idea was to tap the commercial potential of the girls' night in, and the jury is still out as to whether this celebrated business model reinforced domestic drudgery or opened a door to female entrepreneurship.

> The only way you could buy Tupperware was through an agent, and the agent wouldn't sell it to you unless you went to a Tupperware party . . .

Often inexperienced, the hostesses who were enlisted to embark on the curious ritual of selling storage containers from the home were supported by the 'Tupperware ladies' who guided them through the intricate maze of Tupperware etiquette. You were expected to serve cheese and pineapple on sticks. This was followed by funny party games, like: 'Cut an image of your husband out of a sheet of newspaper – (we were all assumed to have one).' Only when one had eaten the cheese on sticks and played the funny games, was one allowed to buy any Tupperware.

It sometimes seemed a heavy price to pay. But I loved Tupperware, and all my 1960s purchases are still in regular use over fifty years later.

Kitchens and their contents had the power to communicate women's dreams. From Scandinavian ceramics to spice jars, tinned spaghetti hoops to psychedelic tea caddies, Pyrex to prawn cocktails, the sixties domestic heartland conveyed hints of exotica, modernity-worship, colour, convenience and clean lines.

However, a host of social and behavioural assumptions accompanied the Cinzano cocktails and eggs in aspic. The effusive romantic novelist Barbara Cartland codified these in a 1960s edition of her *Etiquette Handbook*. Here's a flavour:

– Unless she is ill a woman should get up and cook her husband's breakfast before he goes to work in the morning. It is bad manners to do this in curlers, without lipstick . . .

– It is dirty and slovenly for people to have dinner in the clothes they have worn all day . . . I am really shocked by many people who . . . rush into dinner unwashed and with dirty shoes – the men often without a tie.

– I always advise mothers to take their daughters to a Beauty Parlour and have them shown how to make-up properly . . . The great thing is to see that a standard of good taste in lipstick and eyeshade is reached as quickly as possible.

– Generally speaking, I believe that young people will not be involved in immorality or unsuitable love affairs if they have been brought up with high standards.

– When drinking a cocktail or any other drink it is completely wrong to say: 'Cheers!'

Reading Cartland today, it is easy to see why, for a generation of rebels, any amount of indulgence, dissipation, colour, flamboyance and excess was preferable to this.

The Priesthood

The underground all sprang out of the fact that there was a community of people who wanted to see silent Japanese films, and lie on cushions, and smoke dope and take psychedelics.

Somehow, Melissa North sensed that there was more to life than going to dances, having a boyfriend with a Ferrari and holidaying in St Tropez. The marriage market was starting to seem irrelevant. At the age of eighteen she had completed her débutante year, lost her virginity to Nigel Dempster, learnt to type badly, worked for a Mayfair-based publishing company and spent a lot of weekends at posh country houses. In the early and mid-sixties she was sharing a flat near South Kensington tube station with three girlfriends named Jacquetta, Camilla and Theodora. But something was missing: a different kind of fun, a different set of ideas.

By chance, one day at a Chelsea party, she got to know a new crowd. These boys were graduates from the Architectural Association. They came from exotic eastern European and Jewish backgrounds; they spoke differently, they dressed differently from the tweedy boys she knew, and they had names that didn't appear in *Debrett's*. They had fallen under the spell of Le Corbusier's ideas about class, housing and urbanism; while as émigrés they cared deeply about the disadvantaged, about economics and left-wing politics. They were concerned too about the rapid escalation of the ideological East–West conflict in Vietnam. 'And they lived in this mysterious place called north London . . .'

The AA boys seemed to regard women differently too. As Melissa recalls:

They were all educated people, you know? With clever mothers who taught at LSE or whatever . . . They'd been brought up in intellectual, artistic families, in which the women often ruled the roost . . .

And I thought, they're cool. This is where I want to be . . .

Tchaik Chassay was the handsome architecture graduate at the centre of the group; he and Melissa immediately fell for each other.*

> So Nigel Dempster kind of withered away, and I went out with Tchaik and discovered this startling new world, which was incredible fun.

Melissa and Tchaik were at the very heart of what would soon become known as the underground. Their network of friends encompassed a near-indefinable mix of poets, artists, musicians, beats, students, publishers, actors and intellectuals. Today we might use the word 'fringe' or 'bohemian' to describe their world, which both paralleled and intersected that of the Swinging London trend-setters. But, as so often, there was dissociation between the two. 'We thought "Swinging London" was the most ghastly expression,' says Melissa, 'I *mean*, yeuurgh!' In the introduction to *Too Much*, his analysis of the 1960s, the cultural historian Robert Hewison deftly disentangles them:

> From 1964 to 1967 . . . two ideologies were developing in parallel: the affluent and hedonistic Sixties of 'Swinging London', and the oppositional culture of the underground. They have important cross-relationships; they both depended on a particular set of economic circumstances, they were both heralded by particular developments in the arts, and they both aimed at a kind of personal liberation. Yet the logic of the underground was ultimately opposed to the materialism which had created the opportunity for it to flourish.

Swinging London comprised the fashion crowd and the pop crowd. Melissa's circle overlapped, but it was arty, avant-garde and intellectual; a world of blues bands, little magazines, artistic happenings and – until they discovered pound blocks of hashish – ten-bob deals of Jamaican grass purchased from the dealers who hung out at the Rio in Notting Hill Gate.

Melissa North, however, had left publishing behind, and branched into rock'n'roll. A young, cocksure bunch of laddish fortune-hunters

---

* 'Tchaik', shortened from 'Tchaikovsky', was the nickname of Michael Chassay, so called by fellow pupils at their progressive school, Bedales, who had latched on to his Russian-Jewish ancestry.

were moving into the world of agenting and music publishing; and Melissa found her dream job on the top floor of Bryan Morrison's ramshackle new company overlooking Denmark Street – aka Tin Pan Alley. It included booking gigs for the Pretty Things and the newly formed Pink Floyd.

Melissa loved the informality and excitement of her job; the music was a turn-on and she was steeped in it ('though nobody there asked my opinion on anything to do with it, not ever!'). But Bryan Morrison and his swaggery East End mates took a bit of getting used to, even for a rebel débutante. They were a shocking contrast to the poetry-lovers and intellectuals she hung around with, and a reminder that a minority of women might regard respect as their due. Working at the Morrison Duncan agency, Melissa's posh accent made her the office laughing stock, while Bryan would summon her from behind his partition to talk through a contract, with a casual 'Come here, cunt!' His language was larded with 'fucks', and he and his partner made no attempt to suppress their foul-mouthed male banter; so-and-so was 'a dog'; they'd 'given her one'. Some of the musicians were sordid and predatory – 'they'd sit on my desk and say, well, sexist things . . .' – but, not being a dolly bird, Melissa evaded most of their approaches. 'I wasn't their type.'

Her own type was distinctly cultured and thoughtful by comparison.

Most of us had a rather earnest side – however naive it was . . .

she remembers. They were well read, too – 'We . . . were interested in writers who showed how they were challenging "straight" perceptions' – and deeply respected the thinking of writers like P. D. Ouspensky, Wilhelm Reich, Aldous Huxley, William Burroughs, Jean Genet and Carl Jung, who questioned conventional world views.

In the summer of 1965 London was full of poets. As Melissa recalled:

Before the music thing really got huge, poetry was like rock'n'roll. It had a huge following. One went to every poetry thing that was going.

And 11 June 1965 saw the 'poetry thing' to end all poetry things: a pivotal date in the annals of the underground. Somebody had decided an 'International Poetry Incarnation' could fill the Albert Hall. Every poet in sight was rounded up. There were portents of the coming of flower power. The night before the reading, the actress Kate Heliczer and some friends were inspired to salvage leftover blooms from the florists at Covent Garden★ and bring them to distribute at the reading. They painted their faces in psychedelic colours and handed out the flowers. To everyone's astonishment, over 7,000 people came; some even had to be turned away.

No women poets were included in the twenty-odd performers billed to read. But the Albert Hall's vast circular auditorium was liberally decorated not just with flowers but with a sea of shapely legs, flowing locks and false eyelashes. As Allen Ginsberg clanked a set of Tibetan handbells and droned an incomprehensible chant, a young woman in the front row, dressed in matching spotty Quant-style dress and hat, waved her flower hypnotically and dragged on an unspecified roll-up. Then Adrian Mitchell did a crowd-pleasing chorus of 'Tell Me Lies About Vietnam'. Later in the performance Ginsberg, looking like a bespectacled prophet, returned unsteadily to the platform, to declaim his free verse with blurred, fire-and-brimstone intensity:

> *I am that I am I am the*
> *Man and the Adam of hair in*
> *My loins . . .*

while a solitary nymph in a frilled mini-dress, maybe tripping, swayed balletically, rocking, dancing, clasping and fluttering her arms from the front row. Over all hung a haze of reefer smoke.

Melissa's American friend Sue Miles recalled that Ginsberg was drunk. For her, the occasion had little artistic merit –

– ghastly poetry, unbelievably bad . . .

Its significance was of a different nature. It was about 'discovering that there were more of you around than you thought'. It was a moment of sharing: of astonished awareness that here was a previously unsuspected

★ Until 1974 Covent Garden was still a working fruit, vegetable and flower market located in central London.

groundswell of nonconformity, containing the makings of a genuine counterculture, and the reassurance that as rebels and free spirits they were not deviants adrift, but could lay claim to a sense of belonging, a fellowship and a communal homeland.

Most of them were under thirty, and with their new-found sense of empowerment, they set out to live their lives differently.

The underground's moment was brief, according to Melissa. Barely five years, between 1963 and 1968, during which a quite small group of individuals spread their ripples out from a creative heartland located in London. If you knew the people, you knew where to go. In 1963, by her own account, Marianne Faithfull was among those who looked on starry-eyed in a Chelsea coffee bar as the black-clad male priesthood determined the future course of civilisation: '[London's] going to be the psychic bloody centre of the world, man!' declared one of the beatniks. The outcome was Indica Books and Gallery in Southampton Row, which in 1965 supplanted the hot-spot bookshop and performance space Better Books as a magnet for the avant-garde. In 1966 'Hoppy' Hopkins and Joe Boyd founded the music venue UFO in Tottenham Court Road before moving it briefly (prior to its demise) to the Roundhouse in Chalk Farm. The Roundhouse was also the site of one of the counterculture's most famous events, the launch of *IT* magazine in 1966 – 'the *International Times* First All-night rave Pop Op Costume Masque Drag Ball Et Al'. After 1967 it would be the Arts Lab in Drury Lane, founded by Sue and Barry Miles (who was always known simply as Miles) and their fellow networker Jim Haynes. The Arts Lab was a cinema, bookshop, café, rehearsal space, pick-up joint, drug den and crash pad rolled into one: a venue saturated with the scent of hashish, patchouli and unwashed socks.

In this world, fame and wealth blended seamlessly with Bohemia. Seen through Melissa's eyes, it was a community of creativity, idealism and personal liberation with no down side. Sexual freedom was taken for granted. Melissa's beautiful flatmate Celia's love life veered between the extremes of Cockney street cred and blue-blooded royalty, as she alternated liaisons with film star Terence Stamp and Prince William of Gloucester. 'You'd hear them clomping up the stairs, but you never knew which one it was going to be.'

Here's a day in Melissa's life:

A typical evening was, come home from work – go to bed for a couple of hours, and have a snooze. About nine or ten in the evening people would start turning up, and we'd convene in the attic – which we'd converted into this big room with floor cushions. Dress up, change a bit. Then we'd go down to Blaise's club in Queensgate. Might see Ike and Tina Turner, the Byrds . . . the first time I saw Jimi Hendrix was in Blaise's. So then you'd swirl around with all your friends, probably till about two.

Then we would come back to our flat, and we'd go upstairs to the top room, make tea, roll a joint. And then we'd do mad things, I remember we read *The Hobbit* aloud for a month, with people taking turns. And we'd stay up till about five. And then I'd have to be in the office by ten next day to answer the telephone but nobody ever came in till one o'clock.

We thought drinking was boring, it was what old people did, so we didn't do much alcohol. We were dope smokers . . .

Men's Club

In 1965 Melissa first took LSD. Tchaik's uncle returned from California with the drug. 'And he gave it to us and we took it, and it was fantastic.' Next day Melissa didn't get into the office until about two in the afternoon. Bryan, her boss, said, 'Where the fuck've you been?' 'I took LSD last night,' she told him. 'You *did*?' Her status rocketed, as Bryan looked at her with a new respect.

Cool, colourful, transcendent, mind-altering, psychedelic drugs were the portal to the underground; their use was a badge of honour, and a signal to the uninitiated that you were a card-carrying member of the permissive priesthood. Melissa and Tchaik were early adopters. Within a year, as we will see, LSD would start to refashion the world view of her generation.

For me, the beat of sixties permissive culture was at its loudest when I was barely ten years old, living in safe suburbia, but its vibrations penetrated my childhood – in the form of art students. My father was their professor. Every June, disorderly, colourful and loud, his final-year students arrived at our house for a night of post-exam revelry washed down with intoxicating brandy-laced punch. They had long hair, wore velvet, colourful prints and scarves – and that was just the men. They ate, drank, smoked and danced, then they took off all their clothes and piled into the ornamental pond in our back garden. They seemed like another species, but they were incredibly beautiful and gorgeous and I loved them. Though I barely understood it, the word permissive – for me (and I suspect for innumerable others) – meant lovely, colourful, exciting and aspirational.

The idea of the permissive society has become synonymous with the 1960s counterculture – as if a few thousand earnest beatniks, stoned poets, groupies, art students and musicians could be credited with a Year Zero refashioning of the social agenda. As the historian Dominic Sandbrook explains in his book *White Heat*, these were not the people responsible for progressive policies such as the introduction of birth-control measures, the abolition of the death penalty (in 1965), the reform of the abortion laws and laws on homosexuality (in 1967), and of the divorce laws (in 1969). A melting-pot of politicians, campaigners, writers and public intellectuals, stretching back over the twentieth and even into the nineteenth century, should rightly be acknowledged for those achievements.

The permissive society grew out of an opposition. The ultra-conservatives of the post-war Establishment – people like Dr Leslie Weatherhead, Mary Whitehouse and the outspoken Christian journalist Malcolm Muggeridge – equated liberal reforms with moral delinquency. Ironically, it was their public antagonism that would energise the counterculture, helping it to punch above its initially very modest weight, and transforming it, by the end of the decade, from a flimsy sideshow into a barnstorming psychedelic circus. What had been fringe fiction was becoming mainstream reality. Small in number, a clutch of fun-loving, often frivolous and fanciful bohemians found their activities magnified under the full-beam glare of hostile media headlights. Pop stars and models, actors and artists were having a party. Come in fancy dress, said the invitation. Under thirties only. Drugs and rock'n'roll, from midnight, but above all, sex – for nothing could be more seductive than the promise implied in those two words 'Free Love'. The old, the square, the bourgeois, the prudish, the passionless, the provincial, the 'moral majority' were not invited. And if the unregulated, untrammelled free-for-all from which they were excluded seemed all the more enviably enjoyable, then they only had themselves to blame for so vociferously denouncing the whole extravaganza.

The counterculture's colour, music and potently idealistic agenda would capture the imagination of a generation. And yet the concerns of older people were often justifiable – like the fear that attached to the use and abuse of addictive and hallucinogenic drugs: 'an infant playing with a lethal weapon . . .' Books like journalist Alan Bestic's *Turn Me On Man: Face to Face with Young Addicts Today* (1966) gave ammunition to those convinced that society was going to hell in a handcart. 'Every heroin addict I met had taken first either marijuana or one of the amphetamine group like purple hearts . . . There were the two sixteen-year-old girls who were addicted to heroin two months after taking their first purple heart . . . There was the girl who sneered at pills, but loved to smoke pot, and who is now hopelessly hooked . . .' Bestic painted a dire picture of seedy pads in dismal seaside towns, underage sex, addiction, withdrawal and death. Reckless, defiant, semi-criminal drifters, the addicts were on the run from their families, earning what they could working in shops, or stealing. The epidemic was spreading, said Bestic, with frightening rapidity. Alarmed legislators moved with all speed to tighten the law.

The press gave endless column inches to the view that civilisation was now sliding down a perilous slope. There was talk of changing the homosexuality laws; an affluent and permissive society was fostering a pernicious increase in teenage violence and crime; in places of entertainment, on the streets, in the cinema and on the stage decency and polite language had been abandoned; England was fast losing its self-respect, its empire and its way. A typical correspondent wrote:

> We live in a permissive society. We are encouraged to believe that pleasure lies in indulgence and all forms of discipline are the enemies of enjoyment. This propaganda reaches us in many ways – through many forms of advertisement and the content of much of our enter-

tainment. To live above this needs an upbringing which today all too few receive. We seek technological advance while our morals rapidly decline.

H. W. Austin
London SW1

★

Halfway through the 1960s, a social ripple was becoming a small but unstoppable wave. Behaviour and beliefs which would enter the mainstream by the mid-1970s were formed at this time – from the scandalous use of the word 'fuck' on television to the questioning of marriage, from drug use to potent, entitled individualism.

This book has set out to ask the question of women, 'How was it for you?' For lots of women like Melissa North and Sue Miles the emergence of the counterculture was mind-altering, exciting and fantastic fun. But a broader reading of the sources tells us that, in a rapidly changing society, men were lagging behind in adjusting their inbuilt prejudices. For starters, the terminology used by men to describe women – 'chicks', 'dollies', 'birds' or even 'Richards' (the preferred Cockney rhyming term for 'bird', derived from 'Richard the Third') – was depressingly belittling. Jenny Diski:

> Most women who lived through the early and late Sixties whether as political molls or psychedelic chicks can recall that they were mostly of ornamental, sexual, domestic or secretarial value to the men striking out for radical shores. The Left was never known for its willingness to embrace gender equality, but no more were the 'heads' or the entrepreneurs of the counterculture.

To some extent, women were complicit in their oppression. Working wives like Joan Bakewell barely quibbled with the expectations laid on her: 'Each of the different segments of my life, the job, the children, the marriage and more, made different demands. I felt I was up to it . . . The entire domestic routine was my responsibility.' White-gloved values were still exerting an undertow. The wives of professional men continued to accept that they left the room to powder their noses after dinner, leaving their husbands to stretch their legs, pass the port and talk politics. Nobody made a fuss about being excluded from masculine preserves like university unions, or men-only clubs. 'Women are not clubbable,' *The New London Spy* baldly informed its readers.

A tangible disrespect and fear of women lay behind this free-masonry; a brand of misogyny that prevailed even in countercultural circles, as Marianne Faithfull discovered: 'It was a men's club that I couldn't join.' Though Marianne loved to get high on hashish, her husband John Dunbar forbade her to roll joints – 'an incredible piece of drug chauvinism'. Singer George Melly's widow, Diana, agreed: 'The British jazz world was as full of chauvinists as other more conventional worlds,' she wrote. 'Men knew best and I never corrected them.' As we saw earlier, the Beatles also fell into this category, with Cynthia Lennon recalling, '[They] were very happy to have their women subservient in the background,' while Beatles lyrics like those of 'Girl' and 'Run for Your Life'* were also unashamedly misogynistic. Meanwhile, the Mick Jagger/Chrissie Shrimpton relationship lurched into crisis when the serially unfaithful Jagger, discovering that Chrissie was having an affair, demanded that she break it off. 'Mick has to be the one in control, giving the orders, calling the shots,' Shrimpton was quoted as saying.

The culture of male control was not confined to rich, powerful celebrities. The divorce courts highlighted extreme cases like that of a Mr Kenneth Cox who objected strenuously when his wife Dorothy became involved with a local Girl Guide and Brownie group. Having already prohibited Dorothy from getting a job, the dictatorial Cox now refused to let her anywhere near the Girl Guides. He also tried to force her to have sex. But both parties' pleas for a divorce on grounds of cruelty were rejected by the judge. Male jealousy and ownership of women were seen as legitimate – 'In my opinion, a man who isn't jealous of his wife isn't in love,' wrote a Glamorgan reader to a national newspaper. Writing in the *Daily Express*, the columnist Peter Grosvenor pondered the difference between the sexes, and concluded that women couldn't write symphonies, had made no

* Both tracks feature on the album *Rubber Soul*, released in 1965.

contribution to science and were less emotionally stable than men. In the workplace, hypocrisy, subordination, harassment and sexism ran amok, with women still expected to make the tea and agree with the men.

But sex was the cauldron that was threatening to boil over. In the 1950s, whether they liked it or not, women had been insulated and armoured against sexual advances, with rigidly structured underwear designed to discourage all but the most persistent of would-be suitors. Now, in the world of miniskirts, lightweight bras and the Pill, men were reduced to perpetual spoiled adolescents, screaming, 'I want it, and I want it now.' Few were prepared for the onslaught; and with their self-esteem still predicated on pleasing men, women like Kristina Reed pacified the tantrums with sexual sweeties. 'Free love' was the mantra – but free for whom? We have seen how, as the prohibitive climate of the 1950s evaporated, Kristina sleepwalked into sexual laxity. The journalist Virginia Ironside was the same: 'For women, it was absolutely grisly . . . I remember the sixties as an endless round of miserable promiscuity. It often seemed easier and, believe it or not, more polite, to sleep with a man than to chuck him out of your flat.' And worse was to come. But in 1965 there was no solidarity, no channel and no vocabulary with which to express discontent. The sexual power struggle was still in its infancy.

1966

Nightmare

In the winter of 1966, the news featured the usual lucky dip of ephemera. The *Daily Mail* diarist told his readers that the French singing star Françoise Hardy had upset management at the Savoy Hotel in London by arriving there in trousers, and *The Times* reported that a bureau was being set up to help train older women and wives hoping to return to work. In February London Transport held a meeting to consider whether to employ female bus drivers, while in Sheffield a row was brewing after the local Youth Service publicly accused the city's stores of endemic racism against young Asian women applying for jobs as shop assistants: 'We don't know of one shop in the city which has a coloured assistant,' said a spokeswoman. 'Coloured girls have been turned down for no apparent reason.' Meanwhile, the country was in the run-up to another general election, called by Harold Wilson for 31 March, to strengthen his precarious majority. Of 1,500 candidates selected, just seventy-four were women – fifteen fewer than in 1964. Soon after, someone had a great publicity-generating idea for how to put fifteen women to good use: set a world record by stuffing them into a Mini.

But as winter turned to spring, one story dominated the headlines. In April 1966 the *Daily Telegraph* invited the novelist Pamela Hansford Johnson to deliver an account of the trial of the decade, that of the infamous Moors murders. The fifty-four-year-old Johnson took her place in the packed Chester courtroom.

> It seemed to some of us that April that we were seeing one of the results of total permissiveness in a rather comely young man and woman, ill-educated but neither of them stupid, on trial at Chester Assizes for multiple murder. A wound in the flesh of our society had cracked open, we looked into it, and we smelled its sepsis.

From where she sat, the author was able painstakingly to observe the defendant Myra Hindley in the dock:

> Sturdy in build and broad-buttocked, though her face, hands and feet appear to be narrow and delicate, she could have served a nineteenth-century painter as a model for Clytemnestra; but sometimes she looks more terrible, like one of Fuseli's nightmare women drawn giant-size ... She wears a grey double-breasted suit with six buttons, a sky-blue shirt open at the neck ... She was dark, once; now she is a Nordic blonde. Her hair is styled into a huge puff-ball, with a fringe across her brows. At the beginning of the trial it was rinsed to a lilac shade, now it is melon-yellow ... But it is the lines of this porce-lained face which are extraordinary. Brows, eyes, mouth are all quite straight, precisely parallel ...
>
> In the dock, she has a great strangeness, and the kind of authority one might expect to find in a woman guard of a concentration camp.

Hindley and her boyfriend Ian Brady had both been arrested in October 1965; investigations provided police with sufficient evidence to charge the pair with the murders of seventeen-year-old Edward Evans, ten-year-old Lesley Ann Downey and twelve-year-old John Kilbride. (Though suspected of the murders of two further victims – Keith Bennett aged twelve, and Pauline Reade, the pretty sixteen-year-old who had gone missing on her way to a Gorton jive club in July 1963 – it was not until the 1980s that their disappearance could be attributed to the pair.) In court that spring, harrowing details emerged of the pitiless cruelty and abuse inflicted on these children. Those in the chamber found it particularly hard to listen when tape recordings were played of Lesley Ann begging her tortur-ers for mercy, while Hindley's voice could be heard telling her, 'Hush, hush, shut up or I will forget myself and hit you one, I will hit you one.' Four of the young victims (as it eventually turned out) had been buried in shallow graves on the lonely heights of Saddleworth Moor.

Today, long after their conviction, and though the murderers are themselves dead, this notorious case leaves us still struggling to make sense of the questions it raised more than fifty years ago: questions of the genesis of evil, of societal responsibility, of media conditioning, of free will, and of clichéd notions of gender. There is general agreement that Ian Brady instigated the crimes, and that he was an unrepentant psychopath, a devil. As a woman, an accomplice, Hindley's role appeared far more complex, yet also more corrupt and treacherous.

On one level, Hindley did what post-war society expected its women to do. Her own family background in a deprived area of Manchester had taught her to suppress her emotions. 'Friday and Saturday nights were known as "wife-beating" nights . . . Pub closing times were dreaded, because we all knew what would happen. Women ran out into the street, trying to escape from being beaten . . .' If you wanted to save your skin, you bottled up your reactions, and you didn't challenge your lord and master. Growing up in the 1950s, the young Hindley had learnt to protect herself by complying with male directives. When she met Brady, she surrendered herself to his world view, swayed and manipulated by his assertive personality. If Brady wanted to abuse, torture and destroy, she had to appease him by wanting those things too. Under his maleficent guidance, she had led the children to their fates. In the role of witch not woman, Hindley could be viewed as even more culpably infamous than Brady. By this construction, she was an apostate, who had betrayed all that women were supposed, biologically, to be: caring, nurturing and tender-hearted. While Brady's crimes bore the plausible taint of male anger and brutality, hers appeared as crimes against nature.

For surely it was Hindley's role in the murder of children that made those acts uniquely chilling, uniquely odious and uniquely transgressive – more so than if Brady had perpetrated them alone.

Many years later, Myra Hindley admitted to her absolute complicity: 'Without me,' she wrote, 'those crimes could probably not have been committed. It was I who was instrumental in procuring the children, children who would more readily accompany strangers if they were a woman and a man than they would a man on his own.' And she is reported to have told her solicitor, 'I have always regarded myself as worse than Brady.'

Myra Hindley's peroxided hair, her dead, implacable eyes, concentration-camp rigour and blackened brows: the horrifying image of this woman is the indelible imprint of her time on this earth. Pamela Hansford Johnson came away from the Chester courtroom convinced that she was living in a sick world. Hansford Johnson's youth was in a past era, before the war; around her, she saw the rules she had grown up with crumbling, new freedoms breaking out, fashions shortening, morals contracting and values eroding. It was all too easy to connect the repulsive, piteous crimes being laid bare in the Chester courtroom with the society that she seemed to observe unravelling before her eyes:

We are in danger . . .

she wrote . . .

. . . of creating an Affectless Society, in which nobody cares for anyone but himself, or for anything but instant self-gratification. We demand sex without love, violence for 'kicks' . . .

As she saw it, the dark side of permissiveness was societal breakdown. Amorality and atrocity seemed to be the consequences of liberality. Even before the murders Ian Brady was a convicted criminal, who had read works by Hitler and the Marquis de Sade; he owned a library of horrors about torture and was fascinated by Nazism; he accumulated pornography and sadistic apparatus. Hindley's glaringly blonde coiffure referenced Aryan supremacy; she acquired guns and acquiesced to Brady's extreme sexual demands. But the Moors Murders happened at a time when some felt that society itself was staring into the abyss. From its depths, a distorting mirror reflected back one ghastly image: a fiend with a chalk-white mask, a surly red gash for a mouth and pitiless black eyes: the woman of our nightmares.

In 1966, fearful mothers held their children closer.

*

Myra Hindley would die in prison in 2002, having been sentenced to two concurrent life sentences. To some, even that punishment seemed insufficient for her unforgivable defection from the ideal of womanhood. The horror-monster Hindley was a measure of how invincible that ideal remained, at a time when women's cosy perfect-wife and nurturing-mother identity seemed, on so many fronts, to be diminishing.

For, tracking the 1960s, it might appear as if women were at last starting to taste liberty, with increased access to education, entry into the workplace and greater availability of contraception. Trousers, miniskirts, the jettisoning of corsetry and virginity, all seemed to point to new, joyful freedoms. A female Utopia seemed possible. Our towns and cities would be full of sexually abandoned *Nova* women with higher thoughts on their minds than what to cook for dinner or potty-training. They would be having gratifying orgasms with their many lovers, going to films by Jean-Luc Godard, and working to make the world a better place. Maybe.

Unsurprisingly, as we will discover, the ascent to female fulfilment was steeper, slower and much more of a struggle than it at first appeared. For the men standing on top of the mountain, the sight of all those armies of approaching women in miniskirts was a gladsome one indeed. But when it came to relinquishing any ground, that was another matter altogether. Mastery of women would remain the acceptable norm – and men had much to fear. Myra Hindley's exercise of brutal force against her victims had broken all the rules of female behaviour. As a society, in 1966, nobody was yet ready for real womanpower, no matter what form it might take.

Party Time

Mavis Wilson felt as free as a bird. If you were pretty, had a glamorous job, a flat and a pay packet, life seemed simple. She had all those things. At the age of seventeen, it felt good to be alive:

> And I was aware what a fabulous time the sixties were for creating, risk-taking, making things and daring to experiment . . .

We have already caught some glimpses of 'dolly bird' Mavis, with her long dark hair and wide blue eyes, shimmying in her mock-croc winkle-pickers past the Kingston Recreation Ground to the sound of the Ronettes on a Saturday morning in 1960. In 1964 she was cheering Harold Wilson to victory to the tune of 'A Hard Day's Night'.

Two years after that, consumed with old-age phobia, she was weeping uncontrollably into her red wine at a party to celebrate her eighteenth birthday:

I'd had such a wonderful year – such a brilliant year of fun and excitement. It had been the best time of my life. At eighteen – it just seemed to me that I was getting so *old* . . .

What did it feel like to be part of 'Swinging London'? For the cocktail of creativity and fashion that had been fermenting since 1963 had now won its label. There are a number of claimants to be its originator. Was it Diana Vreeland in 1965, describing London as 'the most swinging city in the world'? Was it nudged into being that same year by the country-music vocalist Roger Miller, singing 'England Swings'? Or should we credit the bearded British-based American intellectual and editor of *Encounter*, Melvin Lasky, who gave *Time* magazine its April 1966 cover quote: 'London: the Swinging city'? Piri Halasz, who wrote that piece, says, '*Time* didn't create "Swinging London". We only popularised it . . . People were already speaking of "Swinging London" by the time I started work on the cover; the phrase was in the air and being used by my colleagues before we went into print.'

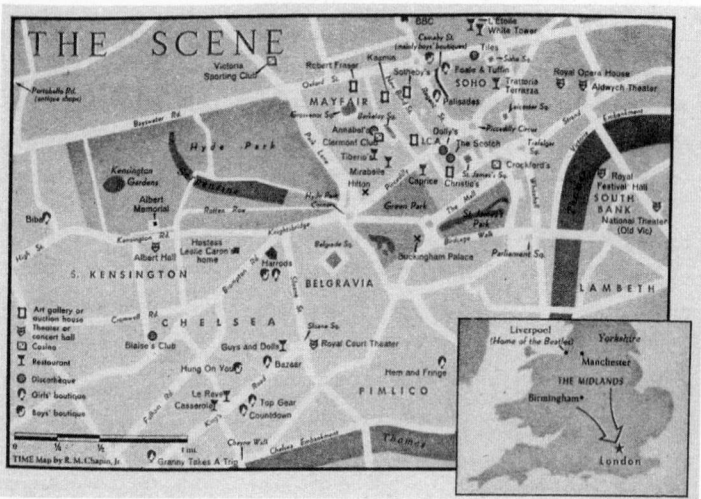

From Tiberio's to Trattoria Terrazza, Blaise's to Biba – where to see and be seen in mid-sixties London. The inset provides a reminder of England's other cultural nerve centre, Liverpool.

Fifty years on, Mavis Wilson (today she is the novelist Mavis Cheek) paints a vivid insider picture of mid-sixties life in our pulsing, rock 'n' rolling, wacky and kaleidoscopic capital city. Nothing could ever be quite so good again.

Mavis had left school at sixteen. The omens for her future weren't bright. Her family background was working class and dysfunctional. Her teachers considered her too weak a student to sit O levels, or even to train to be a secretary, so in 1964 she started job-hunting. 'But can you imagine a better time to hit the ground running?' When she answered an advert for an art gallery receptionist, the new permeability of class divisions worked in Mavis's favour. Editions Alecto were Kensington-based print publishers who sold contemporary lithographs and the like by a range of high-ranking artists from the sixties pop- and op-art scene. And because débutantes in pearls no longer fitted the street-credible image that upmarket art venues like this wanted to project, Mavis – despite being abysmally under-qualified – got the job. 'I was the world's worst typist, I pretended I was capable of transferring a phone call, and I was a complete wide-eyed innocent. But I was pretty, I had long hair, and I was a working-class girl who spoke well. And that was good enough.'

So Mavis learnt to be a social chameleon, and her wonderful new life began. To her astonishment, it was all Christian names. Her bosses were called Joe, Paul and Laurie. Alecto's stable included a roll call of the best contemporary artists: Eduardo Paolozzi, David Hockney, Patrick Caulfield, Gillian Ayres, Jim Dine, Jean Dubuffet, Peter Sedgley and Bridget Riley. Notably, there were few women artists in the top league. Though greatly admired, Ayres and Riley were held up as examples of tough women who had sacrificed their femininity on the altar of their art. Meanwhile, Alecto's clients were a sophisticated mix of the wealthy, the cultured and the celebrated. Kensington was Mavis's stepping-stone to their smart new Mayfair gallery in Albemarle Street. Each day brought delights; from the pleasure of her morning walk to work across Green Park to meeting collectors and dealers who might buy a work of art. The clue to their wealth, she observed, was their shoes. 'Even if they came in looking pretty scruffy, if they'd got a decent pair of shoes on, you could tell they were rich . . . And people were really spending money in the sixties.' At about eleven in the morning Elizabeth, one of the gallery associates, would call out, 'OK, girls, we're all going to have a glass of sherry now,' and crack open a bottle of González Byass. At lunchtime, 'completely plastered', Mavis would roll up Bond Street on the hunt for cheap additions to her wardrobe, or over to Berwick Street fruit and vegetable market, often catching sight of Soho's resident drunken bohemians en route: Francis Bacon or the photographer Dan Farson.

> And if I had a late lunch I would see the tired working girls who'd just woken up, tottering out of their doors to get their coffee or their cigarettes . . .

Then it was back to the gallery for an afternoon familiarising herself with the needs of Alecto's next wave of clients. Six o'clock: time for a mascara top-up ('no girl went anywhere without her make-up bag'); then straight on to an opening.

> You just got invitations to every single opening that happened – and loads happened. So you could go to a party every night.

These ranged from trays of red wine in aid of the latest wannabe abstract expressionist at a neighbouring Cork Street gallery, to the launch of the Space and Air studios at St Katharine's Dock, to an iconoclastic outdoor 'happening' created by light artist Peter Sedgley at Alecto's Kensington premises. On this occasion the guy ropes anchoring Sedgley's giant inflatable artwork completely failed to prevent it going out of control and flattening the string quartet who had been hired to play decorous chamber music in a corner of the courtyard. 'Pete was very radical . . .' Whatever the cultural celebration, Mavis was there. Patrick Caulfield would roll up in a taxi carrying his glass of whisky aloft. David Hockney 'was lovely, absolutely lovely, just a nice guy. Very funny, very witty, very cool . . . Allen Jones – well, one just knew that he liked high heels, big breasts and leather. I mean, that was just Allen. I adored the parties, and people would ask me, "What do you do?" and I would say, "Well, I work in an art gallery . . ." which really gave one kudos.'

Mavis's false eyelashes and short skirts got her plenty of attention too. The cult poet and writer Christopher Logue bought works from Alecto, and was a voyeur. When mini-clad Mavis was sent to deliver some art to his flat he cunningly urged her to climb up the steep steps onto the roof terrace ahead of him. 'Er, no thank you.' She also rejected his offer to get stoned together. In any case, she had a handsome, clever boyfriend of her own, whom she'd met at an offbeat New Year's Eve party in west London full of Communist Party, Ramblers' Association, wholemeal types. By 1965 they were a couple, cohabiting in a 'grotty' Pimlico basement. Mavis's boyfriend, for all his earnest left-wingery, had embarked on a laborious career path, taking a Physics degree, which would lead to a post with the British Iron and Steel Research Association. Nevertheless, he brought with him a democratic band of friends from a wide social range. 'There were about eight of us, a mix of middle class and working class and, for whatever reason, I was included in this group . . .'

Alecto didn't pay a fortune, but Mavis quickly discovered that it wasn't expensive to be hip and 'in it'. The Beautiful People picked up the tab, and it was almost as much fun to window-shop in King's Road as it was to buy the gear in its boutiques. Continental food was fashionable. A bowl of spaghetti or a plate of *huevos a la flamenca* was so much more exotic than egg and chips – and just as cheap. Whatever money you did have, you spent on music. In 1966 the Beatles album *Revolver* was released. 'Yellow Submarine' caught a happy spirit of playfulness, while tracks like 'Eleanor Rigby' and 'She Said She Said' showed that the band were at the top of their game. Mavis and the gang got their copies the minute it came out. 'We just sat and listened to "Eleanor Rigby" again and again.' When they wearied of sitting and listening, dancing took over. Mavis loved the Beatles, but the Rolling Stones had more exciting rhythms.

> I used to dance with a member of our group called Stuart, and he was a great dancer. My boyfriend wasn't. He just jigged around. But Stu and I – well, Pan's People★ had nothing on us!

Mavis remembers how her long, dark hair would cascade wildly down her broderie anglaise 'dolly rocker' frock.

★ Pan's People were a hugely successful all-girl dance line-up, who would become best known after 1968 for their heavily choreographed, synchronised and high-energy appearances on *Top of the Pops*.

We used to really *dance*! We were pretty uninhibited too. You know, gyrating hip movements and all that. It was just incredibly sexy. We went back to the cave. It was – mm – good . . .

Many years later, Stu told me how much he fancied me . . .

Her soul was in her dancing. But her fastidious boyfriend was calling the tune. It never occurred to Mavis – for all their democracy and 'Eleanor Rigby' sessions – that she stood on an equal footing with him. She failed to spot the signs. It suited him very well to have a willing, pretty girlfriend in a miniskirt who could cook 'bits-and-pieces risotto', who took their bedlinen to the launderette, who was less educated than he was – and who was unaware of his infidelities. However, it suited him less that she was at ease among glamorous, artistic, beautiful and talented people; or that she was, by now, becoming a respected professional in her field.

My boyfriend failed to enthuse about my job, my milieu. Notions of liberation and equality came later. They just weren't there in the sixties. I don't think any of us stopped to think about the balance that was going on between the sexes. The blokes were still the ones that had the main jobs, and women were still earning less than men.

In reality, he was envious of the world I lived in, and the fact that I was having this amazing, exciting time . . . Iron and steel didn't measure up by comparison.

My popularity didn't help either. I think he didn't like the idea that I might get out of control.

He screwed around. And he held me back.

*

But ask Mavis, and she will tell you that, at the time, the Swinging London myth lived up to the hype.

There was always something brilliant happening with the artists, and being with them, putting on all the shows, made one feel this incredible hope and positivity.

I had clothes which I adored. There were so many parties. In London we were just having this high old time.

1966. The faces, the places, the parties, the shops, the colours, the cars, the freedom and the fashions . . .

It was the year that Twiggy was taken to have her hair styled at Leonard's Mayfair salon. Eight hours later she emerged with the sleekest of precision-cut elfin caps:

> There was this little Cockney girl in a little white gown, with her long neck and her huge, huge eyes . . . She looked like Bambi . . .

Her then boyfriend, Nigel Davies aka Justin de Villeneuve, was bowled over:

> I knew then that she really was going to make it.

Barry Lategan photographed her. On 23 February the *Daily Express* ran a full page entitled 'This is the Face of '66' and after that the phone didn't stop ringing. Every morning Twiggy spent an hour glueing on three layers of false eyelashes, resulting in a look that one fashion editor described as 'a cherub on speed'. *Vogue* and *Elle* arranged shoots; companies invited her to endorse their products, and she could command £80 an hour.* 'That whole summer was non-stop . . .'

The rise of the celebrity model helped boost boutiques. Hitherto, the fashion-conscious had made do with C&A, but now department-store so-called fashion began to look pompous and silly. Independent, colourful, subversive and transient, with names like Palisades, Granny Takes a Trip, Snob, Top Gear, Glad Rags, Clobber, Pollyanna, Sweet Fanny Adams and Lady Jane's Birdcage, the boutique phenomenon played a vibrant and central part in the shifting scenery of the sixties. Young women barely out of their teens took over poky, groovy, fly-by-night little cupboards in marginal neighbourhoods, which rapidly became trendy or lost status as these ephemeral shops with their disposable merchandise opened and, almost as quickly, closed. Few of their customers were any older, and few of the clothes were above size 12. With the optimism of youth, anyone who could raise a loan found cheap premises, took out a short lease and dreamed up a crazy fascia.

Kristina Reed was lured by a couple of her society contacts into

---

* Now worth over £1,400.

Theatrical publicity stunts accompanied the opening of new boutiques. For the launch of Lady Jane's Birdcage in 1966, the owners put a bikini-clad model in a cage and hoisted it above the street.

an amateurish fashion venture in a mews off Gloucester Road; she hadn't the faintest idea how to manage a shop, but persuaded 'somebody's brother to come in and do some rather cool things in the window with wood, and we hung dresses on it . . .' How to get stock was a puzzle. Kristina arranged to visit the companies whose labels were on her own dresses, and chose styles she liked, but was taken aback when they suggested she order 1,000. 'Oh, no thank you, just <u>two</u>!' A few designers left stuff on sale or return. 'And I sat there looking pretty, and most of the time there were not enough customers.' On one lucky occasion a transvestite came in, tried on five dresses and bought the lot. The job lasted about nine months before she quit.

Biba, Barbara Hulanicki's store, which started out in Abingdon Road in 1964, had more staying power. Named by *Time* magazine as

London's 'most *in* shop for gear', it moved to bigger premises in Church Street, Kensington, in 1966 and eventually to Kensington High Street in 1969, after which, so Hulanicki claimed, over 100,000 shoppers a week stepped through their doors. In some cases, like that of Carnaby Street – which had been a down-at-heel inner-city quarter of bakers and cobblers – the infiltration of fashion would famously become permanent. Deirdre McSharry, the *Daily Express* fashion editor, wrote:

> In the past year hundreds of boutiques have opened all over Britain. Lots of them in London . . . They are vulgar, brash, loud (literally – they find sales increase in direct ratio to the volume of the record player), and great fun.

Model Grace Coddington was an habituée of all the most achingly trendy ones, King's Road being her preferred beat. She would stop for coffee at the Fantasie or the Tortuga, while at the end of the day the creative Chelsea crowd congregated at the Markham Arms in King's Road. 'I hung out at all the King's Road hot spots, which were full of experimental young artists, writers, people working in advertising agencies, fashion and film, and I found it all madly existential.' In the wake of the Teddy boys and Mod fashions, men were discovering their inner dandy. 'He thinks he is a flower to be looked at . . .' sang the Kinks in their 1966 hit, 'Dedicated Follower of Fashion'. Male narcissism found a new flamboyance, catered for by shops like I Was Lord Kitchener's Valet and Lord John.

This was a magic kingdom where grown women wanted to look like adolescents: where girls were elves, boys were fairies and fashion was art.

Pattie and George were living the dream. The model and the Beatle were high on the 'A' list of the gilded power couples (Paul McCartney and Jane Asher, Mark and Annabel Birley, Twiggy and Justin, Mary Quant and Alexander Plunket Greene, Bailey and the Shrimp, Mick and Marianne . . .) who epitomised Swinging London. They were in love, famous, gorgeous and rich. Above all they were young.

Pattie Boyd remembers:

I was with the Beatles, and all these musicians – and it was a very merry group of people.

And I did feel, we are the leaders, the world is ours, and it'll always be like this. I couldn't see it crumbling, I couldn't see it disintegrating. I just thought, this is wonderful! It's not my parents' world which is so grey and dull, with no colour, no music, not much laughter. I felt at last I'd arrived in the 'proper' world.

With money irrelevant, and privacy a priority, the Beatles' manager Brian Epstein – by now more a father figure than a manager – helped the couple locate a gated bungalow in Esher, Surrey, with a swimming pool and a large garden. But London was near enough for clubs, parties and celebrity screenings. Pattie acquired a white Persian cat called Korky, while George bought an E-type Jaguar and later an Aston Martin DB5. They became vegetarians – but 'we didn't eat much . . .' Pattie's favourite was still sweets. The house resonated with the sound of George's guitar.

We were really happy at that time. We were young and creative, and we had lots of friends and musicians who would come over all the time – Mick Jagger for example, and Brian Jones would come quite often, and my brothers and sisters.

With George, I could play! I could be a child again. Those were the times I thought would never end.

One evening George and Pattie were driving through Belgravia when George stopped the car.

'Let's get married. I'll speak to Brian.' He pulled up in Chapel Street, outside Brian's house, rushed in, leaving me in the car, came back fifteen minutes later and said, 'Brian says it's OK. Will you marry me? We can get married in January.'

'Oh, yes!' I said. 'That would be fabulous!'

George took Pattie to Garrard's to buy an unusual multi-hued gold wedding ring. For her outfit she chose a striped pink-and-red shot-silk mini-dress from Mary Quant, paired with red shoes and a tufted fox 'Mod fur'. The cute, chocolate-boxy look was emphasised with a silky pussy-bow atop her cascading hair, intense pencilling swished along the sockets of her blue eyes and the palest of pink lipstick. Then, as if to insist that the couple were rock royalty juniors, a Rolls-Royce Princess was supplied as transport to and from the register office.

Afterwards, frozen with terror, Pattie endured a press conference organised by Brian. 'This is the happiest day of my life,' the bride told reporters. 'George is wonderful.' But the news footage tells a different story, with the look on her face one of dazed bewilderment: a china doll with glass eyes. The pair perch on a table-edge, surrounded by pushy men with cameras. Pattie puckers her lips, turns to George, he leans in, they kiss. And then again, and again, craving cuddles, craving love. They are indeed like children, absurdly young, needy and naive: babes in the wood lost and abandoned to the wild beasts.

> At twenty-one [I was] marrying George, who was all of twenty-two . . . I was so happy and so much in love . . . We would be together and happy for ever.

Hotbed

Beauty, talent and glamour were sufficient to erase the boundaries in this classless marriage between a colonial daughter and the son of a bus driver. Their union spoke of new values. London was a demolition ball in action, violently swinging, bashing up the raw and the polished, the plebeian and the patrician, the rough and the smooth. Hierarchies, controls, traditions, respect and rules lay in a heap of rubble. Pattie later recalled:

> Bohemian baronets smoked grass openly, dukes' daughters went out with hairdressers and everyone put two fingers up to the conventions of their youth and the expectations of their families . . .

In January 1966 old-school photographer and royal habitué Cecil Beaton commented wearily in his diary on 'the changes that have taken place in the new world'. Just two days before the Beatle wedding, Beaton attended an élite party thrown by the Marquess of Dufferin and Ava for two upper-class about-to-be-weds, Lord Henry

Herbert and Miss Claire Pelly. Miss Pelly, apparently, had been snubbed by her future parents-in-law for being a 'beatnik', but had eventually been 'welcomed into the upper echelons'. The celebration, however, was a litmus paper of social change, with no sign of any grand floral arrangements, or buffet with iced fancies, or evening dress. Instead, the guests were 'beats' wearing 'open necks, blue jeans, sweaters, shoulder-length hair for men and women, Shrimpton the model, in football boots'. Whatever next? Would those 'echelons' start buying Bridget Rileys and David Hockneys to hang in their statelys?

But in 1966 it wasn't the aristos who got the public salivating. Television had created a new monster, the celebrity. It too was released from the prison of class, and it came in a number of guises. For example, in the all-too-recent past, footballers had been working-class lads who played for their local team and were to be seen off-duty buying rounds in the local. Now, Belfast-born Manchester United player George Best was earning nearly £1,000 a week* and competing with the Fab Four for the front pages. His talent and good looks won him a fan club of his own, while a mop top paired with a sombrero – following his decisive goals in a 1966 match against Portuguese team Benfica – earned him the nickname El Beatle. In 1965 Best appeared on *Top of the Pops*, and you could buy check jackets or leather trousers in his personal Manchester boutique, Edwardia. 'I spent a lot of money on booze, birds and fast cars. The rest I just squandered . . .' he was reported as saying. In the year that the World Cup was won by England the clubs started to market footballers as sex symbols, encouraging girl supporters to vote for the most attractive player. Saturday 30 July 1966 was a day of national celebration as the home team defeated Germany at Wembley, 4–2. It was also the day of Anthea Martinsmith's long-awaited marriage to Anthony Millican, now curate of St Giles-in-the-Fields, High Holborn: the day for which she had saved herself. 'And all through the reception there were guests were running between the main room and the television room, shouting: "One-all!", "Two-one!", "We've WON!!" – and there was me thinking, "But it's my <u>wedding day</u> . . .!"'

* Now worth about £17,800.

But rock had the edge even on football. The pop aristocracy was setting the pace – and it was speeding up. On 22 September 1966 Kathleen Etchingham's life changed for ever, when talent scout and band manager Chas Chandler stopped off on his way from the airport to introduce his latest American find to his friends in Hammersmith. Kathy, hung over from a night on the town, was barely conscious. Her flatmate Angie shook her awake: 'Come downstairs and meet this guy Chas has turned up with. He looks like the wild man of Borneo.' Who? What? Go away . . . 'He's called Jimi Hendrix, he's a guitarist . . .' 'I went straight back to sleep.' Before the day ended Kathy and Jimi had reached an understanding. 'You're beautiful,' he told her. 'That night was a revelation to me. Jimi was far more sexually experienced and imaginative than any of the friends I had been to bed with . . . I wanted him to be my lover as well as my friend.'

Liverpudlian singer Beryl Marsden was drawn to the Hendrix circle. The music was a turn-on, though, being adamantly casual in her clothes, their flamboyance wasn't quite her style. A King's Road boutique managed to sell her a velvety long-sleeved lilac fur, but it lasted only a week before she sold it on to Jimi's bass player – 'It looked better on him than on me.' Beryl's career had taken off in 1962. In December 1965, after accompanying the Beatles on their last UK tour, she made her professional base in London, flat-sharing in St John's Wood with two girlfriends from Liverpool. When she wasn't on the motorway between gigs the flat was Party Central – 'crazy fun' – for Keith Richards, Eric Clapton, Pattie Boyd's beautiful sister Jenny, the singer-songwriter Twinkle, Peter Green from Fleetwood Mac: a roll call of the young, talented and groovy.

Marianne Faithfull, who had moved in with Rolling Stone Brian Jones and his fascinating, mercurial girlfriend Anita Pallenberg, paints her own picture of Swinging London:

Courtfield Road, Brian Jones and Anita Pallenberg's flat off Gloucester Road during the heady Paint-It-Black summer of 1966 . . . In my mind's eye I open the door. Peeling paint, clothes, newspapers and magazines strewn everywhere. A grotesque little stuffed goat standing on an amp, two huge tulle sunflowers, a Moroccan tambourine, lamps draped with scarves . . . At the centre, like a phoenix on her nest of flames . . . the wicked Anita. I'm here somewhere, too, looking up with hashish-glazed eyes from the Moroccan rug . . .

We were young, rich and beautiful, and the tide was turning in our favour. We were going to change everything, of course, but mostly we were going to change the rules.

By 1966, where Mick Jagger was concerned, Marianne was now the royal favourite. The star's explosive affair with Chrissie Shrimpton was unravelling, and she was going haywire, but the Stones' new album, *Aftermath*, with its venomous lyrics to tracks like 'Stupid Girl', 'Doncha Bother Me', 'Under My Thumb' and 'Out of Time', could only have fuelled her fire.

This was the year the Speakeasy Club ('the Speak') opened in Margaret Street, quickly becoming a nucleus for the music industry. '[It] was *bliss*,' remembered one regular, who freeloaded on her looks. 'When you're young and vivacious and you don't get pissed, clubs absolutely adore to have you. You're just a sparkly young thing, you're not a tart – so they give you free memberships.' Brian Jones usually unwittingly picked up the tab; Jimi Hendrix would show up and exude charm.

In 1966 the streets were coming alive. In September the sun shone over Notting Hill Gate when a melting-pot of local residents, Irish and Caribbean, Spanish and Ukrainian, answered the call of the neighbourhood's most dynamic voice, that of Rhaune Laslett. Of mixed race herself (she was half Native American, half Russian), Laslett's vision was of a carnival and fair that would bring together the hugely diverse west London community. There would be a New Orleans-style marching band, a Trinidadian steelpan procession, fancy dress, floats and children dressed as characters from Charles Dickens all parading through the streets around Portobello. Around a thousand people turned up. There was dancing in the streets, and the sweet scent of ganja wafted from the basements in All Saints Road.

It was also in 1966 that the artist's model and muse Henrietta Moraes observed that 'there was a new look on the streets'. Kids younger than her (in 1966 Henrietta was thirty-five) sat in the parks smoking joints. Their vocabulary had morphed from the days of 'super' and 'golly'. They talked a language of freaks, vibes, bread and trips; of digging, scoring, grooving and shagging. 'Hallo, man, meet my chick. You know this is where it's all at.' Long-haired, radiant and festooned with shimmering fabrics, they told each other that money was the root of all evil. Around this time Henrietta got the first inklings of an unheard-of substance called lysergic acid, LSD 25. 'It's not exactly a drug,' she was told. 'You take it on a sugar cube and go to heaven or something.' For a while it was just a rumour. Then one day her friend Bill led her to his bathroom, showed her a bottle of colourless liquid, filled up a medicine dropper from the bottle and administered the hallucinogen onto her tongue . . .

*

The Beautiful People were all there when film director Michelangelo Antonioni came to town to shoot his oblique, fascinatingly layered portrayal of their milieu: the 1966 movie *Blow-Up*, often cited as the embodiment of Swinging London. *Blow-Up* took David Bailey, the fashion scene's hippest paparazzo, as its starting point, with photographer 'Thomas' played by a languid, kiss-blistered David Hemmings in tight white jeans. The film had a clever post-modern, hall-of-mirrors vibe that bought it many admirers – many of those same admirers being actual walk-on participants. In this respect the film could have been a happening; the *beau monde* were rounded up to play themselves, among them aspiring actress Patricia Quinn:

> So, Antonioni is <u>doing</u> Swinging London. And Antonioni is sent the extras from the extra agency. Well, they were professional extras. They were NOT Swinging London! So Antonioni said, 'I don't want <u>any</u> of those!'
>
> So we were called in from the Drama Centre, art schools, anywhere. And we are the most <u>amazing</u> looking bunch of people you've ever seen; and we're in feather boas, and I'm in my Biba shirt dress, you know, black and yellow with a white collar trim, and we are <u>the</u> *crème de la crème* of Swinging London! And Antonioni walks in and looks at us, and he goes, 'Oh, I want <u>all</u> of them!'

For the shoot, Antonioni's team also corralled the model Veruschka and a bunch of heavily made-up debs in a Cheyne Walk bedroom, gave them some kilo bags of grass and cases of wine, and told them, 'Right, get on with it.'

Blow-Up is a voyeur's film in every sense. The murder mystery element resolves as Thomas's negatives expand and pixillate revealing an unseen corpse, while live bodies are equally subject matter for his inquisitive camera. One memorable scene shows Veruschka in a revealing black sequinned dress writhing on the floor below his probing lens. But even without his finger on the shutter Thomas's own sex life is raw material for the images uncovered by the director, and shared with his audience. One of the most controversial (for the time) sequences shows Thomas watching a pair of dishevelled 'dolly bird' models, stripped down to their pink and lime-green tights, bitch-fighting in the torn chaos of a dismantled mauve backdrop. Thomas urges on the girl-on-girl action from a safe distance before leaping in fully clothed and removing their tights. There's a glimpse of pubic hair. Soon he too has his shirt off.

If Swinging London existed through its window-dressings, its furs, velvets and purple curtains, its art, its fashion and its photography, then *Blow-Up* helped in perpetuating and validating the brand. Unmistakably, part of that brand was gorgeous women spread-eagled on the floor, romps with undressed nymphets, and available sex.

Two other films that piggy-backed on the relaxed sexual climate of 1966 were *Modesty Blaise* and *Alfie*. The time was ripe for a futuristic movie version of the successful British comic strip featuring a female secret agent in false eyelashes, fishnet tights and space-age yellow Bri-Nylon, and director Joseph Losey laid it on with a trowel. *Modesty Blaise* is a camp, exotic-location fantasy in which the heroine (Monica Vitti) is modelled on James Bond, though she leaves all the macho stunts and weaponry to her serial bed-hopping partner, Willie, played by Terence Stamp. By contrast, *Alfie* (the screenplay by Bill Naughton was based on his book of the same name) depicts a fog-laden London of tower blocks and seedy alleyways. Michael Caine made his name playing the 'cheeky chappy' lead, frequently breaking the cinematic 'fourth wall' and addressing the audience – which he does right at the start of the film, when we see him emerge from a steamed-up car in which he has been having it off with the comely Siddie, played by Millicent Martin:

> ALFIE (to camera): A married woman, see. They're every one of them in need of a good laugh. It don't never strike their husbands. I always say, make a married woman laugh, and you're halfway there with her. Course, it don't work with a single bird. Start you off on the wrong foot. You get one of them laughing, you won't get nothing else.

> *[Siddie is heard warbling a cheerful song from inside the car]*

> ALFIE (to camera): There you are, just listen to it. It was dead glum when I met it tonight. I listened to all its problems, then I got it laughing. It'll go home happy.

> *[The pair chat, then with a peck on the cheek he drops her off at the station]*

> ALFIE (to camera): What she don't know is, she's on her way out. When a married woman gets too hot on, it's time to cool off.

Alfie's story is that of an unrepentant Cockney Casanova, working his way through the female sex with callous lack of feeling. After Siddie there's Gilda, who has his child; Ruby the plump American tourist; Lily, who has an abortion; and Annie the pretty teenage hitch-hiker he picks up at a service station and takes back to keep house for him. Annie is seen on hands and knees scrubbing the lino, while Alfie, watching her, invites the audience to share in approval of his new trophy girlfriend:

> ALFIE (to camera): It ain't come up too bad has it? All it needed was a bit of care and attention. It's quite dainty, you know what I mean? Here, I no sooner take a pair of socks off than it washes them. And it can cook too. A bit limited on the menu – it goes in mostly for Lancashire hot-pot and steak and kidney pie . . . they blow you out a bit. But it does do a marvellous egg custard. I ain't never tasted nothing like it.
>
> It's pretty fair on 'the other' an' all. A bit on the shy side, but I find that makes quite a change these days.

As a rake, Alfie was a recognisable type ('There's a little bit of Alfie in everybody', claimed his creator). Though the script ultimately punished him, showing him as lonely and lost, it did not unpack the broader implications of a time in history when the predator male had, perhaps, greater licence to exploit women than ever before or since. That analysis of the film was made, much later, by the novelist Fay Weldon, writing in *The Guardian*. It is worth quoting at length:

> It was the original *Alfie* that started me, and many of my generation, on the road to feminism. We watched it and left the cinema trembling. We saw that the indignity, emotional pain and helplessness that went with being a woman in the 1960s was monstrous and couldn't, mustn't last. It fell to writer Bill Naughton to speak for us: very few women wrote for the screen in the sixties – the job was 'technical' and therefore not for females, who couldn't understand cameras. But Naughton could not appreciate, as only a woman could, that there was a new, more pernicious twist to the timeless Don Juan archetype. Sure, there had always been men who kissed and left. But this was something worse.
>
> The pill had come along. Women, not men, were now 'responsible for contraception', so men, relieved of the duty of care, and with no sanctions to restrain them, took advantage of this new arrangement and behaved disgracefully. Male respect for women diminished. Unmarried women who had sex were slags, and those who did not were frigid. How could you win? Those with any aspiration beyond admiring and serving a man were dismissed (and openly described) as ugly, unable to get a man, or in need of a good lay. Young men, outnumbered by young women, as they now are not, did the sexual picking and choosing. 'Sisterhood' as a concept had not been invented: all women were assumed to be in constant competition for the attention of a man, and indeed were. The man was their meal ticket.
>
> 'Sexism' as a word did not exist.

The Weaker Sex

But it needed to.

In 1966, the Fawcett Society (named in honour of its most influential campaigning member Millicent Fawcett, and previously the

National Society for Women's Suffrage) celebrated its centenary. A hundred years on, its members recognised that – though women had been granted the vote in 1918, and the full franchise ten years later – they still had a serious fight on their hands. In the home, in the workplace, in public life, in relationships and in society in general, the Britain of the mid-sixties remained a country where the odds were stacked against women; where one sex was marginalised, derided, exploited, discriminated against, used and feared by the other.

It is shocking today to encounter some of the instances of abuse and oppression inflicted on women in the mid-1960s. Attitudes were casual and contemptuous. The Mod and Rocker clans took female subordination for granted. A journalist investigating youth cultures quoted his seventeen-year-old source as saying:

> I don't mind girls, but men are more intelligent and I think they're meant to be set above.
>
> I'd like to meet a girl who wasn't a slag . . .

One respondent in an oral history told the interviewer how, as a teenager, he and his group were in the habit of climbing a local vantage point to spit on any girls passing beneath 'like camels'. Another, talking to the authors of *Generation X*, was full of the risks he incurred by sleeping around. 'You never know what you might catch . . .' was his view, though he pointed out that 'toffy [sic] nosed bitches who work in shops and offices' were far smellier and liable to infect you with crabs than Borstal girls. 'If I got a girl pregnant I wouldn't marry her,' said a third. 'If that ever happened I'd be miles away . . .'

Which was why many women took responsibility for contraception. However, the Family Planning Association denied contraceptive services to women who weren't married. In 1963 the Marie Stopes clinic in London had taken the controversial step of starting up an advisory clinic for young people, though it was not until 1964, when Helen Brook took the bold step of opening the (private) Brook Advisory Centres, that young single women could gain confidential and risk-free access to contraceptive advice. But these clinics were unable to see more than a tiny proportion of the women who needed their help. The year 1967 would see the government finally taking responsibility for family planning for all under the terms of the Family

Planning Act, but local authorities were given the choice as to whether to set up clinics, and few did. The Pill was often in the headlines – but it still wasn't in wide circulation. The abortion toll remained high.

Obstetrics and gynaecology was an area where women – as patients – were placed at a distressing disadvantage by the preponderance of male consultants. For example, the novelist Doris Lessing reacted with horror and helplessness when she found herself in a gynaecological ward being subjected to an examination by the male consultant, accompanied by twelve young male medical students. 'Surely I'm not going to be expected to open my legs in front of all these pimply youths?' But she was. And the 'great man' was indignant when he realised he was dealing with a reluctant patient: 'Do you expect me to instruct my students while your legs are crossed?' Lorna Sage, a teenage mother, recalled that she was treated as 'a peasant'. The male professionals in charge of her ward regarded pregnant women as 'walking wombs'. After a week enduring punitive discipline she decided to discharge herself, only to be told that she couldn't do so without her husband's permission. Meanwhile, there were no sanctions against an employer who sacked a woman from her job because she was pregnant.

Prejudice against women was deeply embedded in law and practice. At this time it was legal to turn down an application by a woman for a mortgage, and to grant it only if countersigned by her husband. Unmarried women couldn't get mortgages. Ann Leslie was incandescent to be told by a 'building society twerp': 'Pretty young women don't need to bother their heads with things like that! Why not find yourself a nice husband and let him deal with it?' At this time she was the highest-paid feature writer on a leading national newspaper. And any woman who fell through the safety net found that disability allowances granted to men were not granted to women on the equivalent basis.

Change was slow. It was not unusual for women applying for jobs to be interrogated about their marital prospects, and in 1961 Shell rejected all the women candidates who applied to be interviewed. In the 1960s it was also quite normal for job adverts to be overtly gendered, as in: 'Top Jobs for Top Girls', or 'Theatrical company require girl of attractive appearance with initiative'. Commenting on the employment situation for women in 1966, journalist Hunter Davies advised:

> [Women] are not encouraged to go into industry, political commentating, or economic advising. It is not exactly forbidden. If you are ambitious, you will need to be devious. American style go-getters and career girls are not popular, so never openly compete with men, always appear surprised at the least success, and be grateful for crumbs of praise.

Mary Ingham described how the division of labour in an office reflected that in the home. There were certain tasks that men regarded as beneath their dignity:

> Being a woman and a secretary landed you with jobs like answering the telephone, making tea, taking visitors into the big chief's office, things it just wouldn't have done for a man to do, no matter how junior . . .

In the world before the Sex Discrimination Act, women's pay remained on average 25 per cent less than men's.* Jobs, the national wage bill, retail prices and the nation's exports were predicated on women earning around 40 per cent less than men. In some cases a woman might earn half the pay packet of a man, for doing the same work. The ineradicable assumption was that women were parasitical beings who didn't need to earn. Though the BBC claimed to operate an identical salary scale for men and women, on *Late Night Line-Up* Joan Bakewell was paid less than her male co-presenters. 'I overheard someone say, "She does it for the pin money."' Were employers as ready to employ women as men? asked the *Daily Mail*. 'It's a hypothetical question,' replied an executive at ICI. 'I think you would have to say, they'd choose the man. Women are very conscientious, very tidy. They make great assistants . . .'

Married women were still regarded as dependants and treated

---

* Equal pay remains a vexed issue. Thousands of cases still go before tribunals every year, but the complexity of proving 'equal work' means that most are settled outside the tribunal. It's also necessary to distinguish cases of individual unfairness from the reality of the gender pay gap. The campaign group, The Women's Resource Centre, believes that it will take another century to close that gap.

accordingly, such that – despite paying full National Insurance contributions – they were not entitled to full benefits. And a tax policy that (incredibly) still regarded a married woman's income as being not her own but her husband's disincentivised such women from aiming high.

In any case, many top jobs remained barred to women; the Stock Exchange and the Church were notable examples. The Foreign Office continued to impose a marriage bar, and many ambassadors were hostile to female recruits being posted to their embassies. In sectors like the law and medicine, particularly in the higher grades, women were conspicuously outnumbered by men. At this time, less than 10 per cent of women held positions as hospital consultants. Less than 1 per cent of practitioners at the Self-Employed Bar (about a hundred) were women, and up to 1969 only three women would take silk; while at this date barely 2 per cent of the total number of solicitors were women. In white-collar jobs, of those classified as 'higher professionals', only 9.4 per cent were women – but nearly 70 per cent were employed as 'clerks'.

Dignity, status, authority: these were all labels that automatically attached to men – along with the respect and courtesy that accompanied them. Not so for the other half of the human race. Women who trespassed on male territory posed a threat, and the best way to neutralise it was through mockery. British Pathé Cinemagazine producers knew what their audience wanted. Women police motorcyclists, a 'harbourmistress', a female thatcher, a woman scrap-metal dealer, 'girls' who played football, and a woman who competed in motorcycle races – all got the 'pretty little freak' treatment, and the commentators took every opportunity to poke patronisingly jovial fun at them: 'Slowly but surely women, the weaker sex, are muscling in on man's domain – practically no sport is sacred! Thank goodness for dear old rugby league!'

Even women who doggedly made it to the top often discovered, when they got there, that they were cold-shouldered. When Helen Bentwich was chair of the London County Council she was pointedly not invited to the Royal Academy dinner (and neither, for the record, was the artist Dame Laura Knight). Even after Professor Dorothy Hodgkin won the Nobel Prize for Chemistry in 1964 she was excluded from joining her male colleagues to dine at all but three of the Oxford men's colleges.

In Parliament, not much had shifted since a House of Lords debate ten years earlier, in which one young hereditary peer had complained that women MPs were 'not an exciting example of the attractiveness of the opposite sex . . . Frankly, I find women in politics highly distasteful.' As for inviting them into the House of Lords: 'We like women; we admire them; sometimes we even grow fond of them; but we do not want them here.' After the 1966 election, there were only twenty-six women MPs in parliament – just over 4 per cent – and three fewer than in 1964.* These 'curiosities' were generally made responsible for 'women's interest subjects'. But even where matters of direct interest to women were being investigated by Parliament, they had little say. For example, a twelve-person committee examining matrimonial proceedings had just one woman member, while another committee of twelve, looking into artificial insemination, was composed of nine men and three women. Attitudes to women MPs were a combination of sleazy and belittling. Barbara Castle was only the fourth woman in British history to hold a cabinet position. As Minister of Transport under Harold Wilson, Castle was on the receiving end of both lust and distrust. According to her biographer, the Tories would have preferred even a left-winger to a woman, while quoting her as saying: 'Men are so terribly sex-conscious. If a man disagrees with you in public life, he's also probably resenting you sexually.'

*

For, as innumerable women found out, prejudice, discrimination and resentment inevitably extended to men helping themselves gluttonously from the all-you-can-eat buffet of available sex.

---

* Following the 2017 election, there were 208 women MPs elected to Parliament: a new high of 32 per cent. However, even after that election the chief executive of the Fawcett Society commented: 'The real story is that progress has stalled . . . As we approach the centenary of women first getting to vote in general elections, we cannot wait for another nine elections to achieve equality.'

> I took it for granted. A quick squeeze, a salacious leer, an unlooked-for
> pinch, a remark on one's cleavage, speculation about one's sex life . . .

recalled Joan Bakewell. One day Joan took a taxi to the House of Commons to collect cabinet minister Douglas Jay and bring him back to
Television Centre to take part in *Late Night Line-Up*. In the short ride
before they arrived it took all her efforts to fend off his lunging body.
On another occasion she was halfway through a live studio interview
with the libertinous archaeologist Mortimer Wheeler,* only to find his
hand crawling up her skirt while they were actually on air.

For Joan, and innumerable other women, 'sexual harassment was a
matter of routine'.

> [We] learned to deploy a range of diversionary tactics, to duck and
> weave, to reject, repel and discourage without creating an 'incident'.

In other words, to continue behaving as women were expected to
behave, and not kick up a fuss.

In 1966 Pauline O'Mahony was still working for the Lambeth Housing Department. She was eighteen and deeply committed to her job,
which involved a combination of house visits and stress-inducing interviews with evicted tenants in desperate need of accommodation. That
year, her motivation was further sharpened after watching the harrowing BBC1 drama *Cathy Come Home*, written by Jeremy Sandford.
Directed by Ken Loach, the ground-breaking documentary-style story
of a young wife with two small children made homeless through no
fault of her own told Pauline nothing she didn't know. 'I cried so much
at that film – there was so much I recognised.' The charity Shelter had
been launched at the same time. But Pauline knew that the only way
forward in helping society's thousands of Cathys lay in getting them
access to resources. She had to be compassionate and work the system
in their interests, but she also had to be seen to be professional.

And this was not easy. Pauline was an attractive teenager, but she
was working in an overwhelmingly male environment. 'The amount
of sexism that was around then – it was big time!' She understood that

---

* The suave Sir Robert Eric Mortimer Wheeler (1890–1976) was a broadcaster and
pop-archaeologist who acquired a reputation for widespread promiscuity; after
his death one of his colleagues described him as 'a groper and a sex pest'.

"They're fifteen denier, actually. But to get back to your views on early Byzantine wood-carving . . ."

From 1964 *Late Night Line-Up* presenter Joan Bakewell became a household name – but fame came at a price.

being viewed as sexy would detract from her ability to do her job. So she deliberately distanced herself from the groovy, colourful, Carnaby Street world that was luring in so many of her contemporaries. Instead, she dressed in long brown clothes, wore clumpy shoes and thick hosiery, scraped her long hair back severely and hid her face behind imitation spectacles. 'I wanted to be taken seriously as a competent professional woman. The message was "Don't touch me".' She was scared too.

And yet, knocking on doors around her south London community beat, Pauline rarely felt threatened; it seemed the dowdy 'Welfare Lady' disguise was working. On the contrary, it was among her male colleagues at the Lambeth headquarters that a frightening level of harassment was the norm. All too often she was outnumbered – in the Architectural Department, for example, where she was the only woman. Walking through the open-plan office was a daily ordeal. The men made suggestive comments, followed her, touched her. Undeterred by the unflattering brown garments, they would send her to get the step ladder to climb up and reach a top-shelf file, making it easy for them to grope under her skirt and get their hands up her knickers. 'That was the sport of the day.' But even more dreaded were the 'empty property inspections'. Pauline's boss made a point of assigning her to accompany him on such inspections, because then they would be alone and nobody could see them. On these occasions 'Titter Fox' from the Leicester Police, with his breast-groping habit, looked harmless by comparison. Behind closed doors, this man took advantage of his position of power. 'I don't remember any threat or violence – but he would maul me about, masturbate himself. It was awful, horrible.' But she too felt it was impossible to complain.

> I never told anybody. He was an older married man. I tried to avoid it – I'd do anything not to go on empty property inspections with him. But when it happened, I just thought, well he's my boss, I've got to go along with this.
>
> Why did I feel I couldn't say anything? I was a very junior member of staff really, and I had no power. I valued my job. He was in a position of power – and he could have taken that job away from me.
>
> So I stayed completely silent.

Theresa Tyrell was another young woman who learnt the hard way about female powerlessness. At the opening of this book we saw Theresa as she is today – a stylish, assured, creative woman wearing scarlet tights, surrounded by colourful furnishings and decorative ceramics of her own making. In the mid-sixties Theresa – who is half-Scottish and half-Jamaican – was working towards a Dip Ed in Ceramics at the Art School in her home town of Leeds. Her Scottish mother worked in an old folk's home in the outlying suburb of Seacroft. Nearby, one sunny summer day, the crowds gathered to watch the opening of a neighbourhood fête by celebrity DJ Jimmy Savile, accompanied by a teenage carnival queen. Savile came from Leeds; his wacky bottled hair colour, blingy sunglasses and catchphrases ('How's about that then, guys and gals?') had earned him an adoring public, locally and nationally. So, when his Rolls-Royce drove past the home, the staff waylaid him and persuaded him to come in to meet and greet the old people.

> Well, I happened to be there, so when I heard excited noises in the lobby I came down to see what was going on. And oh God, Savile just kind of grabbed me, and started kissing me all the way up my arm, in front of everyone including my mother. Right up towards my

neck – and he had this awful soft, soft, soft skin. Hands that had never done anything. He was ghastly, *ghastly*. And he was, sort of, 'Oi, oi, what have we got 'ere then? Oi, oi, oi!'

And my mum had some reports or something in her hand, and she went, 'Hey, oof! STOP!' and slapped him off. And everybody just sort of laughed.

And that was my Jimmy Savile encounter.*

Once she'd got her diploma, Theresa Tyrell decamped to London. With no obvious direction of travel, she did what so many optimistic young women did in the 1960s, and got a job as sales assistant in a trendy boutique, where she was expected to look pretty and flog outlandish gear to unsuspecting fashion victims. 'I was a dolly bird.' Unfortunately the shop – the Butterfly Boutique on Chalk Farm Road – was managed by a villainous character called Derek, who lurked in a small room behind the shop reading pornography and visibly masturbating. Every so often he would open his shirt up to show Theresa his stab wounds, while telling her tales of his pimping days in Soho.

'Men were *awful* in those days . . .' says Theresa. Being followed home by a man was an occupational hazard of walking from the tube station, and all too often Theresa got accosted by some dubious character inviting her to earn a bit of extra by 'modelling'. 'They were brazen about trying to pick you up off the street. I'd get harassed, touched up and so on – and guys would flash you on the tube.'

Theresa lasted just six weeks at the Butterfly Boutique before moving on to a seemingly more congenial job at Heal's emporium in Tottenham Court Road. It was low-paid, but working in the prints and art books department felt like a better use of her talents. Yet even here, some customers thought it was all right to lech across the counter, like the popular artist and children's TV presenter Rolf Harris, who came into the shop and – in Theresa's account – suggestively flipped open a book of Aubrey Beardsley prints in front of her, to a

---

* Savile died in 2011. Despite allegations of sexual abuse made against him during his lifetime, no action was taken. After his death hundreds of further allegations were made against him, including thirty-one of rape, a large number of them being by underage girls.

page showing a giant phallus.* 'And he licked all around the outside of his lips with his tongue, gave me a horrible leer, and just said, "*Very* talented man, Beardsley." I mean, I was at work! So I just clammed up – but thank God the counter was between us.' She had problems too with one member of the sales team, who would engage her in prolonged conversation across the shop counter, with one hand concealed in his flies, out of her line of vision. At one point, Heal's switchboard had to block calls from customers asking to be put through to 'Theresa' (the staff all had name badges). 'I had a lot of those: you know, customers asking me out . . .' One was particularly persistent. He wanted her to be in a porn film, and wouldn't take no for an answer. Theresa's manager told her that this kind of behaviour was widespread in the large London stores, and nothing could be done about it. He recommended her to wear longer skirts, and she reluctantly abandoned her minis in favour of a pair of midi culottes, which seemed less provocative when climbing ladders to hang pictures.

So what was going on? Being mixed race was, Theresa believed, part of the answer. If white meant pure, then being black signalled the opposite. As one of the male *Generation X* interviewees signalled, 'Going out with a Spade is something to be proud of . . . They're so way out.' In societies that had slavery or racial apartheid, women were routinely regarded as subject to their masters' whims and desires.

> No white women I knew seemed to get as much unwanted sexual attention as I did. I think I must have seemed more easy and available – and also, somehow, exotic . . .

But it was also about envy of, and power over, the young. The majority of men who approached her were no longer youthful. Theresa feels that her visible 'foreignness' held out a promise of the relaxation of sexual rules not generally on offer to a generation of middle-aged men.

> I think it looked to older guys as if everybody younger than them was having a riot, a free-for-all. And I think a lot of older people, or married men, thought they were missing out on all the fun . . .

* In 2014, aged 84, Rolf Harris was jailed on twelve counts of indecent assault that had taken place between the 1960s and the 1980s. He was stripped of his honours.

In a world where women – black or white – had no sense of rights, few eighteen-year-olds had the courage to make a stand.

Floella Benjamin was another young woman who discovered that being black sent out unwelcome and dangerous messages.

Floella had always been a devotee of dancing, and Dardie, who played in a jazz band, had provided her with a platform for her resounding mezzo to help entertain at West Indian weddings. She adored singing and never felt stage fright. But Marmie was always clear that she could not have a career in the limelight; showbiz was not 'a proper job'.

So in 1965 Floella left school and started work in the accounting office of Barclays Bank in the City of London. The money was good. She saved her pay packet, passed her driving test and bought a lovely yellow Ford Anglia. This was freedom indeed. Floella's siblings now depended on her for their Saturday evening social life, and there was always a dance on. Unfortunately one Saturday morning the car developed engine problems; getting it fixed was a matter of urgency – 'or there would be huge disappointment'. She felt lucky to find a mechanic who promised to have it ready by five that afternoon. But when she arrived to pick the car up, and asked the mechanic what she owed him, the answer was, 'You!' Trapped in his poky office, Floella drew on all her presence of mind and self-preserving instincts to escape unmolested. The man had his flies open – 'he was ready for action should he have got his way'. 'Now, now, my good man, don't be foolish,' she responded, with crushing hauteur.

> 'Please let me have you,' he said, now with a desperate note in his voice; 'I've never had a coloured girl before.'
>
> 'Well, you're not about to fulfil your fantasy now,' I said firmly. 'How much do I owe you?'
>
> 'Just let me touch you,' he pleaded. I came straight back at him with an air of superiority. 'My good man, if you so much as lay one finger on me, my three large six-foot brothers will come round and teach you a lesson you will never forget. Now pull yourself together and tell me how much I owe you.'

The peril over, Floella released all her bottled-up emotions as she drove home at high speed, heart pounding, stomach heaving and tears rolling down her cheeks. But she had proved to herself that she could take control. 'I realised that adversities . . . happen for a reason. They could either break my spirit and drive me crazy or make me strong and resilient. I had chosen the latter.'

Can there ever have been another period in British history when men felt permitted to treat women with such crass contempt? In 1966, many of the protective fences of gallantry, honour, virtue and chastity had been torn down, leaving a landscape denuded of moral signposting. Though the vista offered glorious unbounded freedoms, the assumptions of the past remained. The newly liberated horde reverted to a caveman morality, believing themselves entitled to plunder and pillage, to take and to rape – but not to pay the price. Meanwhile, their victims lacked a vocabulary of rights and justice, they lacked a community to speak for them, and they lacked a voice.

There was work to be done.

Brain Bunnies

Where women's education was concerned, however, the scenery was slowly, if very creakily, starting to change. In the mid-1950s the proportion of women enrolling in UK universities stood at just over 25 per cent; by 1965 this had crept up to nearly 30 per cent. Though many (if not all) universities welcomed women students, far too often schools discouraged them from applying, particularly working-class girls like Rosalind Delmar:

> The head teacher at my school told me that girls like me went to teacher's training college and not to university.

Nevertheless, Rosalind persisted with her ambition, and obtained a place at Manchester. Sophie Jenkins, despite top-notch A-level results ('I could have gone anywhere I wanted . . .'), was also deterred from applying for Oxford because they told her that at seventeen she was too young. Instead, she applied to and was accepted by Keele.

Keele, along with Sussex, Warwick, East Anglia and a number of others, was one of the modern 'plate-glass' universities that set out deliberately to appeal to a new generation of women. When Sussex

1. 'A woman came in . . . and asked if I had *Lady Chatterley* . . .' recalled the owner of the Paperback Bookshop in Edinburgh. 'She picked it up with tongs and carried it out in front of the bookshop. There she poured . . . kerosene on top of the book and proceeded to rant and rave and put a match to it, "this iniquitous document".'

2. In 1961 matching frilly frocks were still the undisputed 'look' for female singers. At the height of her short-lived fame Helen Shapiro topped the bill at the London Palladium. 'It never occurred to me to think, "Who are you, a fifteen-year-old, to go out on that stage?" I just went out there and socked it to them.'

3. A Raymond Revuebar dancer recalls her glory days at the club: 'We had the most wonderful costumes. Money was no object. It was all sparkling high-cut leotards and beautiful headdresses. And we could dance our heads off!'

4. Poise, lacquered hairdo and long, white, unblemished gloves: society photographer Tom Hustler captures the essentials of the 1961 débutante.

5. The cover of Floella Benjamin's childhood memoir, *Coming to England*. Floella was eleven when the children sailed to rejoin their parents in the Mother Country.

6. Marianne Faithfull came packaged as a ready-made myth. 'I first met Mick Jagger [in March 1964],' she recalled. 'Mick fell in love with me on the spot . . . and wrote "As Tears Go By". I, on the other hand, immediately began taking drugs and having a lot of sex.'

7. 'I'd never wanted to be a journalist, I was just filling in time before I decided what I really wanted to do.' But by 1966 Ann Leslie was a star of the *Daily Express*. Smoking still went unquestioned.

8. 'I'm just a mum, I got on wi' it. You're a mum and you do it.'
Margaret Hogg with her son David and his younger brother.

9. Liverpool star Beryl Marsden, aged sixteen, in 1963.

10. Kristina Reid – a résumé for the 1960s: 'I was a deb in '64, dated a drummer, saw the Beatles, didn't have the Pill and bore the consequences, and so on!'

11. Melissa North combined a freewheeling life of fun with a love of poetry and philosophy. 'We had an earnest side. And we made things; we were creative.'

12. Rosalyn Palmer's graduation photo, taken on 20 July 1964. Five days later she gave birth. Note the wedding ring.

13. *Left* The press pack having a feast: Mandy Rice-Davies leaves the Old Bailey after giving evidence at the trial of Stephen Ward on vice charges.

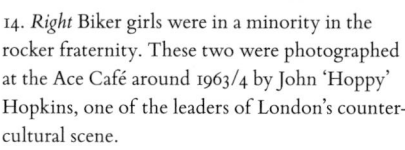

14. *Right* Biker girls were in a minority in the rocker fraternity. These two were photographed at the Ace Café around 1963/4 by John 'Hoppy' Hopkins, one of the leaders of London's counter-cultural scene.

15. *Below* In 1966 Britain had a massive housing crisis, with three million people living in slums. Families were frequently pulled apart. Women were on the front line.

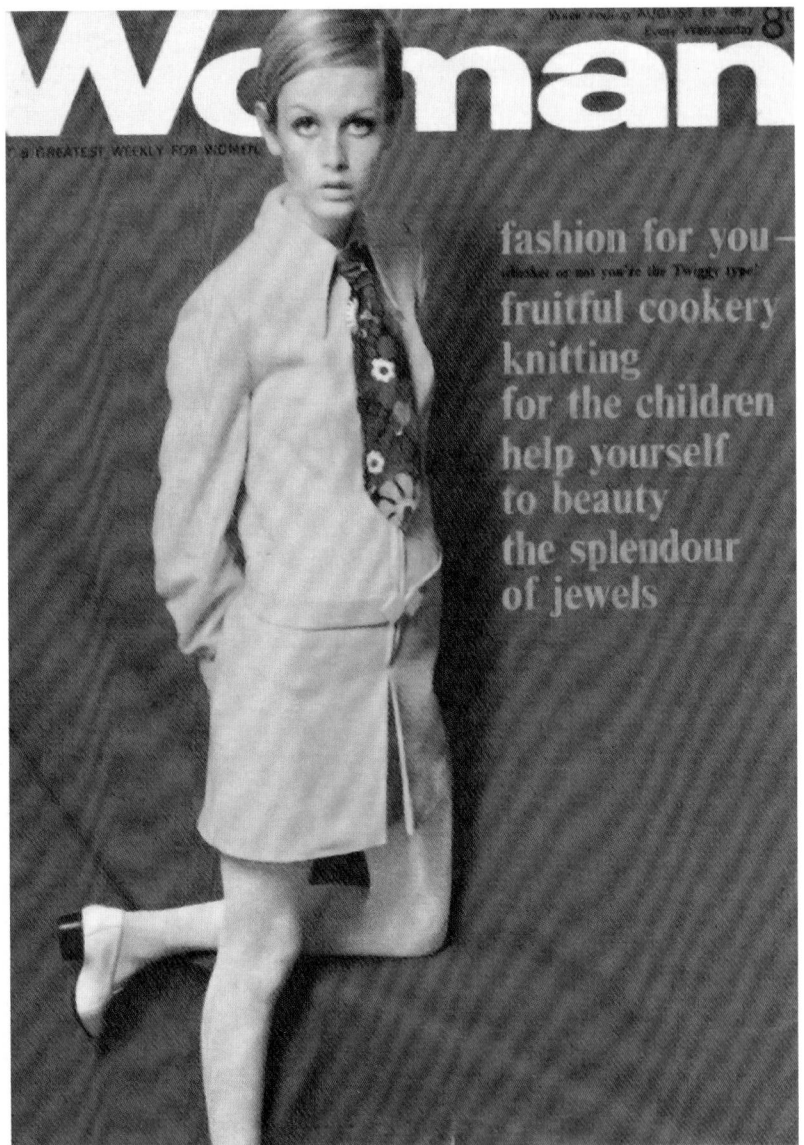

16. 'A little Cockney girl . . . with her long neck and her huge huge eyes . . .'
In 1966 Twiggy's look was the quintessence of modern. But within a year Mod had gone
mainstream: here, the teen icon shares the cover of *Woman* with recipes and knitting patterns.

17. Unafraid of culture, colour, contraception or Italian cookery, *Nova*, launched in 1965, set a new agenda for women's magazines.

18. 'She was one of us.' Cathy McGowan, presenter of *Ready Steady Go*, was both approachable and hip. In 1965, when this publicity picture was taken, trouser suits were still cutting edge, while Cathy's pose seems to echo the notorious portrayal of a naked Christine Keeler astride a modernist chair.

19. 'All eyes will be riveted on the legs and feet . . .' (*News of the World*, 1965).

20. Australian matrons in 1965, scandalised by Jean Shrimpton's hatless, gloveless, stockingless and mini-skirted appearance at the Melbourne races.

21. Mavis Wilson started work at the contemporary print publishers Editions Alecto in 1964: 'Can you imagine a better time to hit the ground running?'

22. Model Pattie Boyd and Beatle George Harrison married on 21 January 1966. Her limpid beauty inspired George to compose 'Something', the most successful song he ever wrote.

23. Art school graduate Theresa Tyrell, around the time she started working as an illustrator on the Beatles' hippie-trippy animation *Yellow Submarine*.

24. A long way from Chelsea: Scottish nurserymaid Veronica MacNab's career took her to Sussex, Swinging London and back to Edinburgh, where she cared for sick and neglected children in a Barnardo's home.

GRAN PREMIO INTERNAZIONALE DEL FESTIVAL DI CANNES 1967

METRO-GOLDWYN-MAYER PRESENTA UNA PRODUZIONE **CARLO PONTI**

UN FILM DIRETTO DA **MICHELANGELO ANTONIONI**

BLOW-UP

VANESSA **REDGRAVE** DAVID **HEMMINGS** SARAH **MILES**

METROCOLOR

25. A good angle? David Hemmings probes a prone Veruschka with his lens in Antonioni's self-conscious movie 'happening' *Blow-Up*.

26. Sexist, slapstick and silly, the *Carry On . . .* films were the longest-running British comedy franchise, with thirty-one interchangeably inane variants on the formula between 1958 and 1992.

SIDNEY **JAMES**
KENNETH **CONNOR**
CHARLES **HAWTREY**
JOAN **SIMS**
KENNETH **WILLIAMS**
BILL **OWEN**
LIZ **FRASER**
TERENCE **LONGDON**

A PETER ROGERS *production*

CARRY ON REGARDLESS

Funniest Carry on EVER!

ANGLO AMALGAMATED FILM DISTRIBUTORS LTD.

27. *Right* Dons and dollies. 'Typical' Cambridge students doing a fashion shoot with bicycles for *Honey*'s 1966 feature on women in higher education.

28. *Below* Around 1967, to her mother's horror, Caroline Harper (*far right, with cigarette*) started to reject the approaches of 'suitable' men. 'I was far more attracted to the colourful guys in the corner of the room.'

The brain bunnies

Whether the
many rags,
always make
their morals
scandals bl
outside the
picion, with
want to kno
we visited Fl

29. 'The sheer happiness that began then . . . ': On 30 July 1966 English Literature graduate Anthea Martinsmith stepped out of the church door with the love of her life, curate Anthony Millican (accompanied by a bonny bagpiper).

30. Love, peace and a universal panacea. Ahead of the Legalise Pot rally, held on 16 July 1967, the *Sunday Times* reported that 'pot fanciers proffer evidence that cannabis relieves tension, cures sleeplessness, aids digestion and has even helped convert a sad homosexual into a happy hetero'.

31. February 1968. After skipper's wife Mary Denness spoke out for the trawlermen, her picture appeared in the *Hull Daily Mail*.

32. Susannah York, Beryl Reid and Coral Browne starred in *The Killing of Sister George* (1969). Members of the Gateways Club played themselves.

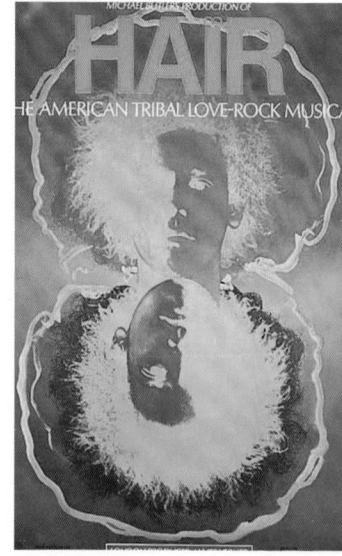

33. Was the hugely successful musical *Hair* a sell-out? 'The real hippies were repelled by its banalities,' wrote one.

34. 'Things – having them and wanting them' were what defined the sixties (according to journalist Peter York) . . .

35. . . . but renouncing materialism was also a key tenet of the Underground. Jenny Fabian's pad sums it up. Here she has the bare necessities: cigarettes, a stereo, Eastern imagery and a floor-level mattress.

36. In 1969 I was fourteen; the untamed hair and Indian-print mini-dress betray my romantic leanings – but the body language is anxious.

37. Atlantic City, 1968 – angry women dumping 'the degrading Mindless-Boob-Girlie-Symbol'. This was the electrifying moment when American feminists sparked a new movement.

38. Oxford, 1970: the life-changing conference which kicked-started British Women's Liberation. 'The whole thing had such an air of excitement . . . it was a breakthrough,' remembered one participant. A smiling Sheila Rowbotham can be identified sitting near the end of the front row.

University opened in 1961, it was deluged with female applicants. This may have had something to do with their promotional pamphlets and branding, which borrowed teen magazine-style imagery featuring sexy, fashion-conscious female applicants with curtains of blonde hair and miniskirts photographed in attractive poses next to senior members of staff, or engaged in earnest discussions on the library steps.★ 'On my first day at Keele,' remembered Sophie Jenkins, 'I turned up in a shocking-pink and navy-blue large houndstooth check trouser suit, and I can remember everyone just staring at me. And I really liked the attention, especially from the boys . . .'

Sophie was an eager and diligent student. But as her comments indicate, far from being a hotbed of clever talk about feminism and the sisterhood, social life at university was – just as Fay Weldon highlighted – a cut-and-thrust competition to attract men. Sophie felt alienated by the idea of equality for women:

> I can remember when I was at university, some people started talking about feminism, and I was just completely horrified, because I thought of women as rivals and enemies, and I actually thought that women *were* slightly inferior. The cool people to be with were the men. I didn't want to be hanging around with a load of women.
>
> I felt I did well out of sexism! Because one was competing for the attention of men, and I was doing quite well. I was pretty, and I knew how to make the most of myself. And, like a lot of women my age, I'd learnt to be quite good at pretending to be stupider than I was. So, I could still get high grades, and at the same time I could flirt with the blokes and seem unthreatening.
>
> What a long journey I've come since then . . .

In 1966, during Sophie's time at Keele, the top-selling teens and twenty-somethings magazine *Honey* ran a prominent colour photo feature entitled 'The Brain Bunnies', a light-hearted round-up of women in higher education: 'What, we want to know, is it all about?' To find out, *Honey*'s team visited five universities: Cambridge, Keele,

★ Professor Carol Dyhouse of Sussex University, who has specialised in the history of women's education, documented this and many other relevant points in her book *Students: A Gendered History* (2006). She writes: 'The "dollybird" was effectively part of the branding image of the new university.'

St Andrews, Leeds and Aberystwyth. If the picture content was any-thing to judge by, what it was all about was the clothes. Posing with their bicycles, on a punt, or in the forbidden ritual of 'climbing in' over their college wall, they modelled trouser suits, crushed-velvet mini-dresses and a 'Sambo Dollyrocker (6 gns)'.

Sophie herself appeared in the section on Keele, wearing a Don-egal tweed skinny sweater, flared corduroy pants and patent lace-up shoes. The accompanying text of the article gave an upbeat account of spaghetti supper parties, coffee lounges, beans on toast, girly gos-sip, and sport – though fencing was demonstrably men-only, and 'the sailing club flourishes, even if the girls stand around looking glamor-ous while the men do the real work'. *Honey* also assessed the boyfriend ratio and husband opportunities at the various universities. At Cam-bridge there were ten men to every girl, but this was offset by the fact that 'some of the men are awful, some work all the time, and some decide to do without a girl during term'. At Keele there were lots of student engagements, while Aberystwyth had one of the highest rates of marriage among alumni. The article wound up with some handy beauty tips for students who might otherwise fall into the unglamorous trap of not only being a bluestocking but also looking like one: so, apply a face-pack while you read; let your nail varnish dry while memorising a page of Latin; spend ten minutes backcomb-ing your hair and spraying it thoroughly – then it won't budge during your busy day of lectures. And never forget, 'study-time can be beauty-time as well'.

*

What about student morals? Beware of getting through too many relationships, cautioned *Honey* – 'Everyone knows everyone else . . . and if you keep changing around you get a bad reputation.' Curfews were imposed at all halls of residence – but, as one girl interviewed by *Honey* put it, 'There's nothing you can do at night that you can't do in the afternoon.'

In her memoir of the bulge baby generation, Mary Ingham (who studied Social Sciences at Liverpool) unpacked the experiences of her women contemporaries at college between 1965 and 1968. It was a time of severing home ties and putting boy-next-door relationships on hold to pursue aspirations. But course tutors still discriminated, while in tutorials women were discouraged from contributing, particularly on scientific or technical subjects.

In other ways the playing-field was levelling out. Women were expected to reach the same academic standard as men, pass the same exams and achieve the same degrees. Rules regarding *in loco parentis* were discriminatory, however. Women (but not men) were required to live in halls, and their male visitors were monitored (Mary's hall was nicknamed 'the Convent'). But as the outside world relaxed its grip on the young the strict curfew rules became less and less bearable, and tensions ran high as students protested that they were being treated like prisoners.

In all too many cases that ship had sailed. Mary's friend Vicky was hauled before the principal when a young man was caught leaving her room. Carried away by physical desire, she'd thrown caution to the winds. She simply owned up, and got let off. The climate of sanctions, punishments and inhibitions was cooling. Instant Nescafé, single beds and Bob Dylan records ('If you gotta go, go now, / Or else you gotta stay all night . . .') were the familiar backdrop to many an inept student sex encounter. One mattress manufacturer even proudly publicised the development of a special new bed designed for students 'to withstand very hard wear'. In Mary Ingham's words:

> Student rooms all over the country were to become the battle/testing/playgrounds for the determination of the New Morality.

How fortunate for men, away from home for the first time, that that testing process now had so few penalties. As Mary Ingham reported, 'College girls were so much fruit, ripe for picking, to be discarded, unfeelingly and insensitively, once appetite was satisfied.'

The vacillating sexual compass of the times left many young women at sea. Specifically, Mary Ingham pointed out that women were hurling themselves over the cliff with abandon, and urging their friends to follow them – 'Losing your virginity had become for some a status symbol.' For liberated students, it was easier to have another Nescafé and stay the night than to head back across town on the late-night bus and take risks by breaking the curfew. (Sheila Rowbotham recalled an unlucky contemporary who had attempted to scale her college railings after hours and impaled herself on them, desperately mopping at the bloody wound between her breasts with a sodden towel, too terrified to see a doctor.)

But nothing seems to have deterred the journalist Lynn Barber. We heard how, in 1961, she was pressured by her controlling parents to get married in preference to going to Oxford. Fortunately for her (since her dodgy boyfriend turned out to have a wife already), she stuck to her guns. However, Lynn arrived at St Anne's College with just one aim, and it wasn't studying for her degree. The message of Lynn's home upbringing had been self-denial, but that was behind her now. The doors of university opened up to freedom, fun, champagne cocktails and seven males to every female – and she was determined to take full advantage of all it had to offer.

> The rule from now on would be that I would go to every party I was invited to, flirt with every man I ever met, drink every drink, smoke every joint, never sacrifice a lunch for a lecture, or a party for a tutorial . . .
>
> I was going to work really hard at this pleasure lark. And I would study men, men, men . . .

Lynn was a fast learner. She filled her diary with dates, often three a day; she made notes on the male species as if they were a new genus of ape. She also quickly picked up how important it was not to show off her intellect, but to appear stupid. By her second year she'd fallen in love, been dumped and had unapologetically come up with a whole new approach to finding a boyfriend. Dates were a waste of time, she decided; better to have sex first, talk afterwards and reputation be damned. She later claimed to have had sex with about fifty men in just two terms at Oxford – 'It was quite good going – I was jamming them in.'

Three male Oxbridge undergraduates interviewed by the *Generation X* researchers shed an interesting light on Lynn Barber's experience. Twenty-year-old Peter Buckton said that he found most of the female students were fixated on 'hooking a mate' in order to settle down, marry and breed. From where he stood, women were dishonest, predatory and an overall bad bet. 'I couldn't be faithful to any one girl,' he explained, '– the whole idea is repulsive to me . . .' Graham Roberts, a third-year doing English, thought men resented women students for being more intelligent than men, but you couldn't pick and choose, because it was a competitive field. 'I like them well-upholstered,' he told the interviewer. 'But there are seven times as many fellows as girls at Oxford, so any old bag gets pounced on.' Another of their interviewees was Marianne Faithfull's husband-to-be, John Dunbar, who reported:

> Girl students at Cambridge are a pretty grim lot. Only one in a thousand is worth looking at. They all tend to work hard – probably . . . as a reaction against their ugliness . . .

As for Lynn, after two terms of sustained promiscuity she met The One, a farouchely handsome undergraduate from New College, and promptly ended her short-lived career as a good-time girl.

Bewilderment came with the territory. Women students with less ruthless energy than Lynn Barber couldn't handle the combination of sex and studying. Negotiating contraception, curfews and a pre-marital relationship alongside biochemistry or the Venerable Bede could leave you a nervous wreck. 'How can I risk getting chucked out in my first term?' said one. 'I've already been caught once, emerging from the men's block at 7.30 a.m. I've never smoked so many ciggies or eaten the skin around my nails so much in my life.' In the hothouse of parties, alcohol and essays, the patiently waiting boy-next-door was almost invariably jettisoned. When Mary Ingham's boyfriend back home suggested they get engaged she panicked. She was having far too much fun to contemplate settling down.

> 1966 was the year that the tables were turned . . . Our generation was learning to play the system to get what it wanted, a reflection of our growing sense of our own power . . .

In 1966 the student population was starting to flex its muscles.

★

Meanwhile, Juliet Mitchell had a project.

Juliet Mitchell was a young academic based at Reading University. The women's cause was in her bloodstream: 'I had a very proto-feminist mother.' At Oxford, where she went to study English in 1959, she was told, ' "men get first and fourth class degrees; women get seconds and thirds". They did, we did.' Juliet remembers herself as 'gender-naive and wondering'. Being mercilessly teased and taunted by a young, entitled public-school boyfriend and his group of male friends was, to her, a baffling experience. She started to question what was going on; to discuss, to challenge, and to read.

Juliet herself was a true intellectual: a well-presented, well-spoken young woman whose unruly dark-blonde hair tumbled across her unmade-up face, and whose intelligent grey eyes questioned and defied. She had a trenchant, confident manner, and she exuded a certain contained power.

After graduating, Juliet fell in with a coterie of 'new left' Marxists, gained a post teaching English Literature at Leeds University and began work on a book about women. But it wasn't always easy to beat a path through the thicket of doubt, dissent and prejudice surrounding her chosen subject. The Marxist orthodoxy denounced 'bourgeois feminism', and remained stuck in a past where women were subordinate to the male party élite. Finding source material was a challenge. On one occasion an assistant ejected her from his bookshop because she asked for a copy of Simone de Beauvoir's *The Second Sex*. Researching the rise of suffrage, she spent hours in the 'dusty and largely unused Fawcett Library near Victoria station . . .', while ploughing determinedly through government blue books to disentangle the historical complexities of women's education: 'There were no secondary sources.'

> Between de Beauvoir in 1949, and Betty Friedan's *The Feminine Mystique* in 1963, one could count the books addressing the discriminatory treatment of women on the fingers of one hand.

It was a time when making the world a better place through the power of ideas seemed entirely possible and likely. As Juliet's academic career lifted off – in 1965 she got a teaching post at Reading and embarked on a PhD on 'Childhood in the English Novel' – most of her time away from her desk was spent excitedly discussing radical politics. At this time Juliet's new-left friends, nearly all men, were embarking on a research project to analyse post-colonial Third World inequalities, supplementing work that had already been done on class. But when it came to inequality, there was one glaring omission.

There's women who also don't fit into a class analysis. I'll do women . . .

said Juliet.

Her long-nurtured ideas started to fall into place. The result, *Women: The Longest Revolution*, first appeared in the November 1966 issue of the *New Left Review*. Much later, she told an interviewer that 'hidden beneath the article and the questions it raised, there is unacknowledged anger and pain'.

Juliet Mitchell wrote *The Longest Revolution* when she was twenty-five years old. She has described it as 'a tract for dark times'. It's a densely argued and scholarly analysis of women's position in society, directed largely at her political comrades, that draws on historical, anthropological and sociological strands of Marxist thinking to question and explain women as workers, as family members, as mothers, as partners and as fully contributing human beings: as one half of the human race. Women were not, she reminded her readers, a minority, but fundamental to human existence. And yet they continued to be treated as a minority, with their own dedicated little universe: the family. And on that front, a wake-up call was needed:

> The 'true' woman and the 'true' family are images of peace and plenty: in actuality they may both be sites of violence and despair.

Women: The Longest Revolution lays down a fundamental challenge to what had, until then, gone under the name of feminism. Juliet Mitchell took on Marx, Engels, Bebel and de Beauvoir to present a new, interdisciplinary take on a tired topic. Don't compartmentalise, she urged. And don't swallow the prevailing ideologies whole. She disputed the assumption that bearing children, childcare and domesticity was women's 'natural' and true vocation. These ideas were demonstrably conditional on circumstances. Look at how the introduction of effective contraception had changed things in a hundred years, she declared. And look how that, in its turn, had dissociated sex from its hitherto inevitable consequence: a baby. And she resisted mainstream Marx by stressing how inadequately he and his followers had dealt with the exploitation of women as sexual objects. She also let off a prophetic warning shot:

The current wave of sexual liberalisation, in the present context, could become conducive to the greater general freedom of women. Equally, it could presage new forms of oppression . . .

But gender equality *could* be achieved – if only socialists recognised that production (work), reproduction, sex and the socialisation of children were all shifting and amorphous by their nature, and were also interdependent social structures. To combat inequality, and achieve women's liberation, change had to be political, concrete and radical. Women's manifold discontents needed to be addressed through realigning, restructuring and legislation. A transformation was needed across all areas.

In 1966 there were already stirrings in the United States. Equality was on the agenda. Riding high on her feminist credentials, Betty Friedan assumed the leadership of NOW, the National Organisation for Women – but it was still early days. The phrase 'the Personal is Political' had not been coined. The label 'Women's Liberation' didn't exist either. But, though they as yet had no names, both those ideas now had life, planted between the bold blue covers of a small-circulation journal aimed at the upper echelons of the left-wing commentariat. The Winter edition of *New Left Review* contained in its pages the radical embryo of second-wave feminism: an idea like fruit on a branch, blossoming, growing, sweetening, maturing – and waiting to fall ripe from its tree.

1967

Things

The era of acquisition had dawned. 'In the capitalist world there had never been a period of expansion and prosperity to compare with the 1950s and 1960s . . . If ever capitalism looked as though it worked, it was in these decades,' reflected the historian Eric Hobsbawm.* By 1967 rationing and making-do were well and truly consigned to the past. One ninety-one-year-old lady recently told me, 'Oh yes – that was the first time since the war that you could really buy whatever you wanted.'

In *Style Wars* (1980) the journalist Peter York writes:

> The reality of the sixties was new money, new technology, *things* – and the choices they implied.

At that time Peter York was working in advertising. *Things* were his handle on reality, from Wrighton kitchens to Hoover Keymatics, prawn cocktails to real cream – 'a veritable cornucopia of consumer goodies'.

My family were not immune to this *embarras de richesses*. We too wanted the things we saw in the new, glossy Sunday supplements. Though my parents (like many of their high-minded ilk) were resistant to watching commercial television, its consumerist agenda filtered through, subtly reshaping their lives. The adverts for After Eight Mints and Cadbury's Drinking Chocolate, for Vesta Chow Mein and Heinz Sandwich Spread all worked their magic on us, and we wanted our share. True, shopping was still recognisably 1950s in style, and most women shopped daily. Having moved from suburban Leeds to rural Sussex in 1967, this was not an easy proposition for my mother. But the local market town had five butchers (one of which delivered to villages

* In *The Age of Extremes: The Short Twentieth Century, 1914–1991* (1994).

like ours), two fishmongers and half a dozen greengrocers, and my mother phoned through her weekly grocery order to the village shop.★ Our liking for foreign food was a challenge to them, but they did their best, providing vermouth, tinned beansprouts and Kraft ready-grated parmesan which had the consistency of sawdust and smelled weirdly rancid. But they also delivered essentials: bacon, Summer County margarine, Ajax powder and twenty filter-tipped Players Navy Cut.

Supermarkets, however, were slowly advancing. A little further afield there was a small branch of Sainsbury's. In those days the shop was nothing more streamlined than a self-service but still old-fashioned grocery with an impressive cheese counter where you could buy Camembert. There were other signs of the times. My parents' wine consumption increased – by 1970 people like them would be getting through twice the amount of wine they had drunk in 1960 – and in the local town a health-food shop and a delicatessen opened. Now adventurous cooks could buy brown rice, Gruyère, tinned olives and *pâté de campagne* by the ounce.

For inspiration and aspiration, one cookery writer was ahead of all the others. Lynn Barber didn't like cooking. But David Cardiff, whom she later married, did. Soon after they moved to run-down Stockwell he brought home a strange purple vegetable he'd found in the local greengrocer's and told Lynn it was called an aubergine.

> He explained it meant there must be other middle-class people in the area, people who read Elizabeth David, people who knew what to do with an aubergine. It meant the area was 'coming up'.

My mother too worshipped at Mrs David's shrine. Author Margaret Forster was the same. 'I had cookery books, mostly Elizabeth David's, and I'd pore over them and experiment.' Hunter happily opened a bottle of something at table most evenings and Margaret flung wine and herbs into her dishes with abandon. Joan Bakewell too had fallen under David's spell. She cooked lasagne and minestrone for her dinner parties, and made pilgrimages to the eponymous Greek Street emporium to buy *petits pots* and *mouli-légumes*.

★ Amazingly, as I write, this wonderful small shop still makes weekly rural deliveries to my mother's home.

Though this kind of eating and drinking had been the preserve of those with wider horizons, by the mid-1960s the continental influence was percolating downwards. Avocados were starting to appear, served with vinaigrette or prawns, on sophisticated menus even in the provinces, and no restaurant was complete without scampi. In oral histories of the period one encounters piquant memories:

– I was astonished when I saw [my sister] feeding long, stiff strands of pasta into a pan of boiling water, because I'd only ever seen or tasted tinned spaghetti before that . . .

– People were just starting to go out to eat. I remember the Berni Inn in Worcester, where we'd go on Friday nights to have chicken in a basket and a glass of red wine, followed by an Irish coffee. Great fun.

In 1967 my parents bought a second car – since the end of the war car ownership had rocketed from 1.5 million to nearly 11 million – and an automatic washing machine. In the new house we had no fewer than three telephone extensions installed, one upstairs and two downstairs, and for her custom-built kitchen my mother joyfully selected a marble-effect Formica worktop. She also found that the Brighton branch of Habitat had caught up with her taste in stripped pine, bentwood rocking chairs and William Morris curtain fabric.

Just a bus ride away, my sister and I were also able to indulge our retail dreams. For sub-teens, half in love with Mick Jagger, rock'n'roll credibility was of pressing importance, and it didn't take long to locate an address in the quaint grid of Brighton city-centre alleyways known as The Lanes where we could buy into the latest trends. This shop was called Gamut. It smelled intensely of sandalwood joss sticks and patchouli oil, which it displayed in ranks of little blue bottles alongside more pop items: Union Jack coffee mugs, Snoopy Dog merchandise and self-adhesive multi-coloured psychedelic butterfly stickers made by a firm called Hunky Dory, which I applied to my wardrobe doors. I also bought spherical turquoise blue Japanese lampshades and a chunky stand-up alarm clock with twin bells, enamelled in clashing pink and orange. My younger sister was the lucky one though: she had a wonderful, all-enveloping yellow 'sag bag' in the corner of her room. Then there were occasional trips to London, now within reach. In Fulham Road I discovered a revelatory shop called Laura Ashley, where it was possible to buy Victorian milkmaid-style floral frocks with flouncy frills. For some reason, everyone wanted to look like this.

By now my parents had caved in and joined the 90 per cent of British households who had a television. They also owned a Morphy Richards steam iron, a second-hand Kenwood chef with a blender attachment, a portable Hacker radio and a stereo record player, beside which were scattered my brother's LPs, mostly Beatles and Stones.

★

This gallop through the products and possessions of the mid-1960s is a personal one, and every reader who lived through those years will surely have their own list of the food, fashions and furnishing that cluttered their homes, or headed their wish lists. Dreams were for sale at this time. Illusions too – for the façade of wealth was a thin one, plastered over a rickety pound, growing unemployment and a tanking economy. When I interviewed Kimberley Saunders about her time with the Rocker fraternity, one of the stories that seemed to me most suggestive of the consumerist 1960s was her account of how she met Dave, whom she later married. They got together through Sindy dolls.

Sindy, 'the doll you love to dress', had been launched in 1963.

> Sindy is the free, swinging girl that every little girl longs to be . . .

the promotional text declared.

> Sindy has sports clothes, glamour clothes, everyday clothes – a dog, skates, a gramophone – everything . . . Every genuine Sindy outfit is a child's dream come true.

Sindy also had a boyfriend called Paul, and her range of plastic accessories gave her the marketing edge over her competitors. This healthy-living, clean-limbed dolly could go skiing, swimming, or to the bowling alley. Like her mass-produced rivals, Barbie and Tressy, she had a ready-made name and off-the-peg characteristics; her owner was not expected to individualise her, but would join a club of other Sindy-owners. However, unlike Barbie or Tressy, who had

Sindy: plastic perfection, packaged for a generation of pre-teens.

alluring make-up, waspy waists and prominent busts, she was not overtly sexualised. Sindy, though slender, looked more like a wide-eyed baby in a bra. All this made her lovable, unthreatening, enviably within reach and utterly desirable, to me and all my school friends. There can't have been a girl in the land who didn't want to own her, and she quickly became a bestseller. I was ten when some generous family friends made me a gift of my first Sindy in her 'Happy Traveller' outfit, featuring tailored coat, pleated skirt, red turtle-neck, plus holdall and camera: a joyful moment indeed.

Teenager Kimberley Saunders had moved way beyond the doll stage. Virginal and wide-eyed she was not, following a wild sex life conducted on the London-to-Hastings line and the shingle of the Essex coast. On top of that, an unplanned pregnancy had made her a mother at fifteen. Her daughter was placed in foster care, and Kimberley went back to school in Bracknell '– as though nothing had happened'.*

> After that I didn't want nothing to do with men. And when I had my sixteenth birthday I didn't invite any boyfriends. Just women friends.

It was a chastening experience. But Kimberley's deflated mood was short lived, and before long she was out looking for fun again. Money, however, was in short supply. Girls like Kimberley traded their attractions for a night out in the dance hall or the bowling alley, which had to be paid for by whichever passing big spender you could entice into getting out his wallet. Saturday evening came, and she and her friend Janice dolled themselves up nicely.

---

* In the 1980s, mother and daughter were reunited.

And we went down to the town to see if we could pick up a couple of geezers. And lo and behold, I tell you, that was the luckiest night of my life.

There was these two blokes, pulled up at the side of the road . . .

The big Ford Zephyr, with its elaborate grille and chrome trim, spoke of cash flow. It looked as if these guys were up on their luck. As it turned out, they were indeed looking to do a deal, but had got lost. They'd come from Kilburn in north-west London with a bootful of goods due to be delivered to some shady contact in Bracknell who would pay ready money for them. One of them, Dave, the good-looking one, rolled down the window and asked the girls for directions.

He said, 'We're looking for so and so, we've got an order for him . . .' It was a racket – a bit like *Minder*, you know? He'd get a load of stuff one day, and a load of stuff another day, probably knocked off the back of a lorry or something. So he says, 'Well, we've got some stuff we need to offload, we're dropping it off with this geezer down 'ere. Then we'll go out for a meal.'

So I said, 'Well, get rid of it first.'

And they opened the boot, and I said, 'What *have* you got in there?' And he said 'Oh, we've got a load of Sindy dolls . . .'

Piled up in their cardboard and cellophane packaging in the back of the Zephyr, Dave and his mate had a ready supply of the toys, a dream cargo of nylon hair and plastic smiles.

So we all went out for a drink or something, and I took Dave's phone number . . .

Happily, Dave was up for it. As for Kimberley, she was seriously interested. So when Saturday rolled around again he showed up in the Zephyr to take her out. But Kimberley's mum was adamant that she wasn't going to have her wayward daughter 'in trouble' a second time. Yes, he could stay the night, but on the settee, not in her bedroom. That evening she was off to the pub herself, but left the pair with Kimberley's little half-sister, five-year-old Heather. With the child around to look after, it was unlikely they could get up to too much mischief. But she'd reckoned without Dave's charm and resourcefulness.

> He bribed my little sister with a Sindy doll. He sent her out so we could be on our own. He said, 'All right, Heather, I'll give you two Sindy dolls if you'll stay out of the room for a few hours, and *three* Sindy dolls if you'll just go upstairs and stay there . . .'
>
> But I mean, it's not as if we needed a bed. He had a great big Zephyr, didn't he, we could just go in the back of his car, or the woods, or something, you know?
>
> Actually, it was the love affair of the century. He was very romantic, wrote letters . . . very poetic. He loved me so much, and I loved him. And when I was sixteen we was engaged.

There is something eloquent about Sindy as intermediary in this short tale of boy-meets-girl. Dollies in the 1960s were not just what many girls wanted to have, it was how they themselves were seen: as plastic playthings. From dressing up to go out on the pick-up in Bracknell on a Saturday night, to the trade-off of a mute, placid, unconfrontational dummy in exchange for sex in the back of the Zephyr, the whole episode is freighted with uncomfortable symbolism.

And even from the early days the clues were there: 'For example, I told Dave, "Look, I'm going to art college," but – typical man – he didn't want me to have a career.' In reality Kimberley was no Sindy, and she was strong-minded. Behind the backcombed hair and high-heeled boots, there was a feminist waiting to get out.

> In the Rocker world you had a passive role. But I wasn't passive. I've always been a feminist, but I didn't know what the word meant. Sexism was seen as normal, but even in those days I wouldn't take it. I remember being in a bar with Dave when we was engaged. He said, 'Innit about time you bought us a round of drinks?' I said, 'Do *what*?' I said, 'When women get equal pay, then I'll be buying the drinks!'
>
> I told Dave I was learning to drive. He said, 'You can't drive, you're a woman!' I said, 'Do you mind, you'd better rephrase that,' I says: 'You can drive, why can't I drive?' And he tried to stop me. I said, 'You can't stop me. If I want to do something, I'll do it.'

Plus, I wasn't the typical woman his mother was looking for. His mum wanted a woman who would boost her son's career. A domesticated woman, with huge whatsits, which I didn't have either. So I didn't quite fit in that role.

And when we did eventually split up, he said, 'The trouble with you, Kim, is you're too much of a feminist.'

So I said, 'Oh, tough, get over it.'

Fun, Fun, FUN!

In a society where the idea of women as plastic playthings was a factor in the sex deal, feminism would have a steep hill to climb. Sanitised and cosmeticised, messy real life took cover behind uniform, unthreatening, smiling mannequins with improbable body types. For now the perfect wife of the 1950s had given way to the fluffed-up, deferential dolly bird. And nowhere was this type more in evidence than at Hugh Hefner's Playboy Club.

The Hefner empire had been expanding. With a new club opening at 45 Park Lane in 1966, a recruitment drive had been launched, and the Great London Bunny Hunt was on. *Playboy* magazine invited England's 'most beautiful and charming young ladies' to send their photographs to the Bunny Mother. From these, six British beauties were pre-selected to be flown to Chicago to train as bunny girls, qualifying them to train another ninety-four applicants who, with their instructors, would make up the 100 bunnies required to wait at tables, direct the clientele and act as casino croupiers, wearing ears, a cotton-wool tail and a tight pink corset.

The lucky six returned to Heathrow airport fresh from their bunny immersion course, stepping off the plane complete in high heels and pompoms, to be greeted like stars by a seething crowd of photographers with flashguns.* Advertisements were then placed in

---

* My thanks to producer and director Philippa Walker, who showed me her fascinating 1999 documentary 'Bunny Girls' (Philippa Walker Productions, made for Channel 4's *Secret History* strand), which colourfully illustrates and contextualises the world of the bunnies.

The excitement mounts: Hugh Hefner was spending over £1.5 million bringing his Playboy Club to London, and staffing it with bunnies.

the press and on radio, and the publicity ensured a deluge of 30,000 candidates competing for the coveted post of rabbit-waitress.

Today, blonde, blue-eyed Patsy Reading – who now runs a quaint bed-and-breakfast in the south of England – still possesses the warm, effusive charm and generous figure that appear to have got her the job back in 1967 when she was twenty.

I must have heard about it on the grapevine. So I went along there, green as green. And it was this huge place, and I went in and I thought, Oh gosh! And I was introduced to the man who was going to interview me, and I thought, Oh dear, is he going to ask me to undress? But he was very nice to me – and I did have, you know . . . [*she smilingly mimes her curves*] – and I suppose he thought, well, maybe she might do –

Student actress Pat Quinn from Belfast had made Swinging London her adopted city at this time, and was living with her friend Melissa in a with-it flat in World's End, Chelsea. Like all theatre people, Pat bought *The Stage* religiously every Thursday, and it was through its pages that she applied for and got a bunny interview:

> I hadn't even read *Playboy*. It was just a club that was opening and they needed some very pretty girls to work in it. And it said you had to bring a swimsuit and high heels.
>
> So off I went and the panel said, 'Could you just walk up and down.' And they muttered a bit. 'Croupier?' they said. And then they said, 'Yes, you're in. Thank you. Next!'

Having made it through the selection process, each bunny was sent to be individually fitted for her costume. Pat Quinn was petite; Patsy Reading more ample of figure. But everyone was expected to be slender and shapely, and the rigidly whaleboned, tight-laced satin corsets they were given to wear ensured the uniformity of the bunny body brand. 'It was like a scaffolding really,' recalled the seamstress who worked backstage at the Playboy Club. 'If the costumes weren't fitted properly, the girls used to get a pain in their hip – the bones used to lay on a nerve – and they used to be in agony.' 'I nearly fainted on several occasions during my first month on duty and would have to leave my post to get unlaced for a while,' recalled another bunny, Carol Cleveland.* All this at a time when the fashion world was abandoning wiring and heavy elastic in favour of minimal underwear, and replacing shapely voluptuousness with unisex jeans and androgyny.

Once strapped in you added accessories: a servile, slightly fetishistic bow tie plus starched white collar and cuffs, a bandeau with floppy satin ears attached, and the famous tail. Pat Quinn:

> We had a wire brush for our tails – and you brushed it till it got bigger and bigger. And eventually you'd get marks for your tail, and then you'd get a prize if yours was the best tail at the end of however long . . .

---

* Carol Cleveland is the actress and comedian best remembered for her appearances, from 1969, in *Monty Python's Flying Circus*. She is the author of a memoir, *Pompoms Up!* (2014).

Why rabbits? Whatever Hugh Hefner had in mind, it wasn't the rodents' famed reputation for reproducing quickly. Bunnies, however, are cute, fluffy, appealingly wide-eyed and soft, with floppy ears, adorable little cottontails, defenceless – and hard to tell apart. In other words pets in a petting zoo, not people.

Almost as soon as she joined the Playboy Club Patsy Reading discovered that all was not as it seemed.

> When I arrived, I was taken to the bunny girls' dressing room. And there were these bunny girls coming off a session . . . Imagine them all, with the most beautiful hair, and beautiful long eyelashes, and beautiful make-up – and boobs up to here! And I thought: these women, they're just amazing, they're fantastic.
>
> So I stood there watching them getting out of their costumes. And this very beautiful girl sat down, and OFF came the hair. And it was a wig! Off it came! And then off came the eyelashes. And then the face – the mask was wiped clean. And then, from out of these wonderful costumes – pushing their breasts up – I watched as they delved into the bra cups, and pulled out all these tissues and socks – and things they'd stuffed in to pump them up! And do you know, underneath all that, none of it was real, it was all an illusion. The high heels, everything. Everything was false.
>
> And I just remember seeing this wonderful image disappearing before my eyes. And underneath it all there was this very nice girl, who couldn't have been more ordinary.
>
> So then I had my fitting – and I didn't need any socks or tissues at all!

As a croupier, Pat Quinn now had to put in a further six weeks' training to acquire the specialised skills needed at the tables. It was exacting work, with shifts of twenty minutes on, twenty minutes off, till the small hours. Waitressing, Patsy Reading had a different challenge on her hands. Serving a tray of drinks dressed in the tightest of corsets and five-inch heels was hard enough. The bunnies were instructed in the art of the 'bunny dip', a complex curtsey-like manoeuvre that involved a graceful bend of the knees without intruding your behind, coupled with the fluid backwards arm gesture that delivered Martini to customer without spilling a drop. '[It] was a way of serving the drinks so that the bourbon hit the table before the boobie did!' recalled Carol Cleveland. Practice made perfect. But Patsy struggled to master the drinks themselves. The club was famed for its superbly stocked bar, comprising a thirty-foot wall of bottles, of every shape, size and colour. 'Whatever exotic cocktail somebody wanted, from a screwdriver to a mai tai, you had to know exactly what it was, and I just could not master it. So what a *hopeless* bunny girl was I!'

With its bars, restaurants and casino, the Park Lane club was regarded as the ultimate exclusive venue for rich sophisticates. The sex divide was surely never more explicitly highlighted than in this dark, mirrored, chrome-and-marble interior: a space where male and female appeared almost as different species. Here in its plush, shadowy recesses men in black tuxedos talked business, made deals and made money, ate, drank and played, while shimmering, semi-naked, improbably curvaceous women in shades of pastel satin tottered past, waiting upon them. The Playboy Club worked because it created an environment in which a man could live out his own James Bond fantasy of the Martini-drinking playboy and bon viveur, complete with suave suit, cigar, roulette and an attitude to women that cramped, crippled, stifled and depersonalised them, and varnished over their imperfections. In the war of the sexes, it decisively handed men the power. An ex-bunny interviewed for Walker's documentary explains:

> A playboy is potent – in every way, I think. He's potent in the workplace, his sexual aura is potent . . .
>
> A playboy knows how to live.
>
> Marilyn Cole

But as one of her colleagues comments, it also worked because it was the embodiment of one man's consumerist vision:

> Well, it is all down to Hugh Hefner, and his notion, his vision of the perfect world, the perfect woman, and the perfect lifestyle.
>
> It was a perfect life for a man. So whatever our own internal conceptions of ourselves were, as women, the original idea was yet another, perfect Thing – or Adjunct – for the perfect man.
>
> Liz Flower

Meanwhile, the mix of provocative lingerie, alcohol and money created an intoxicating cocktail. The steamy atmosphere of sex had the potential to ignite, and Playboy's managers found it expedient to damp things down. Patsy Reading explained:

> The clientele were all these smooth James Bond types, you can imagine – very nice! And you were supposed to be this lovely object, who would come at their command when you were sent for. However, they were not supposed to touch you. And you learnt to duck and dive, to stop them touching.
>
> Also you were made very aware that a lot of them would be wanting to see you outside work. So if one of the men who came in liked you and said, 'Oh, may I have your phone number?' we couldn't give it. And we were taught on pain of death that we would be instantly dismissed if we did.
>
> In other words, they could look, but NO touching.

Pat Quinn was even more blunt:

> No, there was no fraternising – even though we were quite with-it girls! Well, nobody ever bloody approached me. I mean, working there was like being in church, *sorry* . . .
>
> Maybe it's just 'frosty Pat' or something. Anyway, they would have been thrown out on their ear if they'd had their hand up *my* bunny tail!

So, while the outside world was a ferment of free love, the portals of 45 Park Lane concealed a sanctum of Victorian values. Imagine a nineteenth-century society drawing room, strip its occupants of their mutton-chop whiskers and rip off their crinolines, add in some false eyelashes, and you have the Playboy Club. From tight-laced corsets to prohibitive codes of conduct, from D-cup bras to deferential curtseys, the bunny girls lived out a glamorised fantasy in which men-about-town could buy an updated version of the sexually unavailable, heavily supervised Victorian handmaiden. The discreet blush, the feminine flirtation, the billowing bosoms – combined with a strict 'look but don't touch' diktat: a hundred years earlier, this was the way their grandmothers had flattered men into marriage. And not so very much had changed. As Patsy Reading recalls:

I suppose I'm a bit of a flirt – and I suppose I thought, Oh I might meet Mr Right here. *Might*. And I had watched all the Disney films, and – Yes! Of course my prince was coming on his white charger, it was just a matter of time.

But then, in a way, you knew you were safe – because it was just looking and no touching . . .

(though according to Carol Cleveland, the 'wealthy Arabs' paid scant attention to this rule. 'I was always getting my tail tweaked . . .'). Of course, outside working hours was a different matter, and Victor Lownes, the club's chief executive and Hugh Hefner's right-hand man, became renowned for his party-giving and philandering ways. 'It was pretty amazing – it was hot and cold running girls,' remembered Angela Pitt, Lownes's housekeeper at the time. He could take his pick. 'It's like a harem, isn't it? And the guy was extraordinarily attractive and charismatic – *and* he was your boss!'

Pat Quinn and Patsy Reading felt no qualms about how they earned their living. 'I loved being a rabbit,' says Pat:

Those ears were great. We were the *crème de la crème* of rabbits. Oh yes. Very proud of being a rabbit.

And Patsy:

The costume? It was such fun. Who would *not* like wearing a bunny costume? Just imagine the fun of it! – And doing the dip, being charming. Who would *not* enjoy all that?

And I know the feminists would be appalled – but we didn't feel that way. We didn't see it that we were prostituting ourselves, or that it was sleazy.

It was a job, it was good pay – and all I can tell you is that it was FUN. It really was. Fun, *fun*, <u>fun</u>.

*

Smashing time, smashing time,
We're gonna have a –
Smashing time, smashing time
We're gonna have a
SMASHING TIME!

Silly lyrics bubbled from the opening titles of an equally silly film (entitled, unsurprisingly, *Smashing Time*) starring Rita Tushingham and Lynn Redgrave. This undemanding slapstick romp from the 'Ingénues-take-on-London' genre was billed as a satire on Swinging London. But George Melly's script is sadly heavy-handed and, by the time it was released in 1967, it was already passé; the world of hip photographers and dolly birds it purported to satirise had already been subjected to Antonioni's more searching lens. The film's value is its sequences that recapture times and places from the past. The urban locations of *Smashing Time* include the blackened exterior of pre-renovation St Pancras, traffic-free thoroughfares, Battersea Power Station belching vapour, that symbol of modernity the Post Office Tower, and riverscapes of the Thames without skyscrapers. This London still had subterranean public conveniences, barrow-boys were common sights selling their wares along the Camden pavements, conductors patrolled double-deckers collecting fourpenny fares in leather satchels, and black faces on the streets had shock value. Then there's Brenda (Rita Tushingham) being put in charge of a pretentious boutique done up with Victoriana and funky cushions – surely modelled on the Chelsea Mecca, Granny Takes a Trip? – and Yvonne (Lynn Redgrave), dressed in a red-and-white geometric mini prancing down a colourful Carnaby Street with its wacky shop fascias and window dressings. Another sequence shows Brenda kitted out in a fluffy pussy-catsuit with pointy ears and a long curly tail, playing hostess in a glamorous nightclub. Cinema audiences would certainly have caught the reference.

But the tempo of smashing, zany, dolled-up Swinging London was slowing, giving way to a new, more placid and inward mood. 1967 was a year of extremes. Is it possible to reconcile the backward-looking glamour world of the bunny girl with the emergence of the hippie? How does Hugh Hefner's vision co-exist with that of *Sergeant Pepper's Lonely Hearts Club Band*; or those false, contorted bodies with free-floating flower children? Before they descended on our grey island, both hippies and bunnies had arisen out of the USA. Until 1967, for a few short years, Liverpool and London had driven the cultural agenda. Now the reset button had been pressed on style, pop, drugs and philosophy, reinstating America at the cutting edge of change. Students and bohemians who appropriated the fashionable 'hipster' idioms of African Americans had evolved into 'hippies', and reports reached these shores of the Summer of Love, the Human Be-In in Golden Gate Park, and the invasion of Haight-Ashbury by thousands of footloose teens in pursuit of transcendence and cheap hash, irresistibly drawn by Scott McKenzie's summertime music and lyrics: 'If you're going to San Francisco / Be sure to wear some flowers in your hair . . .' The hippie orthodoxy lined up young against old, cool against square, and its gurus endorsed the use of psychedelic drugs, exhorting their followers to 'Turn on, tune in, drop out'. Their peace-and-love, flower-power message was anti-capitalist and nature-worshipping; like bright blades, the fragile daffodils they brandished told of yin and yang, female and male, aggression and submission.

What could be more captivating? Fashion éditor Felicity Green charted the change on the British side of the pond:

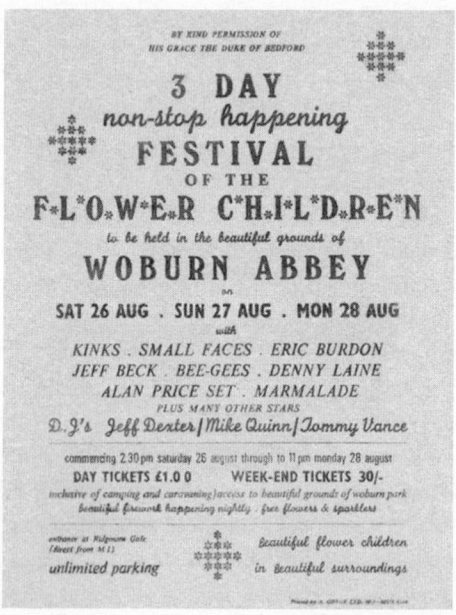

Beautiful flower children, in beautiful surroundings. In August 1967, at the height of the Summer of Love, the Duke of Bedford opened his grounds to an invasion of weekend hippies.

Striped plastic trouser suits in Op or Pop are Old Hat. Out. Finished.

The kookie kids of '66 have been replaced by the flower girls of '67 . . . Short sharp hairdos are now freaked out in a riot of fuzz or curls . . .

Twiggy changed her look from gamine waif to Dame aux Camélias. At the height of flower power, Janey Ironside, professor of Fashion at the Royal College of Art, was called upon to contribute a section about our relationship with clothes to a high-profile television documentary. Ironside immediately proposed featuring a couple of 'flower people'. Unfortunately, it proved difficult to find anyone willing to participate. Ironside scoured her hippie contacts for flower children, but kept getting turned down, despite the generous payment on offer. 'No, I don't know any, and in any case they are against all that sort of thing . . .' was the typical reaction.

I had forgotten that their clothes did not indicate a passing fashion among hippies but denoted an anti-capitalist but peaceful philosophy.

Eventually she tracked down a young man and woman who not only possessed the exotic gear but were also bona fide flower people. At the BBC, the normally blasé receptionists were duly thrilled at the spectacle:

The very pretty girl wore her hair straight – short and straggly – and her feet bare. Her clothes were many coloured, long, on the whole unidentifiable, with a mass of Eastern jewellery. The thin attractive young man wore purple satin women's trousers covered in frills, with a sleeveless Afghan embroidered sheepskin jacket and a pendant round his neck, while his hair was freaked out into a huge frizzy halo round his head.

In her memoir Ironside did not comment on the breakdown of gender boundaries that this look exemplified. Nor did she expound on the anti-fashion ethos now emerging: low-maintenance, do-it-yourself, individualistic style. For many under twenty-five, the alternative way to be and to dress was hard to resist.

A Calm Sea

We'll return to the hippies, the flower children and the permissive society. For now, it should be acknowledged – as an important corrective to a widely held view that hippie-freakydom, sex and drug culture dominated the decade – that even in 1967 there were innumerable other ways to live. Against the background of a deficit and a devalued pound, the mood was becoming decidedly anti-frivolous. Certainly, paisley bedspreads, flowers and free love were not for everybody.

In 1967 we were still a nation of Mrs Grundys and domestic goddesses, with fidelity, patriotism, uniformity, thrift and tedium alive and well in suburbs and villages across the land. As for turning your back on capitalism, that was a luxury few could afford; while for busy wage-earners dangly jewellery and freaked-out locks just got in the way. Paying the rent was hard enough, but marriage and motherhood cramped one's style even more. And where Miss Dropout opted for narcotics, Miss Normal preferred booze (as Melissa North said, 'alcohol was for old people . . .').

For me, uniformity meant exactly that: being uniform. That was the year I first became a pupil at a deeply traditional girls' grammar school situated at the foot of a hill in our quiet town. Here, daily, 400 pink-faced, velour-hatted, adolescent girls clad in identical navy-blue gabardines, blazers and box-pleated serge skirts trooped beneath the arched gateway to the school, whose motto, spelled out in wrought iron, read 'By Love Serve One Another'. Each morning we prayed and sang, with the mistresses joining in. Those schoolmistresses were spinsters, the 'unclaimed treasures' of the First World War,[*] each one buttoned up, across her capacious bosom, in impregnable tweed: Miss Brinkworth with her club foot who knew all about Roman roads; Miss Nicklin who taught us to sew flat fell seams and bind buttonholes; and the dubiously named gym mistress, Miss Pinchin, who chivvied us naked into a post-hockey shower and then stood sentinel.

[*] Such women inspired the subject of my earlier book, *Singled Out: How Two Million Women Survived Without Men After the First World War* (2007).

Here, house ties were worn, lots of hockey was played and the corridors were hung with solemn lettered Boards honouring the Old Girls who had passed on to 'Cantab', 'Lond' and 'Oxon'.

The last chapter described what happened when those pink-faced maidens got there. Beyond the portals of education, the adult world that awaited them was one of stultifying tedium. A 'little job' – often a secretarial one – would tide them through until marriage. In *An Education* Lynn Barber describes being an office junior: the segregation of 'girls' from men, the mind-numbing tedium of taking dictation, of typing it out with multiple sheets of inky carbon paper, the utilitarian workspaces furnished with metal filing cabinets, spider plants and ashtrays. Being able to smoke – as everyone did – was the one redeeming feature.

But apparently it was patriotism, not ennui, that motivated five public-spirited typists, employed in the Surbiton offices of a heating and ventilation company, to demonstrate the spirit of the Blitz by using their tea-breaks to work an extra half hour every day, for nothing. Overcome by anxieties about national decline, the women got together in the winter of 1967 and spontaneously offered their additional services gratis to the firm's marketing director. In the space of a week they had a national campaign on their hands: 'I'm backing Britain', complete with Union Jack imagery and badges. But, quashed by trades unions, it died as quickly as it had started. It was back to the desk job and the dark winter evenings, back to the rush-hour commute, back to your flat, strap-hanging on the suburban trains.

Nevertheless, for wage-earning women, this life might offer a glimpse of freedom. Mary Ingham described her move into an unfurnished flat with two girlfriends as 'the first true stirrings of emancipation'. 'Flat-sharing . . .' *The New London Spy* tells us, 'is a special feature of the London domestic scene . . .' And a perfect example of flatshare life jumps from between the covers of an October 1967 issue of *Woman's Own*. Five student nurses – Liz, Janet, Jane, Jenny and Looby – wrote in to the magazine's 'The Way We Live' page, describing their everyday lives 'on the wrong side of Hampstead Heath'. 'Straight' or 'square' is how Melissa North and her friends would have described them. In their group shot, Liz, Janet and co. project a far-from-trendy image, dressed for off-duty in daintily patterned shirtwaisters. But, though the haircuts are 'square', the dresses are mini, and topping the stack of vinyl LPs artlessly scattered on the coffee table before them is the unmistakably iconic cover of *Sergeant Pepper*. Their little flat is the realisation of a dream of independence – 'We get a great kick from fending for ourselves and find it great fun doing housework to the liveliest records.' Nevertheless, the big excitement is Liz's imminent marriage in December. Looby is going to be her bridesmaid, and the others will be making the dresses.

Carmen Callil set little store by wedding dresses, though she loved nice clothes and continental holidays. By 1967 Carmen was twenty-nine, with a foot firmly on her chosen career ladder; in any case, her well-off boyfriend was already married. A lucky chance got her the job as publicity manager for Panther Books; publicists tended to be pretty young women. On the receiving end were a lot of older male journalists, many of whom were serial gropers. Carmen's office was round the corner from a clutch of Soho pubs, and she learnt to keep up drink-for-drink, at lunchtime and post-work, with the publishing and media men who propped up their bars. No hippie, her day was fuelled by alcohol and a passionate love of her work, but never by drugs. 'Somebody once forced some pot onto me, and I hated it. It made things come out of my fingers. It's always been my way to have one glass too many. I'd wake up in the morning feeling terrible. But that was when my proper life really began.' Carmen formed tight friendships with the other females in her line of work. 'We laughed, we read. It was an education . . .'

Up in Manchester, rookie journalist Ann Leslie's flatshare friend was the actress Janet Suzman; behind lace curtains the pair created a refuge together from the pressures of carving out a career, negotiating the everyday with the help of comfort food and booze. Their speciality was 'spag bol' made with tinned mince and brandy; their Sunday treat, toast and marmalade topped with whipped cream, was also heavily brandy-laced. 'Our drunken cookery was divine, wasn't it? Everyone adored it!' Janet recalled. From 1963 the guru for single working women like these was the redoubtable journalist Katharine Whitehorn, whose chatty and eminently practical manual, *Cooking in a Bedsitter*, was targeted at city survivors in need of a square meal.

In the 1960s fast food meant fish-and-chip shops, period. Ready meals were decades away. Most bedsits were minimally equipped with little more than a single gas ring, and the water supply was often at the end of the corridor in a shared bathroom. Whitehorn's sympathetic understanding of her readers' problems – lack of money and refrigerators, lack of space and lack of little porcelain ramekins – made *Cooking in a Bedsitter* an instant bestseller, as she showed readers how to do creative, thrifty things with tinned soup, bacon and half a cauliflower. They were urged to befriend the casserole and to try using teabags. Whitehorn also understood the complex imperatives of being a young woman, so there were helpful sections on 'Cooking to Impress', 'Cooking for a Man' and 'Asking Him Up' ('The problem here is to make sure that everything is looking nice without anything looking planned . . . Dig in your food box as if you had no idea what was there and you just often do have a tin of foie gras handy'). Independent women who wanted to manoeuvre their man into making a move were learning a new set of rules in the how-to-catch-your-man game. But it was still a game.

Once you'd caught him, the social norms made it ever harder to break loose or live like a butterfly while, for those who hankered for hippie freedoms, getting married and breeding were particularly restricting. After Cynthia Lennon gave birth to their son, John took off on tour, leaving her in Liverpool with an infant who howled incessantly. She was a nervous wreck, seeing double with exhaustion. John dropped in intermittently, but was unwilling to do his share – 'He would leave the room whenever I changed a nappy.' Even if you weren't an aspirant hippie, the 'sour milk, urinous nappies [and] bits of lint . . .' (as Sylvia Plath described them) could drive one deranged. Audrey Battersby, later a vocal feminist, was going 'quietly crazy' with three small children in north London when she started to meet other mothers, mainly to talk about child-rearing. Out of their conversations emerged a growing anger.

Three years later, provision of free twenty-four-hour nurseries would be one of the fundamental demands made by the nascent Women's Liberation movement. The voices of Hannah Gavron's interviewees (in *The Captive Wife*) remind us how the mothering-versus-work dilemma, with which so many women are familiar today, was already becoming acute in the mid-1960s:

> I wanted to work but [my husband] would not hear of it . . .
>
> When they are young children need their mother, and it's doing them a wrong if she isn't there . . .
>
> You've no idea what it's like to spend all day in one room trying to keep the children quiet because the landlady can't bear noise. I feel like I'm in a cage . . .

No wonder hallucinogens and floaty frocks were the preserve of the few.

But Harriet Lear never complained, because her exemplary married life was the one she had chosen. At the age of twenty-six Harriet put her youthful adventurousness behind her, and married a country solicitor. In 1967 motherhood was yet to come (she would eventually have five children). She and Nick were on a tight income, paying off £1 a week for their car. 'As for the various youth cultures of the time – my mother would sometimes say, "Things are going to the dogs" – but it absolutely bypassed me . . . You see, I didn't read the newspapers.' Harriet joined the Women's Royal Voluntary Service to help with meals-on-wheels; friendships evolved through the church. Mainly, she was blissful, tending to a neglected home, an abandoned garden and – until the longed-for babies arrived – orphan lambs. The Lears were frugal in the extreme, growing their own vegetables.

> We had no television. Really, I was absolutely happy, just waiting for my husband to come home at night . . .

Emma Codrington was another who felt slight regret, but mainly detachment, as a generation of young women shifted their focus from respect for their elders, to indifference or hostility. The 'Youthquake' seemed faint and distant in the safe Tory world of her Wiltshire community:

> This is a very nice, conventional little market town. I've always felt very lucky to live in Wilton. We didn't have any bells and beads here!

When the news brought stories of rejection and rebellion, Emma shut her ears.

I thought they were complete idiots, making an unnecessary commotion. I didn't think they were really achieving anything – just disrupting a calm sea.

In her late thirties, Emma had worked all her life to instil certain values – teamwork, duty, responsibility, good deeds, plus the quality she describes as 'stickability' – in her groups of Girl Guides. Sitting round a campfire singing and eating sausages; holding the end of a rope ladder; working with Meg, her lifelong companion, to build up their old folk's home: these were the activities that made sense of her life.

Meanwhile, Scottish nursery maid Veronica MacNab had turned her back on Chelsea and all it stood for. Veronica had aims, and she needed qualifications. From 1965 she resumed her life north of the border, where she found employment as a trainee in a Barnardo's home just outside Edinburgh. Ravelrig housed kids who were deaf, coeliac and hydrocephalic, and she had one small boy affected by thalidomide, who had been dumped because his mother couldn't cope. 'Most of them were from the most sordid, god-awful, atrocious family backgrounds that you could ever, *ever* imagine. They arrived with scabies, eczema, nits, the lot. They had been living on crusts, lying on urine-soaked mattresses. One child whose mother had committed suicide had lain beside the corpse for three days. She screamed and screamed and screamed.' Veronica's new working environment reinforced the values she had grown up with: family, hierarchy and hard work. Prayers were said every morning before breakfast with Matron, and six days a week the trainees worked a twelve-hour day. The home reeked of polish and disinfectant.

But slowly, very slowly, the sounds of the sixties penetrated Veronica's consciousness. On precious evenings off, she went with friends to hear folk music in the Edinburgh pubs, and she started to spend her meagre salary on music. 'My much-prized first record was "Blowin' in the Wind".' At work, Dylan's deadpan lyrics and skirling harmonica drifted down the scrubbed linoleum corridors – 'I played it on the record player in the nurses' staff room.' Ambiguous, bittersweet and uplifting, Dylan's poem of protest spoke to all of hope, humanity and the empowerment of the meek; a transcendent anthem of freedom.

Lucy in the Sky

Which brings us back to the free spirits.

Drugs and hippies are inseparable, which might explain the rarity of the full-time hippie, who could afford his or her highs without holding down a day job. For the majority, the tie-dyes and marijuana were an add-on, brought out for the weekend and on special occasions. On one level, the anti-materialism of hippie culture was itself delivered via *things*: your sandals, beads, albums and wind-chimes were signifiers of your identity. The historian Dominic Sandbrook also points out that only a small number of the rich and young had the wherewithal to follow the path of 'true' peace-and-love hippiedom, while their fellow-travellers were fair-weather hippies, for whom '[flower power] became a form of consumerism'. True – and this is borne out in Michael Schofield's important survey of British teenagers, which shows how few hard drug addicts there were in Britain in 1967 – just 395 – while the proportion of teens turning to cannabis remained overall extremely small.

But it is important to appreciate that there was more to hippiedom than bells, patchouli oil and druggy oblivion. The hippies' anti-Establishment, anti-war and anti-materialist messages were then, and remain to this day, components of a tenacious ideology that – for millions of people – does not lie down. Also, at its best, this was a peace-and-love Utopia that outlawed the constructs of masculinity: greed and violence. Even more importantly, the money men and playboys, with their fat cigars and fast cars, were regarded as tainted. The evils of capitalism, the things, the property, the robotic work and the poisoning of the planet were laid at the door of the heartless patriarchy – 'The Man', as he was sometimes known. Virtuous, unworldly hippies had a psychic distaste for Mammon and all his accompanying machismo, preferring to exist like the flowers of the field, independent of jobs-for-life, mortgages and the trappings of affluence. You did your own thing. You trod lightly on the earth, meditated, read *The Hobbit* and the *I Ching*, sought out ley lines, made art. You cultivated domestic, 'womanly' pursuits: cooking wholefoods, singing, sewing, planting beans according to the phases of the moon, weaving bags. The alternative sixties society was stumbling uncertainly towards a green, anti-macho, anti-materialist creed:

> There was an urge to be less consumer-orientated, to lead a more communal life, to care . . .
>
> Andrea Adam

> You put all your effort into not being employed, not becoming an accountant.
>
> Sue Miles

> How little you could do with, rather than how much you could get, became in itself a kind of status.
>
> Julie Christie

But it was Pattie Boyd, cushioned as she was by her marriage to a Beatle, and despite a love of Charles Jourdan shoes, who expressed it best:

> In the sixties nobody did anything for money. The main goal was spirituality – and creativity. And not caring about money channelled our creativity . . . If I needed some money then George or somebody in the office would give it to me.
>
> Why was this? I think it was because there were more jobs available. If you needed money, it was, 'Oh, I'll just work in this shop because I know the owners and they sell really cool clothes . . .'
>
> Whoever had money would pay for it all . . . If I was out with girlfriends, I'd say, 'Oh, I'll pay, don't worry . . .' I don't know why money wasn't a big issue. But it wasn't.
>
> And everybody of my generation feels the same way . . .

The aggression associated with money-making was also dampened in this time of gentle, scrawny, long-haired, dreamy-eyed dope heads, more concerned with the latest batch of Afghan herb than pumping dollars through the system. Androgyny was trending in the pop world; men and women danced in the same way, but apart. Male stars embraced female vanity, wearing Biba, applying eyeliner and sequins. Jimi Hendrix fussed over his immaculately ironed shirt frills, Mick Jagger adopted Shakespearean blouses while Donovan and Marc Bolan projected a clean-shaven, feminised, soft-focussed romanticism to their legions of besotted teen fans. 'See Emily Play', sung by Syd

Barrett of Pink Floyd, and 'Lucy in the Sky With Diamonds' on the
Beatles' *Sergeant Pepper* album (both released in 1967) were distillations
of a gentle, druggy whimsicality. The hippie sound had a gypsy, vaga-
bond bohemianism which made Elvis's stomping phallic rock of just a
few years earlier seem gross and showy. Ruffled blouses and long curly
hair blurred the sex lines, and male serenity and inertia appeared to
hand the power balance across to the female. As colours, forms and
music fused under the influence of mind-altering substances, it sometimes seemed as if gender, too, could be merged, freed from the past.

That notion of freedom was mesmerising. Freedom to move at
will, freedom of the mind, but above all freedom of the body. Women
like Sheila Rowbotham could see that in certain ways the hippie
counterculture benefited women. The sprouting of unorthodox new
spaces extended women's options. In the old world, it was unacceptable for a woman to go to a club or a pub on her own. She would be
made to feel awkward and vulnerable. But drifting gently through a
haze of joss sticks at the Arts Lab, or leafing through *The Lord of the
Rings* in Better Books, those conventions no longer applied.

> As everything in the counterculture was meant to be weird and mys-
> tical, you could take cover under the imperative on everyone to be a
> free spirit. You could hang around alone, bump into people you
> knew, pirouette in the light shows to music, hide in a corner or meet
> someone new.

So were the male hippies relinquishing masculine power along
with mortgages and market forces? Would marriage and motherhood
become the old world order? Or was it all a mirage, as illusory as the
flying saucers, Middle-Earthers and magicians so beloved of the
'heads' and freaks? Predictably, where freedom was concerned, not
everyone got an equal share of it; these men's attitude to women was
as stuck in the past as the fairy tales they treasured.

*

In 1967 the rarefied aristo-hippies were the ones in the vanguard. (In
this context, it's worth remembering that women from the social
élites have always had possibilities denied to their rank-and-file sisters: like money, domestic help, childcare, leisure – and freedom to

dream.) Novelist and scion of a barony, Emma Tennant recalls watching the ' "real" Sixties' unfold before her, hanging out with galleristas and artists. Cecil Beaton recorded in his diary a visit to the upper-class ' "dopists" of a certain young set in London', where one of the guests was the socialite and beauty Jane Ormsby-Gore, daughter of Lady Harlech – recently killed in a car crash – who was tranquillising herself with reefers. ('We were seeking the Holy Grail at that moment, and always very high-minded and spiritual . . .' remembered Ms Ormsby-Gore). Later Mick and Marianne arrived. Most preposterous of the blue-blooded tearaways was Viscount Weymouth, who took his *droit de seigneur* to extremes, collecting over seventy 'wifelets' together to form one big happy family on his Longleat estate.

Another diarist, the Bloomsbury intellectual Frances Partridge,* paints a vivid picture of advantaged youth gathered on a summer's day at her brother-in-law's country home in an East Anglian village:

May 30th 1967

The younger generation seem like opium-smokers, lying about soaking up sensations, pouring cigarettes, drink, cinema, television and marijuana in at the portals of their senses until near-satiation is reached.

Later that summer, with friends, she returned to the same subject:

July 30th 1967

We talked of the burning, everlasting topic of the drug-taking, flower-loving, Zen-Buddhist young . . . [Ed] mentioned someone who 'was very much "turned on" '. F: 'What does that mean, exactly?' 'Taking drugs and wearing flowers and bells and loving each other and calling each other beautiful.' According to Ed, bells are the badge of drugs . . .

---

* In *All Dressed Up: The Sixties and the Counterculture* (1998), Jonathon Green makes a fascinating and persuasive case for the Bloomsbury Group as precursors of the 1960s rebels and proto-hippies. Both groups were pioneers, dealing in shock; they were modernists, espousers of the avant-garde, reformers, challengers of authority, and believers in passion and self-expression. And they were 'cultural patricides'. Melissa North, a central countercultural character, also told me, 'Holroyd's biography of Strachey and the other Bloomsbury biographies influenced me hugely. It was their bohemianism and so on. Incredible. I thought, wow, this is how I want to live . . .'

That evening, as if to demonstrate how 'turned on' she was, Frances's young daughter-in-law announced her arrival with the sound of tinkling:

> Susan said, 'Oh, here come the bells.' It was Henrietta with two friends, wearing a bell on a string round her neck like a farm animal. She looked lovely and came up and kissed me warmly.

Caroline Harper's story is also an illustration of how privilege begets rebellion. 'Looking back,' she says, 'I was a hideous little snob. I was very right wing, and really rather ghastly . . .' But much in her entitled background would conspire to propel her in the opposite direction.

At the beginning of this book, we briefly saw Caroline as she is today, an elegant, confident woman who exudes warmth and wit, as if to the manner born. Caroline's father was club chairman of an illustrious polo ground in the south of England; her mother gladly took on the role of polo hostess, entertaining a glittering array of spectators and players from the upper echelons of international society. From the age of four the backdrop to Caroline's life was the playboy world of polo.

Of course, she herself didn't compete. 'Some girls played polo, but my father was very against it – he said they ruined the game for the men.' In the early sixties Caroline was sent away to boarding school. But every summer weekend she returned, accompanied by a gaggle of breathless girlfriends:

> I was hugely popular. Everyone wanted to stay with me because of the polo players. The glamour of them! The Argentines particularly. They were all amazingly good-looking. And me and my girlfriends would mill about swooning. And there were definitely some kisses. And sometimes coming close, and sometimes a bit too close . . .
>
> Sex, glamour and horses. I loved it all. I loved the life – and I didn't question it in any shape or form.

Ten years earlier, and – living in this milieu – Caroline would probably have fallen into line with her parents' expectations for her, which were to leave school, do the season, and make a suitable match with the wealthy polo-playing heir to a grouse moor. But by then it was

1966. Almost imperceptibly, the rebel in Caroline Harper was beginning to awaken.

> I was reading *The Carpetbaggers*★ to my riveted dormitory – and getting it confiscated. So the whole sort of sexual freedom thing was definitely hitting . . .

Ignoring her headmistress's advice to try for Oxford ('I was only interested in having fun'), Caroline left school at sixteen and submitted to another of society's rituals ordained for the perfection of womankind: the Tante Marie School of Cooking in Woking. There she learnt to make a very good white sauce. But for a girl of Caroline's class, there was really only one place to be: London, which by 1967 was the centre of the social universe. After some nagging, her parents caved in; it was agreed she would go through the motions of attending secretarial college, while in reality marking time until marriage. Her mother had a handsome, asset-rich aristocrat lined up for her and had taught her that a woman's value lies in externals:

> The women I knew were of a type. They were often very good-looking, glamorous and good hostesses – funny – often sexy. In some ways, they were quite free-spirited, as were my parents, but all within a certain parameter. Mum got a lot of air time because she was funny. My value was to be pretty and sexy.
>
> But the serious opinions were all offered by the men. What they said went. I never thought my opinion had any value at all.
>
> The men had all the power. And I fed it to them.

Caroline describes herself as 'a well-trained people-pleaser'.

And so, what was supposed to be the transitional, débutante phase of life for an extremely pretty, privileged and popular young woman got underway. So far, so familiar: shopping, soirées, dances, flirting and drinks parties consumed Caroline's free time. But something had changed. As Cecil Beaton had noted, upper-crust gatherings had acquired a new, narcissistic character. The 'dopists' had begun to infiltrate high society. Dandified and highly styled young men were

---

★ *The Carpetbaggers* (1961), Harold Robbins's sizzling bestseller, included explicit language, imagery and scenes of fellatio.

appearing, stoned, wearing flamboyant floral finery. The day of the peacock had dawned.

And Caroline was fascinated:

> From fairly early on, I was aware that I seemed to be far more attracted to the colourful guys in the corner of the room. They represented something 'other' than the stuffy, tight, restrained, inhibited, perfectly behaved world I belonged to.
>
> You sort of just know, don't you? They wear different clothes for a start.

For Caroline was now discovering that the aristo-hippies differed in a number of ways from the testosterone-charged Argentines and macho, opinionated Etonians who had been her model of manhood up to now: 'only interested in sex'. The long-haired *roués* she had started to meet were also interesting and deep, and they were searching – like her – for meaning.

> And so I moved towards these 'unsuitable' men. They were the reprobates of the deb world, the dangerous ones on the edge who were experimenting with dope.
>
> One of them quickly became a best friend, a wonderful colourful character – a peacock – who was trying out drugs. And once I had a best friend to laugh with I could start to explore.

Dope suppressed their sexual aggression, and they looked like Jesus: 'These were the kind of men I went for: feminine, introverted, gentle and androgynous.' Among them, she found her opinions listened to, her views shared. As idealists, they wanted to change the world. 'I basically bought into everything that the young of my time believed.' She and her friends cared about the planet, hated the Vietnam War, were anti-materialistic and anti-Establishment.

> There was huge anger with the older generation. We called them the Straights, as in 'Oh, he's terribly straight . . .' or 'She's *so* straight . . .'
>
> Now, looking back, I know my parents just wanted the best for me – it's just that our ideas of what was best differed so greatly. And I had so little understanding then of what they'd fought for – and

given their lives to – to produce, actually, a stable launch pad for us to take off from, like a lot of colourful butterflies.

Along with her friends, Caroline experimented with free love, and she tells me that, looking back at her several dozen lovers, she recalls some memorable moments. But sex was not a driver. The game-changer was drugs:

And so I started smoking. And it was soon after that I started to take drugs more seriously . . .

★

Like Caroline Harper, Melissa North was a boarding-school girl who had hung around the posh party circuit. She and her counterculture friends had been rolling joints since 1965, and that same year she tried LSD for the first time. She was also holding down a decent if rackety job at a music agency, booking gigs for top bands. By 1967 acid (LSD) was regularly on the menu.

Yes, I took it all the time. Well, not every day, but certainly if you went to UFO to see the Floyd, you would take acid because you were going to see a psychedelic band . . .

And bands were Melissa's world.

Taking an acid trip was an intense, ceremonial rite of passage that dissolved the confines of convention. For the post-war housewife, a fitted kitchen with picture windows had offered dream-come-true normality. Melissa and her group were stepping beyond the plate glass, discovering a layered, coloured, ecstatic reality that made home improvements and Hoover Keymatics seem trivial and superfluous. And now it appeared that the locks imprisoning women within four walls were actually flimsy, brittle and impermanent. As Jenny Diski wrote in *The Sixties* (2009):

The middle sixties was that moment when Dorothy stepped through her front door, out of Kansas, on to the undreamed-of yellowness of the brick road on her way to the Emerald City, and the heart burst with pleasure at the sudden busting out of a full-blown Technicolor world.

Melissa North was ecstatic. One could spend hours mesmerised by the beautiful purple tendrils of a fuchsia, enraptured by the slurred, slow-motion resonances of a guitar solo, mindblown by the multi-hued grandeur of a sunset, in love with the turning, wheeling motion of the planet itself. And as bourgeois dreams were replaced by hippie hallucinations, things that seemed important to the mediocre masses – like safety, morality, legality, Tupperware and what to do about dinner – were jettisoned. After Jimi Hendrix arrived in the UK Melissa got close to Howard Parker (aka 'H'), his roadie, and accompanied him on gigs round the country. They took the gear in a van, and Melissa would help set up the amps and speakers on stage.

> And once the gear was up we'd take acid, and then we'd stand behind the amps and Jimi would play. And afterwards we'd load up all the things – on the acid! – and then drive back to London to meet Jimi at the Speakeasy for dinner.
>
> We always drove on acid. The whole of the M1 was nothing but vans driving up and down on acid. And we'd stop off at the Blue Boar transport café for, you know, egg and chips, and there'd be all kinds of encounters, like, 'Oh, hi Dick, I haven't seen you!' And it'd be, like, 'Oh, man, I'm so tripping. I mean, I'm so tripping, I mean, even these baked beans are *speaking* to me man . . .'

Returning at three in the morning from Manchester, H missed a turning and hit the kerb; a wheel flew off the van. As they scrambled to look for it in the dark, life seemed astonishing, peculiar and wonderfully freaky. H and Melissa lay in the road laughing uncontrollably.

> Everything was so much FUN! I mean one was in such high spirits. I always think of acid as being hysterical with laughter . . . I mean, we were very young, and it was just, like, oh – joyous.

This way of life was mind-altering and exhilarating if your day job permitted, if you had wealthy parents or were a pop star. Rainbows, mystical perceptions and cosmic visions were luxury add-ons that came with the affluent rock'n'roll lifestyle. Though the term 'recreational' was not then in currency, drugs, like Sindy dolls, were magical toys that acquired a projected life outside your head. Unlike prescription tranquillisers – ('Mother's Little Helper') – they weren't there to prop you up through the day's drudgery, they were there to validate your rejection of the mundane, the trivial and the domestic. As Melissa North says:

> We took drugs not just to fall around laughing but because we thought they made us think better – and bigger.

The washload could wait. Interiority took on a new meaning. Who needed the joyless drudgery, the petty battles with dirt, disorder and dust endured by a myriad of crushed housewives? There was a different way to look at inhabited spaces. Hallucinating on 6,000 micrograms of LSD, Henrietta Moraes was awestruck by the 'silken, silvery cobwebs, glittering with diamond drops . . .' strewn across her room. Marianne Faithfull stared with distended eyes as the rose-and-trellis Sanderson wallpaper of her bedroom started to dance a mystic ballet that revealed the secrets of the universe through its intricate choreography.

But, just as a spotless home transmitted messages of virtue and right-eousness to the world, the slovenly and neglectful drug-user was inevitably associated with immorality and degeneracy. Marianne saw her pretty nest in Chelsea descend into squalor, the draining board 'strewn with bloody needles', junkies stupefied on the floor. Peak deca-dence was reached when, famously, the police busted Mick Jagger and Keith Richards at Redlands, Keith Richards's home. Marianne Faith-full was there, adding to the debauched frisson of the occasion by exhibiting the fact that she was naked under a fur rug. The press gorged on it, and Jagger and Richards were given custodial sentences.

Cynthia Powell fought a losing battle to keep house, in the face of John Lennon's pot habit, tidying, cooking and trying to minimise interruptions so that John could sleep till two in the afternoon; when he woke she would bring him breakfast in bed. Following the release of *Sergeant Pepper* the drug-taking was escalating; John would pick up glassy-eyed drifters at night clubs and bring them home for all-night sessions listening to loud music, drinking, drugging and raiding the larder. Brick by brick, narcotics were building an ever-growing wall between them.

George Harrison would ultimately retreat behind a different bar-rier. But in 1967 he and Pattie Boyd were still newlyweds, drugs were built into their lives, and they were having fun. Pattie described acid as 'part of the creative process' for the Beatles; though both she and George were disillusioned when they visited the hippie district of San Francisco in the summer of 1967:

> We were expecting Haight-Ashbury to be special, a creative and artistic place, filled with Beautiful People, but it was horrible – full of ghastly dropouts, bums and spotty youths, all out of their brains.

For the same reason Melissa North is reluctant to describe herself as a hippie, seeing the label as belonging to the Haight-Ashbury movement. 'Our culture was more about people sharing. People came to your house, and if you hadn't any dope, they brought some and you shared it.'

Melissa stresses that art, originality and vision were what differentiated her set from the spotty dropouts. 'It was about people doing things. We made things, we were creative.' The youth rebellion found expression through music, but also through little illustrated magazines, album-cover design, batik patchwork skirts, silver puzzle rings, face-paint, funky typography, surreal 'happenings', and décor that took art out of the frame and onto the walls of shabby flats in Hackney, Chelsea, Fulham and Brighton.

In 1967 Celia Birtwell and Zandra Rhodes were rethinking textile design with a new emphasis on whimsicality and psychedelia, Yoko Ono was being censored for her films showing close-ups of buttocks walking away from camera, while the artist Joan Hills was directing light shows for Soft Machine and Jimi Hendrix. But women were still up against the rigid attitudes of the art Establishment. When pop artist Jann Haworth applied to the Slade she asked whether she should submit her work. 'Well, no,' came the reply, 'we don't really need to see portfolios of the women students. We just need to see their photographs because they're here to keep the boys happy.'

> I promise you – not a word of a lie. At the Slade, for sure, there was this kind of separation, that somehow the male students knew about paint. [The tutors] would say, 'Men just know about paint, and women don't.'
>
> From that point, it was head-on competition with the male students . . .

Spurred by indignation, Haworth pioneered outrageous soft sculptures crafted from latex and fabrics – 'a female language to which the male students didn't have access . . .' – and went on to find fame collaborating with Peter Blake on the album cover for *Sergeant Pepper*.

Vultures

In many a dingy basement the bohemian garret dream took shape. But it wasn't always romantic.

This was the heyday of the short-lived Covent Garden Arts Lab, conceived ('[it] was my baby') by underground celebrity Jim Haynes. It was envisioned as an 'energy centre', always ready to embrace the weird and the wacky, the hip and the happening. According to one of its chroniclers, the drifters who used the Arts Lab as a crash pad existed in a permanent fug of marijuana. Quintessentially, the venue offered rich pickings for sexual buccaneers, notably Jim Haynes himself and his comrade-in-arms the talented but quarrelsome theatre director Charles Marowitz. Both were American. Marowitz, another indispensable underground character, had arrived in London in the 1950s. His description of the Arts Lab as an old warehouse cheaply done out with rotting foam rubber mattresses, thick with the reek of pot smoke and unwashed socks, has all the sex appeal of a pigsty; nevertheless, according to him, its high-minded countercultural aims and 'New Bohemianism' were a veneer masking its real purpose:

> It became a kind of sexual seraglio for itinerant potheads and students . . . who perceived it mainly as a convenient place to 'pull birds'.

In this field, Marowitz and Haynes were close collaborators, though they often purloined each other's spoils.

> Our deepest bond was the mutual adoration of pussy and, in pursuit of this object, we frequently roamed the town together reconnoitring some of the loveliest, sexiest, most voluptuous and often most impregnable women in London.

They lured their prey with tempting morsels of rock'n'roll culture, pirated Beatles recordings and the like. But behind the bait of soft-porn Super-8s and poetry readings was that unwavering purpose: 'the quest for pussy . . .'

> – the insatiable (though regularly sated) desire to gobble up as much as one could decently consume and then some.

The carnal greed of these two vultures is of its time, and it is of a piece with the affluence and consumerism rampaging through the shopping streets of the later sixties. And if men were the consumers, women were, like a cargo of knock-off Sindys, the things they acquired.

Marowitz describes how he and Haynes were in a constant state of hungry arousal – 'wanting to touch, to taste, to savour, to consume . . .' from the inexhaustible supermarket of bra-less dolly birds that rolled past them on a seemingly never-ending conveyor belt, packaged in dainty Laura Ashley prints, tactile legs exposed by the briefest of minis (or 'pussy pelmets') which in turn barely concealed the scantiest of knickers. A feast of fresh meat, delectable and juicy, lay temptingly before them, young flesh that had to be eaten before it perished. This was a moment when a certain kind of man ceased to question whether or not he was entitled to whatever erotic satisfactions he happened to crave. A man has to eat, doesn't he? Wanting and taking was enough.

In this context, it's hard not to recall the qualms of Mary Whitehouse and others regarding the permissive society, and their fears that once women were pulled off their pedestals, they would be in danger of maltreatment and abuse. But Marowitz, who wrote his memoir of the 1960s twenty years after they ended, took care to add a disclaimer 'for those feminists who immediately construe this as the insensitive objectification of women'.[*] In it, he explained that he and Jim Haynes maintained an almost religious veneration for the women who inspired their passion. 'Our erotic activities were invariably recalled with awe.'

Unluckily for them, it seems the huntsmen's trophies themselves didn't always see their capture and submission in quite the same light. One Arts Lab habituée recalls the milieu created by Jim Haynes: 'You lay . . . watching these third-rate, amateurish porn films, while people

---

[*] Charles Marowitz, *Burnt Bridges: A Souvenir of the Swinging Sixties and Beyond* (1990).

were actually doing it in front of you, which I thought was really rude.' 'Haynes was the horrible old man who prowled the Arts Lab in search of chicks,' wrote Linda Grant in *Sexing the Millennium: A Political History of the Sexual Revolution* (1993). Wryly, she notes that Haynes had a knack of interpreting the sexual revolution of the 1960s in a way that served his libido. 'Sexual repression and frustration and ignorance' were, for him, the root of society's problems. Banish repression and the rest, let rip with lust, and uncomplicated fun would ensue.

Jim Haynes tried to sleep with me . . .

recalled art student Cheryll Park:

> I wasn't alone, there were about six other women in the bed. I said, 'No.' He humiliated me. He seemed to think it was all so easy to be permissive and free with your body. I was only nineteen and I'd come down from the north of England and it was . . . all too much. I thought that there was something wrong with me, because I wasn't going to go along with it. I told him he was a pervert and to get out of my bed.
>
> I'd love to meet Haynes again, now that he's a shrivelled-up old man, and humiliate him in the way he humiliated me.

★

The trouble was, nobody wanted to look uncool, straight, or behind the times. 'Part of the newness of the world we were creating was the abolition of jealousy, and the idea of possessing other people,' wrote Jenny Diski. Born in 1947, Diski bought into the revolutionary ideals of her generation. Her 1960s were spent in London, 'buying clothes, going to movies, dropping out, reading, taking drugs, spending time in mental hospitals, demonstrating, having sex, teaching . . .' She and her friends aspired to the hippie ideal of unfettered freedom for mind and body.

But over the years Diski's perspective shifted. Her memoir angrily unpicks the permissive experiment, holding up an unforgiving mirror to her own generation. Around 1967 she moved into a squat in Long Acre that she had found through a methedrine dealer who hung out at the Arts Lab. Here she felt curiously at home, in a smoky room full of 'stoned strangers'. But regardless of their favourite mantra, there doesn't seem to have been a lot of peace and love happening among its occupants. 'Our youthful cruelty was boundless,' she wrote, referring to the contemptuous dismissal of middle-aged bourgeois values by the young, whose ideals were formed by anger and indignation at how their parents seemed to have mishandled everything. 'It is not the job of the young to be grateful, it is their job to tear up the world and start again.'

The received idea among peace-and-love merchants was that society's problems could be solved by abolishing sexual repression. The pioneering poet and author Jeff Nuttall agreed. In *Bomb Culture* (1968), he explained how his generation, in thrall to Wilhelm Reich (whose *The Function of the Orgasm* was reissued in 1968), saw the sexual climax as both a window onto the eternal and a quick fix for Mr and Mrs Average – 'who are largely so suicidal because they never get a good fuck'. Nuttall appealed to his underground comrades to save the world through an eight-point plan, which included:

(g) To institute a sense of festivity into public life whereby people could fuck freely and guiltlessly, dance wildly and wear fancy dress all the time.

(h) To eradicate utterly and forever the Pauline lie implicit in Christian conventions, that people neither shit, piss nor fuck . . . To reinstate a sense of health and beauty pertaining to the genitals and the arsehole.

Nuttall's promised land would be constructed around an erect penis:

Can we apply a quivering phallic strength to our civic organisation and our economy?

Fifty years down the line, the damage wrought by a supremacist, patriarchal, phallocentric culture has still to be contained.

Another, less macho way to understand the world was the adoption of pagan and Eastern religions. The past, in the form of ancient texts such as the *I Ching*, the *Vedas* and the *Bhagavad Gita*, provided the young with visions, and the human hunger for answers was sated with arcane lore: horoscopes and the like. This was the time when the Beatles were seeking enlightenment through transcendental meditation, under the guidance of the Maharishi. In the relentless quest for inner development, joints merged with prayer wheels, and ancient wisdom with LSD, against a continuo of twanging sitar music.

But Jenny Diski tells us that ultimately it was all about the self, about doing your own thing. Thus the daily stresses of life – piled-up plates in the sink, grime round the bath – got left to those who cared for trivial matters like order and hygiene. 'That's your problem, *man . . .*' was the banal dismissal routinely dished out – to the women.

And sexism went deep. In the minds of many men, sex was tangled up with social anger and youthful entitlement, and norms like making demands, possession, infidelity and betrayal were supposed to have been jettisoned along with the old world order. In reality, insofar as it meant self-interest, dissipation and misogyny, that old world order seems to have been alive and kicking. Despite moving in a group that professed to have thrown out the formalities, Jenny Diski – like debutante Kristina Reed – still felt hampered by the old-fashioned courtesies. And, though her icy description of sexual power play among the caftan-and-velvet brigade questions all of their claims, it also sounds a doleful echo of Kristina's predicament:

> Sex was a way of being polite to those who suggested it or who got into your bed. It was very difficult not to fuck someone who wanted to fuck you without feeling you were being very rude. My guess, no, my certainty, is that large numbers of people slept with friends, acquaintances and strangers they had no desire for . . .
>
> There was a large principle at stake. If sex was no longer going to be a taboo then it was hard to think of a good reason not to have it with anyone who came along. It was uncool to say no . . .
>
> The idea that rape was having sex with someone who didn't want to do it didn't apply very much in the late sixties. On the basis that no means no, I was raped several times by men who arrived in my bed and wouldn't take no for an answer . . .

★

As liberalisation gathered pace, the male mindset had a lot of catching up to do. Diski's take on the hippie dreamers raises questions about the influence of their radicalism. 'We had about as much effect on the world as someone jumping from a plane does,' was her view.

So, was their opposition to their elders, and to mainstream society, a waste of time? Arguably, yes. Roy Jenkins, the Labour government's Home Secretary between 1965 and 1967, probably delivered more tangible permissive reforms than a field full of hippies. But that permissiveness had consequences – for women. Glaring injustice came in its wake. The hideous, sexist, misogynistic violations Jenny Diski (like so many others) describes would provide fuel for one of the most important social changes of the twentieth century. But first, women had to learn how to give a name to their oppression, and their oppressors. After centuries of subservience, it couldn't happen overnight.

Come Together

In 1967 a reporter from the *Daily Mail* came to interview the principal of Felixstowe College about her views on permissiveness among her students. Miss Elizabeth Manners was an advocate of strict Christian discipline. She was worried, she told the journalist, to see parents allowing their daughters to experiment. 'The more you give way, the more they try on,' she said, and she urged parents to 'fight rebellion – even if this does cause rows at home'.

But the misgivings of the older generation rang hollow as new freedoms accelerated. And the demand for sex without consequences was beginning to force the authorities to grapple with change. Following a heated debate, October 1967 saw the passing of the Abortion Law Reform Act; it would come into effect from April 1968, permitting termination of pregnancy up to twenty-four weeks' gestation. The number of abortions rose almost immediately, but there was a corresponding drop in the incidence of sepsis and death related to illegal terminations. The more tolerant climate also extended to homosexuals, and a bill to decriminalise homosexual acts in private between men over the age of twenty-one (in England and Wales) was passed into law in July 1967.

Generational tension was *the* hot topic. In that year's Reith Lectures the anthropologist and public intellectual Edmund Leach addressed the alienation of the young, and the hostility of parents towards rebellious children. He blamed the family: 'Far from being the basis of the good society, the family, with its narrow privacy and tawdry secrets, is the source of all our discontents.' Leach's inner hippie turned for answers to the tribal societies he had studied. Should we run our lives differently, like the Israelis with their kibbutzim, the Chinese with their communes?

Among dreamers and idealists that very question was already being posed with growing urgency. Unstitching the family itself was a way to challenge capitalism and all its ills, and collective living – the commune – seemed to be the answer. One of the earliest was the Selene Community. It was started in a tumbledown Welsh farmhouse thirty miles from Carmarthen in 1967. One is tempted to wonder what Edmund Leach would have made of the members of this pioneering collective, who apparently wandered nude in the fields and embraced the idea of group marriage. Selene's architect, Tony Kelly, had two 'wives'. Nineteen fellow pagans shared a back-to-the-land existence, which also involved a pantheistic belief system based on the moon goddess Selene and Mother Nature. In their Welsh wilderness, Tony Kelly and his tribe sought oneness with 'the otherworld of faery', communed with Pan, Lord of the Forest, and worshipped the Earth Mother: 'the great womb in which all her children still have their roots'. We don't know whether Kelly's real-life female cohabitants shared in the oneness, but Edmund Leach would surely have seen eye-to-eye with the fundamentals of Selene's creed:

> The monogamous family in its traditional isolation is the greatest barrier to all social reform as well as, ultimately, the instrument of the most devastating form of grief known to man and we urge its abolition . . .

Eccentric though it sounds, Selene was a trailblazer, seeking to close the gap between reality and the ideal. Within five years around a hundred similar collective households, rural and urban, would self-generate across the British Isles. For women, they were to prove a mixed blessing, the lure of collaborative childcare and domesticity being offset by conflict, sexual jealousy and fear of rejection. Male dominance continued to prove a hard plant to uproot. But in 1967 communes were still few and far between.

As Christine Hugh-Jones comments:

> The thing with utopian movements – they're all like this – was that
> you wanted a different society, but you didn't know *how* it was going
> to be run . . .

Today, Christine (a noted social anthropologist) is retired and lives in
Wales – with her husband. In 1967, as Christine Williams, she was
studying for her degree at the London School of Economics. The
LSE in the second half of the 1960s was becoming a beacon for radical activism. But as she recalls, it radiated more heat than light.

> There was a feeling that the world was being run for you, and you
> didn't have any say in its running. The Establishment was what you
> didn't like, and what you had to get rid of. It was a kicking against
> authority. More then, than at any time before . . .

Strong-minded, resourceful and outgoing, Christine was finding her
political feet. Her roots were in Derbyshire. The daughter of a self-
made industrialist and a thrifty housewife who kept a close eye on
the price of apples, she was conflicted in her class allegiances. Wealth
and white gloves pulled one way, hippie-ish bohemia another. Ambitious and driven, Christine shelved her parental model at the earliest
opportunity. A private education (with a scholarship) secured her
entrance first to art school, and thence to the LSE, where she enrolled
in 1965.

Living in London, Christine revelled in her own independence,
beachcombing on the shores of the Thames for driftwood to make
shelves, living off vegetables discarded on the pavements of Berwick
Street market, and sprats at fourpence a pound. Her frugality fed into
a sense of left-wing virtue. 'I saw myself as a good egalitarian socialist; I read the *New Statesman* . . .' The LSE was formative. The school
in those days was a seething, crowded melting pot of students and
staff. In what she describes as her 'worthy middle-middle-class background' foreigners and dark faces were so rare as to be regarded with
fear and consternation, but Christine took the buzz and cosmopolitan atmosphere at the LSE in her stride, remembering the excitement
of being squashed in the canteen conversing with people of various
colours and backgrounds. The course itself was broad in scope,

encompassing sociology, moral philosophy, statistics, economics – 'You did a bit of everything. The teachers were brilliant.' But among this community of excited, young, multi-cultural intellectuals, it was impossible to ignore the prevailing anti-authoritarian current that was gathering force, stronger by the day.

> It was happening in all the universities. It was about having student representation on the board and the councils and that sort of thing – which was a long hard thing to achieve.
>
> And then there was the revolution, which seemed to be about some huge dissatisfaction . . .
>
> Actually I don't know if anybody really knew what the revolution was about. But certainly we all felt unbelievably strongly about it.

To be young, clever and away from home was electrifying. In a world where loud music, free sex, denim and drugs were emblems of prestige, college students nationwide felt that they were the drivers of change. Christine Williams never contemplated the idea that, as a woman, she might be second-class:

> In the life I led at the LSE sexism wasn't an issue. And even though my mother had been a housewife and had done nothing beyond her family sphere all her life, it never occurred to me that I wasn't as good as a man, that I couldn't do the same things as them and so on . . .

She was not alone. The sixties generation clash saw young lined up against old, but within those ranks were daughters lined up against their mothers and grandmothers. In their early twenties, many of those daughters were determined not to be confined by the domesticity that had held their mothers captive. And that meant embracing equality.

One woman whose hippie beliefs underlay her activism was Caroline Coon. Both in the 1960s and beyond, she would make important differences to the society she lived in. In 1967 Caroline was a twenty-two-year-old art-student-turned-underground-activist. Later, she would become a vocal feminist. As she saw it, the two were linked. Caroline now understands that her 1960s fervour for change was a reaction against parental expectation, and against 'the prison that I saw my mother and my grandmother in'. Her wealthy, posh, Home

Counties, landowning parents regarded daughters as 'marriage-meat'. At the age of sixteen, in protest at their expectation that she would accept a millionaire neighbour as her future husband, Caroline stormed out, moved to London, got involved with the underground and started a relationship with a Jamaican musician. It was when her boyfriend was arrested for possession of marijuana and sentenced to two and a half years in prison that she realised how powerless minorities in this country could be. Release, an organisation formed to help young people in trouble with the law (particularly over drugs), was her brainchild.

The breakthrough moment for Release came in July 1967, at the first Legalise Pot rally. 'It was one of those brilliant Peace and Love sunny summer days . . .' remembered Caroline. That summer people were tripping to the sounds of Procul Harum's 'A Whiter Shade of Pale', Jimi Hendrix's 'Purple Haze', the Rolling Stones' 'Let's Spend the Night Together', and – as ever, capturing the mood of the moment – the Beatles were chanting 'All You Need is Love'. On that day 5,000 optimistic hippies in robes and caftans converged on Hyde Park with flowers, macrobiotic picnics and poetry books. 'Change the Drugs Laws', 'Flower Power' and 'Love, Love, Love' were painted in bright colours on their posters.

Among them, handing out Release 'Bust Cards' and leaflets, was Caroline, with a team of helpers. There could be no more palpable demonstration of young versus old, minority versus authority, the rebel versus the Establishment, the freaky versus the fuddy-duddy. At the end of that day Caroline went back to her basement flat in Notting Hill, and the phone didn't stop ringing.

Caroline saw Release as essentially about civil liberties and human rights. People needed to know what to do, and who to talk to if they were arrested. The organisation helped everyone from homeless runaways to heroin addicts. They provided information, and lawyers on tap. 'We were the welfare branch of the alternative society.'

Inevitably, any woman spearheading an organisation of this nature was liable to run up against male resentment. Joe Boyd, a close colleague, was one who admired her unreservedly: '[She] did a magnificent job for Release . . . All she was interested in was answering the phone and getting people a lawyer.'* But her gender and posh accent also won her enemies. A splinter group, apparently led by Mick Farren, attempted a takeover of Release.† Caroline reacted by very calmly handing over the office keys, the account books, the banking details, filing systems, addresses, volunteer rotas and phone listings. 'If you have any questions, give me a call,' she said, and left. Within a day it dawned on the mutineers that they couldn't function without her; they begged her to come back.

Speaking to an interviewer in 2016, Caroline Coon describes her youthful passion for liberty and rights as being inextricable from what, then, were still barely articulated feelings about Women's Liberation.‡ She and her countercultural friends were stumbling towards a way of life in which, as she saw it, people of all colours, orientations, genders and beliefs could live together more equally, more peacefully and more humanely.

> This was absolutely key to what I thought the hippie generation of peace and love was actually about.

And yet . . .

> Looking back on it, that era was an era of <u>male</u> liberation. Men wanted to be liberated from their marriages and to have as much sex as possible. But they weren't going to liberate women as well . . .
>
> The shock to women in the sixties was that our male colleagues were just as misogynistic as any patriarchy of the past . . . But in the sixties we didn't have the <u>language</u>, we didn't have the critical mass with which to combat misogyny and sexism.

---

* Joe Boyd arrived from the USA in 1964, like many others avoiding the Vietnam draft. He was co-founder with 'Hoppy' Hopkins of UFO, London's psychedelic ballroom, and worked at Release alongside Caroline Coon from 1967.

† Mick Farren, lead singer of the proto-punk band the Deviants, was another underground 'character' famed for his outspokenness, sexual appetite and methedrine habit.

‡ Caroline Coon recalled her activist youth as part of a video project made for the 2016 V&A exhibition, 'You Say You Want a Revolution? Records and Rebels, 1966–1970'.

It's the same story that we heard from Kristina Reed in the 1965 chapter, from the victims of sexual harassment in 1966, from Jenny Diski and the Arts Lab trophies. It's about free love. But free for whom?

Release, however, found its voice in 1967 and has been giving legal advice, on-call assistance and specialist counselling, and speaking out for drug offenders, for over fifty years.

★

Harrowing news was unfolding on the world stage. In July 1967, as Caroline Coon and her comrades were assembling their Legalise Pot propaganda and painting posters, the US Marines had suffered their single worst day in Operation Buffalo, conducted north of their base at Con Thien in the Vietnam Demilitarised Zone. On that summer's day, as the hippies in Hyde Park chanted 'Change the Drug Laws', families across America were mourning 159 Marines killed and 345 wounded. But the losses to Vietnamese troops were far worse, with US authorities claiming 1,290 dead. The casualties among civilians at that time were appalling. In 1967 US officials in Saigon estimated that 50,000 civilians, including 10,000 children, would be treated for war injuries; but the civilian death count has never been accurately calculated. The war's dreadful toll was a spur to action, to those who espoused peace and love, and many more besides.

As a virtuous left-winger Sheila Rowbotham joined the East London Vietnam Solidarity Committee; she was invited to attend its first meeting, convened in December 1967. The festive season was approaching, but that evening the streets of Hackney were raw and dank, and Sheila muffled herself up when she set out, reluctantly, to brave the chill of Mare Street. Unsurprisingly, the meeting was male-dominated, and predictably the first item on the agenda was the organisation's dire lack of funds. Equally predictably, in an episode that may sound very familiar, even fifty years later, to women who attend committees or try to contribute to public life, she quickly found herself running up against the men in the driving seat. These ones were Trotskyists too, and they had views that overrode those of their female comrades.

I brightly suggested a jumble sale; no one responded, so I piped up again. They kept cutting me out of the discussion as if I had never spoken.

Jumble sales, it appeared, involved women, particularly old women, and were therefore insufficiently revolutionary. But nobody else had any other fundraising ideas. Feeling herself becoming shrill, Sheila took a righteous stand; voices were raised. At last, grudgingly, the men agreed that she could go ahead with the jumble sale, and the agenda proceeded. The platform then invited a sub-committee representative to take the floor and give his report. To Sheila's surprise a gentle-looking, long-haired hippie guy in a caftan and beads muttered a hesitant response from the back of the room. He had a soft American accent, punctuated by the word 'like'; the gist being that he didn't, like, need to talk from the front, like, and might as well speak from where he was sitting. This man certainly wasn't given to macho assertiveness.

His name was Henry Wortis. At the end of the meeting Henry offered Sheila a ride home. 'It was cold and a lift was welcome.'

> I liked this American man with his quiet air of authority despite the libertarian front. He proceeded to tell me they were shutting me up at the meeting. I grinned. People were always telling me I talked too much . . . But, Henry went on, it was because I was a woman. I couldn't believe my ears. This was an extraordinary thing for a left man to be saying. According to Henry, there was this thing called 'male chauvinism' and that's what had been going on in that VSC meeting . . .
>
> He explained that he knew this because his wife, Shelley, had been in a Women's Liberation group in Boston. Several groups in the United States had been started by women from the new left.

For Sheila, it was like switching on all the Christmas lights at once.

The mounting feeling that, as a political woman, she was out on a limb, that her reluctance to adopt strident asexual postures was causing men to ignore her views, that the behaviour of men who disagreed with each other was different when they disagreed with women – all this suddenly now had a name.

Till now, Sheila had had no posture on feminism. As she saw it, the word belonged to history – 'I knew it only as the suffrage movement of long ago or as a lobby of professional women for advancement at work.' Emancipation had similar connotations. Both terms failed to address the chasm that she and so many women like her experienced in personal relationships between the sexes.

For months now, Sheila had been quietly arguing with herself, cluttering her mind with complexities. She had been reading male literature that typecast women as 'good' and 'bad', and found herself wondering how much these clichés were projections. The empty misrepresentations and pejorative labels had percolated aggressively into the everyday: '– a man at a party talking about a woman's buttocks as if she was meat, another calling girls "bits"'. Women, it seemed to her, were cast in their narrow, off-the-peg roles by men. They didn't know how to be, or who to be. They were things, dolls, possessions, who seemed to have no identity they could call their own. Sheila cast about with increasing urgency, searching for ways to deal with the overlap between class and gender; rereading Simone de Beauvoir, plunging into Doris Lessing's *The Golden Notebook* and the essays on 'feminine psychology' by German psychoanalyst Karen Horney with a growing sense of community and recognition.

But sex was yet another minefield. Sheila's self-questioning led her to recognise that a woman like her could be as detached in her physical desires as a man – 'but this was more or less impossible to assert publicly in 1967'. The power game between the sexes was, she observed, complex: men had vulnerabilities and fears, while women often colluded in their subservience. Anyway, what was to be gained by women becoming the ascendant sex, if what she craved was sexual and emotional closeness? How did one reconcile the overwhelming longing to lose oneself in passion, with the equally passionate attempt to find oneself?

As 1967 slipped into history, Sheila Rowbotham continued to brood over a host of such unanswered questions. But something had shifted. In the bedroom of her dilapidated communal house in Dalston, the floor was obscured by the ever growing mountain of bags and boxes containing outgrown plimsolls, unwanted woollies and discarded pyjama bottoms, all awaiting the Vietnam Solidarity Committee Jumble Sale. In her mind, though, the mountains were rolling away: 'as if some hidden plate deep under the surface of appearances had moved irrevocably, sending out tiny, barely perceptible seismic shocks which were shortly to contribute to an earthquake . . .'

After this politics was never to be quite the same.

1968

Big Lil

Mary Denness had grown up among seafarers. Since childhood, the backdrop to her existence had been the North Sea, whose stormy, icy waters stretched from Hull's familiar docks and estuary to the rich cod-fishing grounds of Iceland and Scandinavia. In 1959 Mary married skipper Barry Denness. But by 1967 she felt utterly trapped, constrained by two young children and a husband who oppressed her with his obsessive fear that she was cheating on him.

Trawler families were not renowned for their harmony, and in the mid-twentieth century the character of Hull's trawling community set it apart from other industries and other tribes. The men employed in it were away for three weeks at a time. Once home, they often drank heavily, brawled and squandered their takings. Back on shore, their womenfolk were expected to await their return while keeping house and minding the family. But the industry itself was flawed by lack of regulation.* From galley boy to skipper, every member of a trawler crew was taken on as casual labour. He had no rights, no work status, no job security. Men often spent weeks unemployed on the whim of a trawler owner. Safety laws were equally hit and miss. Working conditions on board could be unthinkably dangerous and frightening, as the vessel ploughed and dropped over the crest of mighty waves that threatened to send her to the bottom in seconds. In winter one of the worst hazards was ice build-up on the deck and rigging. Its very weight could topple a ship; the only way to defend against this peril was for all hands to hack it off physically with picks

* For help with background relating to the Hull trawler industry and the women who contributed to changing it, I am greatly indebted to Dr Brian W. Lavery, author of the evocative and authoritative *The Headscarf Revolutionaries: Lillian Bilocca and the Hull Triple-Trawler Disaster* (2015), from which I have also quoted certain passages.

and axes. Meanwhile, trawler owners were notorious for cutting corners on working practices such as making regular ship-to-shore contact, ensuring fire drills and providing onboard medical care.

But the men's wives had been taught never to worry. As Mary explains:

> If you did, you'd have finished up a basket case. Every time the wind blew, every time there was a gale, you'd be thinking, 'Oh God, are they safe?' You'd go scatty.
>
> We all accepted it, because that's how the men earned their living, and that's what kept food on the table.

In the early hours of 10 January 1968 the trawler *St Romanus* blasted her foghorn and made her way down the Humber estuary with twenty crew on board destined for the Arctic waters off the north of Norway. There was no dedicated radio operator on board, and the transmitter was faulty. On the following tide, the *Kingston Peridot* set out, also with a crew of twenty, heading for Iceland. For all trawlers, there were protocols that required daily contact to be made by radio, but – where it happened to suit – those protocols were ignored. So, though conditions were terrible, with sub-zero temperatures and battling waves, nobody was unduly worried when the *St Romanus* lost all contact after just a day at sea. On 20 January a third trawler, the *Ross Cleveland*, put out to sea, only to be hit by the same freezing gales off north-west Iceland.

It was not until sixteen days into the voyage that the *St Romanus* was assumed to be missing, by which time the *Kingston Peridot* was no longer responding to radio messages. On 30 January the families of the crew of *St Romanus* were told there was no hope; it was also announced that the *Kingston Peridot* was missing.

Mrs Lillian Bilocca now enters the story.* Like her comrade-in-arms Mary Denness, 'Big Lil' – so named because of her seventeen-stone frame – came from a fishing family; her husband Charlie Bilocca was Maltese and worked in the Merchant Navy. Their son, Ernie, lived by seafaring, and their daughter, Virginia, was an office junior. For twenty years Lil herself had worked as a cod skinner in a fish house: it was arduous, cold and treacherous employment, in which the slip of a knife

---

* Lillian Bilocca died in 1988 aged fifty-nine.

could do you out of wages for weeks. By the end of January she, like the rest of the fishing community in Hull, could think of little else but the looming tragedy. But something inside Lil could no longer accept it with silent fatalism. Her action would change a city's history. Lil left the fish house one evening never to return, picked up a Biro, and started to lay out her concerns. 'Right, Virginia,' she told her daughter . . .

> 'Enough's enough. Something has to get done. I'm starting a petition to get the gaffers to make them trawlers safer. That could be our Ernie or your dad out there, God forbid.'
>
> 'A petition . . . is that a good idea?' said the girl.
>
> 'I am goin' to do it, our Virginia. I have got nowt to lose, have I?'
>
> 'Folk might get upset, Mam.'
>
> 'To hell with what they bloody think. I'm goin' to do what's right.'

Next day Virginia sneaked into the office early to copy the forms on her boss's duplicating machine; Lil rallied her friends and started to gather signatures. In the space of a few days 2,000 had added their names to the petition; under 'occupation' the majority had written 'housewife'. Its rapid growth encouraged support; vocal and energetic women in the community were spurred to her side, bringing with them skills and contacts. The National Transport and General Workers' Union, who were already in a fight for trawler safety, could see that these angry headscarved wives would bring their cause much-needed publicity. With union cooperation, a public meeting was organised at the ramshackle Victoria Hall in Hessle Road, for the women to air their grievances. By the time of the meeting on 2 February Lil's petition had grown to 6,000 signatures. Television cameras and reporters crammed into the hall alongside a huge jostling mob of fishwives and well-wishers. Lil took the platform and spoke from the heart.

> We need to take action . . . I'll board any unsafe trawler in the country to stop an unsafe ship sailing. I pledge my life to get better and safer conditions . . . I'll hitchhike to London if I have to, to make my case in front of Parliament.

John Prescott (later to become Tony Blair's deputy prime minister) stood up to represent the National Union of Seamen in support of the campaign. An impromptu march led by Lil set out to confront the

Hull Fishing Vessel Owners' Association in their offices, but was stonewalled. Undefeated, the marchers returned to Victoria Hall, where Lil summoned two of her most committed supporters, Yvonne Blenkinsop and Chrissie Smallbone, to her side. Lil then called for one more volunteer to carry the fishing wives' petition to London.

Mary Denness takes up the tale:

> I was in the audience, with my brother's wife. 'Go on, Mary,' she said, 'you're a nice talker . . .' But I said I would only go if the majority were for me being elected. So I stayed back. But Chrissie Smallbone said, 'Yes, come up, you've as much right up here as anybody else.'
>
> So then I started to move towards the stairs onto the stage. And one woman's dissenting voice came from the audience saying, 'We don't want a load of bloody skippers' wives up there representing us!'

Lil, however, had no time for divisions in her ranks. 'Look,' she shouted into the microphone, 'two ships have gone down with all hands. Have the skippers come back? No, they haven't! So since they have gone down with their ships, they've a right to be represented.' There was applause. Mary took her turn on the platform, calling for unity in the campaign, and with solidarity established the meeting disbanded. Already, Mary knew that her bold stand could cost her dear. Skipper Barry Denness was not the type to accept his wife playing an interfering role in men's affairs. But Mary was brave, and she was outspoken. If this was going to turn into a marital battle, she was determined to win it.

Early next morning Lil Bilocca and a team of women protesters broke every seafaring taboo in the book by appearing on the dockside at dawn, braving the media scrum and police, to ensure that the departing ships were properly equipped. As the *St Keverne* drew away from the dock a crew member shouted to the protesters onshore, 'We ant got no radio man, Lily!' Lillian struggled with police, swearing like a trooper as they tried to prevent her jumping aboard, and the press photographers went wild trying to capture a spectacle that they knew would make all the front pages.

On 4 February the people of Hull heard with shocked disbelief that the third trawler, the *Ross Cleveland*, skippered by Chrissie Smallbone's brother, was missing in a gale off Iceland. If the ship had indeed

GUARDIAN

Manchester Saturday February 3 1968   Price 6d

| 7,000 jobs at stake in closures | **Militant Hull wives aim at making shipowners listen** | £22M jump in gold reserves |

The media revelled in the spectacle of high-heeled and headscarved fishermen's wives heading for the docks – a no-go area for women.

gone down, fifty-eight men would have lost their lives in the space of three weeks.

Chrissie wept uncontrollably as she and the three other lead women confronted the trawler bosses in their boardroom. This time around they got a hearing, and an understanding that there would be concessions, which remained to be secured through the minister in London. There was work to be done. But that day there were prayers and heartbreak the length of Hessle Road.

Tuesday 6 February was a bitterly cold day with snow in the air. Mary's best coat was thin navy-blue silk shantung, but she took good care to wear a wool suit underneath for warmth. Her Hessle Road hairdresser had backcombed and lacquered her red hair into a bouffant pompadour. As they boarded the 7.55 a.m. train to London, Lil Bilocca, Chrissie Smallbone, Yvonne Blenkinsop and Mary Denness were crowded out by journalists and television crews jostling for their stories. They had become a media sensation.

> But – when we pulled into King's Cross station, there wasn't a soul. I spoke to the guard as we came onto the platform, and I said, 'Where *is* everybody?'

And he said, 'We've had to pull them back off the platform, because it became dangerously overcrowded,' he said. 'So we've pushed them all back onto the concourse, and put barriers up there to hold them back. We only do that for the Queen!'

And I said, 'You're *joking* . . .!'

The women got a pop-star welcome – and the headline 'BIG LIL HITS TOWN' was plastered across the *Evening Standard*'s billboard. Then, with John Prescott and the union bosses, they were driven to the Houses of Parliament where their MP was waiting for them.

Though I'd lived in London I'd never been to the Houses of Parliament before . . .

remembered Mary.

We were treated royally. The MPs we met were all Labourites, all very nice . . . And yes, we felt they treated us right – that they were not simply giving in to us because we were a bit of a novelty.

You know, I really did feel then that I'd come a long way.

Because it was, honestly, quite extraordinary. I mean, if anybody'd said to us, before we'd done this, do you know who Lillian Bilocca and Mary Denness met? We were just ordinary, insignificant, working-class northern women . . .

Harold Wilson was away. 'Look after the girls,' he'd told Fred Peart, Minister of Agriculture and Fisheries. 'Try and see things from their point of view.' After an hour and a half going through the women's demands, Peart made them a promise. Fishing fleets would be grounded until the safety measures had been enacted and the weather improved. 'You've got it, ladies,' he told them. 'You have got it all.' Afterwards, Mary told the press, 'Three women have achieved more in one day than anything that has ever been done in the trawler industry in sixty years.'

Bringing the entire Hull trawler operation to a standstill was an imperative while the authorities made sure safety was implemented. But though it made her and her team front-page news, it wasn't an action that was going to make Lil Bilocca popular. On the night that she returned from London, Lil found three death threats among the stack of post on her doormat. While top columnists and TV hosts lionised Lil, the restriction was having an immediate economic effect, as skippers watched Icelandic vessels bringing in prime catches to sell for high prices on the British market. The tide was turning against Lil and her campaign. Poison-pen letters started to pile up –

> Madam, Why don't the people of Hull kidnap you, tie some bricks round your neck and drop you in the Humber, you big, fat, greasy Maltese whore . . .

– and much more of the same.

The local secretary of the Trawler Officers' Guild was more restrained, but equally damning:

> The idea of forming a women's committee to fight battles for the men is, to my mind, completely ludicrous.

The flak in the local paper was flying too, much of it drawing attention to Lil's plebeian accent and appearance.

Mary Denness, better read and more worldly than the others, could understand why many of the men whose interests they believed themselves to be serving were far from grateful, her husband being one:

> Well, Barry hated it! He thought that the men should fight their own battles. Let them *be* men. And there were plenty of old-fashioned men that still thought that way.
>
> But with Barry, well, mostly he hated it because of his possessiveness of me. He saw the campaign as a threat – that I was going to see a wider world. He just thought, 'That's my wife, I don't want her roaming around all over the place. I want her at home.'
>
> And I think that's when I started to see things in the marriage from a very different angle. And that's when the rot set in.

The euphoria was dissolving. Lil, inexperienced, naive and tactless, was out of her depth, battling abuse and press distortion. Her employers took advantage of the situation to hand her her cards. Mary was fire fighting, trying to rescue a situation that had rebounded on the four women.

It was impossible to really win, without getting the men's full support, and indeed the women's as well, the wives. But how CAN you
fight casual labour? You've got to destroy the casual part of it. And
the trawler owners weren't going to have that. No way, they'd have
had to regulate the industry for a start. No, it was a bridge too far. It
couldn't be achieved by four women.

Nevertheless, their campaign was taking effect. A Committee of
Inquiry was briefed to find ways to make the fishing industry safer.
Even before it reported, a converted vessel, *Orsino*, was equipped
with state-of-the-art medical and meteorological technology and
designated as a 'mother ship' to accompany trawlers to the most dangerous Arctic waters. Lil Bilocca stood on the dock as *Orsino* sailed
and told reporters, 'I am chuffed. Never mind them calling us silly
women, this is what we have fought for.'

Many years later, Mary Denness would reflect on that fight, and
on how Lil, Chrissie, Yvonne and herself – four 'ordinary, insignificant, working-class northern women' – had the courage to invade
one of the most segregated of Britain's industries and start making
demands:

All we were promoting was safety at sea.

Somebody had to speak up for the men, because they had no time
for campaigning – they were only at home for two days in every
three weeks.

But it was more than that. I do think my generation was influenced
by a modern way of thinking. We felt significant all of a sudden. Did
it come from the women's rights campaign in America? It might
have . . . But somehow, the thought of all those students and protesters and so forth was sustaining to the women's campaign for better
conditions for trawlermen.

All of us ladies felt the same. We felt unstoppable. Like we couldn't
turn back, or let go.

You know, as a little girl I'd been forever put down by my mother,
and now finally I'd found something inside myself that I could
accomplish.

But you got so far – and then everything went pear-shaped for you
in your private life. Because from then on, it was constant rows in my

household. Barry would be at me saying, you know, 'You've been interfering again, haven't you?'

And I'd say, 'No. I'm not interfering. I'm involved. I've got a mind. I can think! Can't you accept that?'

'No, I bloody well can't.'

'Right.'

So then you knew, you were on opposite sides.

My husband never recognised any little bit of intelligence I might have. He seemed to regard me as his galley slave. And I think this hit a lot of the ladies the way it did me. We couldn't accept that we should settle for the life that we'd had before, as housewives: just going home to our kitchen sinks, and looking after our kids, and taking no further interest in what we'd actually achieved. Not any more.

That would have been impossible. For me, it changed my life.

'For We Were Young and Sure to Have Our Way . . .'

Half a century after women were first granted the vote, the feeling of having a mind, of being able to think and of reaching beyond the kitchen sink was something more working-class women were experiencing, along with the accompanying rows and tumult.

Rosie Boland and Lil O'Callaghan, shop stewards at Ford's Dagenham plant, brought the factory to a halt when they called 187 women sewing-machinists out on strike that year in protest against sex discrimination in job grading. The women were defined as unskilled, and paid 85 per cent of the male rate. The dispute was resolved with the help of the fiery employment secretary, Barbara Castle, who sidestepped complex union processes and called a face-to-face meeting with the key women. They all gathered for the photocall round a cosy teapot, which Mrs Castle then had removed before settling down to talks over 'a real drink'. Together, they reached an agreement by which the women strikers were promised near parity with the men (in reality, management didn't go the final mile, and progress stalled). But Dagenham became a *cause célèbre*, unfairness to women in industry took hold in the public mind, and Mrs Castle gained sufficient support among women MPs to push for an Equal Pay Act.

At the same time, the slow-burning question of whether women bus conductors should be permitted to drive buses became crucial, as 77,000 London busmen threatened strike action in July 1968. The women conductors aired their grievances in front of the press, but they were up against entrenched attitudes. When would-be bus driver Brenda Armstrong from Yarmouth took on the male drivers she was defeated by their bigotry, with the branch secretary of the Transport and General Workers' Union explaining that, although there was an acute shortage of drivers, it would be 'humiliating for a man to have a woman driver'.

Increasingly, the battle lines were forming between the sexes, as women from Dagenham to Hull discovered unsuspected wells of power and protest within themselves. Male authority was being challenged as never before; disobedience and demonstration were becoming the currency. Both for the women who participated in the 1968 upheavals, and for those who didn't, a new, radical future – in which kitchen-sink subordination was consigned to history – seemed within reach. The days of sober columns of pram-pushing marchers respectfully wending their way from Aldermaston to Trafalgar Square to air their views were being superseded by the new tactics of angry confrontation. For women seeking to resist unfairness and authoritarianism in their own lives, the 1968 protests presented a new, far less passive model.

★

The first anti-Vietnam War demonstration was scheduled for Sunday 17 March. The night before, Sheila Rowbotham attended a VSC meeting to confer on tactics. She learnt how to form a human wedge to push through police lines, and how to lock arms while chanting 'Ho, Ho, Ho Chi Minh'. 'Its ethos contrasted with CND's "We the good people bearing witness" style. We were more angry than good . . .'

On the day, Granada Television's current affairs programme *World in Action* followed a coachload of student protesters travelling down the M1 from Manchester for the demonstration, and spoke to their leader. The unnamed young interviewee is moustachioed, side-burned, good-looking and terse. He was clearly expecting trouble:

I shan't be at all surprised if there's violence today. And I shan't – how shall I put this? I shan't be condemnatory of it . . .

With that in mind, he and his comrades had a job to do, and it was a strictly traditional one:

We have to have someone who's responsible for anybody who gets arrested, and we have to have someone to look after the girls . . .

Just like their fathers, these young men wanted to be good soldiers:

I think that the time has come for all of us . . . to unite and to try and bring about a radical social change – and if violence is a part of it, well, violence is a part of it.

People are starting to fight back. This demonstration is a strengthening of my muscles for the sort of society I want to see later . . .

It was as if men, in the post-war era, had for too long been deprived of their weaponry and their fists; now, they eagerly absorbed lessons from their American counterparts in the student movement, who taught them how to pull policemen off their horses, and how to use banners as lances and spears. The urge to assail and batter seemed ineradicable in the male psyche.

Back on the M1, the Manchester student leader solemnly instructed his fellow-travelling comrades how to repulse the aggressors:

The police are going to try and provoke us . . . If they start using the horses, charging into us, just link arms with the person next to you . . .

As Martin Luther King said, a riot is the voice of the unheard . . .

That Sunday, over 25,000 people set out from Trafalgar Square with actress Vanessa Redgrave at their head, heading for the American embassy in Grosvenor Square. The size and public impact of the demonstration would give feminists like Sheila Rowbotham a taste of what power and strength-in-numbers felt like. 'It fizzled with defiance from the start . . .' she wrote, while an LSE-based oral history respondent, Rachel Dyne, confirmed, 'It was one of the happiest moments of my life . . . We took over the whole street as though we could do what we liked; it echoed to the chanting. I felt we were a real force, part of an international movement that could change the course of events on a worldwide scale.' It also gave radical women like this a lesson in what to expect from those they opposed.

'The old manners didn't apply,' recalled Nina Fishman, an American student activist, then at Sussex University. 'I was kicked by a policeman . . . I still have the scar.' A photographer who witnessed the charge told how 'there was one girl that was shouting and screaming . . . and about five police really laid into her and really kicked her about on the ground . . .' One of the injured was heavily pregnant. The day after the protest, newspapers carried a picture of a young woman demonstrator being grappled by three helmeted policemen; her miniskirt had ridden up exposing pants and suspenders, and one of the officers had his arm raised over her semi-uncovered bottom. The headline was 'Spanked'.

Sophie Jenkins was able to look back at the respectful Ban-the-Bomb campaign of her teenage days, and compare it at first hand with her introduction to the embattled activism of '68:

> Well, I was such a silly girl. I wore high heels, because even if you're going on a demo you have to look nice, don't you? So there I was tripping along in the bright sunshine wearing high heels, and chanting and shouting. But then – I was pushed by the crowd, and I can remember being much closer to a hedge than I would ever like to be again.
>
> It was absolutely terrifying.

Mick Jagger was spotted somewhere in the crowd.* Though Redgrave was permitted to deliver a protest to the embassy, the police urged the demonstrators to back off. Stones and smoke bombs were thrown by the crowd. Famously, many of the police were mounted, and the cavalry charge that flattened long-haired protesters beneath its hooves didn't differentiate between the sexes.

> I remember the horses. I mean, seeing the policemen on their great big black horses, with their brute strength, kind of rushing at people, and people being carted off in police vans. It was really alarming . . .

* The rally inspired the lyrics to Jagger's song 'Street Fighting Man', recorded in April 1968 and released later that year on the Rolling Stones' album *Beggars Banquet*. It also added to his reputation as a 'bad boy' and dangerous delinquent.

Inevitably, the national media fed its readers with the desired fare – plaudits for the boys in blue and sympathy for the plight of the horses. Ann Leslie, by now working for the *Daily Express* as the highest-paid woman journalist in Fleet Street, took a wry view of the disturbances:

> The 1968 'revolution' was largely a male thing: girls were mainly there to paint the posters and provide R and R for their hairy young warriors, who readily concurred with the view of Black Panther Eldridge Cleaver that 'the position of women in the revolution is on their backs'.*

In May 1968 the revolutionary rhetoric erupted again into violence and damage on the streets of Paris, soon spreading to other cities across France. Students were at the forefront of the '68 '*événements*', protesting against a raft of perceived evils from American imperialism to archaic university curriculums. But as ever, sexual freedom was central to the movement, with free access to women's campus dormitories heading the list of students' demands. Soon, industrial workers joined in, calling for better pay and conditions. The protests were on such a scale that the French economy was brought to a virtual standstill, nearly toppling the government. 'Please don't let them be defeated,' prayed Sheila Rowbotham back in Hackney. There were strikes, and savage clashes on the streets involving barricades, torn-up paving stones, burning cars, fire bombs, police charges, tear gas and multiple arrests, making Grosvenor Square look like a picnic. *The Guardian* newspaper's coverage of the riots was filed by their Paris correspondent, fifty-five-year-old Welshwoman Nesta Roberts, who dodged *pavés* and tear-gas canisters to tell the story of the movement. Roberts painted an expressive picture of Paris *in extremis*, sharing with her readers the chaos and the calm, the momentous and the trivial. Her eyes were still stinging with the gas as she listened to the platitudes of the French Minister for Education, while in the background 'the mob

* Ann Leslie has misattributed and misquoted. The comment originated with Black Panther leader Stokely Carmichael, who told his comrades in the SNCC (Student Non-Violent Coordinating Committee) 'The position of women in the SNCC is prone' – though he probably meant 'supine'.

was roaring like surf'. Across the pavement, 'the rubbish of five days is suppurating. Mingling with its stench was the acrid scent of burning lingering around four carcasses that had once been motor vehicles.' And she met the students, in the Sorbonne and the Odéon:

> Both are populated with girls and young men living on sandwiches and oranges, and looking as if they had not slept for months . . .
>
> On the walls of the Odéon are written all the rude words that these mostly bourgeois young people have since the nursery been forbidden to use, but the boys still bow a visitor through the doors, and the girls have charmingly frivolous necklaces showing beneath the red scarves of revolution.
>
> 'You know they killed several people last night, don't you?' says one of them.

Though British student bodies mounted solidarity demonstrations, few on the English side of the Channel had the appetite for Parisian-style *lutte*. Shortly after the *événements* subsided, Sophie Jenkins truanted from her waitress job in London and snuck off with her boyfriend to the Left Bank to see for herself. But by the time they arrived there had been a clean-up.

> The roads looked a bit unmade, but apart from that all you could see was the slogans on the walls.
>
> I'd wanted to go because, well, it felt like – *us*. I thought, this is *my* time. This is *my* generation.
>
> And I regretted not taking part.

★

Nevertheless, by 1968, a doorway of tempting choices and aspirations lay open to Sophie Jenkins and her generation. Many of the tiresome prohibitions had been jettisoned. You could study, sit in, take action, explore relationships, make love, take psychedelic drugs, join the Tribe of the Sacred Mushroom, embrace Sanskrit chants, auras and extra-planetary beings, greet the dawn on Glastonbury Tor. For some women, freedom and fulfilment felt within reach, and if you were lucky like Melissa North, everyday life felt like a party: happy drugs, happy clothes, happy sex, happy music. I'm sure I was one of thousands who spent a lazy summer in 1968 playing and replaying Paul McCartney's upbeat, self-believing ballad 'Hey Jude' till it was imprinted into memory. (Better, better, *better, better, better, better* – *OH!*) The same applied as everyone sang along to 'Those Were the Days', Mary Hopkin's bewitching, elegiac vocal produced by McCartney, which reached number 1 in August.

> *Those were the days my friend:*
> *We thought they'd never end,*
> *We'd sing and dance for ever and a day.*
> *We'd live the life we choose,*
> *We'd fight and never lose,*
> *For we were young and sure to have our way . . .*

Next up on the turntable that year were two nutty oom-pah classics, the Bonzo Dog Doo-Dah Band's 'I'm the Urban Spaceman' and the Scaffold's 'Lily the Pink'. A leisurely vibe permeated The Small Faces' 'Lazy Sunday' (Here we all are sittin' in a rainbow . . .), the Kinks' wonderful, dreamy song, 'Days' (Thank you for the days / Those endless days, those sacred days you gave me . . .), and Otis Redding's languid 'Sittin' On the Dock of the Bay'. As always, pop captured the cultural essentials: groovy, fantastical, laid-back, hedonistic and druggy. Even a clean-living short-hair like Cliff Richard managed to make his bubbly 1968 Eurovision Song Contest submission, 'Congratulations', sound ridiculously light-headed and effervescent – as if he'd had a reefer or two before the performance.

A sense of joyful release and stardust is palpable in many memories of that time, particularly among educated women. Optimistic and aware, they belonged to a sector of society that felt buoyed up by the zeitgeist, and they express the invulnerability of the young:

> The sixties was one long Indian summer of shining brightness, long hair, short dresses, long legs. It was also an experience of metaphysical joy and utopian sharing.

> Marsha Rowe

The relaxation of manners, the sense of intellectual excitement, even the way, oh, God, you didn't have to shave your *armpits* . . .

> Angela Carter

In *The Young Meteors*, his 1967 cyclorama of England's sexual capital, Jonathan Aitken interviewed more than 200 young Londoners, and caught their mood of elated abandon:

> [You can have] a man a night if you can find attractive ones. Why not have a ball? You're only young once.

> Boutique assistant, 20

I go to orgy parties once a fortnight for kicks . . .

> Pool typist in an employment bureau, 17

> The thing that's great about this town is that the chicks are so cool about sex. At a party you can come up to someone and say within a couple of minutes of meeting her, 'How about coming back to my place?' . . .
>
> When you get back, there's no cock-teasing pantomime. It's action all the way.

> Actor, 24

'If there is any moral virtue left in the youth of London, it has been brilliantly camouflaged,' commented Aitken dryly. By 1968 cases of gonorrhoea in the UK were set to exceed the wartime peak of 50,000 a year; it was a common experience for such metropolitan action-lovers to find themselves at the VD clinic: 'A quick jab, a course of antibiotics, a spell of abstinence and then . . . back to the fray.' For Amanda Brooke-Dales, whom we last saw recovering from having an abortion in a private clinic in 1966, it wasn't a question of virtue; she'd thrown that out along with her cocktail suits back in 1963. It was a question of having fun.

> A feeling that we could do whatever we liked swept through some of us in the sixties – and that we were admired for it, you know, as these new, free creatures . . .

The abortion didn't deter her from continuing with a freewheeling love life.

I had LOTS of boyfriends. I just went to bed with people if I felt like it.

I mean, it was simply in the air, for girls to behave with more sexual freedom than they had. For me it was part of this new loosening-up of everything . . .

I just let things happen really, and got away with it. I did what I liked.

And Amanda liked sex. By now she was on the Pill, and taking advantage of the liberty it offered:

Actually, it felt that I was more like a man – I had my 'wild oats' period. I was always treating men rather badly. Turning them down, going off with another one. I didn't feel remotely guilty. I just had a good time . . .

Men have behaved in this manner since time immemorial – but in a post-HIV world blind irresponsibility is no longer an option. When, before or since, have women been able to take control of their own desires with such impunity and disregard for consequences? The permissive climate of the late sixties encouraged Amanda Brooke-Dales to turn the tables on her sexual partners with detachment and insouciance. Blessed with a happy and optimistic nature, from the age of nineteen Amanda spent the best part of ten years feeling that life had spread its bounty before her, to savour as she pleased. How glorious it was to be part of a generation that questioned everything. Hypocrisy, repression and unhappiness were being replaced by liberty and openness – 'I had the sense of not needing to play by the rules any more, and of being free to do whatever I wanted, when I wanted it . . .' Hadn't men felt this for centuries? Now women too could feel what it was like to pick and choose, to try without buying, to love and to leave. There would be no more pretending, and no promises.

The Rule Book

People who think anything goes – people who want to indulge their every whim, their every desire, immediately: they have a philosophy that is entirely self-centred, entirely self-indulgent.

And self-indulgence stems from fallen human nature. Fallen human nature is in need of redemption. And that is the nub of the Christian faith.

The speaker is vicar's wife Anthea Millican.* Anthea never had any urge to sow wild oats, nor did she ever so much as come near a barricade, a demo or an *événement*. Her joys were different. In 1966 Anthea left Reading University and, with a sense of absolute rightness, joined her heart and her hand to her first love, Anthony Millican, on World Cup Final Day at St Giles-in-the-Fields in London's West End, where Anthony was curate.

The couple started their married life in a small flat just off Shaftesbury Avenue, on the borders of London's 'vice' district, Soho. As a young newlywed Anthea would often venture out to Soho's produce markets and grocery stores, braving the excesses of Carnaby Street, the explicit imagery of the sleaze-merchants, and the gaudy flashing lights advertising sex in all its incarnations. As dusk approached the neon shone brighter; now was the time for respectable solo females to retreat to safety. In the morning, heading downstairs on his way to work, Anthony often found used syringes on the doorstep. The world that Anthea had grown up in – a world of Christian belief, of respect for family, of discretion and dignity – seemed to her to be slipping away.

> It all made me feel very sad and very sorry. There was a wholesale rejection of everything else, except what was pertinent to the sixties.
>
> But of course, that was nonsense. How can we completely ignore our wellsprings, and our history? Break up our family lives and snub our parents . . . ?
>
> It wasn't just sex. Anything that wasn't Carnaby Street was 'square'. It was rebellion against the older generation. It was drugs, and philosophy, and fashion, and music.

But much of the pop scene seemed to her aggressively sexual and gross, self-indulgence gone mad.

* Revd Anthony Millican died in 1991, and Anthea later remarried. For simplicity I refer to her here by her first married name.

Anthea's unease with sixties culture is partly hindsight. Today, she sees it as the time the rot set in, and the beginning of a descent towards the far worse tendencies of the 1970s. But she was and is too intelligent to condemn without trying to comprehend. And she was no puritan. Life's comforts and rewards – an appetising meal, a glass of wine – are, in Anthea's book, good. 'Jesus said, "I come to give you life more abundantly." We need to look after ourselves.' But the rejection of rules, and the greedy quest for self-gratification seemed to her to be at odds with the nature of the cosmos as she understood it.

> The Christian faith puts God, and his wisdom, and his provision for mankind at the centre of everything. Self-indulgence is completely humanist. And I would contend that you can't be a Christian humanist, because humanism is, in the last analysis, human-centred not God-centred.

Anthea's own sense of well-being grew around her faith, her family and her marriage: 'My darling Anthony, father of my children . . . He held the central tenets of the Christian faith very sincerely: he was a wonderful clergyman and a wonderful father.' And she sees their marriage as an unequivocal partnership; they were companions, collaborators, a team.

> I loved being married.
>   You know, waking up in the morning, and just being able to say, 'Shall I get the tea, dear? Is it hot enough?'

*

For the old values were slow to release their grip. When Mary Ingham tracked her personal path through the 1960s, 1968 was the year at which she shuddered to a halt. On degree day, it dawned on Mary that, though she was carrying away a scroll of paper endorsing three years of intellectual effort and the passport to the world of work, she was not taking with her that which, deep down, she had hoped for: a husband.

Pinning down a man was getting harder. Under the new morality, men were less motivated to tie the knot. With metropolitan, no-strings, living-in-sin appearing to be more fun and fashionable than provincial married life, the late sixties were no time for educated women to be competing in the marriage stakes.

'Oh God,' wrote Mary in her diary, 'why am I not married and happy with two kids?' For many like her, the sexual revolution was skin deep. 'Emotionally and sexually, we were still looking for the awe-inspiring Mr Right – a man you could put on a pedestal.' When Mary looked around at her peer group, it was not the computer scientists and medics she envied – it was the wives. Gillian had had a marvellous white wedding, and had given up her job to have babies. Glenda, Liz and Kath had all three landed teaching jobs *and* husbands. Janet was a high-flyer who had traded work for wedlock. Why could she not be like them?

Fiancé-less, and released from the comforting confines of the lecture hall, Mary gazed at her own future with terror. 'I was at last facing adult life, free and on my own – and I longed to be rescued from that awful responsibility.'

But there was no guarantee that marriages that started out with high hopes would stay the course. In 1968 10 per cent of marriages ended in divorce, an increase of more than 50 per cent from 1962. Living fashionably in sin in Chelsea was one thing. But living under a stigma was still, for many, tough. Middle England wasn't yet ready for the threat posed by the divorcée, who was still seen as an offender against Christian ethics – like Kathleen Christiansen, whose son, the critic Rupert Christiansen, wrote a precise and poignant memoir of his beloved mother's life in a leafy backwater of south London where time stood still. Christiansen's parents had married in 1948. In 1959 his father left his mother. Rupert was four; his little sister just seven months. All through the 1960s Kathleen shouldered the burdens of single motherhood in this rigid suburban bastion of entrenched 'breeding', where a fortress mentality prevailed. In Petts Wood Kathleen's divorced status was, for her, a source of subtle, awful angst. She wasn't so much shunned, as quietly sneered at and pitied. The neighbourhood kept its distance. When the Church of England vicar paid her a call soon after the divorce to offer his commiserations, he dropped into the conversation the hint that she would no longer be welcome to take communion 'or – ahem! – belong to the Mothers' Union'. There was the persistent intimation that as a divorcée she was a threat to the sacred institution of marriage, and also somehow deficient, having failed to keep her man. Kathleen, isolated, kept a stiff upper lip and barely complained. Only twice did the young Rupert see her weeping, silently and without explanation. This was a breeding ground for narrow-mindedness and conformism; a 1950s world of fish knives, matching accessories and female dependence:

> I don't think that the sixties – that glibly packaged but leaky concept – meant anything much here beyond racier pop music, tighter trousers and shorter skirts . . .

writes Christiansen.

But the Mothers' Union mindset applied beyond Petts Wood. Five years after it had exploded onto Britain's streets, the puritans were still policing young women who liked wearing the mini. In January 1968 staff at Birmingham law courts were threatened with the sack. The clerk to the justices told the *Daily Telegraph*: 'I expect a reasonable standard of dress in the office and skirts have now become so short that comment is being made . . .' Trousers were still controversial. In March 1969 a college principal in Macclesfield provoked a walk-out by banning female students from wearing them, while Mr John Hewlett from Earls Court wrote to the *Daily Mail* to denounce trousered women: 'Am I the only man in Britain who actively hates them?' he asked, explaining that he had twice refused to escort girls on dates until they changed into a dress. Indeed you didn't have to look beyond the columns of the *Daily Telegraph* to find a deluge of correspondence from the likes of retired schoolmaster Mr Thomas Peacocke:

> Britain is sinking into a state of decadence never before reached in her history . . . The Britain of today is just drifting. We have lost belief in ourselves and are fast losing all sense of moral values. Something needs to be done . . .

*

Mr Peacocke, a confirmed bachelor of sixty-five who had taught chemistry at a boys' school in Leatherhead, probably felt left behind by the speed of change in the era of self-gratification. What to do, other than pour out one's frustration to the editor of a national newspaper? But the loss of a rule book could be just as hard to handle for these distressed young problem-page correspondents (writing to the *Woman's Own* and *Woman's Weekly* agony aunts in 1967/68):

I have been going out with a member of a 'beat group' for a month and I like him a lot, but he's always asking me if I would go to bed with him and I really don't want to.

Now he says I'm old-fashioned and that virgins are thought little of today. He's got me confused . . .

Deborah

I am almost 17 . . . My question is, should I tell my parents that my boyfriend used to smoke 'hash'?

Bridget

I am sixteen and I know girls of my age who have had intercourse with different boys. To hear them talk makes me feel sick, but they still egg me on to try it. Of course I know all the reasons against it, but I will admit I have sometimes been tempted to copy them . . .

Sally

A few weeks ago my boyfriend begged me to let him make love to me and I agreed . . .

Do you think he still loves me after what happened? I am worried sick in case he gives me up . . .

'Worried'

Three months ago I met a very nice young man from London and we went out together a few times . . . He told me he had a comfortable sofa in his flat and, if I ever came to London, he would be glad to put me up. Would it be immoral to go and stay with this boy? Do you think it might end by sleeping with him?

I can't tell my mother, as she would be very shocked . . .

Lucy

Recently my boyfriend has been very passionate when we are alone together and a few days ago he asked me if I believed in sex before marriage. I did not answer but he told me he did.

He seems as though he wants to have intercourse with me and I do not know what to do about this.

Anne

Here, and in thousands of other *cris de coeur* sent to the magazine agony aunts, we hear the unheard voices, and catch glimpses of a lesser-known 1968 – one inhabited by reticent, unhappy and fearful young women who feel that the sexual revolution is leaving them behind. Their stories, or what they hint at, are the time-immemorial tales of the betrayed virgin, the abandoned maiden, the deceived, dependent female forever prey to the desires and duplicity of the inviolable male.

'Wait until you are husband and wife . . .'; 'Sex is an important and sacred thing . . .'; 'Enjoy London – but go to bed – alone!' urged *Woman's Weekly*'s Mary Marryat in her auntly way. It was no good. You only have to look at Mrs Marryat's by-line photograph – showing a poised, elderly woman with a nicely permed helmet of white hair and a print blouse with a polite sash neckline – to see that she was hopelessly behind the times. 'Ignore this boy's taunt about being "old-fashioned", it's just nonsense . . .' she advises Deborah. But in 1968 Deborah's sense of virginal value is ebbing, and we can be pretty certain that the beat-group boyfriend is unlikely to stick around waiting to lead her to the altar. What was to be gained by old-fashioned commitment, if you could have all the sex you wanted with nothing to lose except the good opinion of some moralising auntie? Why wait on Deborah's scruples when the beat groups had Sally's sixteen-year-old friends – girls willing and ready 'to have intercourse with different boys' – queuing at the stage door?

Honky Tonk Women

1960s rock sexism is a complex topic. Its themes are lust, misogyny, contempt, irresponsibility, objectification, male supremacism – and raw power. Ruth Padel, the author of an insightful study of maleness in rock'n'roll,* quotes Eric Clapton:

* *I'm a Man: Sex, Gods and Rock'n'Roll* (2000), which is an excellent book on the subject.

You get into a group and you've got thousands of chicks there. There you are with thousands of girls screaming their heads off at you. Man, it's power . . . *phew*!

Or enter into the fantasy world of this rock fan:

I went to every Dylan concert. I made a vow that if I ever got to lay him I'd have myself sewn up . . .

or this one, writing to Lennon:

Dear John,

. . . I am lying here in my bed naked, just waiting for you to make love to my beautiful body. I'm hungry for your mouth. My measurements are: 38–22–36, my hair is blonde and it reaches my waist. My friends say I'm beautiful. If you want me any time my address is –

The music itself was electrifying. Had there ever before been songs as sexy as 'Light My Fire', 'Sunshine of Your Love', 'Honky Tonk Women', 'Foxy Lady' or 'Born to be Wild'? – whose earthy lyrics, humping beat and slipping, sliding, spurting riffs made the older generation's stars (Frank Sinatra, Tony Bennett . . .) sound spineless and sugary. Then there was penis worship. Rock stars like Jimi Hendrix, Eric Clapton and Keith Richards not only prodded their erectile guitars at the audience, they also put their own virility on blatant display, thinly concealed in skin-tight and spotlight-catching velvet and satin. There was no escaping the vanity of those pelvic bulges, as aspirational for teenage male fans as for the bad girls who'd screamed and gone haywire at Beatles concerts a few years earlier. But by 1968 the fan-fantasy directed at the cheeky mop tops in their button-up party suits had changed its character. And sexism was becoming sexy.

Take groupies. Jenny Fabian's sensational *Groupie* (co-written with her friend Johnny Byrne), a thinly fictionalised account of the author's rock'n'roll adventures, is eye-wateringly explicit. Much later, Fabian would freely allow that her 'novel' was autobiographical. And the authors capture London's underground rock culture as few other books have done, using hippie-speak that dates the book to 1968 (it was published in 1969). This is the language of breadheads and spliffs, aggro and downers, plating* and pads. The clothes are embroidered, the trousers crotch-crushingly tight. People talk Zodiac signs and take large quantities of drugs. Her characters have easy-to-decipher pseudonyms. The Jacklin H. Event is the Jimi Hendrix Experience; Satin Odyssey is Pink Floyd, with 'Ben' masquerading as the band's ill-fated singer and lead guitarist, Syd Barrett. Celebrity and one-upmanship are the turn-ons. In the novel, nineteen-year-old journalist 'Katie' (Jenny Fabian) has got into the groupie scene after pulling Nigel, the manager of Satin Odyssey, whom she sees as a route to the star himself. 'Although I dug the status I got from being Nigel's chick there was even more prestige in being Ben's.' But soon after they have sex, Ben falls apart mentally from an overindulgence in psychedelic drugs.

Katie moves on, finds a job in the music world and a groupie mentor in gorgeous Roxanna, who explains the hierarchy. A groupie who slept with a Group Member (GM) was expected to stay at that level, and not slip down the ranking to PM or RM (Personal Manager or Road Manager). At times the content is painfully squalid and scary, with unsparing descriptions of VD clinics, drug busts, sadistic sex and overdoses. Trailing after the leader of the band inevitably led to jealous recriminations; a rock star who wanted to please his fans had to look available, so it was no good his girl getting too attached. But attending to the man's needs was generally expected too, whether that meant rolling his joints, getting his tea, giving him blow-jobs, or ensuring he took his allergy pills. Rather than have a row when a prestigious rock guitarist tells her he has a venereal disease, Katie gives in and masturbates him – 'There wasn't much else I could do . . .' The room is far from fresh, and the mattress sags, but she stays over. In the morning, she masturbates him some more, washes her hands, makes toast and coffee. 'When I'd finished [he] made me sew and press some trousers for him.'

The groupie needs to feel useful. She wants to prove to her rock star that she can not only give him great sex but also rustle up a sausage sarnie and wash up afterwards. But though the groupie might

* Plating: not familiar today, but a term much used in Fabian's lexicon to denote fellatio or cunnilingus.

play house, she was far from being a wife. She might well be under
the age of consent. Other members of the band might expect her to
give them pleasure. Where fidelity was concerned, there were no
rules. The only rules there were, were ordained by the guys – 'It's
what I decide that counts,' says authoritarian rock manager Grant.
The primary relationships in the book are ones in which Katie is
used, and Grant has a hold over her that scarcely lets up:

> He . . . hadn't changed at all. He was still aggressive and bossy, but if he
> had treated me like dirt before, he was treating me like nice dirt now.

As 'nice dirt', she is expected to wash and mend his socks, as well as
find women for him – 'birds with big tits, because he liked big tits
and mine were too small'.

However, for all her cool, Katie is clingy and possessive: this is
Katie struggling to anchor her intimacy with Joe (based on Ric
Grech, bass guitar player with the rock group Family):

> [Joe] started grumbling that chicks shouldn't come on gigs anyway,
> it's a drag having someone sitting in a corner watching you with a
> possessive glint in her eye.
>
> 'OK, I'll wait at home,' I said, desperate to please.

But it's a no-win. Joe can't handle the wife-type.

> 'What do you feel for me?' [she asks]
> 'You're a groove in bed.' What an answer, I thought.
> 'Do you like screwing all that much?'
> 'I'm easy,' said Joe. 'I make out with you all right.'
> '. . . That's only because I work so hard at it.'
> 'That's what you're here for.'

Many years after *Groupie* had become a cult bestseller, Jenny Fabian
told an interviewer, 'I felt I still had something to prove. Like I had
the right to fuck around just like the guys did. I suppose all this is
leading up to the fact that as often as not my day would start with
some strange guy in the bed beside me whom I'd pulled the night
before in the Speak.'

At the end of *Groupie*, the reader is left with unanswered questions
about sex, fame, free love, equality and power – and wondering who

has won. 'Sam' (based on Mitch Mitchell, drummer of the Jimi Hendrix Experience, aka the Jacklin H. Event) is her last conquest – or is she his? After the gig, Katie makes the first move. Back at the band's luxury flat she realises this one's so stoned it's scarcely worth bothering, and he'll have forgotten her by tomorrow. She weighs up the options. What would it be like to have sex with a drummer? But morality is starting to mess with her targets; she is through with 'anonymous fucking', or so she believes. To Sam's bewilderment, she puts her coat on to leave; he pleads with her to stay:

> 'I'm not going to sleep with you,' I said.
> He laughed. 'Why not?'
> 'Because I'm not an easy pull.'
> Sam frowned. 'Then why did you come back with me?'
> 'Well, you are one of the Event,' I said, matter-of-factly.

So is Katie leaving because she has bought out of the groupie ethos? Is she moving beyond her 'wild oats period'? Maybe this female rake will conform to the traditional morality tale, mend her ways, renounce promiscuity and find the true love of a good man. But there's a final twist. Katie walks out on Sam, but we know she's not setting out to tread the path of virtue. She has unfinished business. And she's hardly out of the door before her mind summons up an image of a leg in velvet trousers and groovy boots, faceless, with long dark hair and agile fingers coaxing lustrous chords from a keyboard. 'There's that organist from The Shadow Cabinet to be pulled. Yes.'

Groupie is about the unadorned essentials of the sex transaction, stripped of consequences, and were it not for the suspicion that Jenny Fabian's heroine has both a streak of masochism as well as a remnant of morality, the book would be little more than an observational guidebook to extreme sex circa 1968: 'a social document of our times . . .' as Desmond Morris described it in *The Observer*. But Katie's complex needs and desires give *Groupie* depth. In reality, our intrepid free love champion is not free from inherited baggage. Emotional connections, even love, accompany her encounters, and her partners' infidelities rankle. And when Hunter Davies lifted the lid on Jenny Fabian for the *Sunday Times*, he revealed, not so much an incorrigible adventuress, more a sulky, confused, battle-scarred young woman, stubbornly trying to navigate a pathway through the anarchic sexual minefield of the late sixties, and retreating, defeated, to the safety zone of monogamy:

> Me, I'm just waiting for the right geezer to come along, like every other chick. I'm very persistent when I want a man. I've no pride. It takes a lot of courage to have no pride.
>   That's how I see it anyway.

★

In the episode with Sam, the Event drummer, the author alludes to 'Jacklin' himself with awe. As we know, he's Jimi Hendrix, here seen with a 'chick he's had for some time now . . .', doubtless Kathy Etchingham. Kathy didn't describe herself as a groupie – she'd got involved with Jimi in 1966 shortly before he became a rock phenomenon in Britain – but the relationship was as no-strings as any one-nighter. All the same, it is revealing just how uncommitted they both were to the principle of non-commitment. Jimi was massively promiscuous – he was reputed to have 'balled seven chicks in three hours' – and when Kathy discovered him entwined with some girl in a state of semi-undress a screaming shouting row ensued, after which she refused to speak to him for twenty-four hours. For Jimi it was normal to flirt with anyone in the room, while protesting bemused innocence when Kathy levelled accusations at him. But he himself was consumed with jealousy and distrust, unable to stand her talking to other men. Both were serially unfaithful. When the relationship inevitably fell apart Jimi was uncomprehending. 'He expected me to behave like a saint [but] he wanted to be totally free himself.' Once more, 1960s freedoms were highlighting the massive gulf between male and female expectations. The world's greatest guitarist felt more than entitled to call the tune, on stage and off.

★

By 1968, macho rock-star culture was starting to get to Beryl Marsden.
    Liverpudlian Beryl had started her singing career in 1961 at the amazingly young age of fourteen, becoming a girl in a man's world. Her preference for a casual, low-key look, jeans and sweaters, came

from the desire to blend in, to be 'one of the guys'. But though the singing never let her down, the guy stuff could get irksome.

> When you're in vans up and down the motorway, it's not wondrous, is it? I think people sometimes think it's very glam – and it's not.
>
> 'Cos, being mostly with guys all the time, they were a bit, duh . . . Though you did get used to it, you know, the burping and the farting.
>
> And I'd tell them, 'If you want to talk about what you do with girls, just leave it till I'm asleep. I don't want to know; it's too much information.'

She was all too familiar with the groupie scene.

> Yeah . . . I mean, some of them were hilarious, don't get me wrong, and they would sleep with anyone. They would say, 'I've slept with him, 'cos he's in that band, or this band . . .'

Trophy hunting had no meaning for Beryl. Bands were her everyday reality, and why anyone would want to go to bed with some mal-odorous bloke in a trance state just because he played a guitar was beyond her. But she wasn't immune to the free-love argument.

> Everyone was doing it – and I got caught up in it. You just thought, huh, it's free now – no need to hold back. You met someone, you had a few drinks, you'd go back and chat, chat, chat – and you'd end up sleeping with them . . . I mean, you think you're invincible when you're young . . .
>
> But you'd wake up next day, and you'd think, duh, what did I do that for?

So, why *did* she do it? Now over seventy, Beryl has done a lot of thinking about human psychology and motivation. With hindsight, she thinks that performers, male as well as female, have a particular vulnerability and need for attention that transfers to sex relation-ships, as in 'if you sleep with me, it proves you think I'm a good person'. She recognises that artists of any kind are needy people. 'I'm sure part of it was wanting some gratification about who you are and what you're doing . . .' In her own case, she believes having one-night stands was a way of seeking a substitute for the parental affection she'd lacked as a child. But women had few weapons in their armoury, and Beryl also suspects that, in the match between the sexes, women were playing for a draw:

> I think it was this equality thing going on. I think women wanted to feel empowered – like, if men can do it, then I can do it too.

But evening the score didn't bring any sense of triumph.

> These one-night stands didn't make you feel nice, or good. I didn't even enjoy sex then! I thought it was horrible really. Mad, isn't it?
>
> I mean, it was like somebody should have said, 'Are you actually enjoying this? Because I'm not, so shall we just stop doing it then?'
>
> And I don't think it was a very healthy thing at all. But I think for women it was a lot more damaging.
>
> 'Cos obviously, you don't really get to have great sex, unless you really love somebody. And then it's a really beautiful thing, an emotional, loving caring thing. But that wasn't happening.

Beryl had always had a rebellious streak. And yet again, her contrariness carried her away from the prevailing current. At just twenty, the drinking, the clubs, and life on the road were wearing her down. The promiscuity felt increasingly destructive, a Russian roulette of risk. She was an onlooker as increasing numbers of rock musicians she knew fell prey to drugs – 'the heroin thing scared the shit out of me . . .' – wantonly abusing their bodies. In 1968 she baled out of the London music scene, got on a train and went back to her mum in Liverpool.

Say It Loud

Scalp-collecting, drugs, alcohol, the counterculture and one-night stands represent everything that Floella Benjamin had been brought up to deplore. From an early age Marmie and Dardie encouraged their clever daughter to study hard and work hard, and expected her to observe the three Cs: 'Consideration, Contentment with your lot, and Confidence'. The family were good Christians. Marmie was strict about who her daughters socialised with, though she gave her blessing to their visits to the West Indian Students' Centre in Earls Court, which she saw as being frequented by 'decent, intelligent young people'. Floella and her sister Sandra also observed their mother's ruling that they must have nothing to do with boys, at the risk of ending up as teenage mothers. So, where sexual contact was concerned, Floella had no time for random approaches. When a groper tried to touch her up on the Underground, she shamed him with a resoundingly public rebuke: 'Excuse me, I don't remember giving you permission to touch my bottom. So stop it!' In other words, the world of this sporty, punctual, good-as-gold, teetotal, white-collar worker in a City bank was in every way different from that of the hippie minority, whose mind-bending acid reality suffused daily life with psychedelic colour. Floella 'never needed to drink alcohol to feel good or to dance the night away'. Nor drugs either. Which may explain how this dauntless, moral and ambitious young woman came to take a step that she knew would dismay and disappoint her loving mother, and would associate her indelibly with the very culture that Marmie had so firmly spurned. At the age of twenty, Floella Benjamin joined the cast of the racially integrated musical *Hair*.

We have already seen, through Floella's eyes (and those of her contemporary Theresa Tyrell), some examples of the way in which racism's toxic stain had spread and infected British society in the 1960s. Both young women were subjected to gratuitous attentions, partly owing to the colour of their skin. Through the decade, Britain was accepting around 75,000 Commonwealth immigrants a year, and the *News of the World* cited a statistic predicting three million 'coloured people' living in Britain by the turn of the century. In April 1968 (a fortnight after the assassination of Martin Luther King), Enoch Powell, the Member of Parliament for Wolverhampton South West and Opposition spokesman on Defence, spoke out. Native-born Britons were becoming 'strangers in their own country', he said. Powell looked on with foreboding and imagined, in the words of Virgil, 'the River Tiber foaming with much blood'. Powell's speech heated existing tensions to boiling point. But though he was sacked from the Shadow Cabinet, for weeks his postbag swelled with

Illustration to a *News of the World* investigation into 'Our Coloured Neighbours' (1965). 'There is a very strong hidden colour bar in Britain,' wrote the journalist – 'a cold, stand-offish determination to have nothing to do with "those blacks".'

letters of support. Barbara Castle was one who saw his influence as irreparably destructive. 'I believe he has helped to make a race war, not only in Britain but perhaps in the world, inevitable.'

Race was the hottest of topics. From the late 1950s, the ripples from across the pond – in the form of the marches, movements and riots of the Civil Rights movement – had been spreading and gathering hurricane force. For, if women in the white community felt misused, marginalised and treated as an oppressed minority, then how much more did our genuine minorities suffer under brutal abuse, both racist and sexist? Assaults on black women were all too common; prejudice and hatred damaged their lives and those of their children. The 1960s emergence of left-wing protest – anti-nuclear, anti-Vietnam, anti-apartheid – was paralleled among immigrant women's groups which saw the various movements of Black Power as giving them a voice. From 1968, Altheia Jones-LeCointe from Trinidad deployed her skills in oratory to become a leading figure in the British Black Panther movement, energetically championing women's involvement; fellow recruits included Olive Morris (who later helped set up the Brixton Black Women's Group) and Beverley Bryan, both from Jamaica, who had joined the Black Arts Workshop in 1966.

There were many more.* Beverley's strong sense of black pride grew from her community, and from a justifiable immodesty:

> It was the time, the only period when to be a black-skinned girl was the most powerful and the most beautiful thing.
>
> You could hold your head, you felt – you know – you were a Queen. People used to call me Empress . . .

When male disputes threatened to capsize the movement, she and her female comrades kept things afloat. She believed, too, that women were less egotistic, and better at working together than men.

For Beverley, Olive, Altheia and others like Floella Benjamin, the sense of black female pride – accompanied by dignity, power, gifts and potential – was tangible. At the Earls Court West Indian Students' Centre Floella and Sandra sang along to soul singer James Brown's 1968 funk civil rights hit, 'Say It Loud, I'm Black and I'm Proud'. Since Elvis, imported black music had already stamped its white counterpart with indelible rhythms – but by '68 record buyers and concert goers were in love with Nina Simone, Aretha Franklin, the Miracles, Jimi Hendrix, Stevie Wonder and too many other great black artists to mention. Black was minority, black was underprivileged; but black was dangerously, indisputably cool.

For this traffic across the Atlantic brought with it more than great music; it brought a look, a glamour and an attitude. Fringing, embroidery, beading, batik and ethnic motifs broke away from their roots and appeared on the clothes and cushions of fashion-conscious hippies. Black women groups like the Supremes who had assimilated white styling by straightening their hair, now unstraightened it and re-embraced African-ness. Their springy, curled hair, which until now had been the despair of many a hairdresser, suddenly became enviable. Black model Marsha Hunt had arrived in England in 1966 and was quickly adopted in alternative circles. 'Black is beautiful' was the slogan on innumerable lips. It perfectly described Marsha's sultry loveliness, lithe limbs and Afro halo; at Christmas 1968 her black face

---

* They have been inspiringly chronicled in *The Heart of the Race: Black Women's Lives in Britain* (1985), by Beverley Bryan, Stella Dadzie and Suzanne Scafe, three women who came together through their involvement in black women's politics.

was blazoned across the cover of *Queen* magazine. It was cool to be a 'Spade chick'. But it worked both ways – and white women who slept with black men reaped the associated glamour. For Kathy Etchingham – a white working-class girl from Derby – Jimi Hendrix's 'otherness' (as it was then perceived) was undoubtedly part of the allure:

> I had never seen such an exotic man before. To my naive and unso-
> phisticated eyes he seemed dangerous and exciting . . . His hair was
> standing up from his head in his own version of the Afro style, [a]
> new concept in London.

Though Kathy doesn't go into detail, it's clear that – compared with her white lovers – Jimi's sexual technique was on a different, mythic plane. We are left to imagine whether or not the crushed velvet skin-tight red loons concealed unusual prowess, but the implication is that they did.

All of these themes and many more, from illegal drugs to astrology, from environmentalism to the anti-Vietnam protest movement, collided in *Hair*. The musical starred Marsha Hunt, and was notorious for its profanity, for bringing black actors onto the stage in leading roles and, above all, for a blink-and-you-miss-it scene at the end of Act 1 in which cast members stripped naked. However, unwary audience members might well have taken more offence at the candid lyrics of such songs as 'Black Boys' and 'Sodomy'. For the finale, the audience was invited onto the stage to groove with the cast and join in with 'Let the Sunshine In'.

The first night at the Shaftesbury Theatre was 27 September 1968. In the event, few critics objected to the show's morality, though some were bored. The majority applauded its spirit, charm and energy. *The Times'* critic gave it the ultimate Establishment accolade, writing – 'Its honesty and passion give it the quality of a true theatrical celebration – the joyous sound of a group of people telling the world exactly what they feel.' Unsurprisingly, card-carrying hippies regarded the musical as execrable, its commercialism and huge success (it would run in the West End for five years, with a total of 1,997 performances) utterly damning it. The chronicler of the underground, Jonathon Green, dismissed it as 'middle-of-the-road pap'. Personally, I remember being taken to the show as a treat by a broad-minded relative when I was about fourteen – it must have been 1969 – and being bewildered by its highly coloured, exuberant but incoherent razzmatazz. Yet even then something jarred for me, in seeing the alternative society boiled down to a sensational, shouty chorus, all fine feathers, caftans and fringes: hippies reconfigured as spectator sport for the coach-party market. I had little contact with the hippie universe, but had imagined something more numinous, gentle and profound. Surely hippies didn't need to show off?

No hippie herself, Floella Benjamin was untroubled by the thought of prostituting principles for the sake of entertainment. It was soon after her twentieth birthday that Floella spotted the casting-call advert in an evening newspaper. 'Singers and Dancers wanted. No experience necessary.' All her secret ambitions, her self-belief, her drive, her itch to dance and her craving to perform crystallised as she read the words. 'I got the feeling it was a personal message to me.' To proclaim before an audience her beauty, her power, her talent, her femininity and her skin colour would be the summit of her dreams. On the day, Floella took time out in her lunch hour to head for the West End theatre where the hopefuls were waiting in line. At last it was her turn to demonstrate her audition piece, 'I've Got You Under My Skin'. She gave it her all, following it up with a bopping, fizzing, free-style demonstration of her dancing skills, and finishing with a reading from the part of 'Abie Baby' in her best American accent.

As she waited for the reaction, Floella reached in her mind for what she now sensed would be her future. Somehow, this was going to happen. But how would Marmie deal with her daughter's change of course? *Hair* was everything Mrs Benjamin considered indecent, a blasphemous show that had almost been banned for celebrating free love, drug-taking and nudity. Floella was undeterred. There could be no going back to the bank. But how could she persuade her mother to agree to such a step, or give her blessing to a showbusiness career that she had always opposed?

> For her to share the vision I had of my future, I would have to re-assure her that I would keep intact the principles, integrity, beliefs and values she had instilled in me . . .

There was one way this could be achieved. Marmie had taught her daughter fearless confidence and a sense of her own value. She was beautiful and she was black. As she stood impatiently, staring into the darkened auditorium, hanging on the verdict on her performance, Floella Benjamin decided that the show's producers could take her or leave her. It was *Hair*, or a desk job. She was still on her lunch hour, but time was running short. They needed to make up their minds:

> So with a smile on my face, joy in my voice and happiness in my soul, I announced to the listener in the darkness, '. . . so if you do want me to be in your show, you had better tell me right now. Oh and by the way, I want thirty pounds a week – and I'm not taking my clothes off!'

★

Hair pulled in the coach parties. It even – to the disgust of many genuine hippies, but to the delight of the press – appealed to the embodiment of 'square': royalty. Eighteen-year-old Princess Anne was seen shaking a hip on stage alongside the stars, Marsha Hunt and Jamaican-born Peter Straker. For many, *Hair* spelled the death of flower power. Peace and love had become irretrievably vulgarised. The advertisement for the original production at the Shaftesbury Theatre – mirror images in posterised fluorescent colours, of a blissed-out woman's head surrounded by a halo of Afro hair – drew from the art of the counterculture. Easy to copy as it was, the groovy, psychedelic, Beardsley-inspired hippie aesthetic was becoming degraded and popularised. One very noticeable aspect of this iconography is its appropriation of a kind of comic-book eroticism. Record sleeves, textiles, and posters exhorting 'Make Love Not War' brandished glamorised, gaudy imagery of leggy women with perky breasts in various states of overheated ecstasy: psychedelic beauty queens. Reproduced on everything from magazines to merchandise, the visual shorthand for revolution was fast becoming an empty-headed, glassy-eyed, available naked woman.

The straight press were early adopters of the graphic design style pioneered by the underground. But salesmen too were getting in on the act, pirating the concepts, imagery, deliquescent typography and vocabulary of youthful trendsetters to peddle slimming aids, sports-wear, lipstick, canned soup, spare parts for cars, Pepsi Cola and the Yellow Pages. 'Join the cola dropouts,' urged the marketing men behind a highly coloured flower-filled advert for a Canada Dry product called Wink. 'You don't just drink Wink. You feel it. A million liquid diamonds turn on all at once . . . Wink is where it's at!' 'Hippy?' challenged the makers of a low-calorie snack, over a picture of a woman struggling with her skirt zip – 'Get into shape with Limmits Chocolate Wafer'. Meanwhile, as censorship eased, film-makers cashed in with movies like *Barbarella*, *Candy* and *If* . . . , which broke barriers with their airbrushed portrayal of female nudity and semi-obscured scenes of love-making.

The Beatles too seemed to be selling out. They had created a tax-efficient company, Apple, and opened a well-intentioned store staffed by beautiful dolly birds. But exorbitant prices and a permissive attitude to shoplifting brought the Apple boutique to its knees within months. Nevertheless, the Beatles' creativity continued to be astounding. This was the year of the double ('White') album, and of the animated film *Yellow Submarine*, an innovative hippie-lite fairy tale with a tum-ti-tum-ti, all-together-now signature tune. The making of the film employed a huge team of young animation artists to colour in the verdant underwater landscapes of Pepperland, the Sea of Green and the Blue Meanies (evildoers who plot to drain the country of colour). Theresa Tyrell was one of many art-school graduates who applied to work on it. For months she didn't hear back.

Then, when she was on the point of accepting a promotion at Heal's furniture and design store, the call came.

> I got home to a telegram, saying, you can start work on *A Yellow Submarine* in a week's time . . .

It was too good to turn down. The pay was excellent; her wages went from £9 to £15 a week; if she did overtime she could earn up to £50.* And the animation studio, based in an imposing pillared building in Soho Square, was a crucible of art-school talent.

---

* £15 then is worth approximately £250 today; £50 is worth £850.

Animation used to be done by technicians, but at this time the colleges were spewing out people, so for the first time there was this whole work force, about a hundred of us, who were all from art school.

The surreal, polychrome, poster-art style of the film was inspired by contemporary pop artists like Warhol, Lichtenstein and Alan Aldridge. 'I had friends there, and it was like being back at college but getting paid.' Theresa came in during the final six months of the process, by which time most of the creative basics had been laid down; she was now needed to colour in outlines by hand.

In those days it was very labour intensive – done frame by frame. It was painting by numbers, absolutely – filling in the colours on the reverse of individual cels that had an ink drawing in line on the front.★

The money was good, but wasn't there an irony inherent in working like an automaton to deliver the impression of colourful, trippy spontaneity? Was this the 1960s vision of freedom, individualism and 'doing your own thing'?

Nevertheless, Theresa's days were filled with art students, the Beatles and psychedelia. Working on *Yellow Submarine* ticked a lot of trendy boxes in the late 1960s. 'I guess it was a hoot really – there was such a lot of dope and acid going around . . .' she remembers. LSD wasn't really her scene, though she'd share the odd joint. And being mixed race herself gave her credibility in an environment where, these days, it was cool to have an Afro – even if her cloud of insuperably fine and curly hair more resembled a powder puff than Marsha Hunt's black halo. The team would work late and afterwards head on to parties at the Decca recording studio, where they would smoke dope and hang out with guitarists and DJs. But for Theresa, the atmosphere was often sour and brittle.

★ 'Cel' is short for 'celluloid'. Before computers developed to assist animated production, animated films were made by hand-drawing and hand-colouring the images onto transparent celluloid sheets. A full-length animated feature might require over 100,000 such cels.

The people were quite hippie and druggy. Also, for a gauche girl from Leeds like me, they were all quite sharp, and, you know, 'London' . . . Once I found myself feeling very unwell after smoking dope at some party – and I was begging to be put in a taxi. And the guys were saying, 'Ah, we can't man, 'cos the taxi driver will see that she's been on drugs, and it'll bring the fuzz . . .' And that was that for me.

When completed, the censors gave *Yellow Submarine* a family-friendly 'U' certificate, and on opening the critical reception was positive. Hippie style was losing its power to shock.

Chick Work

But a kernel of dedicated men remained committed to the cause. Revolution hadn't gone away just because the hippies had lost faith in daffodils to deflect the guns. Though its leaders professed anti-violence, there was a war still to be fought: against the Establishment, against institutions, against the fuzz, the straights, capitalists, imperialists, repressed monogamists and the older generation. Politicians, bishops, matrons, walrus-moustached colonels and Mrs Whitehouse still had the upper hand. The counterculture was worth a war with the bourgeoisie. Women were just collateral damage.

That war had been declared in 1967, and it was a war of words, printed beneath swirling, neon-hued, geometric, acid-induced graphics. Its name was *Oz*, a monthly magazine that – for 2s 6d* – offered its readers a phantasmagoria of views on trips, the Vietnam war, Cuba, abortion, flying saucers, the Paris *événements*, the Rolling Stones, communes, cohabitation and breasts, alongside poetry, and a plethora of voyeuristic, sexually sadistic imagery of nubile women. The Classified sections listed pregnancy tests, kooky badges, VD clinics and an excess of advertisements for products that claimed to enlarge the male member ('Magnaphall'). Much of *Oz* was pornography masquerading as sexual liberation.

Its editor, the charismatic Richard Neville, had arrived in London

* Roughly equivalent to £2 today.

from Australia that year, and had quickly recruited a raft of talent, including Robert Hughes, Clive James and Germaine Greer, to staff and write for his new publication.* 'This town needs a bomb under it,' he declared. Felix Dennis (who later became a colossally successful publisher) was his advertising manager. On launch day Dennis used a simple but tried-and-tested sales technique:

> I set myself up in the King's Road with three chicks in short skirts and [rammed] it in the punters' faces.

The rapacious pair described in the last chapter, Haynes and Marowitz, had much in common with Richard Neville and his merry men. 'I loved women and I loved making love to them,' Neville told Jonathon Green. 'I loved fucking and there were lots of people around who felt the same.' *Playpower* (1971) would be Neville's manifesto: a bumptious, cocky, testosterone-fuelled assault on traditional values and virtues. In it he described all the fun, for example, the jollity of gang bangs on the beach –

> On festive occasions . . . a generous girl will 'put on a queue' behind the sand dunes for a seemingly unlimited line-up of young men . . .

or the lightheartedly casual exploitation of an underage schoolgirl –

> I meet a moderately attractive, intelligent, cherubic fourteen-year-old . . . I ask her home, she rolls a joint and we begin to watch the mid-week TV movie . . . Comes the Heinz Souperday commercial, a hurricane fuck, another joint. No feigned love or hollow promises . . .

As editor of *Oz*, Neville professed unfettered, broadminded views. He felt it was time to shake off the 'joyless morality' of the past. 'Open marriage' was the face of the future. The sexual revolution was for everyone. But mainly men.

Having taken full advantage of the liberty this offered him, Richard Neville then went on to give his girlfriend, Louise Ferrier, a lecture on sexual freedom: 'Monogamy and marriage were bywords for "bourgeois". I said it would be fine if she had a bit on the side . . .'

---

* Neville had edited Australian *Oz* in Sydney from 1963 to 1966, and fought two obscenity trials in connection with the flagrancy of its content.

Needless to say, when she took him at his word, such protestations didn't hold up. Richard discovered that Louise had had several flings, and was cut to the quick; he was also tormented by the knowledge that feigned love, jealousy and possessiveness were supposed to be outmoded emotions.

To be fair, it appears that Richard Neville genuinely did wish to run things on progressive lines, and he sincerely wanted people's lives, including his own, to be more pleasure-filled. In his memoir *Hippie Hippie Shake*, Richard Neville portrays himself as a fun-loving, warm-hearted guy always ready for a 'hurricane fuck', but conscientious in toiling away at his writing and editorial work. He paints a joyful picture of a lighthearted three-way relationship that he conducted with Louise and her beautiful friend Jenny Kee (who sold second-hand clothes to a hippie clientele in Chelsea Antique Market):

> Spontaneous joy! No premeditation, no set fantasy, just an entwining of fleshly desires and long-held affection. The three of us tossed about on the sheets until dawn. For me, it was a sensation of wholeness, as if my dislocated yearnings – for a wife, for a mistress – united for once in sweaty tumult, without tears or deceit.

Jenny herself, however, remembers things differently. At that time she was prostrated with guilt and grief following the suicide of a close friend. Aghast with misery, she stumbled over to the flat where Louise and Richard lived. Richard was working on his book, but Louise rallied round like the best of friends; she looked after Jenny, made strong tea for her, rolled a joint, sat with her and hugged her while she cried and cried. Then she tucked her up in bed, cuddled her and told her she could stay.

> Richard . . . saw us in bed and thought all his dreams had come true at once. Needless to say the Great Work was temporarily forgotten while he joined us. It was an intimate time between two women with great feeling for each other, and he was lucky to be there.

The affectionate threesome then take off for a week's idyll in rural Suffolk. Richard spends most of this time thinking deeply about his 'Book', while the girls do girl-stuff – 'Louise and Jenny took amphetamines and made a cake.' There is much nattering and dithering over the ingredients; as Jenny Kee puts it, 'a perfect sixties scene: girls barefoot in the kitchen while the boys changed the world'.★ As 'The Book' progresses there are more country weekends, shared with Richard's theatre director friend Tony Palmer. Again, Louise makes herself useful: '[She] would cycle three miles to the village to buy supplies, and prepare meals. In her spare time she sat picturesquely under the spring blossoms, making her way through *Gone With the Wind*.'

They didn't wear corsets or curlers, and they were promiscuous, but apart from that Louise and her ilk were as much housewives as their mothers. In female terms, this was what being a good hippie was all about. 'Chick work' meant looking decorative, cooking well, scouring the toilet, rolling joints, and above all fucking freely.

Nobody describes the predicament of the hippie women better than the artist Nicola Lane. In 1968 Nicola was living 'in run-down Notting Hill – then the throbbing nerve centre of bohemian and "alternative" life'. She had always wanted to be an artist; in 1967, after a peripatetic and cosmopolitan childhood, she came to London to study at Saint Martins and spent the following decade immersed in the underground art scene. Jonathon Green, who interviewed Nicola twenty years later for his book *Days in the Life: Voices from the English Underground, 1961–1971*, puts her in context as an art student and 'hippie chick'. But Nicola was far from as mindless as that makes her sound. Her interview is worth quoting at some length:

> The important thing to remember about the sixties is that it was totally male-dominated. You had to be an awful lot of things: you had to be sexy, you had to be game for anything, there was pressure for taking drugs, and you had to be an 'old lady' and have the brown rice ready. A lot of girls just rolled joints – it was what you did while you sat quietly in the corner, nodding your head . . . People would

★ 'And I love them both to this day,' adds Kee, who – while observing the double standards enacted by Richard Neville and his friends – didn't feel it necessary to take a stand. For her, the sex divide was incontestable. 'In the sixties women were still largely accessories . . . The girls might have dabbled in studies at art college or university, but they didn't actually have a lot to *do*.'

say, 'Wow, she's so far out, she's so cool, she never makes any waves . . .' And she never speaks.

You were not really encouraged to be a thinker. You were there really for fucks and domesticity. The old lady syndrome. 'My lady': so Guinevere-y. You had to fill so many roles: you had to be pretty and you had to be 'a good fuck', that seemed to be very important. I think it meant mostly that a) you would do it with a lot of people, and also b) that you'd give people blow-jobs. It was paradise for men in their late twenties, all these willing girls. But the trouble with the willing girls was that a lot of the time they were willing not because they particularly fancied the people concerned but because they felt they ought to . . .

[There were] endless nights sitting in rooms with the men smoking joints and talking about mighty things . . . There was a lot of misery. Relationship miseries: ghastly, ghastly jealousy, although there was supposed to be no jealousy, no possessiveness. What it meant was that men fucked around. You'd cry a lot, and you would scream sometimes, and the man would say, 'Don't bring me down, don't lay your bummers on me . . . don't hassle me, don't crowd my space . . .'

And in all the underground newspapers and magazines there was the first stirrings of what is now a full-blown business: pornography . . .

★

Nobody burned a bra on 7 September 1968, nor was it ever part of the plan.

But on that historic day Robin Morgan and several hundred women co-protesters in Atlantic City were on fire with excitement.★ The demonstration against the Miss America beauty contest, held in the Atlantic City Convention Hall, had been weeks in the planning. Posters and leaflets had been printed, banners painted, buses chartered, a megaphone hired. The women were aiming at the perfect target. The contest was manifestly degrading to women. Its winner (a white woman, always) would be packaged by the sponsors as a

---

★ The writer and activist Robin Morgan was a leader of 1960s and '70s second-wave feminism in the USA, and her edited anthology *Sisterhood is Powerful* (1970) is generally recognised as being one of its key texts.

dolly mascot and passively bundled off to Vietnam to entertain the troops. Here was capitalism, militarism, racism and sexism all rolled into one artificially curvaceous, high-heeled, swimsuited female proto-type. Outside the Convention Hall, Morgan and the sisters gathered around their chief prop, a Freedom Trash Can, into which they flung the symbols of their oppression: body-crushing girdles, bras that warped and contorted, shorthand notebooks that imprisoned, mops and scouring pads that enslaved, stiletto shoes that crippled, treacher-ous hair curlers and false eyelashes. Inside, as the glitz and pageantry unrolled, twenty intrepid women let rip with a wild cry of 'Freedom for Women!' while unfurling a huge WOMEN'S LIBERATION banner from the upper balcony rail.

And so it began.

*

The malaise, first identified in America by Betty Friedan in 1963, and fostered by her with the creation of NOW, had generated a movement.

I heard about a course run by Juliet Mitchell, called something like 'The Role of Women in Society' . . .

We always used to sit round the bar afterwards. An American woman came to talk to us about the women's movement in the United States, and said, 'Why haven't you got a women's movement here?' We just gaped at her.

Audrey Battersby

I can date to that time and to that sense of heightened awareness of the society around me in the summer of 1968 my own questioning of the nature of my reality as a woman.

Angela Carter

The student revolution of 1968 opened up the quest for yet new freedoms . . . At the same time Women's Liberation was becoming known in this country, proclaiming the fact, which I found even more extraordinary, that women were an oppressed class, both domestically and in the marketplace.

Patricia Vereker

My son . . . was born [in 1968] . . . I reacted to it very badly . . . I loved him, but I hated the way of life. I was isolated [and] I thought I was going insane. So I was very typical, I think, of people who were ripe for the women's movement.

Val Charlton

In the twelve months since she had begun to feel the first conscious stirrings of feminist awareness and had found a name for them, Sheila Rowbotham had barely paused for breath. 1968 was a year of feverish activism. At marches, at demonstrations, and at student sit-ins, Sheila was there. She organised festivals, sold magazines, painted banners, travelled, wrote, and stood on platforms. She spoke at the founding meeting of the Revolutionary Socialist Students' Federation. Agit Prop taught her that propaganda could take on new forms, while during the Paris revolution she had glimpsed the exhilarating reality that institutions can totter. During the May *événements* Sheila's New Left comrade Tariq Ali started *Black Dwarf*, a radical anti-capitalist broadsheet, and in the autumn he invited her to contribute to it. 'It had never occurred to me to actually write in it. The unstated assumption was that political writing was something men did.' Meanwhile, the incessant feminist refrain in her head was never quiet — just as a seemingly endless stream of laddish banter and machismo issued forth from the political men she associated with. One day Sheila flipped. Did they realise, she demanded to know, that in America an organisation had recently been formed called The Society for Cutting Up Men (SCUM)? If not, it was time they did. Burning with annoyance, she stomped out to the ladies' toilet, taking with her three other indignant women. '[We] began talking. This was really my first-ever women's meeting — a crucial glimpse of how connection to other women makes it much easier to express disgruntlement.'

Nevertheless, Sheila's male colleagues invited her on to *Black Dwarf*'s editorial board, and in December she began commissioning articles for a special women's issue. There would be pieces about contraception, equal pay, the family, and a first-person piece by a single mother. Sheila too would have a go at writing something a bit different, something that came from the inside about how it felt to be a woman in the late sixties.

The gas fire hissed in *Dwarf*'s basement office in Hackney. Sheila Rowbotham hunched beside it, her unruly red hair falling over her eyes. First, she made a list:

> Me
> Hairdressing girl
> Brentford nylons
> Birth control
> Unmarried mothers
> Ford's women
> Striptease girl . . .

Then she started to write, and words – charged with the accumulated intensity of twenty-five years of anger, passion, dreams and discoveries – started to overflow. Sheila felt that she was writing not just for herself, but for her generation.

She headed it WOMEN: A CALL TO REVOLT.

1969

The We Generation

'Sweet Caroline . . .' serenaded Neil Diamond in his famous 1969 hit:

I look at the night and it don't seem so lonely
We filled it up with only two . . .

The decade of the 1960s is often associated with the growth of individualism and self-absorption, as personal freedoms advanced. Being yourself, doing your own thing were the mantras. But a closer look brings us up against a variant of that familiar narcissistic trope. We might label it 'the We Generation' – a cohort as in love with each other as they were with themselves. Of course, there's nothing new about romantic love, but this 1960s version took its cue less from troubadours and *La Traviata*, and more from the idea of togetherness. Underlying togetherness was the revelatory notion that the sexes might be equal.

As the 1960s draw to a close, it's time to explore how real that equality was, and whether the decade really was a turning point for women. Since midway through it, small signs have been indicating that liberation is on its way; but a thousand contradictory factors continue to erode our confidence that it's real. Where do bunny girls fit into progress for women? Surely being a provider of 'fucks and domesticity' isn't compatible with togetherness? Will the We Generation live up to its peace-and-love promises, or are they built upon sand?

Throughout the 1950s, most couples still conformed to the time-honoured ideal, by which the man was expected to be the provider, dominant and aggressive, while the woman was submissive, domestic and often tearful. This ideal was seen as 'natural'; it drew sustenance from the Bible and tradition. 'Men must work and women must

weep . . .' as the poet wrote; 'He for God only, she for God in him.'*
Marriage was assumed to be a lifelong commitment, among a gen-
eration who only had recourse to the divorce courts in extremity.
Divorce was seen as scandalous, tainted and no fun.

In 1969 the indefatigable social anthropologist Geoffrey Gorer
decided to revisit the sexual and marital attitudes of the English public, in a follow-up to a survey he had presented sixteen years earlier.†
What he discovered confirmed that the meaning of commitment had
indeed changed. The stakes had become higher. Geoffrey Gorer now
showed that the historic ideal had been replaced by the wobbly but
heartfelt 'ideal of equality'. When he asked his respondents what
most contributed, in their view, to a happy marriage there was, compared to his 1950s sample, a greatly increased emphasis on comradeship
and partnership. 'Love and affection' came near the top in a lengthy
list of qualities that he suggested to them might be of importance in
a marriage – far above sexual compatibility, a happy home, and interests in common. The word 'togetherness' recurred frequently in the
interview transcripts. Gorer now coined the term 'symmetrical marriage' to describe what he saw as a new state of affairs. In the
symmetrical marriage, the planets of man and woman were travelling through that dark, lonely night on parallel orbits.

The starry, romantic *égotisme-à-deux* of the 1960s is permeated
with the ideal of coupledom. Cohabitation was the exception to marriage, not the rule. Weddings held sway as they always had done. By
the mid-1960s, 96 per cent of women aged forty-five were married.
Almost half of those women had found a husband by the age of
twenty-one. And the days of parental intervention in their daughters'
choices were over, with comedienne Joyce Grenfell catching the 1969
mood: 'Daddy and I are delighted that you are going to marry a
middle-aged Portuguese conjurer, darling. But are you sure he will
make you happy?'

* From Charles Kingsley's 1851 ballad 'Three Fishers'; and Milton, *Paradise Lost*,
Book IV.
† During 1969, 1,987 men and women were questioned about their attitudes; the
results were presented as *Sex and Marriage in England Today* (1971). Gorer's earlier
survey was *Exploring English Character*, published in 1955.

It seemed as if the Merseybeat generation was as attached to the idea of lifelong commitment as their parents' generation had been – with the difference that rose-tinted romantic fulfilment was at the heart of the promise they made to each other. 'Togetherness', peace and love, and compatibility were of the moment, as never before. Music business secretary June Child started living the dream from the moment the seraphically handsome singer and musician Marc Bolan first walked into her office:

> It was like an electric shock, the most extraordinary thing . . .

Within hours, Marc had asked her round:

> It was a beautiful summer's day. He opened the door and said, 'Would you like some muesli . . . ?'
>
> We sat out on the tiny little bit of grass at the back of the house, eating muesli and talking. And then he said, 'I've got something to give you,' and . . . he brought out this little piece of paper and I opened it, and it was the most beautiful love poem. And I looked at him, and he said, 'I'm in love with you,' and I was absolutely speechless.
>
> And I knew, I *knew* that it was right.

From then on Marc and June were inseparable, their marriage ending only with his early death.

But between 1960 and 1969 the number of divorces in England and Wales more than doubled – from 23,868 to 51,310.

When *The Guardian*'s reporter Ann Shearer went to talk to a group of divorcées to find out what was going wrong, one of them – through a cloud of cigarette smoke – told Shearer how she saw things:

> The trouble is, in the West, we're all so hooked on the ideal of romantic love as the only way to live that we're left thinking there's nothing when it lets us down.

It seemed that almost as fast as the knots got tied, they were unravelling. Placing 'togetherness' at the heart of marriage was putting the institution under unprecedented strain, at the same time as making the divorce laws less and less fit for purpose. The boom babies were quick to marry, and quick to part when things went wrong. Many of Geoffrey Gorer's respondents saw adultery as a deal-breaker.

Fidelity ranked almost as high on their scale of priorities in marriage as love and togetherness. A woman who was asked how to deal with an errant husband replied:

> Ignore it if it's a mere flirtation; if it's a lot more than this she should leave him.

A twenty-two-year-old lorry driver was categorical about what should be done with a straying wife:

> Divorce her . . .

he said. He himself had been unfaithful three times in the year that he got married, but seemed unaware of any contradiction; meanwhile a thirty-five-year-old man, asked the same question, saw it as a case of cutting your losses:

> Thump her – then the man. Try to patch it up with the wife . . . if this fails, divorce . . .

The stigma attached to divorce was slowly diminishing. When the etiquette guru Drusilla Beyfus wrote a guide to modern manners in 1969, she commented on the softening of attitudes. Divorcés, who now included many of the great and the good, were finally permitted to enter the Royal Enclosure at Ascot. Some divorcés even remained friends, though others didn't, creating a whole new landscape of social sinkholes to be navigated by the modern hostess.

The debate was shifting too. By the end of the 1960s something had to give, as couples found themselves trapped in loveless unions. If the stardust had dimmed, why – many argued – should such couples be compelled to remain together? From 1966 the term 'irretrievable breakdown' began to enter the vocabulary of churchmen and law-givers. Now came the turning point, when Parliament passed the 1969 Divorce Law Reform Act which allowed for a 'no-fault divorce', provided the pair had lived apart for two years (or five, if only one of them wanted to split up).* Dropping out, tuning in, and peace had

---

* The Act did not become effective until 1 January 1971, after which divorce figures rocketed. Within twenty years of the legislation, the number of yearly divorces was almost equal to the number of marriages.

yet to be embraced by a puritanical and materialistic Establishment who regarded the flower power generation as self-indulgent drifters. But LOVE, heart-shaped, primary-coloured and radiant, had emerged victorious. Its hippie-dippy anthem, 'All You Need is Love', was on everyone's lips. The pick-and-choose generation had been given a legal blessing to opt for togetherness – or, if they preferred, to do their own thing.

★

But seeing love as a right could cause terrible fallout:

> I found the man I wanted to be with and that was that.

recalled Amanda Brooke-Dales:

> I saw it as 'This is Love, and we have to be together.'

Amanda's 'wild oats' period ended abruptly – when she met Bernard Butler. Unfortunately, Bernard, an attractive American and a resident diplomat at the embassy where she now worked, was already married and the father of four children.

Bernard Butler was not a philanderer; he had married young and never before had an extramarital affair. By contrast, Amanda had leapt onto the permissive sixties bandwagon, gone on the Pill and, from about 1966, enjoyed an easy-come, easy-go attitude to relationships – 'I behaved exactly as I wanted, and just had a good time.' Wrecking a marriage was not part of her plan. To begin with, she saw their affair as being no more than an office fling: another in a long list of flings. But this one was different. In a short time the relationship had run out of control, feelings were intense on both sides, and the need to be together outweighed all other considerations. As things accelerated she began to realise that their love was causing dreadful damage to his marriage and, briefly, she tried to pull away. 'But that just made things worse.'

Bernard decided to leave his wife. There was terrible pain, distressing rows, anger and jealousy. 'It was all a big, big mess, and actually the whole thing was about as bad as it could be.'

But today, Amanda, who is in her seventies, cannot regret the long and rewarding marriage that she had with Bernard. Their feelings for each other remained as strong, over the thirty years they spent together until his death in 2000, as in the early days of their illicit romance. As in a fairy tale, 'we lived happily ever after'. But their happiness came at a cost.

For Amanda, widowed now, it has taken time to unscramble the motives and factors that caused two well-meaning and educated people so devastatingly to injure a third. She believes there was something in the air in the 1960s that permitted a type of behaviour of which, today, she would be ashamed.

> It's funny about guilt, isn't it? I didn't feel guilt at the time, because we were in love, and Bernard's marriage wasn't working.
>
> And I thought I knew everything – but really I knew <u>nothing</u> about the importance of a marriage with four children, and what it does to people. And sometimes, for all our happiness, I look back and ask myself: how did you have the nerve to do it? To be the other woman, and to be as ruthless as I was, in thinking, 'Well, bad luck about the wife and kids.' Because certainly, if I'm honest, that is what I thought at the time.
>
> And I would put that down to the sixties zeitgeist.
>
> I am quite critical of my sixties self. I sometimes think: you were a very selfish, spoiled, badly behaved, careless young woman, who thought you could play around with sex and emotions – and I don't think of it as being very admirable. Breaking up a marriage is a pretty serious thing to have on one's conscience, and I do have it on my conscience. I bloody well should too, it caused terrible pain.
>
> And yet – I don't exactly regret it.
>
> I think my generation thought that the old rules had led to a lot of repressions and unhappiness and hypocrisy, and we were going to behave in a more free and open way – and if someone's wife and four small children got in the way that was part of the price that was going to be paid, you know?

Amanda Brooke-Dales is entitled to reproach herself; but, as a woman 'helping herself' to someone else's spouse, wasn't she guilty of something that men have been guilty of for centuries, often unrepentantly? Don Juan refused to see the light, and burned in hell; but he and his smooth-talking colleague Casanova have always been saturated in aspirational glamour, sex appeal and attractive bravado – the Mick Jaggers of their day – while a woman who plays around is seen by others, and by herself, as ruthless, a wrecker, selfish, badly behaved, a Jezebel. Amanda is careful not to criticise Bernard. But it takes two to break a marriage. Why should her trespass be seen as more unforgivable than his – a sin more accountable to women than to men?

*

Marriage in the late 1960s was in a process of reconfiguration. The rumblings of change had been audible over the years since 1945, with a post-war divorce explosion accompanying a baby boom, and the growing belief, as more and more women entered the workplace and labour-saving devices promised to take the effort out of housework, that marriage could and should be a democracy. The Marriage Guidance movement, which had surged in the 1950s, was relevant as never before; its booklet *Sex in Marriage*, advocating 'simultaneous orgasm' as a desirable ideal, sold over half a million copies.

Drusilla Beyfus chose this moment to interview twenty-three married couples and present a composite portrait of 'what it is like to be married today'. Beyfus's case histories show how women in the late sixties were swimming further from the shoreline of old-fashioned respectability, while at the same time wrestling with the undertow of conformity. They also reveal some of the fault lines and fissures opening up in the marital terrain: a volcanic convulsion in slow motion.

Take Jack and Joan, for example, who were both struggling to encompass infidelity within their marriage. Nothing new there. But both adopt the contemporary vocabulary of freedom and togetherness, while Jack's sense of entitlement and his untrammelled access to a bit on the side are very much of their time: 'The trouble is I love girls . . . [and] girls are endlessly available.' Jack was finding it difficult to stay within the limits. 'I know I am a terribly immature person and as I have continued in this boyish vein, freedom has made the marriage viable.' Joan for her part was trying to deal with all the falsehood and cheating. 'Periodically throughout my marriage I feel that if I don't get out of this I shall die.' But she too was open to offers from other men, though she found the practicalities got in the way:

what if it was half-term, what if the children got measles? Despite all this, their marriage stayed alive. Something in Joan craved conflict: 'I feel I've just got to have a quarrel . . . I find real togetherness absolutely suffocating.'

Meanwhile, Frances and Tom had unthinkingly embarked on an incompatible marriage, and were coming unstuck over sex. A decade earlier, and Frances's honesty in expressing her own desires would have been unthinkable. She wanted more fulfilling love-making than Tom was giving her. She had an affair. It was physical, uncomplicated – 'I'm like a man about this. I need a screw every so often and like to have it and get it over with and cheerio. But since men don't expect a woman to feel like this, you can't. You get yourself horribly tied up.' But Frances admitted that Tom's jealousy acted as a check to her excesses, and she remained sufficiently traditional in her views to regard grooming as part of her wifely duty: 'I still have this corny conviction that you have got to look lovely for your husband . . . I take about three-quarters of an hour in the morning to get dressed and made up and hair and everything.'

The relationship of a third couple, Alexander, a long-haired ex-public schoolboy, and Rosie, a working-class shop assistant and occasional model, illustrates a quintessential 1960s conundrum: how can freedom co-exist with commitment? The pair had forged a laid-back marriage via drug use and a mutual love of psychedelic music. 'I love Alexander,' said Rosie, 'and I don't think I shall stop. I give him love, look after him, cook his meals, do his washing and hope he likes me.' Alexander, who admitted to having stolen Rosie from his best friend, was trying hard not to give in to a sense of male ownership – 'You are doomed if you think a person is yours . . . Possession is an illusion. But I find it frustrating because whereas it is clear to me that Rosie is not mine and she belongs to everybody I do suffer from jealousy. She has been whipped off once already . . .' Rosie was on the same bandwidth: 'Ideally, everybody should be able to make it with each other . . . [But] I do get unhappy when I think of him sleeping with another girl because I think he might prefer her to me . . . It's just jealousy. Maybe I can get over this thing.' However, the harmonious vibes soon became discordant when Rosie found out that Alexander was sleeping with a man, and she became so hysterical that he felt forced to hit her.

For most of Beyfus's interviewees, contentment remained elusive. The biblical gender division had been bust up by work and permissiveness. New ideals were at war with old assumptions. And nobody, it seemed, was emerging the victor.

Back to the Garden

When BBC Television screened its much anticipated documentary *Royal Family* in 1969, one of its supposed aims was to demystify the marriage at the heart of the monarchy. *Royal Family* portrayed the daily life of HM the Queen, her husband and four children. About two-thirds of the British public watched the transmission, in which the Duke of Edinburgh was shown barbecuing sausages at a Balmoral picnic, and his wife appeared to serve her breakfast cereal from Tupperware boxes. But, of course, the royals were never 'just like everybody else'. The affected informality was saturated with rank and pedigree, and in 1969 their tweediness, Scottish grouse moors, clipped accents and side partings made them seem more remote than they had ever been.

Caroline Harper's story will take us on a long journey away from that vision of the upper-class marriage. Aged seventeen, and entranced by the colourfully psychedelic group on the periphery of her privileged circle, Caroline had started smoking dope seriously in 1967. From then on, bit by bit, joint by joint, she began to reconfigure how a woman could live, jettisoning the frivolous ephemera of femininity: Cordon bleu cookery, secretarial skills, flirting and the rest. Travel, and drugs, would take Caroline to new places on the planet, liberating her body, her mind and her spirit.

Nevertheless, for a while, grouse moors remained part of her world; and the cultural tug-of-war is perfectly illustrated in 1969 when Caroline attended a weekend gathering held in a baronial property in Argyllshire. The youthful debs and double-barrelled delights who were of the party were all well known to Caroline through her parents' polo world, and they included her exact contemporary, Princess Anne, daughter of the queen. At the age of eighteen, the princess was already old before her time, having embarked that year on a

round of ribbon-cutting and official tours. Princess Anne was trapped
in a privileged time warp from which there was no escape; royalty
had condemned her to a lifetime of equestrianism, eccentric milli-
nery and good works.

That evening the company round the dinner table was divided
between the younger generation, who were all of them, with the
exception of the princess, completely and utterly stoned; and the
parental generation who, as their offspring descended into uncontrollable giggles, soldiered on desperately trying to keep up appearances
in front of Her Royal Highness.

> I was SO – goodness me – <u>GONE</u>! Luckily I had enough buddies
> around me, because when I smoked dope, I was not actually capable
> of holding on to this world as well.
>
>   Poor Princess Anne, she was having a horrible time. I honestly
> think it was hideous for her. I remember feeling sorry for her, though
> I expect the feeling was mutual.

Who knows what went through the princess's mind that evening as
she found herself on the wrong side of the table at Ardchattan Priory:
a helpless witness, as her young contemporaries abandoned every
pretence at formality, rambling dementedly and spouting nonsense,
pop-eyed with the best mind-bending Moroccan? Probably she felt
left out.

Meanwhile, for Caroline, the drug culture of the late sixties was
an irresistible magnetic field, pulling her away from her familiar
world of polo players and landed earls, towards a dimension from
which there would be no going back. With each step she made, she
lost a foothold on the closed Brideshead community that espoused
lineage, land, the season and the cul-de-sac of a 'good' marriage.
Dope was a constant; but for six months amphetamines played a role
in loosening inhibitions and sharpening a consciousness that was
already posing questions about class, identity and belief. On speed,
Caroline and her new friend Sue stayed up talking all one night until,
as dawn broke, with piercing clarity, the existence of God – 'or, as
quantum physics would say, a benign universal intelligence' – became
a demonstrable reality. But that was only the start. Speed had served
its purpose, but LSD was a passport to exploring further realms of

the mind. So, with Sue and her other close friend, Hawke, she entered
the drop zone, stepped over the hallucinogenic threshold and let herself free-fall into the multicoloured skies of innermost spiritual
freedom where time slows, the senses are at their most heightened
and the view of our jewel-like planet is both distant and astonishingly detailed. And where everything she thought she had understood
was transfigured at a molecular level. Solid became fluid, static
became active. 'And – I know it sounds corny – but I was more taken
by the level of inner freedom and love, and a profound, deep, full-
body, mind-soul knowing, that felt a thousand times stronger than
any brain-knowing that I'd had previously.' From here there was no
return: Caroline's path ahead would be defined by the zealous quest
for spiritual revelation.

But first she had some scores to settle.

My mother was very, very, very worried, and she'd say I was killing
her and making her ill. And I do feel so sorry for her! She really had
hoped I would marry the aristocrat! By that time all her friends'
daughters were marrying the right men and doing the right thing –
and they'd ask her rather pointedly, 'How's Caroline?'

And I did something dreadful. I came down for the polo ball. And
I deliberately sought out the most shocking person I could, and
brought him down with me. His name was Ivo. We'd met at some
party or other, and he was from a completely different background.
He had two teeth – I think he must have been in a fight – and bright
orange hair, and skin-tight satin trousers.

My poor mother – I think she cried. It was just SO horrible for
her. I mean, choosing a man who was the polar opposite of what they
wanted for me was a very unkind thing to do to my poor parents.
But I wouldn't have done it if I hadn't been angry with them.

Actually Ivo was a gentle soul . . .

But he was not for keeps. Hawke ('a full-throttle hippie') was in a different league. Thus, after they drifted into bed, she found herself
falling deeply in love with him, and the journey began.

For women who had lived through the Blitz, a dream house was the
summit of aspiration; for their daughters, like Caroline, home might
be under canvas, on a beach, or in a camper van. She and Hawke were

among the thousands who, spaced out on dope, sex and sitar music, set out on the hippie trail, leaving behind the convenient, sanitary society for which their mothers had laboured and penny-pinched.

Trips were not just acid. First, Caroline and Hawke went to Greece with a band of like-minded hippies. It was an idyllic interlude spent in tents on the Albanian border, where Caroline rolled the joints and washed the boys' clothes in crystalline mountain streams. Then, in the second half of 1969, the two of them headed to India – a nation that was being colonised by the counterculture. The Beatles were early adopters, being among those who led the migration to the sub-continent, when they (and their wives and girlfriends) travelled to the Maharishi's Academy of Meditation in Rishikesh in 1968. As Caroline recalls, 'India was the place to go. And Hawke and I were on a "Let's get good dope" quest. There *was* some <u>very</u> good dope.'

Their drug pilgrimage now took shape, carrying them north to Kashmir and Pakistan, stopping in cheap hostels on the way, making friends on the road with the ragged, glazed knots of long-haired, colourful, beaded Westerners with whom they climbed on board trains and buses. 'It was the hippie time, and there would always be deep, earnest, stoned conversations going on, with Americans, Australians, French, Italians . . . plus a lot of laughter. Yes, it was fun, fun, fun.' Next stop was Delhi, where the pair joined the audience for a lecture by the great teacher Jiddu Krishnamurti. 'His voice had the profound ring of truth . . .' Sublime, penetrating and releasing, the guru's words were life-altering.

Soon after, Hawke decided to go back home. After he left, Caroline took the train to Calcutta – a forty-eight-hour journey. 'At this point I went kind of crazy . . .' She felt as if her very mind was being reordered:

> I remember sitting on that train and at some point deciding, well the only thing to do with this is to let it happen. Let go. I thought, if you fight it you'll go mad. And it was as if a molecular structure had been totally melted down and then restructured again but in a different shape. It was SO intense . . .
>
> And by the time I arrived on the Calcutta platform, I was normal and sane. But I was not the same person.

After her stop-off in Calcutta she travelled alone for three months, to Bombay and Goa. The 'straight' world, grouse moors, debs, dinner parties, polo and people-pleasing, had receded to the western hemisphere, and the past. The present, shimmering and ecstatic, took shape among the casuarina pines and coconut palms stretching along the scented Goan shoreline:

> A perfect moment: somebody had lent me an ancient old bike, and I was bicycling along a lane in Goa, heading towards the sea. I was wearing a glorious, full-length blue dress, with a sort of strange red dressing gown on top of it, and – before they got tangled up, predictably, in the bicycle spokes – my clothes were flowing out in exactly the way they ought to. The wind was in my hair.
>
> And everything fitted somehow. The wind, the sun, the beach, the clothes, the freedom. It was just a lovely moment of total freedom. I was living the ideal.

India had got under her skin. Caroline returned to England, but within a year she was back, journeying to the Himalayas with her friend Sue. There she had the trip of a lifetime. They'd saved some acid – 'Was it Californian Sunshine or Pure Light? I can't remember which' – and took it somewhere in a dazzling glade far from all habitation. Here, the triviality of human concerns appeared like thistledown, floating away on the breeze. Caroline tries to explain how this quintessential experience both destroyed and rebuilt:

> It was terrifying and liberating – like being let out of a very tight straitjacket. Something inside me knew that the only safety lay in letting go . . .
>
> And then came the bliss. Love – all-embracing, all-encompassing, unconditional love – with every cell in the body participating . . .

How could a *man* live up to this?

> When the drug wore off, I had this appalling sense of loss, of grief. That's why I searched for it, for years . . .

Caroline Harper has been seeking transcendence ever since.

Her quest was one that many hippies embarked upon at that time. From Marrakech to Kabul, Istanbul to Jalalabad, the escapist impulse took hold of innumerable daydreamers setting out to shake the dust of Western materiality from their sandalled feet. But Caroline's adventure highlights an aspect of that escape story that relates more specially to 1960s women's experiences. This was a true liberation, a release from the pressures imposed by marriage, family alliances, class and convention. Some women in the late 1960s reacted to oppression by becoming feminists and taking up the political cudgels – but this was not for everybody. In Caroline's case, guru wisdom and hallucinogenic drugs turned a life dominated by externals into one of interiority and a profound search for truth and answers. Everything known, everything assumed – from taking a proper partner to a ball, to women's place in the gender hierarchy – was challenged and deconstructed as she re-evaluated her entire identity.

' "We are stardust, we are golden, and we've got to get ourselves back to the garden." It was all about that. We've come from the stars, and we'll return to the stars.' After Calcutta, after Goa, after LSD, Caroline Harper was never the same again.

★

On 20 July 1969 the stars seemed closer than they had ever been before. Three American astronauts conquered a mysterious frontier of space, landing a module on the moon. In the small hours of the morning, British time, Neil Armstrong stepped onto its surface.

My parents woke us early. We had all been invited to a cousin's wedding, and were staying for a few days with relatives in a village not far from Cambridge; they had a television in their sitting room. In blurred black and white, the pale, space-suited figures moving robotically against an inky sky looked like Michelin men, slightly comic. But something of awe and moonshine remains in my memory, associated strongly with the more earthly wedding festivities, held on a mild summer's day in my uncle's garden. Small children bounced ecstatically across the lawn on pneumatic orange space hoppers, the latest toy craze. Older guests, many of them decked out in flamboyant hippie crushed-velvets and lace petticoats, milled on the terrace drinking still champagne. Someone played a lute. The sweet hay scent of hash drifted across the herbaceous borders. There was creamy home-made blackcurrant fool whipped up by Henrietta, the bridegroom's beautiful sister.

In truth, she was the most glamorous person at that party – along with her friends. For that year Henrietta had joined hippieland. The company she mingled with was a Rocker-meets-royalty crowd of romantic dropouts, including Ormsby-Gores, Tennants, Lord Gormanston, Henrietta Moraes and Sir Mark Palmer. Palmer led this pack of aristo-bohemians eager, like many of their arty predecessors, to sample the lawless glamour of gypsy life; and with them my cousin Henrietta had taken to the road ('the chequebook hippies', she now calls them). Over the summer of 1969 much family talk revolved around the doings of her group. Horse fairs, camp fires, Arab stallions, painted wagons and birdsong captured our imagination. At that time I was jittery with nerves. A letter had arrived from the local education authority announcing that my own safe world was under threat. The girls' grammar school I attended was to be amalgamated with two other schools, and reconfigured as one enormous melting pot of a co-educational comprehensive. All my adolescent longings and fears of exclusion were intensified by the imminent and scary prospect of *boys* in the classroom. With all that looming on the horizon, it appeared to me that a life of gypsy camaraderie, bohemian romance and freedom of spirit was surely an ultimately desirable (if utterly unattainable) form of existence.

The same feeling of not being asked to the party was also gnawing at me as the autumn term approached. During the holidays London friends came to visit. Their sophisticated daughter, three years older than me, told me she'd been at the occasion everyone was talking about, the free public concert held on a beautifully sunny day in Hyde Park to welcome the Rolling Stones back on stage after a two-year absence; in the event, following the drowning of band member Brian Jones, the occasion became one of tribute, at which Mick Jagger, robed in white, gave a eulogy and released hundreds of white butterflies over the heads of the transfixed audience. Even though the band was barely visible, she made it sound electrifying: 'Of course the Stones were miles away. It was like looking down a telescope the wrong way, but a tiny Mick Jagger danced like a dervish in his white dress leaping above the heads of the audience. I wore my Indian shirt, very fine pink voile with purple embroidery around the neck, and white jeans . . .' I was green with envy. Why couldn't *I* have been there?

In August 1969 people were also talking about the Isle of Wight Festival, billed for the bank holiday weekend. It followed on from Woodstock, three life-changing 'days of peace and music' which had brought Hendrix, Jefferson Airplane, Joan Baez and Janis Joplin together before an audience of nearly half a million hippies in upstate New York a couple of weeks earlier. Now, just a short journey from home, there was a once-in-a-lifetime chance to hear Joe Cocker, the Who and the Pretty Things, but above all Bob Dylan. It would be the biggest open-air concert in history. I was fourteen, and I knew my entreaties to go would fall on deaf ears. But how could I be alive at such an amazing time, and miss out on all this?

So many of the people I've talked to, and the books I've read, conjure up a picture of youth, beauty, love and elation in the late 1960s. Was it a phantasm? Those late-sixties summers had a heightened quality that sets them apart. But of course, women had other things on their minds.

Time for a reality check. We come down to earth with a crash reading a mundane report in June 1969 of ten women lavatory cleaners in a Birmingham factory going on strike for equal pay. Another small news item from July reminds us that a quarter of a million British women were burdened by caring for their elderly relatives; one told the reporter that she had entirely given up going on dates to look after her sick mother. Or catch the flavour of everyday life for a group of London housewives, via British Pathé's coverage of a hairdressing salon in the East End. The Cinemagazine crew filmed a dozen middle-aged women having their hair washed and rolled up into symmetrical corkscrews, then being placed in a row under identical metallic domed dryers to knit, gossip and read the paper, before emerging, brushed, backcombed and beatific, with lacquered helmets like sculptures.

Nor should we forget Britain's backwaters, like feudal Frampton on Severn, buried in Gloucestershire farmland, where eighteen-year-old Julie Barnfield was growing up just touched by modernity. Here, the high spot of the year was Frampton feast, a line-up of helter-skelters, dodgems and hooking the goldfish that entranced the village girls – as much as the black-leather-jacketed boys who ran the rides:

> Every August these lads arrived with their collars turned up and their drainpipe jeans . . . And these lads were there with their quiffed hair thinking they were real Jack the lads . . . We'd sit on the steps of the dodgems and stare at them in adoration.

This was *Cider with Rosie* country: muddy, superstitious, rumour-mongering and conservative. 'London may have been swinging, but Frampton certainly wasn't . . .' Julie and her friends got no sex education, though in 1960 they weren't so stranded in the sticks as to make *Lady Chatterley's Lover* unobtainable; someone got hold of a copy and read the rude bits aloud, 'giggling hysterically'. The pop magazines reached Frampton too, and the Rolling Stones were popular. At the age of thirteen Julie had her first boyfriend and managed to keep out of 'trouble'; but several of her friends weren't so lucky and found themselves pregnant brides at sixteen. She left school in 1968 and went to work in a shop in Gloucester, spending her wages in the local pub.

> I can remember getting absolutely out of my head on Ponys . . .
> Ponys and Cherry B and Babycham – they used to be the popular drinks.* Awful, used to give you the most terrible hangovers. And cider . . .

Drugs got through to Frampton too, via a lad who had left the village, seen the wider world, and showed up on the village green one day, bearing a marijuana cigarette:

> I can remember him passing it around, and I can remember being frightened to death . . . Oh, it was awful – a terrible thing to be doing, sat out there with this wacky-baccy. Oh no, goodness me, tut, tut!

Julie described Frampton as a 'gluepot' – 'Nobody wanted to leave!'
Far from Chelsea, far from the fleshpots, attitudes remained anchored to the past. In Cardiff, Jenny Sullivan was working in a

---

* These quintessentially sixties drinks were targeted at a female market: Pony was a variant of sweet cream sherry, advertised as 'The little drink with the big kick!' Cherry B was sugary cherry wine, often mixed with lemonade. Babycham – fizzy pear-juice – was famed for its commercials which featured Disney-style Bambi animations and wide-eyed dolly birds, and ended with the breathless catchphrase 'I'd *LOVE* a Babycham!'

typing pool, still living at home aged twenty-four, and submitting to a ten-thirty curfew every time she went out for a date. She would get home to find her mum waiting up in her flannelette nightie with a bottle of aspirin by her side. Finally, in 1968, she informed her parents that she was going to flatshare with a cousin:

> Mother wept ostentatiously in corners, father looked grim-faced . . .
>
> She sobbed, 'What do you want to do in a flat that you can't do at home? The neighbours will think you're a prostitute. I won't be able to look anybody in church in the face any more. I'm so ashamed . . .'

Infrequently, dwellers in the remoter corners of the country caught disturbing glimpses of an alien tribe, like Margaret Lloyd from Merthyr Tydfil, who took her family to the seaside resort of Rhyl on Bank Holiday Monday:

> The whole place was swarming with strange beings in flowing robes, unwashed hair and beads . . .
>
> [We were] not a little frightened of this weird crowd who pushed and shoved on all sides, despite their repeated chants of, 'Peace, Man'.

Sunshine and Rainbows

However, for a whimsical fourteen-year-old, it was the doings of those colourful partygoers that fed my daydreams for several summers, and which remain to this day part of a nostalgic mental hinterland for many of my generation. Swinging London was passé by now. But the out-of-reach minority of Beautiful People still had lots of thrust left in their engine. Marsha Hunt's description of being 'the only girl rocker' at the Isle of Wight brings home what an unmissable occasion it was:

> One could have imagined that our revolutions in music, sex, fashion, drugs and alternative cults were all there was in the world – we were the ruling class.

Fun, fun, fun. For the few, anyway.

Having recounted the bliss of taking acid on the road with Jimi

Hendrix's roadie, Melissa North goes on to describe spending a dream summer in 1969 at an arty retreat in the hills above St Tropez. The pop and cultural aristocracy of the day gathered by the pool, smoked joints, lunched under the almond trees. 'I wouldn't have missed it for anything.' A little further up the Côte d'Azur eighteen-year-old Rosie Boycott had taken a villa for a month with a bunch of wealthy hippy-ish school friends; for three weeks the rent, and a hedonistic lifestyle – 'champagne-soaked peaches, nights on the terrace under the lemon trees, and days on the sun-sparkled beaches' – were subsidised by shipping in dope on flights from London, and selling it for a hefty margin to the clientele of the St Tropez restaurants.

Back in London, Pat Quinn's bunny croupier job kept her out of the red for a couple of months until her return to drama school. Getting Pat to talk about her life in the 1960s is like turning on a tap. Years in London have supplanted her Irish brogue with a posh, throaty, suggestive drawl, and a torrent of starry-eyed, stagy celebrity gossip gushes forth in a breathless stream, with walk-on roles by artists, poets and the leading theatrical luvvies of the day, from Michael York to Tony Richardson, from Ned Sherrin to Zeffirelli. Pat was an exotic bird, flitting from one twig to another. 'We were *it* – we were *everyone* who was <u>anyone</u>. Marc Bolan lived in a basement across the road, and further down the road was David Bowie.' One day, sitting on the top of a double-decker bus, she spotted Terence Stamp on the pavement – 'I ran down the stairs and followed him down the road. I've never done that before!' She sighs. 'He was *so* beautiful . . .' And there were 'wonderful parties', of course. Her crowd hung out in Indian restaurants, jazz clubs, the Opera Tavern, the Royal Court, the Poule au Pot, the Arethusa. Pat's ungovernably curly hair gave her Marsha Hunt-style street cred, and she shopped at Biba – 'FANTASTIC! A trouser suit! A black boa made from sheepskin! And Kensington Market, and Granny Takes a Trip. We *were* the Beautiful People.'

Meanwhile, jet-setting model Grace Coddington also holidayed in über-gregarious St Tropez, where she and her hip restaurateur husband Michael Chow careered around in a grey E-type socialising with Catherine Deneuve, David Bailey and Ali McGraw. Back in their minimalist home in Fulham they posed for the photographers 'as one of London's most happening couples'. And Edna O'Brien, made famous by her ground-breaking novel *The Country Girls* and liberated from her marriage to Ernest Gébler, was celebrating by partying with a galaxy of household names such as Marianne Faithfull, Sean Connery, Roger Vadim and Shirley MacLaine. Puzzled by the prestige of her new circle, O'Brien recalled, 'Some serendipity threw us together . . . It was a more innocent time.'

★

Was it? Ann Leslie thinks so:

> The Sixties . . . were extraordinarily hopeful times, its young almost naively excited by everything new . . .

– as does ex-débutante and biographer Fiona MacCarthy:

> No woman of my generation could be unaffected by the prospect of expanding possibilities that became so potent a feeling in the air.

Since around 1963 the candy-shop door had been thrown open, offering an appetising array of colourful lollipops to the flocks of sweet-toothed passers-by on Freedom Street. From mantras to miniskirts, *Suck* magazine to space travel, gypsy caravans to Californian Sunshine, the universe seemed to be expanding.

Small wonder, then, that in the late 1960s we start to see the homo-sexual woman emerging from her holes and corners: testing a more tolerant climate, reclaiming status and visibility for the lesbian sister-hood, and tentatively advancing in a rainbow T-shirt that she would, one day, wear without shame.

So how far along the road to liberation had gay women travelled in the 1960s? The answer has to be, they were still a very long way from 'Out and Proud'. The advance was happening against a back-ground of hostility and ambivalence towards same-sex relationships among women. Anxiety pervades letters to the magazine agony aunts, like these:

> I'm in my late twenties and intend sharing a flat with another girl of the same age. But so many people have hinted that this will lead to an unhealthy relationship that I'm beginning to worry.

Is there any way of preventing these feelings occurring between women, or any treatment if they do occur?

I'm 14 and am always dreaming about my music teacher. The problem is that she's female, like me. I even get a peculiar feeling when I see her. Am I daft or is it natural to feel like this?

(You will grow out of it, she was assured.)

Even in the permissive world of Jenny Fabian's *Groupie*, lesbianism is regarded as nice – but deeply dodgy. Early in the book, Katie gets initiated into how to 'go with chicks'. To start with, she feels out of her depth, but her friend Roxanna is beautiful and, after all, 'a hand is a hand and a clitoris is a clitoris and when you can feel the pleasure beginning to rise up inside you, it doesn't really matter about the sex of the hand'. Nevertheless, it is emphasised that neither of them is a '*real* dike'. The *real* dike, the 'Les' (Roxanna says), is sick; she wears flecked tweed, and does weird things with rubber strap-ons. 'No, making it with a chick for me is like making it with a guy without the hangups.'

As with the broader women's movement, a key challenge was putting a name to a life choice. The lesbian subculture was shrouded in secrecy, shame and uncertainty. Where establishing their identity was concerned, gay women had a learning curve ahead of them.

In 1963 Esmé Langley had convened the early meetings of the Minorities Research Group, the first social and political organisation in this country dedicated to lesbians. In 1964 she and her colleagues had founded *Arena Three* – twelve sheets of duplicated A4 stapled at the corner – in whose privately circulated pages gay women (and men) could read book reviews, fiction, correspondence and features, and feel that they were not alone. It was a struggle to reach this readership, since the 'respectable' press refused to carry advertisements for the publication. Maureen Duffy's lesbian novel *The Microcosm* (1966) also tapped a well of isolation. 'We read it, reread it, reread it,' remembered the poet U. A. Fanthorpe. Duffy received numerous letters – '[They] wrote and said I had changed their lives and given them courage to be openly themselves . . .'

As the decade progressed, word was spreading that lesbians no longer needed to hide. *Arena Three* came alive with a buzz of opinions about isolation, dress, lesbian heritage and identity; among them was the emerging view that some lesbians experienced their sexual orientation as a kind of freedom, preferable to labouring under the constraints of conventional wife-and-motherhood. Yet still, most contributions to *Arena Three* were pervaded with the assumption that the lesbian was somebody who was basically deficient: a kind of offensive mutant, who at best could only emulate the happy heterosexual.

But, between them, Esmé Langley and Maureen Duffy were raising the profile for lesbians. Over these years there was press coverage of a kind not seen before. Ahead of the decriminalisation of male homosexual acts in 1967, BBC1 screened two *Man Alive* documentaries confronting the topic of 'consenting adults'. The second of these, entitled 'The Women', featured Steve, a twenty-four-year-old with short-back-and-sides, wearing mannish trousers, collar and tie,

The slender pamphlet that, from 1964, first threw a lifeline to women isolated by their incongruent sexuality.

talking about her distress at how society could not accept her for
what she was. What does her mother think about her? asks the interviewer, Angela Huth. 'She just thinks I'm disgusting,' was the reply.
Next, Huth asks a couple named Cynthia and Julie about the early
days of their romance. They are filmed sitting on the couch in their
Wandsworth living room, dressed similarly in woollies and button-
up blouses. Julie glances adoringly at her partner. Cynthia speaks for
them both: 'I just don't see any difference between a normal couple
falling in love and two women falling in love. It's as romantic as the
two people make it.' The BBC cameras were also welcomed in to
film at London's favourite gay women's haunt, the clandestine Gateways Club in King's Road. Huth interviewed a group of its members.
'Why did they need a special club?' asked Huth. Couldn't they just go
to an ordinary pub? 'I like to be in a world which isn't particularly
dominated by men . . . I like to be able to sit there and not have some
man come and try to pick me up, which happens the whole time. I
just happen to like a society where everyone is really equal – quite
apart from being lesbian . . .' The speaker was a long-haired brunette
who resembled a French intellectual with her well-bred, gently
accented voice and fashionable dark glasses; for the televised interviews also provided evidence that 1960s lesbians didn't have to look
like, well, lesbians. The androgyny of the straight world was permissive in the best sense: it allowed homosexual women to be genuinely
unisex, without having to look like short-back-and-sides caricatures
of men.

Following the transmission of 'The Women' there was a *Late Night
Line-Up* discussion in which Maureen Duffy was on the panel, speaking passionately in support of a more open society. However, she was
up against the Tory MP Ray Mawby (an active campaigner against
the Sexual Offences Bill), who put his view that the *Man Alive* programmes should not have gone out before the 9 p.m. watershed – 'This
is dealing with a twilight area of abnormal people, and it's something
that I wouldn't think is up for public discussion.'

But Mr Mawby was out of step, and in 1967 the bill was passed
which partially legalised homosexual acts in private between two
men. Women homosexuals had never had to fear prosecution, but, as

we have seen, the misery and isolation they experienced could be as acute as that of their male counterparts.

Perhaps the most overt airing of gay female relationships came in 1969, when the film version was released of Frank Marcus's 1965 stage play *The Killing of Sister George*. By today's standards the portrayal of the butch, tweedy, gin-and-tonic-swilling George (Beryl Reid), and her kittenish, doll-loving girlfriend Childie (Susannah York) appear heavily stereotyped, locked into a model of lesbianism that hadn't budged since the 1930s. By this model, the couple play out their relationships according to the rigid gender divisions of traditional heterosexual society, the 'butch' taking on the gruff, macho dominant role, while her sweet, 'femme' partner bills and coos in chiffon nighties like any dolly bird. But for its time *The Killing of Sister George* was a pioneer in validating a lesbian relationship, with all its ups and downs, rather than showing it as aberrant. Its drama lay in the central bond, with the audience's sympathies swayed as George and Childie's 'marriage' is invaded and despoiled by the ruthlessly attractive Mercy Croft (played by Coral Browne in a scarlet dress, at her most sinuous and witch-like). It also legitimised lesbianism by filming a protracted, semi-documentary sequence in the Gateways Club, where the clientele were recruited as extras and paid handsomely to be themselves. The footage gives life to a historic club and its regulars in their customary gear, mostly smart trousers, short hair and jackets, doing the 'Gateways grind' on the dance floor. When *The Killing of Sister George* was released it was given an X certificate because of a somewhat clinical scene at the end where Mercy seduces Childie; some local authorities cut this harmless scene, or banned the film altogether. But wherever it was screened it attracted a large lesbian audience. 'The showings of the film seemed like big gay public occasions in an era before such things existed,' remembered one of them.

The straight press remained po-faced. The *Daily Mail* reported that the Bishop of Lichfield felt so overwhelmed by the number of X-rated films like *The Killing of Sister George* that he had become too embarrassed to go to the cinema. He pleaded for the 'so-called permissive society' to be reversed for the sake of the community as a whole, and for there to be more films like *Mary Poppins* and *The Jungle Book*. Even right-on *Nova* sat on its hands, running a feature that insisted, reassuringly, that the three actresses themselves were ultra-heterosexual. It quoted one of them expressing her squeamish distaste for girl-love: '[It's] like being fed marshmallow when you want rock cake.' In the *Daily Mirror*, columnist Marjorie Proops was honest about her responses to the film, which were 'an uncomfortable feeling of disquiet, a feeling of inexplicable uneasiness . . .' But she confessed that it had also shifted her views:

> I, like most other heterosexual women, prefer not to think about lesbianism. This film, which I saw last week, has compelled me to stop fooling myself and pretending it simply doesn't exist.

But her recognition, tolerance and charity had limits:

> The one good thing open discussions of this subject can do is make the rest of us pity, rather than condemn, our less normal sisters.

As 'Steve' told the BBC, '[My mother] can't accept me . . . I've never been really happy. It just makes you feel you might as well be in prison. 'Cos it's a sort of prison anyway.' There was no getting away from it: those sisters still had a long way to travel on the road to toleration, acceptance and the freedom to be themselves.

In the world of the popular press and its readership, women loving women made great entertainment, and it wasn't against the law. But it was still sad, creepy and weird.

You Say You Want a Revolution

Marjorie Proops was struggling to be broad-minded. Female solidarity has never been a given. Fifty years earlier, every stone-throwing suffragette campaigning for the cause was outnumbered by the passive majority who preferred a quiet life; similarly, when it came to women's oppression, there was a lack of consensus.

In March 1969 *The Observer*'s Pendennis column reported the views of a radical, and angry, feminist playwright named Jane Arden.* Arden saw her sex as being members of an underclass:

---

* The column, contributed by a number of different journalists, took its name from the hero of W. M. Thackeray's eponymous novel (1848), a young gentleman who seeks his fortune in London and comments on contemporary society.

Woman, like the Negro, is singled out from the beginning. She's something special: passive, frivolous, weak, lacking in leadership, incapable of dealing with power. Women are seen to be a slave-group, appendages of men without identities of their own . . .

I'm talking about freedom . . .

Jane Arden was also keen to tell readers about her next project, a publication which she hoped would uncover the 'resentment . . . hidden violence . . . [and] pain' that men imposed on women.

However, Pendennis himself took the unrepentant view that no such problem existed:

We haven't met a woman yet who felt 'oppressed' by simply being a woman . . .

We . . . believe that if women feel oppressed it isn't because of men, but life.

Readers were then invited to comment. Pendennis's bulging postbag the following week testified to a wide range of views, from the vehemently feminist to the acquiescent and traditional. Christine Hyatt from London agreed with Jane Arden:

'Woman Power' should be as powerful a slogan as Black Power, but most women just don't want to know.

'Most women' felt deterred by the prospect of turning the sex war into a battleground. But Mrs Mary Wingfield from Suffolk saw nuances in the equality argument:

Those who rant and rave about equal opportunity only seem to have in mind equal opportunity for top jobs and top privileges . . .

They'd be the first to protest about women's rights, she continued, if somebody offered them equal opportunities to become coal miners or morgue attendants. And Mrs J. Reynolds from Derbyshire could see nothing to be gained by freedom:

A true woman can only flower in a state of security and the knowledge of protection of man . . .

but Janet M. Turner from Putney had complicated reservations:

I will happily have my body dominated – but not my mind . . .

Meanwhile, a correspondent from Reading, Mrs M. Allsebrook, put her views succinctly:

What a career woman really needs is a good wife . . .

and Mrs Clare Smith from Surrey was unapologetically rude:

Horrid, nasty, smug Pendennis. Patronising, cocky, sneaky, *masculine* Pendennis.

But Pendennis gave lead position to a letter from the well-regarded *Nova* journalist Irma Kurtz (later to become *Cosmopolitan*'s longest-running agony aunt), who, by contrast, contributed a somewhat aloof overview of the subject:

Sitting here in a world that is infected with injustice and shaking with war, it seems to me very sad that someone with Miss Arden's talent as a writer . . . should devote herself to a crusade which is so beside-the-point as to seem a creation of her own psyche. It is not our identity as women we must find, but our identity as human beings.

Kurtz had no intention of climbing on board the emergent women's movement bandwagon. 'Of course I support wholeheartedly the liberation of women,' she wrote later in her memoirs. 'What woman of spirit does not celebrate release from antiquated restraints? If I never became a ranking member of the movement, that is because I am unable to sit for long in any congregation of made-up minds, no matter how sympathetic their aim.'

*

In 1969 war and injustice continued to preoccupy both women and men. At the London School of Economics the mutterings were vociferous; in the early months of the year they evolved into a head-on collision between the authorities and the Student Union over the college's financial interests in white South African companies that were thought to be complicit in upholding apartheid. There was a stand-off when the college governors had iron security gates erected on the LSE site to deter demonstrations, and a fully policed lock-out followed.

But, like the Pendennis correspondents, not everyone at the LSE was signed up to the congregation of made-up minds. Here are two contrasting stories from women students that perfectly illustrate the divergence between those resolved to jump feet first into a changing world, and those who continued to embrace the set of values they had inherited. And remember that at this time women at the LSE were (inevitably) outnumbered nearly three to one by men.

In 1966 eighteen-year-old Lucy McLaren from Leeds had arrived there to study Sociology, wearing a twinset and pearls. A buoyant, bright, blonde teenager, astute and friendly, Lucy had been sent to a private school by her old-fashioned 'perfect wife'-style mother, who 'could not conceive that my life, clothes, values and views would differ in any way from hers'. 'You mustn't appear too clever, boys won't like it,' she told her daughter. Though Lucy saw the Beatles perform live, the permissive society bypassed her bourgeois world of tennis clubs, church, youth-club breakfasts and vicarage entertainments. Lucy admits that, for a provincial girl, the London School of Economics may not have been her best choice of university. Almost from the start she felt out of her comfort zone, surrounded by leather jackets, blue jeans and 'unshavenness'. 'And I was scared stiff . . .'

The fear Lucy felt was a mixture. The heavily politicised atmosphere at the LSE alarmed her: 'I just wasn't going to stick my neck over the parapet.' Social transgressors – like the young woman in her tutor group who had an affair with the lecturer ('he was revoltingly grubby and never brushed his teeth') – came with a warning light, and she tended to avoid them. And there was the jolt of hearing her contemporaries speaking a taboo language – 'Hearing them say "fuck" was a real shock!' But there were also the rule-breakers and trailblazers:

> I remember feeling 'I wish I was as brave as them.' Like, people who were sleeping with more than one person at a time – and taking *drugs*! I felt challenged by their social ease, and the fact that I didn't smoke, and I was terrified about drug-taking and things. As for having an active sex life, as some women of my age were, I didn't do anything like that.
>
> I always thought that everybody else was having more fun than me . . .

The student movement was anti-adult, anti-authoritarian, but this young woman's conventional posture towards society was not untypical:

> I didn't feel anger towards the older generation. For me, the police were to be trusted, the Royal Family were marvellous – along with all their historical pageantry. I bought into their values – the family, and so on.

1968 passed in a blur. Lucy picked up that there was a 'feeling of energy' on the campus, but was not quite clear what it was about. Once, a friend at another college asked her, 'So, are you going to go and riot?' – but demonstrations were for other people, not her. That summer vacation, when so many of her fellow students were at boiling point, Lucy was quietly supplementing her education grant working in the cardigan department of Selfridges ('to this day I can't leave a cardigan unfolded . . .'). In 1969 she was back studying for her finals, though unable to ignore that her contemporaries – who included Tariq Ali and Robin Blackburn★ – were at the forefront of one of the most heavily publicised student protests of the decade. Life at the School was so disrupted that everyday attendance had become an obstacle course:

> The whole area outside the building was just bodies, everywhere. And there were people sitting inside the building – like a sea of denim really – all over the floor, that you had to climb over.
>
> So I ended up just not going into School. I went and worked in the Senate House Library instead.

Beyond the hurdle of finals a promising future beckoned. In the spring of 1969 Lucy had applied for, and won, a place as a radio studio manager at the BBC: that corporate bastion of middle-class values, popular appeal and political impartiality. In August, a month after graduating, she stepped over the portals of Broadcasting House – 'and that's when my adult life began'. In June 1971 she would meet and

★ Tariq Ali (b. 1943), writer, New Left activist and public intellectual, was a contributor to *New Left Review*. Robin Blackburn (b. 1940) taught Sociology at LSE, and joined his students in the 1969 boycott. He and a colleague were dismissed for supporting the students who had broken down the security gates.

start dating a handsome young producer in Light Entertainment. Six
months later she was married.

Looking at women's relationship with the political protest movement, it's interesting to compare Lucy McLaren's short story with
that of her exact contemporary, the anonymous 'Respondent 13',
who was interviewed in 1984 by the historian Ronald Fraser.*

Let's call this young woman 'Roberta', and let's imagine her in the
late 1960s as warm, confident and powerfully idealistic, with long
dark hair and a miniskirt. Did Lucy and Roberta ever cross paths?
They were born in the same year, 1948; both attended a private girls'
school, both in their early teens saw the Beatles perform live, and
both enrolled in the London School of Economics at the age of eighteen. But the similarity ends there. Roberta had lost her virginity
even before she arrived at LSE, while she was still at school. In 1966
she went on the Pill. And from the beginning of her time at the school
she pitched into the ferment of strikes and occupations. Here is Roberta describing her first sit-in:

> [We were] sitting on the floor and blocking places – everyone
> crowded in, eating rolls and buns, smoking cigarettes and getting
> dirtier and dirtier. I remember wanting to go home for a bath . . . But
> it was very exciting.
>
> It was power – whether we would win or not – but there was also
> the feeling that right was on our side.

Roberta now considered herself a card-carrying Marxist: 'I believed
that capitalism would be overthrown and the working class in alli-
ance with students would stand up and fight it.' Union meetings were
the dynamic place to be; the halls were full of massed students,
Americans and Asians, black Africans and Jews; the atmosphere was
edgy and thrilling. For Roberta, politics were a turn-on: the Marxists were the sexy ones, because despite being unwashed they were
interesting, lively and, as she saw it, open to new ideas. This was
where you had to be to change the world. She soon found a role

* Fraser published *A Student Generation in Revolt* (1968), based on recordings held
at the British Library.

posting smudgy hand-duplicated propaganda leaflets in pigeonholes and on noticeboards. It seemed like a good place to start.

Then the students came back from the Christmas holidays to find that the authorities had put up the gates. Tactics were discussed, and a division of labour agreed. Half a dozen women took up their positions by each gate to stop it being closed, while the men went off to fetch pickaxes and sledgehammers. A smaller group was detailed to carefully unscrew the discriminatory 'Ladies' and 'Gentlemen' signs from the college toilets.

While Lucy McLaren was diligently doing her best to pass her exams, Roberta and her comrades were joining a mêlée of flailing crowbars and clashes with police. Roberta's inner group were the grubby unshaven rule-breakers in blue jeans who had most terrified the timid Lucy. Among these Marxist and anarchist friends she found a sense of fun and imagination. They 'opened themselves out as people more', particularly the women. But where the men were concerned, she had her limits:

> I rarely socialised with those men in the evenings, because I found it difficult to go for eighteen hours at a stretch talking simply about the dialectic, about politics . . .
> There was great male chauvinism.

Turned on as she was by the heady, empowering spirit of protest, Roberta was bored and baffled by much of the blokey baggage that went with it. The beer, the blind certainty, the made-up minds, the propagandist jargon all alienated her. And she felt the way these men treated women was disdainful. '[There] was that macho thing about power and political influence and being hard men . . . [Women] seemed to be appendages . . . there . . . on a sort of sexual sufferance.'

In the tense, combustible atmosphere of student protest, nobody seems to have given women's oppression much airtime. Many a male Marxist ate buns, penned placards and omitted baths on behalf of black people in South Africa, Vietnamese children or the proletariat. But on behalf of women? They didn't count. The attendant girls were there to distribute the leaflets they'd written, act as decoys and listen to them droning on about dialectics. Where women in the protest movement were concerned, liberation had barely begun.

Nevertheless, fifteen years on, Roberta judged that the protest years had given her more than they'd taken away. The interviewer asked her what she had gained of value from that time, that she would pass on to her daughter:

ROBERTA: Being involved, not sitting on the sidelines . . . being free to have ideas which later might seem idealistic, romantic and utopian . . .

We were very free – and that freedom meant one could be very uncompromised. Things were very black and white. We were fired to better the world and make it a better place to live in . . .

Maybe the world had to be made better a step at a time. Roberta had played her part. And she would live to see extraordinary changes.

Birth of a Movement

As the decade drew to a close the message was at last starting to get through.

The voices of women like Juliet Mitchell, Maureen Duffy, Sheila Rowbotham, Lillian Bilocca in Hull and Rosie Boland at the Dagenham works were growing in number, and in volume. As in an orchestra, the ensemble now joined the soloists. Women working in industry started to organise through their unions, and in 1969 formed the National Joint Action Committee for Women's Equal Rights. Their acronym, NJACWER, didn't exactly trip off the tongue, but their chorus – 'What do we say? Equal Pay!' – could be heard fortissimo down Whitehall. On a showery Sunday in May around 1,000 women, conventionally attired in raincoats and high heels, with umbrellas to protect their nicely permed hair, showed up at their first demonstration in Trafalgar Square. Representing affiliated groups from as far afield as Yorkshire and Scotland, they bore banners and hushed their chant as the veteran feminist and politician Baroness Summerskill mounted the steps to address them from the platform: 'You are not only demonstrating on your own behalf, but for all women suffering discrimination in the whole country.'

The spirit of the trades union women heartened those left-wing intellectuals, students and radicals who felt isolated and terrified of being branded feminists – for in Trotskyist circles it still took courage to assert that women had anything to complain about. Juliet Mitchell began to hold classes at the short-lived Anti-University. And in a shambolic terraced house in Islington full of mothers and riotous children, the Women's Liberation Workshop was born. In January 1969 Sheila Rowbotham's special women's issue of *Black Dwarf* had been printed and distributed. It was a plea to rise out of passivity:

> We are the most divided of all oppressed groups . . .
>> We walk and talk and think as living contradictions.
>> We give up struggling on every front . . .

and a pitch for equality –

> We want to drive buses, play football . . . We want men to take the pill.

But it was also a challenge, an entreaty, a rallying cry:

> We must make a new world in which we do not meet each other as exploiters and used objects. Where we love one another and into which a new kind of human being can be born.

In parallel, some American expatriates were transplanting the green shoots of the transatlantic Women's Liberation movement to their Tufnell Park living rooms, where they took new root:

> It was tremendously exciting . . .

wrote one of them:

> No one else seemed to have heard of Women's Liberation – we were freaks. I used to be exhausted and exhilarated after meetings and used to lie awake thinking – couldn't stop . . .
>> We wanted to be able to break down the barriers between private personal life and public political life.

Soon after, Sheila Rowbotham took up a suggestion to attend a discussion of Women's Liberation under the banner of a 'Revolutionary Festival' being held at Essex University. On a slushy, freezing,

February day she shared a ride from London with two women friends, talking all the way, exchanging and comparing the ideas which, in those early days, seemed to fizz from fountains of passion and belief. The concrete-and-glass Essex campus was sodden with melting snow, and their trailing maxi dresses (worn in defiance of the sexually inviting mini) soaked them to the ankles. But the hall was packed for what proved to be a chaotic, urgent and argumentative session; ideas jostled for space. The men there were feeling defensive, accusing the women of giggling like mothers at a tea party. Maoists were at odds with the New Left. Sheila began to wonder whether men needed to be there at all.

As the year progressed more groups were started up across the country. The Women's Liberation Workshop began publishing *Shrew*, which campaigned for local changes in women's lives (contraceptive clinics and the like), as well as providing a forum for divergent views. *Shrew* talked to a seventy-eight-year-old feminist:

> In my view it is futile for women to rely on men to fight their battle for them. They must do it themselves – even at the risk of being dubbed 'battle-axes' . . .

and a housewife –

> I don't think it does a lot of good. I think it's a lot of lesbians getting together for a giggle . . . I can't see any good in Women's Liberation . . .

These were experimental days, with small, intense, splintered clusters who formed and reformed, rambled and rabble-roused, connected and explored. Beginners' mistakes were made. Comically imaginative, publicity-attracting tactics were adopted. The WL Workshop sent a guerrilla group into the lingerie department of a large London store, where they staged a funeral of corsetry, chanting:

> A cup, B cup, C cup, D:
> Breasts support our currency . . .

One young bank employee joined a group who had stickers made saying 'This Exploits Women' and 'A whore makes more'. They got up at five in the morning, walked as unselfconsciously as possible into the Underground and glued the stickers onto sexualised swimwear adverts. 'No doubt [we looked] incredibly conspicuous . . .'

The early months of Women's Lib were illuminating, idealistic, brave, energetic and emotional. Sheila Rowbotham remembers the atmosphere as tentative and democratic rather than militant. She wrote of this time:

> I don't think any of us realised we were starting a movement . . .

The male backlash was immediate. 'Cadres of the Women's Liberation Workshop,' grumbled Peter Simple in the *Daily Telegraph*, 'have been energetically charging up and down escalators decorating the pictures of undressed women with subversive stickers . . . [They] sound a grim lot . . .', while John Crosby in *The Observer* gave vent to some patronising mockery of the liberationists: 'Is it just possible that the greater freedom and power women get, the more revolting they get . . . ? [And] it won't be long – you mark my words – before calling a girl beautiful will get you a swift karate punch in the kidneys.' Some women were also outspoken about their dissatisfied sisters; Mrs Jennifer Daly from Lymington wrote to the *Daily Mail* –

> I am sick of reading about all the discontented, maladjusted, neurotic, inadequate women who have so little self-sufficiency that just the thought of spending one day as a housewife with just the children for company sends them screaming.
>
> Why the majority of them ever get married in the first place beats me.

Irma Kurtz preferred, as before, to stand at a journalistic distance from her subject.* Writing in the *Sunday Times*, she observed that the radicals had emerged from the privileged and educated classes. But there were compelling reasons behind their demands for rights, and there was a tangible discontent underlying the very condition of womanhood.

> The material for a feminist movement is there. The anger is rising. All that is needed are full-time leaders.

* Irma Kurtz contributed a three-part investigation into contemporary feminism to the *Sunday Times* in September 1969; Part 2, 21 September, entitled 'Boadicea Rides Again', focussed on the British movement.

Throughout 1969 Sheila Rowbotham was travelling, part-time teaching, writing and reflecting on what a women's movement might have to offer. Did the oppression of women reduce them to victims, or could they reinvent themselves as purveyors of the Utopia so beloved of the 1960s radicals? And what about sex? 'I was as capable of wanting momentary sensual pleasure as a man, but this was a barely permissible female thought then.' The same honesty compelled Sheila to admit that she was also as capable of inflicting pain on men as they were on her, and she refused to bundle all men together as brutish Neanderthals. 'They are afraid,' she noted in her diary of April 1969. And being a woman wasn't always such a raw deal – she often felt glad to be spared the pressures that she saw men having to deal with.

In the summer of 1969 the dripping taps and rotten joists finally got the better of Sheila's household; the floor of their communal bathroom collapsed. While her friends laboured with saws and screwdrivers reconstructing it, Sheila spent an intense three weeks at her desk wrestling with these thoughts and contradictions. Her new essay opened with a challenge:

> The first question is why do we stand for it? The oppressed are mysteriously quiet . . .

As she wrote, a drumroll of ferocious hammering reverberated across the stairwell. At intervals Sheila left her typewriter and navigated a plank laid across the joists to get to the toilet. 'I felt terribly guilty not helping . . .' The resulting pamphlet, *Women's Liberation and the New Politics*, was an attempt 'to probe beyond what was taken for granted . . .'; 'a message into the unknown'. In a brief thirty-two pages it exposed the nature of women's oppression, delving deep into the condition of the slighted and the subjugated, and their relationship with the wider purposes of revolution. It tore into the gendered vocabulary and thought processes that mirrored a male world view: with words like MANkind, WoMANkind and HuMANity spelling invisibility for half the human race:

> Thinking is difficult when the words are not your own . . .

And it deftly unpacked the sex war, explaining the complex collusions that proceeded within the male/female power relationship: how

This was the pamphlet that launched Women's Lib. Its author, Sheila Rowbotham, wrote: 'All the ideas and reading of the previous few months [were] welling up inside me and tumbling out on to the pages.'

flattery meets vanity halfway, how flirtation elicits obligation, and how woman's tactics – appearing dumb and devious – were inseparable from the achievement of her ends. Where, in our society, she asked, could women find freedom? Everywhere, we are limited, cramped, stultified. The housewife may achieve some limited dignity through placing a cordon bleu *coq au vin* in front of her husband; the 'emancipated' career woman competes for attention in the professional world with her mannish attire and aggression; while the 'liberated' woman asserts herself through sex – an arena in which the game of wanting and being wanted was almost invariably played out in men's favour. The pamphlet addressed housework too. Wasn't it time for society to recognise that scrubbing the steps and bleaching the bath were not only material activities, but also ones that affected a person's understanding of the world, their very consciousness? Capitalism had infiltrated marriage and the home. Wasn't it also time to understand that woman's domestic labour, above all in working-class households, took the shape of an unfair bargain? 'In 1969 [this] still seemed revelatory.'

Meanwhile, the role of the working woman strikingly highlighted her double burden, both inside and outside the home. Equal pay and childcare were necessary, but were not a solution, unless women's social subordination was also addressed. Though earning a wage gave married women a bigger share of power, it wasn't the whole story. The working women carrying placards in Trafalgar Square didn't only want to be paid the same as men – they wanted to prove they could do the same work as a man. Flag-carrying and slogans weren't enough. Some tactical iconoclasm was required – the Atlantic City protesters against Miss America having set the model the previous year. Through swimwear, dolls, adverts, fashions, books and imagery of every kind, the media all unthinkingly expressed the 'thingification' of women. Now the time had come to oppose that unthinkingness, and Sheila Rowbotham urged women in Britain to show the world how they too felt about being sexual commodities and consumer dustbins. But the biggest challenge to this kind of gesture politics was woman herself. The female psyche was formed of stubborn material, in which the legend SEX OBJECT was deeply incised. 'When I go out without my mascara on my eyes I experience myself as I knew myself before puberty. It is inconceivable that any man could desire me sexually . . .' And women seeking a way out of captivity would find themselves in a grotesque looking-glass world where the very concept of freedom was warped and mangled.

This book has told the stories of the real women behind many of those distortions – narratives of indignity and insult that supplement Sheila Rowbotham's necessarily terse polemic. *Women's Liberation and the New Politics* was directed at a self-selecting proto-feminist readership. But surely her words were for them too? For Margaret Hogg in 1960, patronised and shunned by the medical Establishment, or Viv Nicholson in 1961, lonely and afraid, drowning in wealth. For Ann Leslie, baited and tormented by the men in her Manchester news office, and Jean Shrimpton, miserable and reluctant, giving in to David Bailey behind a bush in the park. 1963 saw Mandy Rice-Davies and Christine Keeler stigmatised, bullied, belittled and manipulated for changing the accepted scenario of female shame, and 1965 saw

Kristina Reed, emerging from the posh-deb world, falling on her face because she was too well mannered to say no. Then there was Pauline O'Mahony, suffering the assaults of her groper boss in order to hold down her job in the Housing Department, while Theresa Tyrell and Floella Benjamin were afflicted by the unwelcome attentions they attracted owing to the colour of their skin. Kimberley Saunders's boyfriend got sex in return for Sindys; Hugh Hefner created the fluffy, fake Mayfair bunnies – pets, not people. In 1968 Mary Denness and Lillian Bilocca campaigned for safety at sea – in return for a broken marriage and poison-pen letters – while the magazine agony aunts' postbags bulged with distraught correspondence from hapless teenagers asking whether they should sleep with their boyfriends. Then spin on to Jenny Fabian, ground down by promiscuity, desperate for the right man to come along; Amanda Brooke-Dales destroying a marriage for love; gay women enduring discrimination. The 1960s witnessed confusion, cruelty, indignity, protest, politics and a crescendo of rage.

All of that oppression, and more, Sheila Rowbotham distils into a howl of pain and anger:

> There is a cruel irony in the way the assertion of the dignity and honesty of sexual love has become the freedom for the woman-object to strip to sell the object-commodity, or the freedom for the woman-object to fuck her refracted envy of the dominator man . . .
>
> Modern capitalism beguiles with flickering lights, it mystifies with a giant kaleidoscope . . . We walk into a world of distorting mirrors. We smash the mirrors. Only pain convinces us we are there. But there is still more glass. Your nose is pressing against the glass, the object suddenly finds herself peeping at herself. There is the possibility of a moment of illumination. The feminine voyeur finds her identity as pornography. The 'emancipated' woman sees herself as naked buttocks bursting out of black suspenders, as tits drooping into undulating passive flesh. WHO ME? Comprehension screeches to a halt. She is jerked into watching herself as object watching herself. She is being asked to desire herself. The traditional escape route of 'morality' is blocked. She can either shutter the experience or force some kind of breakthrough.

Women's Liberation and the New Politics is a demonstration of the power of ideas. Before it there were groups, debates, articles, workshops and meetings.

After it there was a manifesto, and a movement.

*

The ideologues of the 1960s gave the world a tenacious vision. But it's one that is open to interpretation. Margaret Thatcher believed that their theories damaged our society; that all their 'permissive claptrap' contributed to a breakdown of old-fashioned morals. But surely Thatcher's own denial of society itself, her libertarianism and the rampant individualism of the 1980s, also owed something to the ego-centricity of the doing-your-own-thing decade?

As Jenny Diski wailed in her final memoir, *The Sixties*, 'That wasn't what we meant . . .'

Perhaps hindsight can help us, today, to distinguish what was damaging from what was valuable in the 1960s. The decade may have fostered misogyny, pornography and objectification. But, at its best, it offered a peace-and-love Utopia that outlawed the constructs of masculinity: intolerance, greed, money and war. And for some that dream wouldn't lie down, giving the barefoot children of the age something precious and enduring, which has guided their lives. 'We wanted to change ourselves . . .' says Melissa North. 'We took drugs not just to fall around laughing but because we thought they made us think better, and bigger . . . And we saw our beliefs expressed by the musicians, artists and poets we followed. It ran through all the tribes of the time. That's why the Beatles were gods. They just kept writing songs that expressed what we all felt at exactly the same moment.' 'Amid all the fun and games we tried to be not so much down in the gutter and more looking at the stars. That was my aim and it still is,' said another contemporary.

The fire stays alight in many a septuagenarian breast. And it's easy to recognise the dreamers in their different guises as, perennially, the ideologies, like the fashions, are resurrected: Eco-warrior, Anti-War demonstrator, New Age bohemian, Global Justice protester, Black Lives Matter activist – and #MeToo Feminist.

Their visions still animate our world, still inspire gratitude – above all perhaps among older women, who espoused Women's Liberation in the early 1970s. These women's daughters and granddaughters may learn to thank them for their attempt to change the world, to remove sexual and racial prejudice, and to bring true equality a step closer.

*

A bitter taste accompanied the waning of the 1960s. Excess was followed by hangover. After Brian Jones died Marianne Faithfull's drug use accelerated; 'I wanted to be a junkie more than I wanted to be with [Mick],' she said. She was with Jagger in Australia when she took an overdose of Tuinal and sank into a coma from which she emerged only after six days, the second of Jagger's girlfriends to attempt suicide.* In August news broke that five people, including the then pregnant actress Sharon Tate, had been victims of a horrifying mass murder in Los Angeles. The crimes led to the arrest and trial of the cult leader Charles Manson and his followers who carried them out. Many would take the view that the Manson murders were the end of everything the hippies had stood for. 'They closed an era,' said the prosecuting lawyer, Vincent Bugliosi. 'The sixties, the decade of love, ended on that night, on 9 August 1969.' Altamont, California, was also the scene of 'rock and roll's all-time worst day', according to *Rolling Stone* magazine, which described the moment when an audience member at a free festival was fatally stabbed yards from the stage by Hell's Angels hired to provide security. There were scores of injuries. The concert, held on 6 December 1969, would equally become synonymous with the collapse of the hippie dream.

*

For me too, a cloud moved across the sun in the last months of 1969. The threatened amalgamation of three schools into one enormous 1,500-pupil, co-educational entity took place in the autumn that I was fourteen. For a timorous, nerdy adolescent, the timing was awful. Being good at Latin and History no longer had status. The

---

* The first was Chrissie Shrimpton, in 1966 (Laura Jackson, *Heart of Stone*, p. 63). A third, the designer L'Wren Scott, hanged herself in her Manhattan apartment in 2014.

exotic presence of a lot of pimply boys sent half my class over the edge; our uniforms had been modernised, and our navy-blue hats and box pleats were replaced with grey A-line skirts that in most cases now hit the knicker-line. Two fifteen-year-olds got expelled for selling cannabis, which turned out to be Oxo cubes. Though I still religiously watched *Top of the Pops*, I felt scared, immature, and completely out of my comfort zone. In 1969 my childhood ended, the giggly girly friendships on the netball pitch evaporated and I retreated into a lonesome world of poetry and stories.

At the beginning of this book I asked myself some questions about the 1960s. Did I miss out on all the fun, from being too young? Did I benefit from the accumulated experience of those women just a few years older than me who lived the 1960s more fully than I ever could? Or was I really the lucky one, to have been spared their experiences? Inevitably, my answers are mixed. I don't envy the bunny girls, or the victims of workplace harassment, and I'm relieved I never had an abortion. I can only admire and wonder, too, at how mothers like Margaret Hogg found the maturity and courage to cope with the stress of caring for a severely and unnecessarily impaired child. And I'm also very glad, as a woman, to have escaped much of the aggression, misogyny, bias, disadvantage, belittlement and sheer hatred that this book has described.

But let's not pretend it all came to an end when the Women's Liberation movement began. Sexism is like a Hydra. Chop off its head and two more grow in its place. The harassment and abuses of power described in these pages, which one might have hoped were consigned to history, are alive and well in the twenty-first century. My grown-up daughters and their generation have new battles to fight, and are discovering a new kind of feminism.

Nevertheless, nearly every woman who talked to me about growing up in the 1960s seemed to think that it was a rich and extraordinary decade; most of them had colourful and intense recollections of their youth between 1960 and 1970. Of course, I wish I had been there when Lulu was belting out 'HEY HEY HEY HEY, Jump up and SHOUT now, everybody SHOUT now,' from the *Ready Steady Go!* stage. I envy those who saw the Beatles and the Rolling Stones. Or, how great to have been Mavis Wilson in 1966, in her false eyelashes and crocheted mini, partying with famous artists, or Kimberley Saunders, heady with speed and excitement astride a Triton on the A23, or Patsy Reading careering round Hyde Park Corner in her Mini on two wheels – 'It was a wonderful life, Virginia! You could do *anything*.' My beautiful gypsyish cousin Henrietta, an unreachable ten years my senior, seemed to live a life like a mirage, incandescent, intensely romantic, always in love. And what teenager wouldn't have stepped into Pattie Boyd's Charles Jourdans? Lovely, creative, young, rich and married to a Beatle, wasn't she the luckiest girl in the world? As for the drugs – when Melissa North told me about her time taking acid she was still intoxicated by the memory, and seemed to pity me for never having had the courage to try it out, while listening to Caroline Harper talking about her quest for enlightenment made me feel I'd only lived half a life. Politically, today, we seem to see the death of idealism – but, amid the ferment of 1968, feeling you were on the right side of the argument must have been mind-blowing. I'd have liked, too, to be with Pat Quinn as she and her celebrity friends riotously celebrated the end of the 1960s at a crazy party on New Year's Eve 1969, even if it meant waking up with a hangover to a sadder, more sober 1970. 'And she'll have FUN FUN FUN . . .' sang Mike Love of the Beach Boys while chewing gum at the same time. These women and many others felt they'd been set free from their cages.

So, yes, I'm envious. Of the joy, of the release, the openness, the love, the colour, candour and courage; the fantasy and guiltless freedom that certainly characterise so much of those years. All that *fun*. And no, the liberated sixties weren't just a myth. Women were like fledglings tipped from the confines of the nest, exhilarated by the sun and the wind on their beautiful feathers, giddy on music, psychedelia and strange pleasures. Many felt rocketed into a brave, glorious firmament, a wonderful space and time in which to be alive. And many found a new honesty, a new language and a new voice.

But the sky was frightening, unknown and full of predators. Real liberation for women was something different.

Real liberation would be a long time coming.

It hasn't come yet.

Aftermath

Why be equal? . . . They've got a very warped view of life in my
opinion . . .

It's 1970, and Les, a hippie, is talking to a social scientist making a study
of youth cultures, about his attitude to women and women's rights:

I mean if somebody had sort of gone to this chick when he first
screwed her and screwed her with absolute tenderness, and showed
the quality of fucking love as much as he could, they wouldn't have
been freaking out all over the place, wanting equal fucking rights,
you know. They just want to be into being women, because it's a
beautiful fucking thing . . .

Take away the slang, take away the obscenities, and we are back in
the pre-suffrage era, when women were dolls in dolls' houses, when
their bodies were regarded as the natural property of their menfolk,
and when the idea of gender equality was seen by men as outlandish
and abnormal.

The time had finally come to change all that.

*

Sheila Rowbotham and the others thought about a hundred women
might show up. It was 28 February 1970, and the organisers of the
first National Women's Liberation Conference quickly realised that
the space they had booked at Ruskin College Oxford was far too
small for the 560-odd women, plus the handful of men that had travelled there that day. The conference decamped to the Oxford Union,
a building hitherto reserved for male orators. Nearby, men students
from Ruskin were (unprecedentedly) running the children's crèche.
The women had come together to make demands: for equal pay, for
equality of education and opportunity, for free contraception and
abortion on demand, and for free twenty-four-hour nurseries.

Picture a Gothic quadrangle and leafless trees; then picture a sombre galleried chamber with Victorian stained glass and sculpted busts of past presidents.* Someone has irreverently cloaked the head of one of these male panjandrums with a stripy towel. The benches are crowded with attentive female faces. They're casually dressed, many with long, loose hair. They lean forward, not missing a word as speaker after speaker takes the microphone in that cavernous panelled space, relieved only with the boldly graphic banners of the movement: WOMEN'S EQUAL RIGHTS CAMPAIGN – an angry face, a raised fist. On the wall they've Sellotaped a scrawled timetable: *Saturday 2 p.m., Women and the Economy – Sunday 3 p.m., Women and Revolution.* Tables are loaded with flyers, leaflets and copies of *Shrew*. Among the crowd milling around after the sessions there's a palpable vehemence and fervour:

> Suddenly we were all together having this enormous buzz of excitement – and then the world started taking notice, often to belittle us – like calling us Women's Lib – but actually from then on they couldn't ignore us.

Participants like this one remember the atmosphere as euphoric, electrifying. Ideas spilled out about what slogans to adopt, how to connect with existing political groups, how to organise and exert influence. A march was planned and a committee formed. 'After Ruskin I felt I had rights . . .' said Audrey Battersby, who had come up to Oxford that weekend from the original Tufnell Park group; 'I didn't feel like a sex object any more . . .' 'Ruskin changed my whole life,' recalled one of the Conference organisers, Sally Alexander. 'I learnt who I was through the Women's Liberation movement.' But Juliet Mitchell remembered above all the sense of solidarity:

> You did feel you could have one feminism. One 'women's liberation'.
> In 1970, at Ruskin, we felt we had one goal, we were unified. Yes, we had that.

*

* The Women's Liberation Conference was filmed by Sue Crockford and her collective Angry Arts. *A Woman's Place* is a unique record of this moment of history.

Germaine Greer had arrived in Britain a couple of years before her compatriot Richard Neville, and almost immediately started to overstep boundaries. But 1970 was the breakthrough year.

That May Neville surpassed himself in putting two fingers up to the Establishment, by giving the world 'Schoolkids *Oz*', a special X-rated edition of the magazine put together by school-age teenagers. His comeuppance in 1971 was the resulting highly publicised obscenity trial at which Neville and his colleagues would be found guilty under the Obscene Publications Act. His book *Playpower* also came out in 1970. Feminism doesn't feature in *Playpower*, though Neville makes passing mention of a 'Female Fuckability Test'.

But hard on the heels of 'Schoolkids *Oz*', in October 1970, he gave page space to Germaine Greer to guest edit a special Women's Liberation issue. Headed 'Cunt Power', its very title was a declaration of war against male phallic domination. Greer – clever, iconoclastic, witty, beautiful and provocative – was a new voice for a new decade, and here, beneath the customary trippy graphics, in an article entitled 'The Politics of Female Sexuality',[*] she called on women to 'dig CUNT' and abandon their knickers for ever. The article coincided with the publication of Greer's first book, *The Female Eunuch* (1970), which used confrontational language to bust the myths of female passivity, to debunk the permissive society that so depressingly favoured men, and to develop her premises about women's libido into a vision of the pleasure principle. Women, she argued, were effectively castrated, raised from birth to be in denial of their sexuality. Smoothed, softened, brushed, tamed, hatted and white-gloved, womankind had been bridled and neutered. Greer urged women to think outside their social conditioning, and to struggle joyfully against their oppressors. Joy, she asserted, was something women were entitled to:

> To be emancipated from helplessness and need and walk freely upon the earth that is your birthright. To refuse hobbles and deformity and take possession of your body and glory in its power, accepting its own laws of loveliness . . . To be freed from guilt and shame . . .

[*] *Oz*'s female writers were usually credited with a forename-only byline ('Germaine', 'Rosie', etc.), whereas the male writers were credited with both forename and surname.

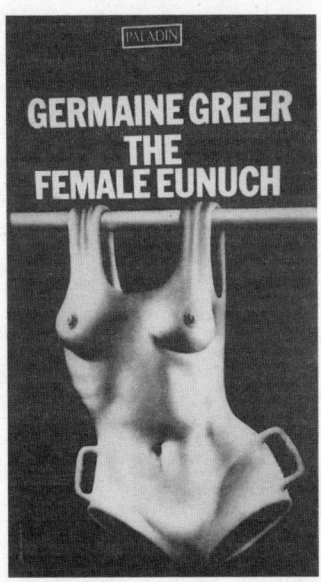

A book whose cover was calculated to affront and challenge.

The Female Eunuch was a bestseller.

At this time feminist militancy was never far from the headlines. In November 1970 members of the Women's Liberation movement infiltrated the audience for the live television broadcast of the Miss World contest held at the Royal Albert Hall, with light relief provided by comedian Bob Hope. Outside, demonstrators held placards proclaiming 'We're not Beautiful – We're not Ugly – We're Angry'. Hope mocked the protesters, quipping: 'I'm very, very happy to be here at this "cattle market" tonight – "*Moo-ooo!*". No, it's *quite* a cattle market – I've been back there checking calves ...' As Hope's commentary descended into innuendo – 'I don't want you to think I'm a dirty old man, because I never give women a second thought – my first thought covers everything' – he was interrupted by the clatter of football rattles. From the auditorium, feminist Jo Robinson watched him beat a hasty retreat. 'I looked up and saw in the floodlights all this flour, smoke bombs and leaflets all coming down ... and there were all these women screaming, and the show stopped – and it was OURS – this was <u>our</u> moment to tell the whole world about feminism!'

But the contest's winner, Miss Grenada, told a journalist, 'I do not think women should ever achieve complete equal rights. I do not want to. I still like a gentleman to hold back my chair for me.'

Nevertheless, progress was inching through Parliament in 1970, with the introduction of the Labour Party's last piece of ground-breaking legislation before their election defeat later that year: the Equal Pay Act, triggered by the Dagenham workers' strike in 1968 and propelled through the Commons by the trailblazing Barbara Castle.* Though the Act laid down a principle of equal pay for equal work of equal value, almost ten years later women in this country would still be relatively worse off than their sisters in Italy, France and Germany. Nor did the 1970 general election do much to amplify the female voice in Parliament: just twenty-six women gained seats in the chamber – barely 4 per cent – to alleviate the 630-strong multitude of grey-suited men who had been voted in to legislate on the fate of the nation. One of them, however, was the independent socialist Bernadette Devlin, at twenty-two the youngest sitting MP, elected to represent Mid Ulster in a 1969 by-election. Devlin, 'the girl from the Bog', became a press sensation – 'I was a mass of flesh which had become public property' – but her record as youngest woman MP would stand for over forty-five years. And at last, after all the gibes about women's 'inability to concentrate', there were signs that local authorities were giving in to pressure, when a Darlington bus company announced (in January 1970) a scheme to train a hundred women bus drivers.

Minorities were getting louder, and more visible. A few months after the 1970 election the first meeting of the Gay Liberation Front was held in a basement room at the London School of Economics. GLF drew inspiration from the revolutionary activism of 1968, aiming to change social attitudes, and giving heartening encouragement to lesbians, as well as homosexual men, to step outside their closets.

But, as the sixties melted into the past, a generation had much to mourn. Rock'n'roll fans were in shock, because this was the year when rumour became certainty that the Beatles as a group were over

---

* That was nearly fifty years ago. According to the Fawcett Society, British women in 2017 still earned just 86 pence for every £1 earned by a man.

and done with. And it was the year when Jimi Hendrix and Janis Joplin died. It also saw Rolling Stone Mick Jagger branching out, with a new film role in the sinister Donald Cammell/Nicholas Roeg art movie *Performance*, which showcased the decadent dark side of late-sixties *jeunesse dorée*. Musically, from 1970, everyone was in thrall to the poetry and melodies of Simon and Garfunkel. But Marcia Griffiths, with her vocal partner Bob Andy, was a young Jamaican singer who better caught the zeitgeist of 1970, with her upbeat hit 'Young, Gifted and Black', while another talented black American singer, Freda Payne, belted out the grief and disillusionment of marriage:

> *Now that you're gone*
> *All that's left is a band of gold . . .*

We've travelled a long road from the diehard devotion and cutesy wifedom of 'Bobby's Girl'.

What will the new decade hold in store for women? A lucky dip into the headlines of 1970 brings up a handful of omens. Altheia Jones-LeCointe was arrested while assisting a woman injured during a Black Power demonstration that had gathered to denounce police raids directed at the Mangrove restaurant in Notting Hill Gate. Jones-LeCointe would later stand accused of riot in a landmark race trial. In the three years since 1967 prosecutions for cannabis offences had risen threefold, to 7,520; and hot pants broke new ground in sexual exposure when they first appeared in fashion collections. Also that year Mary Whitehouse's campaign for standards of taste and decency in the media was getting into its stride. Whitehouse was greatly heartened by the rise, and growth, of the Nationwide Festival of Light, a massed evangelical Christian movement, which took off with two huge rallies the following year. The puritanically minded could see the floodwaters rising. In July 1970 permissiveness had gone mainstream with the opening of the stage revue *Oh! Calcutta!*, Kenneth Tynan's version of a smutty seaside postcard. Popular with those who enjoyed unisex full-frontal exposure, it would run for ten years. Cecil Beaton looked on in dismay:

Nudity is everywhere. Nothing is left unsaid. It is amazing and wherever does it go from here? . . .

It went even more mainstream. In November 1970 *The Sun*'s editor Larry Lamb out-manoeuvred *Oz* and broke new ground for a daily paper by printing a picture of model Stefanie Kahn on Page 3, backlit in a meadow, with a clearly visible nipple. Sales rocketed, and by mid-decade – depending on where you stood – the Page 3 Girl had become synonymous with either a culture of tabloid sexism which demeaned and objectified women, or a celebration of female beauty and 'an innocuous British institution'.★

This was the year when the Family Planning Association finally changed its rules to allow contraceptive advice to be given to un-married women. They also, in 1970, commissioned the poster that brought fame to everyone concerned, portraying a man in a jersey whose repentant expression and swollen tummy hardly needed its inspired caption: 'Would you be more careful if it was you that got pregnant?'

Ten years after oral contraceptives were introduced in Britain, the children of the Pill age were starting to change their minds, some-times dramatically. At the beginning of the decade, nearly 60 per cent of girls who had been asked their opinions of pre-marital sex in a psychological survey considered that it was 'Always wrong'. By 1970 that figure had dropped to under 15 per cent. Young women were not just looking anew at sex; they were starting to analyse the costs and benefits of the permissive society, and to ask the questions about sub-jugation that hadn't been asked before. In 1971 Rosie Boycott was a receptive onlooker at a meeting of women working, like her, for the underground press, as they threw a searchlight on the condition of women in the new decade:

'I expected to be encouraged to write and to edit. Instead all I do is type.'

'I hate being called a chick . . .'

'I'm too embarrassed to say what I like in bed . . . But how to ask?'

'I hate to admit it, but I've never had an orgasm.'

★ BBC News: '*Sun* Editor Dominic Mohan defends Page Three', video footage from the Leveson Inquiry, 7 February 2012.

Rosie came away tingling with excitement. Within a year she and Marsha Rowe, an Australian who had worked as a secretary on *Oz*, had raised the money to start another new magazine, *Spare Rib*. This time the content would be feminism and all it stood for.

But the 1970s are another story.

*

For most of the women whose voices have been heard in this book, the 1960s were a formative time, when they were growing up. Who they became later was determined by those years. So for the curious, the orderly and those who like resolutions, the following paragraphs may help to deliver a kind of dénouement.

*

There are multiple heroines to this story, but the name of Sheila Rowbotham comes high up my list; her insights, expressed in lucid, honest writing, changed the world for women. During the research stage of this book Sheila and I corresponded briefly, and she was right to suggest I drew on her memoir *Promise of a Dream: Remembering the Sixties* (2000), rather than interview her. It proved a rich resource. At its close, Sheila describes the disintegration of her relationship with the male editorial board of *Black Dwarf* and how, after returning from a trip to the dentist, she sat in a café writing them a resignation letter. '[I suggested] that they sit round imagining they had cunts for two minutes in silence so they could understand why it was hard for me to discuss what I had written on women.' The Women's Liberation movement would be her life for the next ten years, until Margaret Thatcher came to power. But Sheila has been a lynchpin for British feminists for nearly half a century. In her long career she has been a campaigner, historian, biographer, journalist and teacher. Much loved at the University of Manchester, where she held the professorship of Gender and Labour History, her compulsory retirement in 2008 at the age of sixty-five provoked a wave of indignant support from students and academics worldwide, who started a 'Save Sheila' campaign on Facebook. The battle was won, and Manchester has now reinstated her as a research professor, confirming her reputation as one of Britain's leading feminist thinkers.

*

Margaret Hogg is a very different kind of heroine. Margaret's son David was born severely disabled because she was prescribed medicine containing thalidomide while pregnant. When David was three, the Hoggs had a second son, and a daughter completed their family in 1972. The doctors predicted that David would not live past his fifth birthday. He is now in his fifties, and still living at home with his parents, who are approaching their diamond wedding and have seven grandchildren. Against the odds, their firstborn son learnt to play football and became a keen swimmer. His mother says, 'What David wants to do, David goes ahead and does it whether he succeeds at it or not. He tries.' In adulthood he has worked on a telephone switchboard for a charity, has travelled, has had 'umpteen girlfriends' (according to his mum) and an excellent social life based at the local pub. As for Margaret, after a lifetime struggling with doctors, lawyers and the daily demands of bringing up a disabled child, she remains as loving, brave, strong and straightforward as ever. Today the campaigning is slowing down, but Margaret is always willing to add her voice to calls for better allowances and disabled facilities. Above all, her outspoken tribute is to the 'thalidomiders' themselves:

> When people speak of thalidomide victims, can I just please plead not to call them victims? They are survivors . . . and all I can say, as a parent – and I speak for all the rest of the parents – is, we are very, very proud of them.

And if she could turn the clock back, would she change anything? The simple answer is, 'No.'

After what she has lived through, one might also expect Pattie Boyd to willingly hit the rewind button, but she too has no regrets. 'Given my life over again, I wouldn't change anything.'

It was after she and George got back from India in late 1968 that things started to go wrong. Chapter 7 of Pattie's memoir is headed 'The Tears Begin'. George, sucked into a hermetic world of meditation and chanting, was neglectful and unfaithful; Pattie felt helpless against his denials. There were lonely days with just the cat for company since, at George's insistence, she had given up modelling. As an antidote to isolation she took up photography. In 1970 Eric Clapton, the guitarist and songwriter of Cream, fell in love with her, pouring his unrequited passion into the heart-rending song 'Layla'. But when Pattie protested that she was married, he threatened to take heroin, and was as good as his word. In 1974 a desperate Pattie left George and joined Eric on tour in the USA. They married in 1979, and the pattern repeated. Eric's drug shifted to brandy – 'life was one big party fuelled by alcohol' – and the rock-star infidelities soon kicked in. For years, as their relationship foundered, it tore at Pattie to listen to the songs she had inspired, like 'Wonderful Tonight'. In 1989 their divorce was finalised. Pattie found herself in meltdown at the age of forty-five, haunted by her empty life, tortured with loss, regret and grief. But she has survived. There have been new relationships, a house in the country, adventures in the Himalayas, Peru, Bali. When she heard of George Harrison's death from cancer in 2001, Pattie burst into tears – 'I couldn't bear the thought of a world without George.' Muse to the greatest performers, inspiration for immortal songs, Pattie Boyd has lived at the heart of a historic moment in music. Today, the ex-model stands on the other side of the photographer's lens, and – though she still has a weakness for glamorous shoes – she has learnt the hard way how beautiful women can be trapped by projection and illusion.

Pattie Boyd, like many of her generation, first married in her early twenties. But Melissa North believes young marriages are a bad idea. 'Nearly all my circle who did that got divorced later,' she says. She and Tchaik had been an item since 1962, but unlike most they waited to marry until she was thirty-two.

> I had this horror of marriage and children. You didn't want the mortgage, the house. We didn't want anything that looked like our parents.

Melissa brings that same sense of defiant stylishness to her work as an interior designer. And when we met at her apartment in a hip west London neighbourhood, its poetry of colour quickened my pulse. Melissa and Tchaik's relationship has lasted, and they have lived in this flat – previously owned by their old friend David Hockney – for fifty years. Recently Melissa had the sitting-room walls painted an intense viridian green as a loving birthday present for Tchaik. 'It took ten coats, and each one had to dry out, so it wasn't ready for his party!' Bold works of art, photographic and abstract, interrupt its expanse, huge mirrors bounce light from floor-to-ceiling windows and pink lilies collide with crimson, lemon-yellow and cobalt-blue armchairs. It's a joyful technicolour mishmash. The bathroom is brilliant with turquoise mosaic, and the kitchen nurtures an indoor jungle of triffid-like house plants which spill into the dining room ('If this table could speak . . .!'). Melissa brings a tripped-out taste to chairs and tables that recalls her exuberant youth. If you could match this interior to a soundtrack, it would be 'Lucy in the Sky With Diamonds'. Everything about Melissa's home sings loud and clear: 'It's party time.'

Theresa Tyrell's marriage also stayed the course. In 1969 she found she was pregnant by Jeff, the boyfriend she had met at art school in 1965. Jeff's mother reacted with alarm when they decided to make it official. 'She didn't know me, and she was scared of her son marrying someone with a different skin colour . . .' Theresa pulls out the group shot from her wedding day to show me – and the clothes say it all. Centre-shot, the happy couple epitomise 1960s Sunday best, with Jeff in a fashionable button-up suit from the men's boutique Take 6, and Theresa in a home-made floral ultra mini-dress, modestly cut under the bust to disguise her pregnancy, with a matching hat, gloveless, and clutching a posy of sweet peas. Flanking them are Jeff's mum in a feathered hat and structured outfit, beadily smiling at her son while keeping a tight grip on her handbag, and Theresa's mum beatific in flyaway spectacles and a turban. Both mothers are wearing the white gloves that defined their generation; her Jamaican dad, standing to one side, has the only noticeably black face in the picture. Theresa and Jeff's son was born in 1970, and they have now been together for over fifty years. Both of them are working artists. Through the seventies, Theresa continued to be employed as an animator. Later, her exuberant sense of design took her back to an early love of ceramics, and today she re-explores her Caribbean heritage through gorgeous textured pottery. On bowls and plates, her fish, parrots, cacti, palm fronds and flowers evoke jungles and sunny shores. In many of her loveliest pieces, the bright pigments sing out against a black background.

Pretty Mavis Wilson nurtured the fantasy of a gift-wrapped wedding and a happy-ever-after ending. 'I wanted to be like Dick Van Dyke and Mary Tyler Moore. You'd be happy together, you'd have a nice house, and you'd have children, and you'd have fun.' Her live-in boyfriend was the kind of card-carrying radical who spurned marriage. But when Mavis's boss at Editions Alecto offered her a job in the company's New York art gallery he changed his tune and proposed. 'I think he thought it was a bit of an imposition for his girlfriend to go off somewhere as exotic as New York. I was a fool really. I was just a bloody idiot.' It was an uneven relationship from the outset. As her marriage floundered, Mavis, soon to be a divorcée at twenty-three, found compensations. There were affairs and, later, a daughter; but also her mental life expanded and she became a voracious reader. Today, alone, but with a complex family and past that she mines for material, Mavis Cheek is a successful author who volunteers her novel *Yesterday's Houses* (2006) as a source of supplementary 1960s socio-biographical information, from serving pimento-stuffed olives with a glass of sherry to having sex wrapped round the banisters. 'But looking back, what I took away from my time working in the sixties art world was the value of exploring, creating, risk-taking and daring to experiment. Society encouraged it. It really was a fabulous ten years.'

After 1971 Mavis, like many of my interviewees, was in a position to take advantage of the easier divorce laws. Like Mavis, Kristina Reed married in 1970. At twenty-two, Kristina was starting to feel the pressure of her friends tying the knot. 'There were a lot of engagement pictures of people one knew in the press . . .' The marriage lasted twenty-three years. Second-wave feminism barely touched her, though she admits that in the 1970s she found it embarrassing, when asked what she did, to have to reply, 'Well, I'm married, and I've got a child.' She solved this by learning a new skill, which led to a modest career in interior decoration – 'So I could say, "Well, I make lampshades."' In 1983 Kristina recognised that the bad in her marriage outweighed the good and decided divorce was the only solution. 'By that time the stigma for a divorced woman had all but disappeared. The relief of being independent was extreme.'

Today Kristina, who dresses with the sober and thoughtful taste of a woman who knows what keeps a seventy-year-old young-looking, has settled in a quiet London town house as neat and petite as she is. She is now remarried to the retired founder of a successful theatrical insurance-broking firm, who still has interests in theatre production. Her second husband appreciates her raw honesty and spicy turn of phrase. They have pretty things, and a small black cat, and they are happy.

Another woman who repented her early marriage was Rosalyn Palmer. Being a clueless newlywed with a baby in a Liverpool slum in 1965 wasn't what she had signed up for when she got her university place there three years earlier. But it had compensations. Her next-door neighbour Millie Sutcliffe, mother of the Beatles' first ill-fated bass guitarist,* was often visited by the Fab Four, and Rosalyn got a thrill from watching the guys, then at the height of their fame, popping in to visit her at the Clarence Street flat, and getting insider gossip from Millie afterwards: ' "That John Lennon," she would say – "he fucks the boys *and* the girls – and not even the cat is safe!" ' In 1967 Rosalyn found work as a teacher. Getting the best out of her deprived inner-city pupils proved inspirational, and gave her the grounding in social justice that has been her guiding principle ever since. Later, both she and her husband, Paul, worked abroad, teaching and travelling. There were sorrows and setbacks. In the 1970s her marriage crashed and burned. In 2000 she remarried and made a home in the south of England, where she served as a popular and effective Liberal Democrat county councillor. I asked for her thoughts on the women's movement. 'What's Women's Liberation? It's about being able to run away. Girls in China have their feet broken. Here in Britain they wear high heels and tight skirts – what's all that about?

---

* Stuart Sutcliffe, often known as 'the fifth Beatle', left the band in 1961. He died in 1962 from a brain aneurysm.

It's about repressing the female so she can't run away. The minute you start wearing jeans and flat shoes you can *run*! And that's freedom.'

Carmen Callil is surely one of the greatest feminist heroines of the last fifty years. In the early 1970s Carmen – like several of her Australian compatriots, Richard Neville, Germaine Greer and Marsha Rowe – was a champion of change. In 1973 she founded Virago Press to 'publish books which celebrated women and women's lives, and which would, by so doing, spread the message of Women's Liberation to the whole population'. Its mission was in character with its founder – an imprint which would shock, provoke, entertain and liberate. In 2017, when she was honoured by the Queen, Carmen's reaction was typical: 'I like the Dame idea – but not so keen on the British Empire . . . I am busy writing furious letters about Grenfell Tower to Kensington Council, and signing them Dame . . .'

A comparable humour and campaigning spirit was in evidence when I met Mary Denness in 2016, though her circumstances were far humbler. Today, the city of Hull celebrates Lillian Bilocca and her female comrades – including Mary. A centrepiece of the city's artistic line-up when it was European City of Culture in 2017 was the impressionistic staging of 'The Last Testament of Lillian Bilocca', by actress and writer Maxine Peake, which played to sell-out audiences. The campaigner's likeness, captured in the form of a pair of massive murals, gazes, complete with headscarf, from the walls of two locations in the centre of Hull, and the city council has honoured her with a commemorative blue plaque – 'In recognition of the contribution to the fishing industry by the women of Hessle Road, led by Lillian Bilocca, who successfully campaigned for better safety measures following the loss of three Hull trawlers in 1968.' Today, the smell of herrings has left the dock area. The 1970s Icelandic cod wars killed off the industry, and a retail park has grown up by the quay where the trawlers lay at anchor. Nevertheless Mary Denness remained immensely proud of the part she played in Lil's campaign. Talking to Mary, it was clear that she had always regarded herself as more educated and experienced than her friend – 'And I put on my lah-di-dah accent because I saw how they treated Lil.' After she and

Barry Denness divorced in 1977, that savvy, and the lah-di-dah accent, stood Mary in good stead. They gained her a job as a matron at a posh public school, and in her sixties she was employed by Eton College, helping to care for Princes William and Harry, ensuring that her unruly royal charges submitted to flu jabs and the like, even if it meant forcibly getting Prince Harry to roll up his sleeve. 'And, whatever you're writing about me,' she insisted, with a rich cackle, 'I'd like it to end with that piece of levity!' Her sense of gratification at having disproved her mother's prediction that she would never amount to anything was even greater than her pride at her triumph over the trawler owners. The remarkable Mary Denness had only a year to live when we spent that memorable afternoon together; in 2017 she died, aged seventy-nine.

Neither Mandy Rice-Davies nor Christine Keeler are here to tell their tales. Mandy died in 2014 and Christine three years later. Their obituaries remained saturated with myth, ungenerously laced with the vocabulary of prostitution, prurient in their use of photographs and irresponsibly prolonging the unproven version of events by which Christine was having simultaneous affairs with Profumo and Ivanov. A surprising number of people still assume that both women were call girls. After the scandal their paths diverged and there was little love lost between them. Christine, her beauty eroded by her tribulations, remained haunted by her past, continually retelling her story in ever more conspiratorial forms in a quest for redress. In later years she worked in telesales and as a school dinner lady. Mandy took a more down-to-earth view of events, but never shunned an opportunity to step back into the limelight, happily collaborating with Andrew Lloyd Webber when he announced a West End musical based on Stephen Ward's story. At the end of her 1980 memoir *Mandy*, she wrote, '[I have been] caught up in a web of fate, not knowing who I really am. It is the oddest thing to experience in life, reading so much about yourself that the line between fact and fiction is blurred.' The conclusion to Christine's book was more fatalistic: 'There are some preconceptions about that will never change; not now and not after I'm gone.'

★

What about the bunny girls?

Patsy Reading married twice, divorced twice, and has two much-loved daughters. At over seventy, blonde Patsy brings an irresistible glamour to her seasonal job taking the public on guided tours round a historic house; while her bunny training contributes grace and allure to her other occupation, hosting a bed-and-breakfast in her pretty cottage near to the South Downs.

Glittery Pat Quinn still dazzles. 'The point is, I always take trouble with my attire, no matter what the occasion.' Her 'interviewee' outfit is a silver lurex mini-dress, belt studded with sparkling diamanté, and gleaming silver leggings, scalloped like fish-scales in black, while her hair, an untamed shock, is the colour Chanel calls 'rouge noir'. Pat's first marriage, to actor Don Hawkins, gave her two children; her second, to Sir Robert Stephens, gave her a title and access to a more aristocratic kind of sparkle. Pat stresses that her job as a bunny croupier occupied a very brief period of her life while she was 'resting'. In 1973 she hit the big time when she was cast as Magenta in *The Rocky Horror Show*, reprising the role when the show was made into a movie in 1975. Her bravura acting and dancing, and her dark-rouged lips, gained her a cult following. Now that she is widowed, Rocky Horror conventions around the world keep Pat, now well into her seventies, insanely busy. 'It's gone stratospheric, it's gone off the planet. I mean, darling, signing my autograph is my occupation now!'

Baroness Benjamin's jet-propelled life also leaves one feeling mildly exhausted. In 2010 Floella Benjamin's Establishment credentials were formalised when she was made a peer: the first Trinidadian woman to join the House of Lords. Her energy – so fizzingly abundant at the age of twenty when she joined the cast of *Hair* – showed no signs of abating in her new career as presenter of the BBC's *Play School* – ('Guess the window!') – which made her a household name. Undoubtedly, she would have made her Marmie proud, for a glance at her website shows her presenting the Commonwealth Cup at Royal Ascot; in her role as chancellor of Exeter University giving honorary degrees to the great and the good; speaking at the Hay Festival; visiting schools nationwide for Black History Month; attending the BAFTA Awards and the Women of the Year Lunch; campaigning for the Liberal Democrats in Hull; donning a hard hat to inspect the Crossrail excavations; and gallivanting to the Monaco Grand Prix to meet Lewis Hamilton. In 2006 Floella ran the London Marathon in four hours forty-six minutes. She sings in a band, runs a production company, writes books, supports charities. She is happily married with two grown-up children, looks fabulous in her late sixties, and has an all-singing, all-dancing philosophy:

> Remember to live your life to the full, giving with the joy and passion you would like to receive. Never become or see yourself as a victim, even when others go out of their way to make you feel like one. Keep on thinking, 'I am worthy; it's not my fault.'

'I've been so blessed.' At the start of Anthea Martinsmith's marriage to her 'lovely curate' Anthony Millican, the couple lived in Soho, but soon after moved to Bristol. At twenty-one, with a baby and another on the way, Anthea was thrown straight into the role of clergy wife, which she performed with such élan that she was made Diocesan Young Wives' representative and entrusted with the writing of a newsletter, a medium for her communication skills and strong-minded views. 'The Bishop called it Mrs Millican's Encyclical.' Anthea has given her devoted all to church and family. But in 1991 tragedy struck. Anthony, who appeared to be a fit man, collapsed. 'I was talking to him one minute, the next minute he was gone. He died in one second.' A year passed, and in her forties she married a second clergyman, widower of a woman who had been in Anthea's tutorial group at Reading University. But my interview with Anthea, conducted in the light-filled conservatory of her Somerset home, was overlaid by the context of a troubled daily life; at this time Anthea was devotedly spending hours each day visiting her husband, who was very ill in a nursing home, witnessing his deterioration with anguish and courage. And this happy marriage also ended with his death in 2017. Twice widowed, Anthea's faith sustains her:

> That, and my philosophy, and my beliefs, are not relativistic. There are many grey areas in life. But there are some absolutes, the most

important of which is the incarnate Son of God, risen, ascended and glorified.

Without the resurrection we are wasting our time.

Some things were right and some things were simply wrong. Veronica MacNab knew from the start that her old-fashioned father would never, never accept her relationship with a married man. In 1965 Veronica's adventure, nannying for wealthy families in the south of England, ended when she returned to Scotland, to train as a Barnardo's nurse. She was still a complete ingénue when she fell giddily in love with the 'wonderful' Steve who – when he wasn't on his speedway motorbike – drove a bright red Triumph Spitfire. The small problem was that he was married – 'and, well, you just *didn't'*. Richard, who asked her to dance at a Student Union hop, seemed a better bet. Torn with misgivings, Veronica let wonderful Steve go. 'I chose Richard, and I chose safety. I was twenty-three and not very brave. The ring was on my finger within three months.' Pregnant, Veronica closed the door on her nursing career in order to bring up a much-loved son; sadly, the marriage did not live up to her hopes. But twenty years in, a new door opened. Out of 'sheer bloody-mindedness' (and to her husband's disgust) Veronica accepted a place on a degree course in Geography at Dundee University, where she got a First. Never did she guess that it would lead her, through brains, determination and serendipity, to a remarkable career: initially as first woman director of National Trust Scotland, then as the first woman bursar of a Cambridge college. Today, Veronica is divorced, and happily remarried. And she smiles to think that most of the dons who later conferred her with an honorary degree had little idea that she had left school at fifteen; and that her taste for great houses, peaches and fine porcelain had been formed on the wrong side of the green baize door, all those years ago, nannying at Knepp.

Nor would it have been easy to predict Kimberley Saunders's self reinvention, from school-shy wild child to student and self-styled radical feminist. In 1969, when she was eighteen, Kimberley married Dave, the Sindy doll seller – it was 'the love affair of the century' – and moved to West London, where she found work in the buying department of a carpet store. But the marriage didn't last. 'I thought Dave was playing away, so I wanted to get my own back on him. And I got bloody pregnant by his best friend . . . I didn't even like him.' As Kimberley says, 'You could write a whole book about my life . . .' With two husbands, one of them Ghanaian – ('I *love* black people!') – neither of whom fathered her two children, her complicated and colourful life is indeed impossible to compress into a paragraph. Meanwhile, her dancing days are far from over – 'I can do the Banga, and the Sega, and the Charleston, and the Can-can, and I've tried a bit of belly dancing.' But the shelves in Kimberley's Hastings flat, crammed as they are with feminist texts, tell a different story. In the 1980s Haringey Council employed her as a social worker. It gave her direction; a lifetime of struggle fuelled a new determination, and she started up a women's centre. 'I went from doing nothing at school to taking an honours degree in Sociology. Back then I didn't know words like patriarchy. I just knew that there were some bloody awful men around who treated us like bastards. And after my marriage to Dave finished I gave my wedding ring as a donation to the National Abortion campaign. Men? I like them as individuals, but not as a species, no. I like my women-only space, I always have done, and I will defend that space until I die.'

Following her second journey to India in 1971, hippie Caroline Harper made a firm decision: 'no more drugs'. LSD had ignited an inextinguishable inner fire – but it could never be compatible with true freedom, true love and true caring: qualities which she has amply demonstrated in her subsequent life. Back in England, Caroline worked as a Montessori teacher, and later as a nurse. Marriage, and the intense joy of motherhood, followed. Later she divorced. For nearly thirty years now, she has been in a relationship with Nick ('who is even more other-worldly than me!'). She also teaches meditation, runs a chanting group and works as a counsellor; her parents, whose polo-playing world she turned her back on, were both devotedly cared for by their daughter till the end. Today, Caroline reflects on the journey that her generation took:

I am now on the threshold of a new phase of my life.

What became of the sixties dream? I think that many seeds were scattered at that time – through music, art and literature and, like all seeds, some have fallen on stony ground and some have taken root and flourished – probably many more than we know. The more recent discoveries in quantum physics verify many of the more 'way out' experiences of LSD, while neuroscience is confirming that we humans can 'change our spots' – with enough vision and dedication.

The sixties ideal, in essence, was to believe in 'the more beautiful world that our hearts know is possible'.* It still seems to me a worthy ideal and one worth having changed the course of my life for . . .

Imagine . . .

Scouse pop singer Beryl Marsden found healing and enlightenment too. But she got there by a very different route. In 1968 Beryl put the sex, drugs and rock 'n' roll of the capital behind her, and went home to Liverpool. 'I got offers to join this band or that band – you know? – as soon as I got back, and I chose not to go with anyone who was going on tour. I just wanted to be home, and have a bit of a normal life.' Unfortunately a dark period ensued when she ill-advisedly married a man who not only resented her work as a performer, but also had unpredictable moods. 'Don't ask me about the 1970s. They were horrendous. I went through hell.' Two children were born, but the marriage ended, leaving Beryl stranded, broken, and with her confidence in rags. Fear drove her back to London with her small family. In the Speakeasy one evening she ran into a musician friend who suggested she come to a meeting with him.

> And out of that terrible, terrible darkness I found Buddhism. It's become key to my life. Stuff that happens in your life can destroy you. Holding on to pain can stop you from enjoying your life. You

---

* *The More Beautiful World Our Hearts Know is Possible* (2013) by Charles Eisenstein, explores the view that humanity can be transformed through small but positive interactions between people. Eisenstein, philosopher, author and public speaker, describes himself as a 'degrowth activist'.

can't let it win. There are things we can learn from, things we can use. All that darkness, all that hurt, all that pain – it hasn't been wasted.

In Beryl's north London flat the little 'shrine' arrangement with its flowers and shimmering tea-lights all come into focus. The Buddhist tradition requires its adherents to perform ritualistic chants. At the first gathering she attended, something in the chorus of vibrating human voices spoke to Beryl:

It stirred something inside of me. I felt, 'I know this . . .' – if that makes any sense?

And literally the next day, I started to chant – every day. And as soon as I started to chant I felt a wonderful, warm feeling, which I hadn't felt for a long, long time. And slowly, little by little, all those terrible feelings of anger and hurt just melted away.

In the same 2011 interview Beryl describes her gradual abandonment to the force of the chant; its capacity to transcend adversity, to heal and to bring peace.

For Beryl Marsden, singing – in every form – has always given her life its meaning.

I've always known that's what I'm here for . . . it's never left me.

If I ever felt nobody was listening to me, or that vocally I couldn't cut it, I would stop. But that's not yet.

And at the age of seventy, casual as ever in jeans and a glitzy T-shirt, Beryl bounced back onto the stage at Liverpool's legendary rock'n'roll venue the Casbah Coffee Club, and belted out the song which launched her career all those years ago when she was fourteen, back in 1961. It was 'Boys':

> Well, I'm talkin' 'bout BOYS – yeah-yeah, BOYS –
> Hey, what a bundle of joy – yeah-yeah, BOYS!

The beat is made for dancing. This tiny, energetic woman fills the one-time coal cellar and early home of the Beatles with her raw, raunchy contralto and infectious gusto. Beryl Marsden's voice is a sexy, whisky voice, full of throat, and full of heart.

'Cos when you're singing, and your heart's pounding, and you're just full of that feelgood feeling, it's quite amazing. And now – to have continued singing through everything – through the ups, through the downs, through the darkness and the light – that's really something.

And, well, it's just an incredible joy . . .

Notes on Sources

The following notes give only principal sources consulted, and are aimed at the general reader rather than the scholar. For all publication details, please refer to the Select Bibliography.

Where reference is made to monetary values I have often referred to what sums in the past would be worth today. These calculations were made at www.thisismoney.co.uk/money/index.html

Statistical references are uncredited throughout. Principal statistical sources consulted are as follows (for publication details, see Select Bibliography):

Booker, Christopher, *The Neophiliacs*
Dyhouse, Carol, *Students: A Gendered History*
Gavron, Hannah, *The Captive Wife*
Gorer, Geoffrey, *Sex and Marriage in England Today*
Green, Jonathon, *All Dressed Up*
Halsey, A. H., *Trends in British Society Since 1900*
Hewison, Robert, *Too Much*
Kynaston, David, *Modernity Britain: 1957–1962*
Laurie, Peter, *The Teenage Revolution*
Lewis, Jane, *Women in Britain Since 1945*
Marsden, Dennis, *Mothers Alone*
Marwick, Arthur, *The Sixties*
Roberts, Elizabeth, *Women and Families*
Robinson, Jane, *In the Family Way*
Sampson, Anthony, *The New Anatomy of Britain*
Sandbrook, Dominic, *Never Had It So Good*
Sandbrook, Dominic, *White Heat*
Schofield, Michael, *The Sexual Behaviour of Young People*

Certain sources recur throughout this book. For the sake of brevity, they are abbreviated as follows:

ABD/A – Amanda Brooke-Dales, author interview
AC/A – Anne Chisholm, author interview

AL/KS – Ann Leslie, *Killing My Own Snakes*

AM/A – Anthea Millican, author interview

AP/CT – Alison Pressley, *Changing Times*

BM/A – Beryl Marsden, author interview

CH/A – Caroline Harper, author interview

CK/TL – Christine Keeler, *The Truth at Last*

CL/TL – Cynthia Lennon, *A Twist of Lennon*

DM/A – Doreen Massey, author interview

FB/AB – Floella Benjamin, *The Arms of Britannia*

FB/CE – Floella Benjamin, *Coming to England*

GC/G – Grace Coddington, *Grace: A Memoir*

JB/CB – Joan Bakewell, *The Centre of the Bed*

JD/S – Jenny Diski, *The Sixties*

JG/DL – Jonathon Green, *Days in the Life*

KE/GE – Kathy Etchingham, *Through Gypsy Eyes*

KR/A – Kristina Reid, author interview

KS/A – Kimberley Saunders, author interview

LB/E – Lynn Barber, *An Education*

MC/A – Mavis Cheek (née Wilson), author interview

MD/A – Mary Denness, author interview

MF/F – Marianne Faithfull, *Faithfull*

MH/A – Margaret Hogg, author interview

MI/NT – Mary Ingham, *Now We are Thirty*

MN/A – Melissa North, author interview

MRD/M – Mandy Rice-Davies, *Mandy*

MW/OF – Michelene Wandor, ed., *Once a Feminist*

P/Cine – Pathé Cinemagazines and newsreels available at www.
  britishpathe.com

PB/A – Pattie Boyd, author interview

PB/WT – Pattie Boyd, *Wonderful Today*

PO/A – Pauline O'Mahony, author interview

PQ/A – Patricia Quinn, author interview

RP/A – Rosalyn Palmer, author interview

SJ/A – Sophie Jenkins, author interview

SM/VH – Sara Maitland, ed., *Very Heaven*

SR/PD – Sheila Rowbotham, *Promise of a Dream*

TT/A – Theresa Tyrell, author interview

VM/A – Veronica MacNab, author interview

Prelude

p. 3 'It was incredibly dull . . .': 'Susan', cited in Cécile Landau, *Growing Up in the Sixties*

p. 4 'I'm a sixties woman . . .': KS/A

p. 5 'Oh my God, yes . . .': TT/A

p. 5 'Whenever I want you . . .': from 'All I Have to Do is Dream', the Everly Brothers

p. 6 'Girls were seen as insignificant': MD/A

p. 8 'I do seem to fit your brief . . .': AM/A

p. 9 'So radio was, well . . .': BM/A

p. 9 'The screaming was so loud . . .': CH/A

1960

p. 11 'Here is London in her pride . . .': P/Cine

p. 13 'In the end it had to be . . .': Margaret Forster, *Hidden Lives*

p. 15 'I can't even remember . . .': 'Elizabeth', cited in Cécile Landau, *Growing Up in the Sixties*

p. 15 'I got married in 1959 . . .': 'Jane', cited in SM/VH

p. 16 'Like a river flows . . .': from 'Can't Help Falling in Love', Elvis Presley

p. 18 'If I had my way . . .': cited in Richard Davenport-Hines, *An English Affair*

p. 19 'You didn't think twice . . .': cited in Ali Haggett, *Desperate Housewives*

p. 19 'When the evening fire glows . . .': Peter Willmott and Michael Young, *Family and Class in a London Suburb*

p. 20 'a historical document of a time now gone . . .': Fay Weldon, *Auto da Fay*

p. 22 'It never struck me . . .': MI/NT

p. 22 'Miss Green, who taught us Domestic Science . . .': DM/A

p. 23 'My periods started at home . . .': RP/A

p. 23 'I thought I came out of a tulip . . .': BM/A

p. 23 'My mother just tutted a lot . . .': MD/A

p. 24 'It all felt very grey . . .': Clare Lane, author interview

p. 24 '. . . shaking with anguish and fury . . .': Sybille Bedford, *The Trial of Lady Chatterley's Lover*

p. 25 'Mellors and Lady Chatterley . . .': Clare Lane, author interview

p. 25 'When I was on the jury once . . .': lyrics by Sydney Carter

p. 26 'Then as he began to move . . .': D. H. Lawrence, *Lady Chatterley's Lover*

p. 27 'I had a right cough . . .': MH/A

p. 32 'I knew we were getting closer to England . . .': FB/AB and FB/CE

p. 34 'Thousands of people marching . . .': Kate Paul, *Journal*

p. 36 'Are we really to go on . . .': *The Times*, 24 June 1960

p. 36 'I think we have reached a stage . . .': *The Times*, 31 March 1960

p. 36 'a very short tight skirt . . .': Kate Paul, *Journal*

p. 38 'We were hoping for boys!': MC/A

p. 39 'I have never done anything . . .': MRD/M

p. 42 'The place was very glamorous . . .': Marjorie Davis, author interview

p. 44 ' "Eighteen," I lied blithely . . .': MRD/M

1961

p. 46 'Walking back to happiness': from 'Walking Back to Happiness', Helen Shapiro

p. 48 'It was tough, in the fifties . . .': Angela Carter, cited in SM/VH

p. 49 'When people ask of me . . .': from 'Bobby's Girl', Susan Maughan

p. 49 'I was a girl, I'd just get married . . .': Margaret Forster, *Hidden Lives*

p. 49 'You don't need to go to university . . .': LB/E

p. 49 'If you hadn't've gone to that university . . .': DM/A

p. 51 'My breasts were developing . . .': Vivian Nicholson and Stephen Smith, *Spend, Spend, Spend*

p. 55 'I started work [in the bank] . . .': cited in AP/CT

p. 55 'In 1961 I earned . . .': cited in AP/CT

p. 55 'I was earning nearly twice as much as my dad . . .': cited in AP/CT

p. 55 'I was sent to some publishing companies . . .': cited in AP/CT

p. 56 'Far from silent . . .': SM/VH

p. 56 'I would walk down . . .': RP/A

p. 59 'Our type don't go to university . . .': DM/A

p. 59 'And having got across the Atlantic . . .': Harriet Lear, author interview

p. 60 'At sixteen I realised . . .': KE/GE

p. 60 '. . . a good conversationalist . . .': MRD/M

p. 61 'I just had this thing . . .': BM/A

p. 65 'I needed to get away . . .': Emma Codrington, author interview

p. 66 'It was [the Chelsea Girl] . . .': Mary Quant, *Quant on Quant*

p. 67 'I drove my mum insane . . .': Twiggy, *An Autobiography*

p. 68 'Some parents would be horrified . . .': *Daily Mail*, 12 September 1961

p. 68 '. . . my staff must be . . . one hundred per cent . . .': Lynne Reid Banks, *The L-Shaped Room*

p. 69 'The poor man was so upset . . .': Eirlys Ellis, cited in Deirdre Beddoe, *Changing Times*

p. 69 'There is a widespread new attitude . . .': *Daily Mail*, 22 March 1961

p. 70 'the gratuitous exhibition . . .': *The Times* 17 May 1960

p. 70 '. . . recently stated that not one girl in her sixth form was a virgin . . .' etc: *The Times*, correspondence columns, September 1961

p. 72 'I'll run away . . .': 'Our Teenage Daughters', *Sunday Times*, 10 and 17 December 1961

p. 73 'I kind of went looking for wildness . . .': MN/A

p. 74 'No amount of information . . .': Anne Edwards and Drusilla Beyfus, *Lady Behave*

p. 76 'The most fundamental thing . . .': 'Anatomy of a Dolly-Bird', in Linda Grant, ed., *Sexing the Millennium*

p. 76 'It was completely wonderful . . .': cited in Gerard DeGroot, *The 60s Unplugged*

1962

p. 77 'The Pill had to be the best thing . . .': VM/A

p. 81 '. . . black stockings and a rather Chelsea-look . . .': cited in Fiona Mac-Carthy, *Last Curtsey*

p. 81 'All us working-class lads . . .': cited in GC/G

p. 82 'Before 1960, a fashion photographer . . .': cited in Eamonn McCabe, obituary of Brian Duffy, *Guardian*, 6 June 2010

p. 82 'I was a naive girl . . .': Jean Shrimpton, *An Autobiography*

p. 82 'There's a hardness to her forehead . . .': *Sunday Times*, 6 October 1963

p. 83 '[It was] quite awful . . .': Jean Shrimpton, *An Autobiography*

p. 84 'I was young, nubile . . .': PB/WT

p. 84 She was clean, fresh and bubbly . . .': Cherry Marshall, *The Cat-Walk*

p. 85 '. . . who, after cutting the customers' hair . . .': GC/G

p. 85 'The photographer must have . . .': Jean Shrimpton, *The Truth About Modelling*

p. 86 'Women are taking the lead . . .': G. M. Carstairs, *This Island Now*

p. 86 '. . . no matter what stage of equality . . .': Eustace Chesser, *Is Chastity Outmoded?*

p. 87 'Our elders and betters . . .': Charles Hamblett and Jane Deverson, *Generation X*

p. 88 'Why can't oldish women *walk*?': Kate Paul, *Journal*

p. 88 'I would never want to grow old . . .': *Daily Express*, 2 June 1964

p. 89 'One officer was a sergeant . . .': Valerie A. Tedder, *You'll Never Last*

p. 90 'I was everything he hated . . .': AL/KS

p. 93 'Ann Leslie – yes, I remember . . .': AC/A

p. 98 'And when they'd finished . . .': RP/A

p. 100 '. . . so you just took off . . .': BM/A

p. 101 'Sick and faint . . .': CL/TL

p. 102 'We were the first generation . . .': Jo Durden-Smith, cited in JG/DL

p. 102 'We thought we would never grow up . . .': SJ/A

p. 103 'Don't you hear the H-bombs thunder . . .': lyrics by John Brunner

p. 105 'I was 14 at the time . . .': 'Zena', cited on BBC website http://news.bbc.co.uk/1/hi/world/americas/2317931.stm

p. 105 'I . . . waited, along with the rest . . .': JD/S

p. 106 'For several days . . .': JB/CB

p. 106 'The question was . . .': MI/NT

p. 106 'I don't care. My husband has just come home . . .': MH/A

1963

p. 111 '. . . a whiteness I had never seen . . .': FB/AB and FB/CE

p. 113 'I need romance . . .': MRD/M

p. 113 'I always wanted a man around . . .': CK/TL

p. 116 'I did not understand . . .': CK/TL

p. 116 'The whole thing . . .': AC/A

p. 118 '[The *Daily Express* men] wanted . . .': CK/TL

p. 118 'She earned top marks . . .': *Daily Express*, 7 June 1963

p. 119 'The voluptuous lips . . .': *Daily Mirror*, 23 July 1963

p. 120 'I wore it to boost . . .': MRD/M

p. 122 '. . . the attitude was simply . . .': CK/TL

p. 123 '*Should a Man Think You are a Virgin?* . . .': Helen Gurley Brown, *Sex and the Single Girl*

p. 124 'It was a strange stirring . . .': Betty Friedan, *The Feminine Mystique*

p. 125 'The pendulum was bound to swing . . .': Anthony Storr, *Sunday Times*, 5 May 1963

p. 125 '. . . a moment of epiphany . . .': JB/CB

p. 125 'Career girls are sexy . . .': Helen Gurley Brown, *Sex and the Single Girl*

p. 126 '. . . [the parents'] immediate reaction . . .': cited in Rebecca Jennings, *Tomboys and Bachelor Girls*

p. 126 'They kept on so!': cited in Rebecca Jennings, *Tomboys and Bachelor Girls*

p. 126 'Pubs are . . . risky places . . .': Maureen Duffy, in Hunter Davies, ed., *The New London Spy*

p. 127 '. . . a sort of lesbian club . . .': Barbara Bell, *Just Take Your Frock Off*

p. 128 'the Sixties did not really begin . . .': Robert Hewison, *Too much*

p. 128 'Sexual intercourse began . . .': Philip Larkin, '*Annus Mirabilis*'

p. 129 'I grew up thinking there was no such thing . . .': MD/A

p. 135 'I wrote it simply . . .': Elizabeth Woodcraft, *The Saturday Girls*

p. 136 'I liked all modern things . . .': Twiggy, *An Autobiography*

p. 138 'It was our bible . . .': Twiggy, *An Autobiography*

p. 138 '1963 was the year . . .': MI/NT

p. 139 'Those who flock . . .': *New Statesman*, 28 February 1964

p. 139 'The girls are subconsciously . . .': cited in Dominic Sandbrook, *Never Had It so Good*

p. 140 'the face contorted . . .': MI/NT

p. 140 'Mine was George . . .' : Jessica Chappell, author interview

p. 141 '. . . lots of lunatic girls . . .': KR/A

p. 141 'I don't remember much . . .': cited in AP/CT

p. 141 'It was what you did . . .': Linda Grant, cited in Dorian Lynskey, 'Beatlemania: "The Screamers" and Other Tales of Fandom', *Guardian*, 29 September 2013

p. 143 'My sister was truly naughty . . .': Jean Shrimpton, *An Autobiography*

p. 143 '. . . very put together . . .': Marianne Faithfull, cited in Shawn Levy, *Ready, Steady, Go!*

p. 144 'The venue was stifling . . .': *Guardian*, 10 July 2013

p. 144 'Mick doesn't really respect women . . .': cited in Shawn Levy, *Ready, Steady, Go!*

p. 145 'They've killed a great man . . .': FB/AB

p. 145 'But the party ended early . . .': KR/A

p. 146 '. . . she had come to realise . . .': Janny Scott, *New York Times*, cited in *Jackie Kennedy's Power Woman Complex*, Jezebel.com, 9 December 2011

1964

p. 147 'Homosexuality, prostitution . . .': Mary Whitehouse, *Quite Contrary*

p. 148 'You see, the BBC say . . .': Mary Whitehouse, *Cleaning-Up TV*

p. 149 'We women of Britain . . .': cited in Ben Thompson, ed., *Ban this Filth!*

p. 149 'It was so fantastic . . .': cited in Michael Tracy and David Morrison, *Whitehouse*

p. 149 'We recognise that the period . . .': www.youtube.com/watch?v=YO_DqJ85jvk

p. 150 'Perhaps never in the history . . .': *The Times*, 6 May 1964

p. 150 'The women of Britain need . . .': cited in Ben Thompson, ed., *Ban this Filth!*

p. 151 'People say this isn't . . .': *Guardian*, 24 April 1965

p. 151 'I go to church . . .': Charles Hamblett and Jane Deverson, *Generation X*

p. 152 'Clunton and Clunbury . . .': A. E. Housman, in *A Shropshire Lad*

p. 152 'I have lived . . .': Ann Gurney, author interview

p. 153 'You will be expected . . .': Angela Patrick, *The Baby Laundry for Unmarried Mothers*

p. 154 'I think that's quite normal . . .': Ann Widdecombe, author interview

p. 155 'There was no expectation . . .': Julia Cumberlege, author interview

p. 156 'I went on holiday . . .': AM/A

p. 159 '[He] shook his head . . .': Ann Widdecombe, *Strictly Ann*

p. 160 'I was sent to a mother-and-baby home . . .': KS/A

p. 161 'A mother trying to rear . . .': *The Times*, 22 May 1964

p. 166 'The young have taken over . . .': Janey Ironside, *Janey*

p. 166 'There was energy then . . .': Jean Shrimpton, cited in Brian Masters, *The Swinging Sixties*

p. 166 '[It was] a time when . . .': Twiggy, cited in JB/CB

p. 166 'There was a yeastiness . . .': Angela Carter, cited in SM/VH

p. 166 'We used to drink and dance . . .': GC/G

p. 166 'It was the women of Chelsea . . .': Alexandra Pringle, cited in SM/VH

p. 166 'Well, five of us girls . . .': PQ/A

p. 167 'You spoke to strangers . . .': PB/WT

p. 167 'Where else can you find Lord Plunkett . . .': cited in Shawn Levy, *Ready, Steady, Go!*

p. 168 'What was once strictly . . .': www.britishpathe.com/video/trouser-fashions/

p. 169 'And George . . . was the best-looking man . . .': PB/WT

p. 170 'It was so pretty . . .': VM/A

p. 174 'Thirteen years of Tory rule . . .': *Observer*, 20 September 1964

p. 175 'I'd live in the future . . .': cited in Janet Mendelsohn, *Varna Road*

p. 175 'I'd just like to . . .': Kathy Collier, cited in Nell Dunn, *Talking to Women*

p. 175 'We lived in a . . .': Paddy Kitchen, cited in Nell Dunn, *Talking to Women*

p. 176 'The numbers of them . . .': PO/A

1965

p. 182 'I got a sense . . .': DM/A

p. 183 'The Beatles thought Wilson was good . . .': MC/A

p. 183 'we didn't realise . . .': RP/A

p. 185 'I was fifteen, sixteen . . .': KR/A

p. 188 'The women who came to my bureau . . .': Margery Hurst, *No Glass Slipper*

p. 192 'Where's it all leading . . .': *Daily Mirror*, 19 May 1964

p. 192 'That little fluted skirt . . .': Barbara Hulanicki, *From A to Biba*

p. 193 'It doesn't matter . . .': Jean Shrimpton, *An Autobiography*

p. 193 '. . . a frenzy of the prettiest legs . . .': 'London: The Most Exciting City', *Sunday Telegraph*, 26 April 1965

p. 193 'They're getting shorter . . .': *News of the World*, 21 March 1965

p. 193 'If it's not for sale . . .': cited in documentary with Michael Caine, *My Generation*

p. 193 'There is only one solution . . .': *Daily Mirror*, 22 February 1965

p. 193 'Every girl with a hope . . .': Mary Quant, *Quant on Quant*

p. 195 'It makes me hopping mad . . .': *Guardian*, 9 March 1964

p. 197 'I never once lay down with him . . .': Nell Dunn, *Up the Junction*

p. 197 'It was quite a lot of money . . .': KR/A

p. 199 'this was one of the worst . . .': Carmen Callil, author interview

p. 200 '. . . and I didn't know enough . . .': SJ/A

p. 201 'I was having an on-off fling . . .': ABD/A

p. 202 'Lots of people got pregnant . . .': MN/A

p. 204 'How, asked one lady correspondent . . .': *The Times*, 13 July 1965

p. 204 'Do disabled people really wish . . .': *The Times*, 10 February 1966

p. 204 'Let us call a spade a spade . . .': *The Times*, 20 July 1966

p. 205 'As I left the abortion ward . . .': cited in AP/CT

p. 205 'Being pregnant was inconvenient . . .': Belinda Mitchell, author interview

p. 206 'And the doctor examined him . . .': MH/A

p. 208 'I wonder if people realise . . .': *News of the World*, 11 April 1965

p. 209 '. . . one of the loneliest people . . .': Edith Summerskill, *Letters to My Daughter*

p. 209 '*Was* it? Swinging London?': Harriet Lear, author interview

p. 210 'The only way you could buy Tupperware . . .': Belinda Mitchell, author interview

p. 211 'Unless she is ill . . .': Barbara Cartland, *Barbara Cartland's Etiquette Handbook*

p. 212 'The underground all sprang . . .': MN/A

p. 215 'I am that I am I am the . . .': Allan Ginsberg, *Collected Poems*, 327

p. 215 '. . . ghastly poetry, unbelievably bad . . .': Sue Miles, cited in JG/DL

p. 216 'You'd hear them clomping . . .': MN/A

p. 219 'We live in a permissive society . . .': *The Times*, 6 July 1965

p. 220 'Most women who lived . . .': JD/S

p. 220 'Each of the different segments . . .': JB/CB

p. 221 'It was a men's club . . .': MF/F

p. 221 'The British jazz world . . .': Diana Melly, *Take a Girl Like Me*

p. 221 '[They] were very happy . . .': CL/TL

p. 221 'Mick has to be the one . . .': cited in Laura Jackson, *Heart of Stone*

p. 221 'In my opinion . . .': *News of the World*, 21 March 1965

p. 222 'For women, it was absolutely grisly . . .': Virginia Ironside, *Daily Mail Online*, 18 January 2011

1966

p. 223 'We don't know of one shop . . .': *Guardian*, 7 March 1966

p. 223 'It seemed to some of us . . .': Pamela Hansford Johnson, *On Iniquity*

p. 224 'Hush, hush, shut up . . .': *The Times*, 27 April 1966

p. 225 'Friday and Saturday nights . . .': *Guardian*, 18 December 1995

p. 225 ' "Without me," she wrote . . .': *Guardian*, 18 December 1995

p. 226 'We are in danger . . . of creating . . .': Pamela Hansford Johnson, *On Iniquity*

p. 227 'And I was aware . . .': MC/A

p. 228 '*Time* didn't create "Swinging London." ': Piri Halasz, *A Memoir of Creativity*

p. 229 'But can you imagine . . .': MC/A

p. 233 'There was this little Cockney girl . . .': Justin de Villeneuve, *An Affectionate Punch*

p. 233 'That whole summer was non-stop . . .': Twiggy, *An Autobiography*

p. 234 '. . . somebody's brother to come in . . .': KR/A

p. 235 'In the past year . . .': Deirdre McSharry, cited in Marnie Fogg, *Boutique: A '60s Cultural Phenomenon*

p. 235 'I hung out at all . . .': GC/G

p. 236 'I was with the Beatles . . .': PB/A

p. 236 'Let's get married . . .': PB/WT

p. 238 '. . . welcomed into the upper echelons . . .': Cecil Beaton, *Beaton in the Sixties*

p. 238 'And all through the reception . . .': AM/A

p. 239 'Come downstairs and meet . . .': KE/GE

p. 239 'It looked better on him . . .': BM/A

p. 239 'Courtfield Road, Brian Jones . . .': MF/F

p. 240 '[It] was *bliss* . . .': Jo Cruickshank, cited in JG/DL

p. 240 '. . . there was a new look . . .': Henrietta Moraes, *Henrietta*

p. 241 'So, Antonioni is <u>doing</u> Swinging London . . .': PQ/A

p. 243 'A married woman, see . . .': Bill Naughton, *Alfie*

p. 243 'There's a little bit of Alfie . . .': cited in documentary with Michael Caine, *My Generation*

p. 244 'It was the original *Alfie* . . .': *Guardian*, 15 October 2004

p. 245 'I don't mind girls . . .': Nik Cohn in *The Observer*, cited in Linda Grant, ed., *Sexing the Millennium*

p. 246 'Surely I'm not going . . .': Doris Lessing, *Walking in the Shade*

p. 246 '. . . she was treated as "a peasant" . . .': Lorna Sage, *Bad Blood*

p. 246 'Pretty young women . . .': AL/KS

p. 247 '[Women] are not encouraged . . .': in Hunter Davies, ed., *The New London Spy*

p. 247 'Being a woman and a secretary . . .': 'Janet', in MI/NT

p. 247 'I overheard someone . . .': JB/CB

p. 248 'Slowly but surely women . . .': www.britishpathe.com/video/girl-racer/

p. 249 '. . . not an exciting example . . .': from House of Lords debate, 3 December 1957, cited in Richard Davenport-Hines, *An English Affair*

p. 249 'Men are so terribly sex-conscious . . .': Anne Perkins, *Red Queen*

p. 250 'I took it for granted . . .': JB/CB

p. 250 'I cried so much . . .': PO/A

p. 252 'Well, I happened to be . . .': TT/A

p. 255 '. . . or there would be huge disappointment . . .': FB/AB

p. 256 'The head teacher at my school . . .': Rosalind Delmar, Millennium Memory Bank, British Library

p. 257 'On my first day at Keele . . .': SJ/A

p. 257 'What, we want to know . . .': *Honey*, October 1966

p. 259 '. . . student rooms all over the country . . .': MI/NT

p. 260 'The rule from now on . . .': LB/E

p. 261 'How can I risk . . .': MI/NT

p. 261 'I had a very proto-feminist mother . . .': Juliet Mitchell, cited in MW/OF

1967

p. 266 'He explained it meant . . .': LB/E

p. 266 'I had cookery books . . .': Margaret Forster, *Hidden Lives*

p. 267 'I was astonished . . .': cited in AP/CT

p. 267 'People were just starting . . .': cited in AP/CT

p. 269 'After that I didn't want . . .': KS/A

p. 273 'I must have heard about it . . .': Patsy Reading, author interview

p. 274 'I hadn't even read *Playboy* . . .': PQ/A

p. 274 'If the costumes weren't fitted . . .': 'Bunny Girls', 1999 (*Secret History*, Channel 4), directed by Philippa Walker

p. 276 'A playboy is potent . . .': Marilyn Cole, in 'Bunny Girls', 1999 (*Secret History*, Channel 4), directed by Philippa Walker

p. 276 'Well, it is all down to Hugh Hefner . . .': Liz Flower, in 'Bunny Girls', 1999 (*Secret History*, Channel 4), directed by Philippa Walker

p. 281 'Striped plastic trouser suits . . .': *Daily Mirror*, 14 December 1967

p. 281 'No, I don't know any . . .': Janey Ironside, *Janey*

p. 284 'Somebody once forced . . .': Carmen Callil, author interview

p. 284 'Our drunken cookery . . .': AL/KS

p. 285 'He would leave the room . . .': CL/TL

p. 285 '. . . sour milk, urinous nappies . . .': Karen V. Kukil, ed., *The Journals of Sylvia Plath, 1950–1962*

p. 285 '. . . going "quietly crazy" . . .': Audrey Battersby, cited in MW/OF

p. 286 'As for the various . . .': Harriet Lear, author interview

p. 286 'This is a very nice . . .': Emma Codrington, author interview

p. 287 'Most of them . . .': VM/A

p. 288 '. . . [flower power] became a form . . .': Dominic Sandbrook, *White Heat*

p. 289 'There was an urge . . .': Andrea Adam, cited in JG/DL

p. 289 'You put all your effort . . .': Sue Miles, cited in JG/DL

p. 289 'How little you could do with . . .': Julie Christie, cited in SM/VH

p. 289 'In the sixties nobody . . .': PB/A

p. 290 'As everything in the counterculture . . .': SR/PD

p. 291 'We were seeking . . .': www.vam.ac.uk/content/articles/i/jane-ormsby-gore/

p. 291 'The younger generation . . .': Frances Partridge, *Good Company, Diaries 1967–70*

p. 292 '. . . I was a hideous little snob . . .': CH/A

p. 295 'Yes, I took it all the time . . .': MN/A

p. 297 '. . . silken, silvery cobwebs . . .': Henrietta Moraes, *Henrietta*

p. 297 '. . . strewn with bloody needles . . .': MF/F

p. 298 '. . . part of the creative process . . .': PB/WT

p. 298 'I promise you . . .': Jann Haworth, cited in Alastair Sooke, *Pop Art, A Colourful History*

p. 299 '. . . [it] was my baby . . .': Jim Haynes, cited in JG/DL

p. 299 'It became a kind of sexual seraglio . . .': Charles Marowitz, *Burnt Bridges*

p. 300 'You lay . . . watching . . .': Jo Cruickshank, cited in JG/DL

p. 301 'Jim Haynes tried to sleep with me . . .': Cheryll Park, cited in JG/DL

p. 301 'Part of the newness . . .': JD/S

p. 304 'The more you give way . . .': *Daily Mail*, 1 March 1967

p. 304 'Far from being the basis . . .': Edmund Leach, *Ourselves and Others*, Reith Lecture 3, transmitted 26 November 1967

p. 305 '. . . the other-world of faery . . .': cited in Andrew Rigby, *Alternative Realities*

p. 306 'The thing with utopian movements . . .': Christine Hugh-Jones, author interview

p. 307 '. . . the prison that I saw . . .': Caroline Coon, cited in www.the-guardian.com/theobserver/2000/jul/30/features.review17

p. 308 '[She] did a magnificent job . . .': Joe Boyd, cited in JG/DL

p. 310 'I brightly suggested . . .': SR/PD

1968

p. 314 'If you did . . .': MD/A

p. 315 'Enough's enough . . .': Brian W. Lavery, *The Headscarf Revolutionaries*

p. 315 'We need to take action . . .': Brian W. Lavery, *The Headscarf Revolutionaries*

p. 316 'I was in the audience . . .': MD/A

p. 316 'two ships have gone down . . .': Brian W. Lavery, *The Headscarf Revolutionaries*

p. 317 'But – when we pulled into . . .': MD/A

p. 319 'Madam, Why don't . . .', and 'The idea of forming . . .': both, Brian W. Lavery, *The Headscarf Revolutionaries*

p. 319 'Well, Barry hated it!': MD/A

p. 322 '. . . humiliating for a man . . .': http://archive.commercialmotor. com/article/5th-july-1968/54/yarmouth-busmen-ban-woman-driver

p. 322 'Its ethos contrasted . . .': SR/PD

p. 323 'I shan't be at all surprised . . .': 'The Demonstration', Granada TV, *World in Action*, Season 4, Episode 18, aired 18 March 1968

p. 323 'It fizzled with defiance . . .': SR/PD

p. 323 'It was one of the happiest . . .': cited in Ronald Fraser, *1968: A Student Generation in Revolt*

p. 324 'The old manners didn't apply . . .': Nina Fishman, cited in JG/DL

p. 324 '. . . there was one girl . . .': Horace Ove, cited in JG/DL

p. 324 'Well, I was such a silly girl . . .': SJ/A

p. 324 'I remember the horses . . .': Christine Hugh-Jones, author interview

p. 325 'The 1968 "revolution" . . .': AL/KS

p. 325 'Please don't let them . . .': SR/PD

p. 325 '. . . the mob was roaring . . .': Nesta Roberts, 8 May 1968

p. 326 'The roads looked a bit unmade . . .': SJ/A

p. 327 'The sixties was one long . . .': Marsha Rowe, cited in SM/VH

p. 328 'The relaxation of manners . . .': Angela Carter, cited in SM/VH

p. 328 'A feeling that we could do . . .': ABD/A

p. 329 'People who think anything goes . . .': AM/A

p. 332 ' "Oh God," wrote Mary . . .': MI/NT

p. 333 'I don't think that the sixties . . .': Rupert Christiansen, *I Know You're Going to be Happy*

p. 333 'I expect a reasonable standard . . .': *Daily Telegraph*, 24 January 1968

p. 333 'Am I the only man . . .': *Daily Mail*, 1 August 1969

p. 333 'Britain is sinking . . .': *Sunday Telegraph*, 7 December 1969

p. 334 'I have been going out . . .': Mary Marryat's Problem Page, *Woman's Weekly*, 10 February 1968

p. 334 'I am almost 17 . . .': Mary Marryat's Problem Page, *Woman's Weekly*, 1 June 1968

p. 334 'I am sixteen . . .': Mary Marryat's Problem Page, *Woman's Weekly*, 11 May 1968

p. 334 'A few weeks ago . . .': Mary Marryat's Problem Page, *Woman's Weekly*, 9 March 1968

p. 334 'Three months ago . . .': Mary Marryat's Problem Page, *Woman's Weekly*, 6 July 1968

p. 334 'Recently my boyfriend . . .': Mary Marryat's Problem Page, *Woman's Weekly*, 13 July 1968

p. 336 'I went to every Dylan concert . . .': Virginia Clive-Smith, cited in JG/DL

p. 336 '. . . I am lying here in my bed . . .': cited in CL/TL

p. 340 'Me, I'm just waiting . . .': *Sunday Times*, 12 October 1969

p. 340 'He expected me . . .': KE/GE

p. 341 'When you're in vans . . .': BM/A

p. 342 'Consideration, Contentment . . .': cited in www.theguardian.com/lifeandstyle/2008/nov/15/family-children-tv-floella-benjamin

p. 343 'Excuse me, I don't remember . . .': FB/AB

p. 344 'I believe he has helped . . .': Barbara Castle, *Diary*, 21 April 1968

p. 345 'It was the time . . .': https://graziadaily.co.uk/life/opinion/forgotten-story-women-behind-british-black-panthers/

p. 346 'It was cool to be a "Spade chick"': Marsha Hunt, *Real Life*

p. 346 'I had never seen . . .': KE/GE

p. 346 'Its honesty and passion . . .': *The Times*, 28 September 1968

p. 346 'middle-of-the-road pap . . .': Jonathon Green, *All Dressed Up*

p. 347 'I got the feeling . . .': FB/AB

p. 349 'I got home to a telegram . . .': TT/A

p. 352 'I set myself up . . .': Richard Neville, *Hippie Hippie Shake*

p. 352 'I loved women . . .': Richard Neville, cited in JG/DL

p. 352 'Monogamy and marriage . . .': Richard Neville, *Hippie Hippie Shake*

p. 353 'Spontaneous joy! . . .': Richard Neville, *Hippie Hippie Shake*

p. 353 'Richard . . . saw us in bed . . .': Jenny Kee, *A Big Life*

p. 353 'Louise and Jenny . . .': Richard Neville, *Hippie Hippie Shake*

p. 356 'I heard about a course . . .': Audrey Battersby, cited in MW/OF

p. 356 'I can date to that time . . .': Angela Carter, cited in SM/VH

p. 356 'The student revolution . . .': Patricia Vereker, cited in SM/VH

p. 357 'My son . . . was born . . .': Val Charlton, cited in SM/VH

p. 357 'It had never occurred . . .': SR/PD

1969

p. 360 'Daddy and I are delighted . . .': cited in Anne Edwards and Drusilla Beyfus, *Lady Behave*

p. 361 'It was like an electric shock . . .': cited in JG/DL

p. 361 'The trouble is . . .': *Guardian*, 2 February 1968

p. 362 'Ignore it if . . .': Geoffrey Gorer, *Sex and Marriage in England Today*

p. 362 'Divorce her . . .': Geoffrey Gorer, *Sex and Marriage in England Today*

p. 362 'Thump her – then the man . . .': Geoffrey Gorer, *Sex and Marriage in England Today*

p. 363 'I found the man I wanted . . .': ABD/A

p. 365 'The trouble is I love girls . . .': Drusilla Beyfus, *The English Marriage*

p. 368 'I was SO – goodness me . . .': CH/A

p. 373 'Of course the Stones were miles away . . .': personal email to author

p. 375 'Every August these lads arrived . . .': Julie Barnfield, Millennium Memory Bank, British Library

p. 376 'Mother wept ostentatiously . . .': Jenny Sullivan, cited in Deirdre Beddoe, *Changing Times*

p. 376 'The whole place was swarming . . .': Margaret Lloyd, cited in Deirdre Beddoe, *Changing Times*

p. 376 'One could have imagined . . .': Marsha Hunt, *Real Life*

p. 377 'I wouldn't have missed it . . .': MN/A

p. 377 '. . . champagne-soaked peaches . . .': Rosie Boycott, *A Nice Girl Like Me*

p. 377 'We were *it* . . .': PQ/A

p. 378 'Some serendipity . . .': Edna O'Brien, *Country Girl, A Memoir*

p. 378 'The Sixties . . . were . . .': AL/KS

p. 378 'No woman of my generation . . .': Fiona MacCarthy, *Last Curtsey*

p. 378 'I'm in my late twenties . . .': *Woman's Own*, 26 November 1967

p. 379 'I'm 14 and am always dreaming . . .': *Woman's Own*, 18 November 1967

p. 379 'We read it, reread it . . .': cited in Jill Gardiner, *From the Closet to the Screen*

p. 379 '[They] wrote and said . . .': cited in Jill Gardiner, *From the Closet to the Screen*

p. 381 'She just thinks I'm disgusting . . .': 'Consenting Adults'; 2, 'The Women', on *Man Alive*, broadcast 1967

p. 381 'This is dealing with . . .': *Late Night Line-Up*, BBC2, broadcast June 1967

p. 382 'The showings of the film . . .': cited in Jill Gardiner, *From the Closet to the Screen*

p. 382 '. . . the "so-called permissive society" . . .': *Daily Mail*, 29 May 1969

p. 383 '[It's] like being fed marshmallow . . .': cited in Jill Gardiner, *From the Closet to the Screen*

p. 383 'I, like most other heterosexual . . .': *Daily Mirror*, 1 April 1969

p. 383 '[My mother] can't accept me . . .': 'Consenting Adults'; 2, 'The Women', on *Man Alive*, broadcast 1967

p. 384 'Woman, like the Negro . . .': *Observer* 9 March 1969

p. 384 'We haven't met a woman . . .': *Observer*, 16 March 1969

p. 384 ' "Woman Power' should be . . .": *Observer*, 16 March 1969

p. 384 'Those who rant and rave . . .': *Observer*, 16 March 1969

p. 384 'A true woman . . .': *Observer*, 16 March 1969

p. 385 'I will happily . . .': *Observer*, 16 March 1969

p. 385 'What a career woman really needs . . .': *Observer*, 16 March 1969

p. 385 'Horrid, nasty, smug Pendennis . . .': *Observer*, 16 March 1969

p. 385 'Sitting here in a world . . .': *Observer*, 16 March 1969

p. 385 'Of course I support . . .': Irma Kurtz, *My Life in Agony*

p. 386 '. . . could not conceive . . .': Lucy Brett, author interview

p. 390 'You are not only demonstrating . . .': *Guardian*, 19 May 1969

p. 391 'It was tremendously exciting . . .': Sheila Rowbotham, cited in MW/OF

p. 392 'In my view it is futile . . .': cited in MW/OF

p. 392 'I don't think it does a lot of good . . .': www.grassrootsfeminism. net/cms/node/520 Shrew: Women's Liberation Workshop

p. 392 'A cup, B cup, C cup, D . . .': 'Boadicea Rides Again', *Sunday Times*, 21 September, 1969

p. 393 'No doubt [we looked] incredibly . . .': Janet Hadley, cited in MW/OF

p. 393 'I don't think any of us . . .': SR/PD

p. 393 'Cadres of the Women's Liberation Workshop . . .': *Daily Telegraph*, 24 June 1969

p. 393 'Is it just possible . . .': *Observer*, 7 September, 1969

p. 393 'I am sick of reading . . .': *Daily Mail*, 5 August 1969

p. 393 'The material for a feminist movement . . .': 'Boadicea Rides Again', *Sunday Times*, 21 September, 1969

p. 394 'I was as capable . . .': SR/PD

p. 394 'The first question is . . .': Sheila Rowbotham, *Women's Liberation and the New Politics*

p. 398 'We wanted to change . . .': MN/A

p. 398 'Amid all the fun . . .': Virginia Clive-Smith, cited in JG/DL

p. 399 'I wanted to be a junkie . . .': MF/F

p. 399 'They closed an era . . .': cited www.theguardian.com/world/2009/aug/02/charles-manson-linda-kasabian-polanski

p. 401 'It was a wonderful life . . .': Patsy Reading, author interview

Aftermath

p. 402 'Why be equal? . . .': cited in Paul E. Willis, *Profane Culture*

p. 403 'Suddenly we were all together . . .': www.bl.uk/sisterhood/articles/activism-and-the-womens-liberation-movement

p. 403 'After Ruskin I felt . . .': Audrey Battersby, cited in MW/OF

p. 403 'Ruskin changed my whole life . . .': Sally Alexander, cited in MW/OF

p. 403 'You did feel you could . . .': Juliet Mitchell, cited in MW/OF

p. 405 'I'm very, very happy . . .': www.youtube.com/watch?v=reCX3_OAkv8

p. 405 'I looked up and saw . . .': www.bl.uk/collection-items/jo-robinson-miss-world-contest

p. 406 'I do not think women . . .': *Observer*, 22 November 1970

p. 406 'I was a mass of flesh . . .': Bernadette Devlin, *The Price of My Soul*

p. 407 'Now that you're gone . . .': 'Band of Gold', Freda Payne

p. 408 'Nudity is everywhere . . .': Cecil Beaton, *Beaton in the Sixties*

p. 408 "I expected to be encouraged . . .': Rosie Boycott, *A Nice Girl Like Me*

p. 409 '[I suggested] that they sit round . . .': SR/PD

p. 410 'When people speak . . .': MH/A

p. 410 'Given my life over again . . .': PB/WT

p. 411 'Nearly all my circle . . .': MN/A

p. 412 'She didn't know me . . .': TT/A

p. 413 'I wanted to be . . .': MC/A

p. 413 'There were a lot of . . .': KR/A

p. 414 ' "That John Lennon,". . .': RP/A

p. 415 'I like the Dame idea . . .': personal email to the author from Carmen Callil

p. 415 'And I put on my . . .': MD/A

p. 416 'There are some preconceptions . . .': CK/TL

p. 417 'The point is . . .': PQ/A

p. 418 'Remember to live your life . . .'; FB/AB

p. 418 'I've been so blessed . . .': AM/A

p. 419 'I chose Richard . . .': VM/A

p. 420 'I thought Dave . . .': KS/A

p. 421 'I am now on the threshold . . .': CH/A

p. 421 'I got offers . . .': BM/A

p. 422 'It stirred something . . .': Beryl Marsden, *Changes*, 2011 interview with Iain McNay www.youtube.com/watch?v=VKBsQ7soNAc

p. 422 'In the same 2011 interview . . .': Beryl Marsden, *Changes*, 2011 interview with Iain McNay www.youtube.com/watch?v=VKBsQ7soNAc

Select Bibliography

Biography, Memoirs, Diaries, Autobiography, Oral Histories

Adie, Kate, *The Kindness of Strangers*, Headline, London, 2002

Bakewell, Joan, *The Centre of the Bed: An Autobiography*, Hodder & Stoughton, London, 2003

Barber, Lynn, *An Education*, Penguin, London, 2009

Beaton, Cecil, *Beaton in the Sixties: The Cecil Beaton Diaries, as They Were Written*, introduced by Hugo Vickers, Weidenfeld & Nicolson, London, 2003

Beddoe, Deirdre, ed., *Changing Times: Welsh Women Writing on the 1950s and 1960s*, Honno, Dinas Powys, 2003

Bell, Barbara, *Just Take Your Frock Off: A Lesbian Life*, Ourstory, Brighton, 1999

Benjamin, Floella, *Coming to England*, Pavilion, London, 1995

———, *The Arms of Britannia: The Teenage Years of Floella Benjamin*, Walker, London, 2010

Bennett, Mary, *An Autobiography*, St Hilda's College, Oxford, 2006

Berry, Mary, *Recipe for Life*, Michael Joseph, London, 2013

Beyfus, Drusilla, *The English Marriage: What It is Like to be Married Today*, Weidenfeld & Nicolson, London, 1968

Black, Cilla, *Step Inside*, Dent, London, 1985

Boycott, Rosie, *A Nice Girl Like Me: A Story of the Seventies*, Chatto & Windus, London, 1984

Boyd, Pattie with Penny Junor, *Wonderful Today: The Autobiography*, Headline Review, London, 2007

Bron, Eleanor, *The Pillow Book of Eleanor Bron – or – An Actress Despairs*, Jonathan Cape, London, 1985

Charles, Caroline, *Fifty Years in Fashion: The Diaries and Scrapbooks of a Leading Designer*, ACC, Woodbridge, 2012

Christiansen, Rupert, *I Know You're Going to be Happy*, Short Books, London, 2013

Clark, Ossie, *The Ossie Clark Diaries*, edited and introduced by Lady Henrietta Rous, Bloomsbury, London, 1998

Cleveland, Carol with Peter Jarrette, *Pompoms Up! From Puberty to Python and Beyond*, Dynasty Press, London, 2014

Coddington, Grace with Michael Roberts, *Grace: A Memoir*, Chatto & Windus, London, 2012

Curtis, Hélène and Mimi Sanderson, eds., *The Unsung Sixties: Memoirs of Social Innovation*, Whiting & Birch, London, 2004

Davies, Hunter, *The Beatles*, revised edition, W. W. Norton, New York, 2002

de Villeneuve, Justin, *An Affectionate Punch*, Sidgwick & Jackson, London, 1986

Des Barres, Pamela, *I'm with the Band: Confessions of a Groupie*, Helter Skelter, London, 2003

Devlin, Bernadette, *The Price of My Soul*, André Deutsch, London, 1969

Diski, Jenny, *The Sixties*, Profile, London, 2009

Dundy, Elaine, *Life Itself!*, Virago, London, 2001

Dunn, Nell, *Talking to Women*, MacGibbon & Kee, London, 1965

Etchingham, Kathy with Andrew Crofts, *Through Gypsy Eyes*, Victor Gollancz, London, 1998

Faithfull, Marianne with David Dalston, *Faithfull*, Michael Joseph, London, 1994

Farquharson, Robin, *Drop Out*, Anthony Blond, London, 1968

Forster, Margaret, *Hidden Lives: A Family Memoir*, Viking, London, 1995

Fryer, Jonathan, *Soho in the Fifties and Sixties*, National Portrait Gallery Publications, London, 1998

Galloway, Janice, *All Made Up*, Granta, London, 2012

Gee, Maggie, *My Animal Life*, Telegram, London, 2010

Goldie, Grace Wyndham, *Facing the Nation: Television and Politics, 1936–1976*, The Bodley Head, London, 1977

Goldsmith, Annabel, *Annabel – An Unconventional Life: The Memoirs of Lady Annabel Goldsmith*, Weidenfeld & Nicolson, London, 2004

Green, Felicity with Sinty Stemp, *Sex, Sense and Nonsense: Felicity Green on the '60s Fashion Scene*, ACC, Woodbridge, 2014

Green, Jonathon, *Days in the Life: Voices from the English Underground, 1961–1971*, Heinemann, London, 1988

Halasz, Piri, *A Memoir of Creativity: Abstract Painting, Politics & the Media, 1956–2008*, iUniverse, New York, 2009

Hamblett, Charles and Jane Deverson, *Generation X*, Tandem, London, 1964

Hart, Jenifer, *Ask Me No More: An Autobiography*, Peter Halban, London, 1998

Haynes, Jim, *'Thanks for Coming': An Autobiography*, Faber & Faber, London, 1984

Healey, Edna, *Part of the Pattern: Memoirs of a Wife at Westminster*, Headline Review, London, 2006

Hughes, Shirley, *A Life Drawing*, The Bodley Head, London, 2002

Hulanicki, Barbara, *From A to Biba: The Autobiography of Barbara Hulanicki*, V&A Publications, London, 2007

Hunt, Marsha, *Real Life*, Chatto & Windus, London, 1986

Hurst, Margery, *No Glass Slipper*, Arlington, London, 1967

Ingham, Mary, *Now We are Thirty: Women of the Breakthrough Generation*, Eyre Methuen, London, 1981

Ironside, Janey, *Janey*, Michael Joseph, London, 1973

Jackson, Laura, *Heart of Stone: The Unauthorised Life of Mick Jagger*, Smith Gryphon, London, 1997

Keeler, Christine with Douglas Thompson, *The Truth at Last: My Story*, Sidgwick & Jackson, London, 2001

Kochan, Nicholas, *Ann Widdecombe: Right from the Beginning*, Politico's, London, 2000

Kukil, Karen V., ed., *The Journals of Sylvia Plath, 1950–1962*, Faber & Faber, London, 2001

Kurtz, Irma, *My Life in Agony*, Alma, Richmond, 2014

Landau, Cécile, ed., *Growing Up in the Sixties*, Macdonald Optima, London, 1991

Lavery, Brian W., *The Headscarf Revolutionaries: Lillian Bilocca and the Hull Triple-Trawler Disaster of 1968*, Barbican Press, London, 2015

Lennon, Cynthia, *A Twist of Lennon*, Star, London, 1978

Leslie, Ann, *Killing My Own Snakes: A Memoir*, Macmillan, London, 2008

Lessing, Doris, *Walking in the Shade: Volume 2 of My Autobiography, 1949–1962*, HarperCollins, London, 1997

MacCarthy, Fiona, *Last Curtsey: The End of the Debutantes*, Faber & Faber, London, 2006

Maitland, Sara, ed., *Very Heaven: Looking Back at the 1960s*, Virago, London, 1988

Marowitz, Charles, *Burnt Bridges: A Souvenir of the Swinging Sixties and Beyond*, Hodder & Stoughton, London, 1990

Martin, Priscilla and Anne Rowe, *Iris Murdoch: A Literary Life*, Palgrave Macmillan, New York, 2010

Melly, Diana, *Take a Girl Like Me: Life with George*, Chatto & Windus, London, 2005

Moraes, Henrietta, *Henrietta*, Hamish Hamilton, London, 1994

Neville, Richard, *Hippie Hippie Shake: The Dreams, the Trips, the Trials, the Love-Ins, the Screw-Ups, the SIXTIES*, Bloomsbury, London, 1995

———, *Playpower*, Jonathan Cape, London, 1970

Nicholson, Vivian and Stephen Smith, *Spend, Spend, Spend*, Jonathan Cape, London, 1977

O'Brien, Edna, *Country Girl: A Memoir*, Faber & Faber, London, 2012

Ollerenshaw, Dame Kathleen, *To Talk of Many Things: An Autobiography*, Manchester University Press, Manchester, 2004

Partridge, Frances, *Good Company: Diaries, 1967–1970*, HarperCollins, London, 1994

Pasle-Green, Jeanne and Jim Haynes, eds., *Hello I Love You: A Collection of Voices*, Almonde, Paris, 1974

Patrick, Angela with Lynne Barrett-Lee, *The Baby Laundry for Unmarried Mothers*, Simon & Schuster, London, 2012

Paul, Kate, *Journal*, Carrington Press, Hay-on-Wye, 1997

Perkins, Anne, *Red Queen: The Authorised Biography of Barbara Castle*, Macmillan, London, 2003

Polhemus, Ted, *Boom! A Baby Boomer Memoir, 1947–2022*, independently published, 2011

Pressley, Alison, *Changing Times: Being Young in Britain in the '6os*, Michael O'Mara, London, 2000

Pullar, Philippa, *The Shortest Journey*, Hamish Hamilton, London, 1981

Quant, Mary, *Quant by Quant*, G. P. Putnam's Sons, New York, 1966

Rankin, Peter, *Joan Littlewood – Dreams and Realities: The Official Biography*, Oberon, London, 2014

Rice-Davies, Mandy with Shirley Flack, *Mandy*, Michael Joseph/Sphere, London, 1980

Rosen Obst, Lynda, ed., *The Sixties: The Decade Remembered Now, by the People Who Lived It Then*, Random House/Rolling Stone, New York, 1977

Rowbotham, Sheila, *Promise of a Dream: Remembering the Sixties*, Allen Lane, London, 2000

Sage, Lorna, *Bad Blood*, Fourth Estate, London, 2000

Sassoon, Vidal, *Sorry I Kept You Waiting, Madam*, Cassell, London, 1968

Shapiro, Helen with Wendy Green, *Walking Back to Happiness: My Story*, HarperCollins, London, 1993

Shrimpton, Jean with Unity Hall, *An Autobiography*, Ebury Press, London, 1990

Sinclair, Andrew, *In Love and Anger: A View of the Sixties*, Sinclair-Stevenson, London, 1994

Stott, Mary, *Before I Go: Reflections on My Life and Times*, Virago London, 1985
———, *Forgetting's No Excuse*, Faber & Faber, London, 1973

Tedder, Valerie A., *You'll Never Last: One Policewoman's Story from 1958–1984*, United Press, London, 2010

Tennant, Emma, *Girlitude: A Memoir of the 50s and 60s*, Jonathan Cape, London, 1999

Twiggy, *Twiggy: An Autobiography*, Hart-Davis, MacGibbon, St Albans, 1975

Wandor, Michelene, ed., *Once a Feminist: Stories of a Generation*, Virago, London, 1990

Warwick, Christopher, *Princess Margaret: A Life of Contrasts*, André Deutsch, London, 2000

Weldon, Fay, *Auto da Fay*, Flamingo, London, 2002

Whitehorn, Katharine, *Selective Memory: An Autobiography*, Virago, London, 2007

Whitehouse, Mary, *Quite Contrary: An Autobiography*, Sidgwick & Jackson, London, 1993

Widdecombe, Ann, *Strictly Ann: The Autobiography*, Weidenfeld & Nicolson, London, 2013

Willetts, Paul, *Members Only: The Life and Times of Paul Raymond, Soho's Billionaire King of Burlesque*, Serpent's Tail, London, 2010

Wood, Martin, *Laura Ashley*, Frances Lincoln, London, 2009

Wyn Ellis, Nesta, *The Marquess of Bath: Lord of Love*, Dynasty, London, 2010

History, Sociology, Psychology, Advice

Aitken, Jonathan, *The Young Meteors*, Secker & Warburg, London, 1967

Akhtar, Miriam and Steve Humphries, *The Fifties and Sixties: A Lifestyle Revolution*, Boxtree, London, 2001

Ali, Tariq and Susan Watkins, *1968: Marching in the Streets*, Bloomsbury, London, 1998

Aquilina Ross, Geoffrey, *The Day of the Peacock: Style for Men, 1963–1973*, V&A Publications, London, 2011

Barnes, Richard, ed., *Mods!*, Plexus, London, 1979

Barrow, Andrew, *Gossip: A History of High Society from 1920 to 1970*, Hamish Hamilton, London, 1978

Bedford, Sybille, *The Trial of Lady Chatterley's Lover*, Daunt, London, 2016

Bestic, Alan, *Turn Me On Man*, Anthony Gibbs/Tandem, London, 1966

Black, Lawrence and Hugh Pemberton, eds., *An Affluent Society? Britain's Post-War 'Golden Age' Revisited*, Ashgate, Aldershot, 2004

Booker, Christopher, *The Neophiliacs: A Study of the Revolution in English Life in the Fifties and Sixties*, Collins, London, 1969

Bowlby, Rachel, *Carried Away: The Invention of Modern Shopping*, Faber & Faber, London, 2000

Bray, Christopher, *1965: The Year Modern Britain was Born*, Simon & Schuster, London, 2014

Broackes, Victoria and Geoffrey Marsh, eds., *You Say You Want a Revolution? Records and Rebels, 1966–1970*, V&A Publications, London, 2016

Bryan, Beverley, Stella Dadzie and Suzanne Scafe, *The Hearts of the Race: Black Women's Lives in Britain*, Virago, London, 1985

Carpenter, Humphrey, *That Was Satire That Was: Beyond the Fringe, The Establishment Club, Private Eye and That Was the Week That Was*, Victor Gollancz, London, 2000

Carstairs, Professor G. M., *This Island Now: The BBC Reith Lectures, 1962*, Hogarth Press, London, 1963

Cartland, Barbara, *Barbara Cartland's Etiquette Handbook: A Guide to Good Behaviour from the Boudoir to the Boardroom*, Paul Hamlyn, London, 1962

Caute, David, *Sixty-Eight: The Year of the Barricades*, Hamish Hamilton, London, 1988

Chesser, Eustace, *Is Chastity Outmoded?*, May Fair, London, 1960

Cohen, Stanley, *Folk Devils and Moral Panics: The Creation of the Mods and Rockers*, MacGibbon & Kee, London, 1972

Collins, Marcus, ed., *The Permissive Society and its Enemies: Sixties British Culture*, Rivers Oram Press, London, 2007

Cross, Tom, *Artists and Bohemians: 100 Years with the Chelsea Arts Club*, Quiller Press, London, 1992

Dallas, Karl, *Swinging London: A Guide to Where the Action Is*, Stanmore Press, London, 1967

Davenport-Hines, Richard, *An English Affair: Sex, Class and Power in the Age of Profumo*, William Collins, London, 2013

Davies, Christie, *Permissive Britain: Social Change in the Sixties and Seventies*, Pitman, London, 1975

Davies, Hunter, ed., *The New London Spy: A Discreet Guide to the City's Pleasures*, Anthony Blond, London, 1966

DeGroot, Gerard, *The 60s Unplugged: A Kaleidoscopic History of a Disorderly Decade*, Macmillan, London, 2008

Dyhouse, Carol, *Girl Trouble: Panic and Progress in the History of Young Women*, Zed, London, 2013

———, *Students: A Gendered History*, Routledge, London, 2006

Edwards, Anne and Drusilla Beyfus, *Lady Behave: A Guide to Modern Manners for the 1970s*, Cassell, London, 1969

Barbara Ehrenreich, 'Screams Heard Around the World', in Barbara Ehrenreich, Elizabeth Hess and Gloria Jacobs, *Re-Making Love*, Doubleday, Garden City, NY, 1986

Ferguson, Marjorie, *Forever Feminine: Women's Magazines and the Cult of Femininity*, Heinemann Educational, London, 1983

Field, Clive D., *Secularization in the Long 1960s: Numerating Religion in Britain*, Oxford University Press, Oxford, 2017

Fogg, Marnie, *Boutique: A '60s Cultural Phenomenon*, Mitchell Beazley, London, 2003

Fountain, Nigel, *Underground: The London Alternative Press, 1966–74*, Routledge, London, 1988

Fraser, Ronald et al., *1968: A Student Generation in Revolt*, Chatto & Windus, London, 1968

Friedan, Betty, *The Feminine Mystique*, Victor Gollancz, London, 1963

Fryer, Peter, *Mrs Grundy: Studies in English Prudery*, Dennis Dobson, London, 1963

Gaar, Gillian G., *She's a Rebel: The History of Women in Rock & Roll*, Seal Press, New York, 1992

Gardiner, Jill, *From the Closet to the Screen: Women at the Gateways Club, 1945–85*, Pandora Press, London, 2003

Gardiner, Juliet, *From the Bomb to the Beatles: The Changing Face of Post-war Britain, 1945–1965*, Collins & Brown, London, 1999

Gavron, Hannah, *The Captive Wife: Conflicts of Housebound Mothers*, Routledge & Kegan Paul, London, 1966

Gorer, Geoffrey, *Sex and Marriage in England Today: A Study of the Views and Experience of the under-45s*, Panther, St Albans, 1973

Grant, Linda, *Sexing the Millennium: A Political History of the Sexual Revolution*, HarperCollins, London, 1993

Green, Jonathon, *All Dressed Up: The Sixties and the Counterculture*, Jonathan Cape, London, 1998

———, *It: Sex Since the Sixties*, Secker & Warburg, London, 1993

Greer, Germaine, *The Female Eunuch*, MacGibbon & Kee, London, 1970

Gurley Brown, Helen, *Sex and the Single Girl*, new edition, Barricade, Fort Lee, NJ, 2003

Haggett, Ali, *Desperate Housewives, Neuroses and the Domestic Environment, 1945–1970*, Pickering & Chatto, London, 2012

Halasz, Piri, *A Swinger's Guide to London*, Coward McCann, New York, 1967

Hall, Lesley A., ed., *Outspoken Women: An Anthology of Women's Writing on Sex, 1870–1969*, Routledge, London and New York, 2005

Halsey, A. H., *Trends in British Society Since 1900*, Macmillan, London, 1972

Hewison, Robert, *Too Much: Art and Society in the Sixties, 1960–75*, Oxford University Press, Oxford, 1987

Hewitt, Paolo, ed., *The Sharper Word: A Mod Anthology*, Helter Skelter, London, 1999

Hills, J., *Inequality and the State*, Oxford, Oxford University Press, 2004

Hobsbawm, Eric, *Age of Extremes: The Short Twentieth Century, 1914–1991*, Michael Joseph, London, 1994

Holdsworth, Angela, *Out of the Doll's House: The Story of Women in the Twentieth Century*, BBC Books, London, 1988

Hulanicki, Barbara and Martin Pel, *The Biba Years: 1963–1975*, V&A Publications, London, 2014

Jennings, Rebecca, *Tomboys and Bachelor Girls: A Lesbian History of Post-war Britain, 1945–71*, Manchester University Press, Manchester, 2007

Johnson, Pamela Hansford, *On Iniquity: Some Personal Reflections Arising Out of the Moors Murders Trial*, Macmillan, London, 1967

Klein, Josephine, *Samples from English Cultures*, Routledge & Kegan Paul, London, 1965

Kynaston, David, *Modernity Britain: A Shake of the Dice, 1959–1962*, Bloomsbury, London, 2014

Laurie, Peter, *The Teenage Revolution*, Anthony Blond, London, 1965

Lawton, John, *1963 – Five Hundred Days: History as Melodrama*, Hodder & Stoughton, London, 1992

Lester, Richard, *Boutique London – A History: King's Road to Carnaby Street*, ACC, Woodbridge, 2010

Levin, Bernard, *The Pendulum Years: Britain and the Sixties*, Jonathan Cape, London, 1971

Levy, Shawn, *Ready, Steady, Go! Swinging London and the Invention of Cool*, Fourth Estate, London, 2003

Lewis, Jane, *Women in Britain Since 1945*, Blackwell, Oxford, 1992

Liddington, Jill, *The Road to Greenham Common: Feminism and Anti-Militarism in Britain Since 1820*, Virago, 1989

Maclean, Rory, *Magic Bus: On the Hippie Trail from Istanbul to India*, Viking, London, 2006

Magee, Bryan, *One in Twenty: A Study of Homosexuality in Men and Women*, Secker & Warburg, London, 1966

Marsden, Dennis, *Mothers Alone: Poverty and the Fatherless Family*, Allen Lane, London, 1969

Marshall, Cherry, *The Cat-Walk*, Hutchinson, London, 1978

Marwick, Arthur, *The Sixties: Cultural Revolution in Britain, France, Italy and the United States, c.1958–c.1974*, Oxford University Press, Oxford, 1998

Masters, Brian, *The Swinging Sixties*, Constable, London, 1985

Mellor, David Alan and Laurent Gervereau, eds., *The Sixties – Britain and France, 1962–1973: The Utopian Years*, Philip Wilson, London, 1997

Mendelsohn, Janet, *Varna Road*, Ikon Gallery, Birmingham, 2016

Metzger, Rainer, *London in the Sixties*, Thames & Hudson, London, 2012

Milburn, Claudia and Louise Weller, eds., *POP! Art in a Changing Britain*, Pallant House Gallery, Chichester, 2018

Mitchell, Juliet, *Women: The Longest Revolution*, Virago, London, 1984

Moorhouse, Geoffrey, *Britain in the Sixties: The Other England*, Penguin, Harmondsworth, 1964

Nuttall, Jeff, *Bomb Culture*, MacGibbon & Kee, London, 1968

Opie, Robert, ed., *The 1960s Scrapbook*, New Cavendish, London, 2000

Oram, Alison and Annemarie Turnbull, *The Lesbian History Sourcebook: Love and Sex Between Women in Britain from 1780 to 1970*, Routledge, London, 2001

Osgerby, Bill, *Youth in Britain Since 1945*, Blackwell, Oxford, 1988

Padel, Ruth, *I'm a Man: Sex, Gods and Rock'n'Roll*, Faber & Faber, London, 2000

Paton, Maureen, *The Best of Women: The History of Women of the Year*, Women's Press, London, 2000

Rigby, Andrew, *Alternative Realities: A Study of Communes and their Members*, Routledge & Kegan Paul, London, 1974

———, *Communes in Britain*, Routledge & Kegan Paul, London, 1974

Roberts, Elizabeth, *Women and Families: An Oral History, 1940–1970*, Blackwell, Oxford, 1995

Robinson, Jane, *In the Family Way: Illegitimacy Between the Great War and the Swinging Sixties*, Viking, London, 2015

Roszak, Theodore, *The Making of a Counter Culture: Reflections on the Technocratic Society and Its Youthful Opposition*, Faber & Faber, London, 1970

Rycroft, Simon, *Swinging City: A Cultural Geography of London, 1950–1974*, Ashgate, Farnham, 2011

Salter, Tom, *Carnaby Street*, ed. David Whitehead, M. & J. Hobbs, Walton-on-Thames, 1970

Sampson, Anthony, *The New Anatomy of Britain*, Hodder & Stoughton, London, 1971

Sandbrook, Dominic, *Never Had It So Good: A History of Britain from Suez to the Beatles*, Abacus, London, 2006

———, *White Heat: A History of Britain in the Swinging Sixties*, Little, Brown, London, 2006

Schofield, Michael, *The Sexual Behaviour of Young People*, Longmans, London, 1965

Segal, Lynne, ed., *What is to be Done About the Family? Crisis in the Eighties*, Penguin, Harmondsworth, 1983

Shapiro, Harry, *Waiting for the Man: The Story of Drugs and Popular Music*, Helter Skelter, London, 1999

Shrimpton, Jean, *The Truth About Modelling*, W. H. Allen, London, 1964

Shteir, Rachel, *Striptease: The Untold History of the Girlie Show*, Oxford University Press, Oxford, 2004

Smith, Evan and Matthew Worley, *Against the Grain: The British Far Left from 1956*, Manchester University Press, Manchester, 2014

Sooke, Alistair, *Pop Art: A Colourful History*, Viking, London, 2015

Tebbutt, Melanie, *Women's Talk? A Social History of 'Gossip' in Working-Class Neighbourhoods, 1880–1960*, Scolar Press, Aldershot, 1995

Thane, Pat and Tanya Evans, *Sinners? Scroungers? Saints? Unmarried Motherhood in Twentieth-Century England*, Oxford University Press, Oxford, 2012

Thompson, Ben, *Ban This Filth! Letters from the Mary Whitehouse Archive*, London, Faber & Faber, 2012

Tobin, Fergal, *The Best of Decades: Ireland in the Nineteen Sixties*, Gill & Macmillan, Dublin, 1984

Tracy, Michael and David Morrison, *Whitehouse*, Macmillan, 1979

Turnock, Rob, *Television and Consumer Culture: Britain and the Transformation of Modernity*, I. B. Tauris, London, 2007

Walford, Jonathan, *Sixties Fashion: From 'Less is More' to Youthquake*, Thames & Hudson, London, 2013

Wandor, Michelene, ed., *The Body Politic: Writings from the Women's Liberation Movement in Britain, 1969–1972*, Stage 1, London, 1972

Wheen, Francis, *The Sixties: A Fresh Look at the Decade of Change*, Century, London, 1982

Whitehorn, Katharine, *Cooking in a Bedsitter*, Penguin, Harmondsworth, 1963

Whitehouse, Mary, *Cleaning-Up TV: From Protest to Participation*, Blandford, London, 1967

———, *Whatever Happened to Sex?*, Hodder & Stoughton, London, 1977

Whiteley, C. J., and Winifred M. Whiteley, *The Permissive Morality*, Methuen, London, 1964

Willis, Paul E., *Profane Culture*, Routledge & Kegan Paul, London, 1978

Willmott, Peter and Michael Young, *Family and Class in a London Suburb*, Routledge & Kegan Paul, London, 1960

Wood, Kay, *Education: The Basics*, Routledge, London, 2011

York, Peter, *Style Wars*, Sidgwick & Jackson, London, 1980

Fiction, Poetry

Cheek, Mavis, *Yesterday's Houses*, Faber & Faber, London, 2006

Duffy, Maureen, *The Microcosm*, Hutchinson, London, 1966

Dunn, Nell, *Up the Junction*, MacGibbon & Kee, London, 1963

Fabian, Jenny and Johnny Byrne, *Groupie*, New English Library, London, 1969

Ironside, Virginia, *Chelsea Bird*, Secker & Warburg, London, 1964

Lucie-Smith, Edward, ed., *The Liverpool Scene*, Donald Carroll, London, 1967

Reid Banks, Lynne, *The L-Shaped Room*, Chatto & Windus, London, 1960

Woodcraft, Elizabeth, *The Saturday Girls*, Bonnier Zaffre, London, 2018

Journals, Scholarly Articles, Theses and Archives

Atkinson, A. B., 'The Distribution of Wealth and the Individual Lifecycle', *Oxford Economic Papers* (n.s.) 23(2), 1971

Atkinson, Anthony B., James P. F. Gordon and Ian A. Harrison, 'Trends in the Shares of Top Wealth-Holders in Britain, 1923–1981', *Oxford Bulletin of Economics and Statistics* 51(3), 1989

Jones, Jennifer and Josephine Castle, 'Women in UK Universities, 1920–1980', *Studies in Higher Education* 11(3), 1986

Millennium Memory Bank Oral History Collection held at the British Library

Mills, Helena, 'Using the Personal to Critique the Popular: Women's Memories of 1960s Youth', *Contemporary British History* 30(4), 2016

Parliamentary Committee on Higher Education, *The Robbins Report*, October 1963 (appointed by the prime minister under the chairmanship of Lord Robbins, 1961–3)

Walton, John K., 'From Institution to Fragmentation: The Making and Unmaking of the British Weekend', *Leisure Studies* 33(2), 2014

Newspapers, Magazines, Journals

Birmingham Evening Mail
Daily Express
Daily Mail
Daily Sketch
Daily Telegraph
Evening Standard
Guardian
Honey
Manchester Evening News
News of the World
Nova
Sunday Telegraph
Sunday Times
The Times
Woman's Own
Woman's Weekly

Useful Websites

British Pathé at www.britishpathe.com
Fashion through history on www.fashion-era.com/index.htm
Historic inflation calculator at www.thisismoney.co.uk
Oxford Dictionary of National Biography online at www.oxforddnb.com
Search UK legislation via www.legislation.gov.uk/

Acknowledgements

As a writer of non-fiction, I lean heavily on others for collaboration and support, and this is my opportunity to thank them all in print. First comes Eleo Gordon. Eleo was my editor, mentor and friend at Viking for sixteen years; *How Was It For You?* was commissioned by her, and though she reached retirement when I was halfway through writing this book, her rocklike belief has been there for me throughout. Daniel Crewe picked up where she left off. He has been supportive, tactful, super-cultured and alert to my shortcomings – what more could one ask for? – and I feel very lucky, too, that clever Connor Brown is his assistant. Fortune has also been my friend in the shape of my stellar agent, Caroline Dawnay. Thanks, too, to Venetia Butterfield for her generous confidence in my books; also to Joanna Prior. My husband William Nicholson has been the wisest, kindest and most loving of critics; I couldn't have done it without him. Claire Singers gave me a boost when it was most needed (and put me in touch with one of my most glamorous interviewees), and my daughter Julia Nicholson has not only been my devoted one-woman focus group, but has also contributed her impressive editorial skills to reading the penultimate draft.

I travelled the country to ask many women the question that this book poses. Those who agreed to share their memories – often intimate ones – were generous, brave and honest. Though some have preferred not to be named here I salute them all. Among others, they are: Pattie Boyd, Lucy Brett, Dame Carmen Callil, Jessica Chappell, Mavis Cheek, Anne Chisholm, Emma Codrington, Baroness Cumberlege, Marjorie Davies, the late Mary Denness, Theresa Edwards, Patsy Embry, the Revd Anne Gurney, Caroline Harper, Margaret Hogg, Dr Christine Hugh-Jones, Harriet Lear, Beryl Marsden, Margaret Masding, Doreen Massey, Clare Morpurgo, Veronica Morriss, Melissa North, Rosalyn St Pierre, Lady Patricia Stevens, Kristina

Walton and the Rt Hon Ann Widdecombe PC DSG. And a special thank you to Kate Clarke for sending me her published *Journal*.

Making contact with women from a wide variety of backgrounds can be difficult. I had help in this from a range of accomplished networkers, who made suggestions, spread the word and set up introductions: my old friend Jane Salvage deserves a special mention in this category, as does Lisa Dando, director of the Brighton Women's Centre. I am also particularly indebted to the Hull-based journalist Dr Brian W. Lavery, who went to unusual lengths in helping a fellow author. Thank you, too, to Julia Aisbitt, Ariane Bankes, Sir Peter Bazalgette, Noelle Beales, Julian Bell, Jane Bonham-Carter, Sam Burnett, Richard Chamberlain, Carolyn Chinn, Julian Henriques, Lucy Hughes-Hallett, Simon Brett, Rosalind Brown, Rupert Christiansen, Macha Ferrant, Jacqueline Fox, Dan Franklin, Susie Freeman, Peter Grimsdale, Janie Hampton, Patsy Hickman, Tom Hollander, Jo Hugh-Jones, Annalena MacAfee, Kinn McIntosh, Joanna Newton, Teddy Nicholson, Maggie Norden, Angie O'Rourke, Leah Romaniello, Georgie Rowse, Barbara Ryrie, Andrew Scadding, Anne Sebba, Paula Thompson, Paul Willetts and Ellis Woodman. I'm also grateful to my cousin Dame Pippa Harris, producer of *Call the Midwife*, for giving me a steer on approaches to women affected by thalidomide in the 1960s, to Mikey Argy of the Thalidomide Trust, but above all to Dr Ruth Blue, Secretary to the Board of Trustees of the Thalidomide Society, for her trust in me, and for her inexhaustible care and attention to detail.

Others took trouble to link me to special resources, ransack their memories, advise, correct, encourage and give technological assistance; my thanks here to Richard Adams, Baroness Kay Andrews, Juliet Annan, Lucy Annan, Maureen Ashby, Desmond Banks, Cressida Bell, Baroness Benjamin, Lucy Bland, Dr John Collins, the late Henrietta Garnett, Orlando Gough, Linda Grant, Jonathon Green, Martin Jennings, Jan Maulden, Hilary Newiss and Maria Nicholson. Special thanks are due to Nicola Lane for authorising the use of her published memory, to Philippa Walker for lending me a VHS of her 1999 documentary *Bunny Girls*, to Kim Fuller for sharing his knowledge of 1960s broadcast media, and to Beatles biographer Hunter Davies for spreading some of the stardust, while, for everyone who knows him, it will come as no surprise to hear that Paul Beecham not only suggested one of my most compelling interviewees, but has also been a go-to resource for 1960s pop arcana. My visit to north Lincolnshire was made extra special by the intervention of two wonderful good Samaritans, June and Carley Taylor, who quite literally went the final mile to ensure that my interviewee Mary Denness didn't fall by the wayside.

Lloyd Ross has been at the end of an email countless times in the making of this book; my thanks to him for his research in the Social Sciences Library of the London School of Economics. Sheila Rowbotham has been an inspiration, and responded generously when I wrote to her. The historian David Kynaston has, as usual, been both an encouragement and a wonderful example.

It would be impossible to list the teams of librarians and archivists who have given time to answering my queries, but their institutions deserve warm mentions: the London Library, the British Library (particularly those in the recorded sound and newspaper collections), Birmingham University archive and the University of Sussex Special Collections.

Thank you, too, to Louisa Brown for her painstaking assistance in dealing with a number of literary and musical estates, and also to the team of staff and freelancers associated with Viking who helped *How Was It For You?* along its journey: copy-editor Trevor Horwood, senior editorial manager Emma Brown, indexer Dave Cradduck and publicist Olivia Mead.

★

In addition, the author gratefully acknowledges the kind permission of copyright holders to quote from a number of authors and sources, as follows: excerpts from *The Centre of the Bed* by Joan Bakewell, copyright © Joan Bakewell 2003, reproduced by permission of Hodder and Stoughton Ltd; excerpts from *An Education* (2009) by Lynn Barber, published by Penguin and reproduced with permission of the author; excerpts from *The Arms of Britannia* © (2010) and *Coming to England* © (1995) by Baroness Floella Benjamin OBE, reproduced by permission of the author; excerpts from *Wonderful Today* by Pattie Boyd with Penny Junor, reproduced by kind permission of Pattie Boyd; excerpts from *Hidden Lives* by Margaret Forster (1997), and from *The New London Spy* by Hunter Davies (1966), reproduced with the kind permission of Hunter Davies; excerpts from *The Sixties* (2010) by Jenny Diski, published by Profile Books, reproduced with permission of the estate of Jenny Diski; excerpt from lyrics of 'Boys', words and music by Luther Dixon and Wes Farrell © 1960, reproduced by EMI Longitude Music, London WIF 9LD; excerpts from *Talking to Women* (1965) and *Up the Junction* (1963) by Nell Dunn, published by MacGibbon & Kee Ltd, reproduced with the generous permission of the author; excerpts from *Through Gypsy Eyes* (2013) by Kathy Etchingham and Andrew Crofts, published by Orion, reproduced with the kind permission of the authors; excerpts from *Groupie* (1969) by Jenny Fabian and Johnny Byrne, published by Omnibus Press, reproduced with permission of the authors; the use of approximately one hundred and forty-one (141) words from *FAITHFULL* by Marianne Faithfull, published by Penguin Books, copyright © Marianne Faithful, 1995; excerpts from *The Captive Wife – Conflicts of Housebound Mothers* (1966) by Hannah Gavron, published by Routledge & Kegan Paul, taken from pp. 51 and 78–9, reprinted by permission of Taylor and Francis on behalf of Routledge & Kegan Paul PLC; all excerpts from *Days In The Life* (1988) by Jonathon Green, published by William Heinemann Ltd, reproduced with the kind permission of the author; extract from 'Mrs Albion You've Got a Lovely Daughter' from *Collected Poems* by Adrian Henri, published by Allison & Busby, copyright © Adrian Henri 1986, reproduced by permission of the estate of the author c/o Rogers, Coleridge & White Ltd, 20 Powis Mews, London W11 1JN; *Now We Are Thirty: Women of the Breakthrough Generation* (1981) by Mary Ingham, published by Eyre Methuen, all excerpts reprinted by kind permission of the author; excerpts from *On Iniquity – Some Personal Reflections* by Pamela Hansford Johnson, reproduced by permission of Curtis Brown Group Ltd on behalf of the literary estate of Pamela Hansford Johnson, copyright © Pamela Hansford Johnson 1967; Christine Keeler's quotations are taken from *Secrets and Lies* by Christine Keeler with Douglas Thompson (2012), published by Blake Publishing and reproduced with permission; a quotation from 'Annus Mirabilis' from *The Complete Poems* by Philip Larkin, published by Faber and Faber Ltd, reproduced with permission from the publisher; excerpts from *Lady Chatterley's Lover* and *A Propos of Lady Chatterley's Lover* (The Cambridge

Edition of the Works of D. H. Lawrence) by D. H. Lawrence, published by Cambridge University Press in 1993 and reproduced by permission of Paper Lion Ltd and the estate of Frieda Lawrence Ravagli and Cambridge University Press; excerpts from *Killing My Own Snakes: A Memoir* (2013) by Ann Leslie, reproduced with permission of the Licensor through PLSclear; a quotation from the lyric *Smashing Time* by George Melly, copyright © George Melly 1967, reproduced by permission of A. M. Heath & Co. Ltd, authors' agents; grateful acknowledgements to Kate Clarke for the use of excerpts from *Journal* (1997) by Kate Paul, first published by Carrington Press, Hay-on-Wye; excerpts from *The 50s & 60s: The Best of Times; Growing Up and Being Young in Britain* (2003) by Alison Pressley, published by Michael O'Mara Books and reproduced with the generous permission of the author; all excerpts from *Promise of a Dream* (2000), published by Allen Lane, and *Women's Liberation and the New Politics* (May Day Manifesto Pamphlet No. 4) by Sheila Rowbotham reproduced with the kind permission of the author; extracts from *Twiggy – An Autobiography* by Twiggy reprinted by permission of Peters Fraser & Dunlop (www.petersfraserdunlop.com) on behalf of Twiggy; excerpts from the article 'Some like it rough' by Fay Weldon, published in *The Guardian* on 15 October 2004, reproduced by kind permission of the author.

Grateful acknowledgement is also due to the BBC for use of extracts from the British Library Millennium Memory Bank Oral History Collection.

Acknowledgements are also due to the following whose works have been quoted from: Jonathan Aitken, *The Young Meteors*; Richard Barnes, *Mods!*; Cecil Beaton, *Beaton in the Sixties: The Cecil Beaton Diaries*; Sybille Bedford, *The Trial of Lady Chatterley's Lover*; Barbara Bell, *Just Take Your Frock Off – A Lesbian Life*; Alan Bestic, *Turn Me On Man – Face to Face with Young Addicts Today*; Drusilla Beyfus, *The English Marriage – What It is Like to be Married Today*; Drusilla Beyfus and Anne Edwards, *Lady Behave – A Guide to Modern Manners for the 1970s*; Rosie Boycott, *A Nice Girl Like Me*; Christopher Bray, *1965 – The Year Modern Britain was Born*; John Brunner, lyrics to 'The H-Bomb's Thunder'; Sydney Carter, lyrics to 'Wicked Lady C'; Barbara Cartland, *Barbara Cartland's Etiquette Handbook: A Guide to Good Behaviour from the Boudoir to the Boardroom*; Rupert Christiansen, *I Know You're Going to be Happy*; Grace Coddington with Michael Roberts, *Grace – A Memoir*; Richard Davenport-Hines, *An English Affair – Sex, Class and Power in the Age of Profumo*; Ron Dunbar and Edith Wayne, lyrics to 'Band of Gold'; Marnie Fogg, *Boutique*; Ronald Fraser, *1968 – A Student Generation in Revolt*; Betty Friedan, *The Feminine Mystique*; Jill Gardiner, *From the Closet to the Screen*; Allan Ginsberg, 'I am that I am', from *Collected Poems*; Linda Grant, *Sexing the Millennium*; Germaine Greer, *The Female Eunuch*; Helen Gurley Brown, *Sex and the Single Girl*; Charles Hamblett and Jane Deverson, *Generation X*; Robert Hewison, *Too Much: Art and Society*; Margery Hurst, *No Glass Slipper*; Janey Ironside, *Janey*; Laura Jackson, *Heart of Stone*; Rebecca Jennings, *Tomboys and Bachelor Girls*; Jenny Kee, *A Big Life*; Cécile Landau, *Growing Up in the Sixties*; Shawn Levy, *Ready Steady Go – Swinging London and the Invention of Cool*; Fiona MacCarthy, *Last Curtsey: The End of the Debutantes*; the words of Angela Carter, Alexandra Pringle, Julie Christie, Marsha Rowe, Patricia Vereker and Sue O'Sullivan in Sara Maitland, *Very Heaven: Looking Back at the 1960s*; Charles Marowitz, *Burnt Bridges: Souvenir of the Swinging Sixties*; Cherry Marshall, *The Cat Walk*; Diana Melly, *Take a Girl Like Me*; Janet Mendelsohn, *Varna Road*; Juliet Mitchell, *Looking Back at Woman's Estate* and *Women – The Longest Revolution*; Geoffrey Moorhouse, *Britain in the Sixties – The Other England*; Henrietta Moraes, *Henrietta*; Richard Neville, *Hippy, Hippy Shake* and *Playpower*; Jeff Nuttall, *Bomb Culture*; Ruth Padel, *I'm a Man – Sex, Gods and Rock'n'Roll*; Frances Partridge, *Good Company – Diaries 1967–70*; Mary Quant, *Quant on Quant*; Eugene Raskin, lyrics to 'Those Were the Days'; Mandy Rice-Davies with Shirley Flack, *Mandy*; Elizabeth Roberts, *Women and Families*; Valerie Tedder, *You'll Never Last*; Ben Thompson, *Ban This Filth*; Michael Tracy and David Morrison *Whitehouse*; Michelene Wandor, *Once a Feminist*; Mary Whitehouse *Quite Contrary*; Ann Widdecombe, *Strictly Ann*; Paul Willis, *Profane Culture*; Elizabeth Woodcraft, *The Saturday Girls*; Peter York, *Style Wars*.

While every effort has been made to obtain permissions from copyright holders, the publishers would be glad to correct any errors of omission or commission in future editions.

Index

Page references in *italic* indicate illustrations.

He just wanted a decent book to read ...

Not too much to ask, is it? It was in 1935 when Allen Lane, Managing
Director of Bodley Head Publishers, stood on a platform at Exeter railway
station looking for something good to read on his journey back to London.
His choice was limited to popular magazines and poor-quality paperbacks –
the same choice faced every day by the vast majority of readers, few of
whom could afford hardbacks. Lane's disappointment and subsequent anger
at the range of books generally available led him to found a company – and
change the world.

*'We believed in the existence in this country of a vast reading public for intelligent
books at a low price, and staked everything on it'*
Sir Allen Lane, 1902–1970, founder of Penguin Books

The quality paperback had arrived – and not just in bookshops. Lane was
adamant that his Penguins should appear in chain stores and tobacconists,
and should cost no more than a packet of cigarettes.

Reading habits (and cigarette prices) have changed since 1935, but
Penguin still believes in publishing the best books for everybody to
enjoy. We still believe that good design costs no more than bad design,
and we still believe that quality books published passionately and responsibly
make the world a better place.

So wherever you see the little bird – whether it's on a piece of
prize-winning literary fiction or a celebrity autobiography, political tour
de force or historical masterpiece, a serial-killer thriller, reference book,
world classic or a piece of pure escapism – you can bet that it represents
the very best that the genre has to offer.

Whatever you like to read – trust Penguin.